ROBERT BROWNING'S LANGUAGE

ROBERT BROWNING'S LANGUAGE

Donald S. Hair

UNIVERSITY OF TORONTO PRESS
Toronto Buffalo London

© University of Toronto Press Incorporated 1999
Toronto Buffalo London
Printed in Canada

ISBN 0-8020-4434-4

Printed on acid-free paper

Canadian Cataloguing in Publication Data

Hair, Donald S., 1937–
  Robert Browning's language

  Includes bibliographical references and index.
  ISBN 0-8020-4434-4

  1. Browning, Robert, 1812–1889 – Language.   2. Browning, Robert,
  1812–1889 – Criticism and interpretation.   I. Title.

  PR4244.H34 1999   821'.8   C98-933051-6

University of Toronto Press acknowledges the financial assistance to its
publishing program of the Canada Council for the Arts and the Ontario Arts
Council.

This book has been published with the help of a grant from the Humanities
and Social Sciences Federation of Canada, using funds provided by the Social
Sciences and Humanities Research Council of Canada.

Contents

Acknowledgments

The origin of *Robert Browning's Language* is a question Northrop Frye asked me years ago, when he was an examiner of my doctoral dissertation at the University of Toronto. The question was about the nature of 'Browning's verbal universe.' The answer I gave him then was inadequate, and his phrase has haunted me ever since. Someone once said about Ruskin – Ruskin himself quotes the comment – that 'when he wants to work out a subject, he writes a book on it.' This book is my working out of 'Browning's verbal universe.'

Doing the work has meant incurring debts which I am happy to acknowledge. At my own university, Jim Horton, Justin Baird, Jason Kuzminski, and Timothy Habinski all worked diligently on the project at various stages. Cory Davies, busy with her own work on the Brownings, followed several lines of inquiry in pursuit of an ultimately elusive reference. Karl Hochmann was an unfailing source of help with my word processing program, and the staff at the D.B. Weldon Library – especially Dave Newman, Ann Morris, and David Murphy – all helped in finding obscure materials. No critic can work without accurate and reliable texts, and I have relied upon the careful editing of the Browning poems and plays, and the immensely useful concordance, of my colleagues Tom Collins and Dick Shroyer.

Beyond the University of Western Ontario, I am grateful to the librarians at the Beinecke Rare Book and Manuscript Library, Yale University, and at the British Library. Rita (Humphrey) Patteson welcomed me to the Armstrong Browning Library, Baylor University, and Paulette Smith brought books I needed, but I am especially indebted to Cynthia Burgess for understanding the directions in which my research was heading and for matching my interests with the resources at Baylor. Katharine Thomson, Modern Manuscripts Assistant, and Alan Daniello, both of Balliol College Library, kindly allowed me to see Browning's own copies of Quarles and other texts, and the Reverend Clive R. Dunnico, warden and minister at The Robert Browning Settlement, Walworth, gave me access to the Settlement's Browning materials, its collection of Clayton's sermons, and its records of the York Street Chapel. I am indebted to Michael Meredith, the Librarian at Eton College, for generously allowing me to see some of the books from his own collection that had once been owned by Browning, and for giving me permission to quote from Browning's annotations in his copy of Donne. Finally, I thank Stephen Crook and Philip Milito of the Berg Collection in the New York Public Library for letting me examine yet other books owned by Browning.

I am grateful to members of both the London and New York Browning Societies for various kindnesses, and in particular to Philip Kelley, Mairi Calcraft-Rennie, and Al Omans. Special thanks are due to Dick Kennedy, the former president of the New York society and Professor Emeritus of Temple University. He generously read early parts of the manuscript, and it has benefited from his correction of fact – any errors which remain are mine – and from his astute questioning of emphases, interpretations, and expressions. He and I enjoyed good literary talk in Waco, and I am grateful for his broad knowledge of Browning and for his magnanimity of spirit.

Much of the research for this book was made possible by a grant from the Social Sciences and Humanities Research Council, and by grants from the Faculty of Arts at the University of Western Ontario. I am grateful for both, and for the sabbatical year arranged by the chair of the Department of English, Paul Gaudet, and the dean of the Faculty of Arts, Jim Good. Isabelle Bossé, Suzanne Rancourt, and Kristen Pederson shepherded the manuscript through the evaluation process, one crucial result of which was a grant in aid of publication from the Humanities and Social Sciences Federation of Canada. Finally, for University of Toronto Press, Suzanne Rancourt, Judy Williams, Barbara Porter, and Jill Foran managed the publication of this book with admirable care and efficiency.

Note on Texts

All quotations from Browning's poetry and from his 'Essay on Shelley' are, unless otherwise indicated, from the Penguin-Yale edition: Robert Browning, *The Poems*, ed. John Pettigrew and Thomas J. Collins, 2 vols. (Harmondsworth: Penguin, 1981) and *The Ring and the Book*, ed. Richard D. Altick (Harmondsworth: Penguin, 1971). Quotations from the plays are from *The Plays of Robert Browning*, ed. Thomas J. Collins and Richard J. Shroyer (New York: Garland, 1988). Philip Kelley's edition of the letters of the Brownings is in progress, and all quotations from letters written up to May 1846 are from the twelve volumes published to date in *The Brownings' Correspondence*, ed. Philip Kelley and Ronald Hudson (vols. 1–8) and Philip Kelley and Scott Lewis (vols. 9–12) (Winfield, Kans.: Wedgestone, 1984–). I refer to these volumes throughout the book as *Correspondence*. For letters written after May 1846, I have relied on other (usually older) collections and editions of letters as specified in the notes. Finally, I have used extensively Philip Kelley and Betty A. Coley's *The Browning Collections: A Reconstruction with Other Memorabilia* (Winfield, Kans.: Armstrong Browning Library, Browning Institute, Mansell, Wedgestone, 1984) and refer to it in both text and notes as 'Kelley and Coley' or *The Browning Collections*.

ROBERT BROWNING'S LANGUAGE

Introduction: 'Sense, sight and song'

This book is a study of Browning's language. Its main concern is Browning's understanding of the nature and function of words and syntax and the discourses they make possible, and I attempt to define that understanding not only through Browning's poems, plays, and letters, but through the books in his library. Browning was, unlike Tennyson, largely untouched by the new philology which had been introduced from Germany into England by Coleridgians such as Kemble and Trench. Instead, his understanding of language belongs in an older context, that of Johnson's *Dictionary*, of the language theory of John Locke (on which the *Dictionary* is to a large extent based), and of the work of followers of Locke, like Collard on logic and Tooke on etymology. Browning approached all of this material in yet another context, that of the dissenting religious tradition in which he was brought up, and Puritanism, as understood by the Congregationalists (the particular denomination to which the Brownings belonged), gives the use of language a moral and spiritual purpose and language itself a double character: words are, on the one hand, empty and foolish, windy things that reflect a fallen humanity; on the other, they are the means of our hard-fought return to God, and they, like the vanities condemned by the preacher of Ecclesiastes, will ultimately be called into judgment. All of these matters I trace through Browning's texts in a roughly chronological way. Browning's actual use of language is another concern of the book, and I attempt to balance the theory, which I give largely in terms with which Browning himself was familiar, with close readings. Browning was not himself a philosopher (in spite of an older tradition in Browning criticism which made him a philosophical and religious teacher) and he was not a systematic thinker about language. Nonetheless, we note how often his poems are self-conscious in their comments on language and especially on the language of poetry, in their exploration of the nature of verbal truth and falsehood, and in their placing of poetry in relation to two other arts which were lifelong passions with Browning, painting and music.

A good introduction to Browning's language concerns is the Prologue to *Ferishtah's Fancies*, a volume published in 1884, late in Browning's career. We might have begun at the beginning, but we have the sanction of the poet himself for starting at the end. In 1875 he told his publisher, George Barnett Smith, that 'I myself have always liked to read a man's *collected* works, of any kind, *backwards*; and what I once thought a fancy I incline now to consider an eminently rational procedure.'[1] So we proceed to the first thirty-two lines of the Prologue:

> Pray, Reader, have you eaten ortolans
>   Ever in Italy?
> Recall how cooks there cook them: for my plan's
>   To – Lyre with Spit ally.
> They pluck the birds, – some dozen luscious lumps,
>   Or more or fewer, –
> Then roast them, heads by heads and rumps by rumps,
>   Stuck on a skewer.
> But first, – and here's the point I fain would press, –
>   Don't think I'm tattling! –
> They interpose, to curb its lusciousness,
>   – What, 'twixt each fatling?
> First comes plain bread, crisp, brown, a toasted square:
>   Then, a strong sage-leaf:
> (So we find books with flowers dried here and there
>   Lest leaf engage leaf.)
> First, food – then, piquancy – and last of all
>   Follows the thirdling:
> Through wholesome hard, sharp soft, your tooth must bite
>   Ere reach the birdling.
> Now, were there only crust to crunch, you'd wince:
>   Unpalatable!
> Sage-leaf is bitter-pungent – so's a quince:
>   Eat each who's able!

But through all three bite boldly – lo, the gust!
    Flavour – no fixture –
Flies, permeating flesh and leaf and crust
    In fine admixture.
So with your meal, my poem: masticate
    Sense, sight and song there!
Digest these, and I praise your peptics' state,
    Nothing found wrong there.

The antepenultimate line of the quotation names the central features of poetry and the three major topics for any discussion of its language. It is, of course, conventional to talk about the appeal of poetry to the sense of sight and to quote the Horatian tag *ut pictura poesis*, just as it is conventional to analyse the sounds and rhythms of poetry and to think that Horace ought also to have said *ut musica poesis*. Browning, however, treats these conventional topics in his own way. When he appeals to the reader's eyes, he frequently proceeds as he does here, by presenting a precise and concrete picture – the ortolans – and then turning it or troping it ('So with your meal, my poem') and stating its meaning ('masticate / Sense, sight and song there!'). This procedure Browning derives, as we shall see, from the emblem tradition, in which picture and motto are placed side by side, with the clear understanding that 'this means that.' So sense is allied with sight. Tennyson, with his leanings towards symbolism and his anticipating of imagist poetry, objected to such interpretation, which seemed to him reductive; he once told the Bishop of Ripon that 'I hate to be tied down to say, "*This* means *that*," because the thought within the image is much more than any one interpretation.'[2] Browning, and the characters he creates, are always saying 'this means that,' because he understands interpretation as the essence of the inner life and the chief activity of the soul. In making sense of sights, men and women have the aid of language, without which we would find ourselves amid a miscellany of sensations, but with which we can name and order things, and so specify their meaning for us. Not that the meaning is ever complete or final. 'The world is not to be learned and thrown aside,' Browning wrote in his 1851 essay on Shelley, 'but reverted to and relearned.' Even so, it remains a riddle, and the 'sense' with which Browning is concerned is a continuing process of interpretation.

There is one final point about interpretation as it is presented in the Prologue we are considering, and that is a point implicit in the emblem:

the close link between interpreting and troping. It is only one step from saying 'this means that' to saying 'this is that,' and so meaning becomes metaphor. Here meal and poem are identified, and Browning extends the metaphor in a suggestive way by saying, 'Digest these.' The words of the sacrament ('take, eat') lie behind Browning's imperative, and they indicate that reading and interpreting are also a process of transforming, the integrating of the text into the very being of the person responding to it, such integration depending upon choices on which he or she will act. The individual expresses such choices in troping, and a trope, we remember, is in Greek a turn. Browning's central concern as a poet is the way in which men and women turn all things, such turning being, in his view, finally a spiral upwards. Language makes possible such versions (a word derived from the Latin verb for turning) as we 'revert' (another turn) to the world and all that is therein; and what is conversion, the central concern of the dissenting religious tradition, but a climactic turn? If we are going to recover from the fall, language provides the means, and we can trope our way to heaven.

Music, like painting, is wordless, and it too needs language if we are to say what it means. Just as images in poetry link that art with painting, so prosody links poetry and music. The most characteristic aspect of Browning's prosody, as we shall see, is his rhyming, and his rhymes are often not just the repetition of one vowel sound, but double and triple, as they are in the Prologue. The music of his poetry lies not in the repeated sounds, and certainly not in sounds which are (in the sentimental understanding of music) smooth or sweet, pleasing or harmonious. Browning understands the music of poetry primarily in its measuring of time, and rhyme is primarily a marker of those measures, as it is in the quotation: iambic pentameter lines played off against hypercatalectic iambic dimeter lines, their boundaries defined by the repetitions in sound. The skilful handling of measured time is an important matter for Browning. He accepted Carlyle's view that time and space are modes of human perception and the conditions under which we live our lives. Just as turning and interpreting visual images are ways by which the soul develops, so are beating and manipulating time. It is not enough simply to keep time, and Browning has only contempt for thumpingly obvious rhythms. Rather, each one of us must struggle with time, as we struggle with meaning, and the struggle will result, as we see in the Prologue, in measures which are rough with clustered consonants and elided vowels.

The Prologue 'allies' music and image, Lyre and Spit, the verb indicating nothing more than the relating of unlike things. The Coleridgian understanding of symbol has nothing to do with this relationship, and yet the verbal act of allying one thing with another thing is, in Browning's view, the essence of the moral and religious life. Browning is characteristically oblique and ironic about such a momentous purpose. He dismisses his troping here as a 'fancy-freak,' and he makes Gressoney – the location of the poem – speak and provide a motto ('"Take what is, trust what may be!"') about which the poet says jauntily, 'That's Life's true lesson – eh?' – as if it were possible to sum up the meaning in a single aphorism. For Browning, as we shall see, distinguishes sharply between truth (the concern of philosophy and theology) and the means of speaking and conveying truth (the concern of rhetoric). Truth is not to be won without struggle, and so Browning creates texts which are all, in a broad sense, riddles. Language is the location of the struggle, for the poet with his material, and for the reader with the poet. The meaning is to be 'seen only by reflexion in details.' That phrase is not Browning's, but it is one he approved of, and he quotes it in a letter to Isabella Blagden in November of 1863. Commenting on a review of his *Poetical Works*, issued that same year, Browning says, 'That critique was fair in giving the right key to my poetry – in as much as it *is* meant to have "one central meaning, seen only by reflexion in details" – "our principle," says the critic – "mine and good" say I ...'[3]

Chapter One

'The world of words':
Johnson, Locke, and Congregationalism

When the first part of the *New English Dictionary* – now the *Oxford English Dictionary* – appeared in 1884, its editor, James A.H. Murray, met Browning, with whom he had already corresponded, in Edinburgh. 'Browning told him that he found the Dictionary "most delightful" and intended to read every word of it.'[1] The poet was expressing more than polite enthusiasm, for he had in fact prepared himself for his life's work by reading the best known of the earlier dictionaries, Dr Johnson's. 'When the die was cast,' Mrs Orr writes in her account of the young Browning, and he 'was definitely to adopt literature as his profession, he qualified himself for it by reading and digesting the whole of Johnson's Dictionary.'[2] Mrs Orr tells us nothing more than that, and the task has seemed so Herculean that critics have not known quite what to make of it. John Maynard in *Browning's Youth* (1977) accepts the statement, and says only that 'from this exercise some of Browning's tendency to long words and obscurity as well as his best successes in finding the right word for a character may possibly stem.'[3] The reading of the dictionary seems to me to have much more profound implications, both for Browning's interests as a poet and for his understanding of language. From the beginning, Browning was comprehensive in his interests, and had an encyclopedic desire to embrace the whole of knowledge and to master all of the arts. Moreover, his knowledge of Johnson's *Dictionary* was one of the major factors which oriented him towards empiricism in philosophy and settled his understanding of language firmly in the tradition of Locke's theory as set out in book 3 of *An Essay Concerning Human Understanding.*

When Browning refers to an English dictionary, it is usually Johnson's. For instance, when Elizabeth asks, in 1846, about the word 'gadge' in *A Soul's Tragedy*, Robert replies that it 'is a real name (in Johnson, too) for a torturing iron' (*Correspondence* 12:241; Kelley and Lewis point out that 'gadge' does not in fact appear in Johnson). Browning's most extended reference to Johnson is in an 1870 letter to Isabella Blagden. There he tells 'dearest Isa' about a letter he has received from one of the readers for the *New English Dictionary*, then in the process of being prepared by the Philological Society. This reader, a Mrs Bathoe, asks Browning about thirty-eight words in *The Ring and the Book* '"whose meaning is by no means clear to me,"' but 'everyone of which,' Browning writes with a tone of disgust, 'is to be found in Johnson's dictionary!' 'There happen to be one or two words in the poem which are really of my own coining for good reasons,' Browning says, but Mrs Bathoe does not list them, and Browning does not hide from Blagden his contempt for someone so ignorant of the language. Blagden no doubt can conceive of 'something more impolite that [*sic*] what I am about to tell Mrs Bathoe, – that people who intend to supplement Johnson would better read him first of all.'[4]

That reading certainly fostered the all-embracing thrust of Browning's interests. Unlike Tennyson, Browning did not have a university education – he spent less than a full academic year at the newly established University of London – and instead he read in his father's library. The collection was extensive – 'one of the finest private libraries in London: some 4,000 volumes, many of fabulous rarity,' according to John Woolford; 'six thousand books and more, we are told,' says John Maynard – with an enormous range: 'books for every interest and books on virtually every subject.'[5] No wonder William Irvine, in describing the Browning cottage 'lined from front to back door with a thick interior epidermis of books,' should say that Browning 'spent a lifetime turning encyclopedias into poetry.'[6] It was Browning's father whose interests were omnivorous. 'Oh that *helluo librorum* [devourer of books] my father, best of men, most indefatigable of book-digesters!'[7] Browning was later to say. The father may have 'confused great knowledge with a great accumulation of information' (Maynard 91), but his aim was to embrace 'the whole round of creation': 'he seems to have been working toward some ultimate and unimaginable goal, an encylopedic grasp of all knowledge, the sum of all the books he could find' (Maynard 88). The son, too, devoured everything, and had a remarkably retentive memory, but the books (and not nature or society) were the primary materials to which his imagination responded. George Bornstein makes a suggestive remark which sums up the importance of the father's library for the son's poetry. 'Each' – Bornstein is here referring to both Browning and Pound – 'was the leading figure of his generation to develop a postromantic substitution of history – particularly the written documents of both social and cultural achievement – for nature as prime stimulus to the poet's internal powers.'[8]

Johnson's *Dictionary* is a compendium of 'the written documents of both social and cultural achievement.' The lexicographer says in his Preface that he wants not only to collect all the words in the language, but to illustrate their various meanings with quotations from a wide range of writers, 'to collect examples and authorities from the writers before the restoration, whose works I regard as *the wells of English undefiled.*'[9] Johnson's aim was encyclopedic. 'When I first collected these authorities,' he writes, 'I was desirous that every quotation should be useful to some other end than the illustration of a word,' and that 'some other end' was both 'a kind of intellectual history' and a survey of all knowledge as it is preserved in words. 'I therefore extracted from philosophers principles of science; from historians remarkable facts; from chymists complete processes; from divines striking exhortations; and from poets beautiful descriptions.' His aim was 'to pierce deep into every science,' but, he says in a suggestive admission of failure, 'these were the dreams of a poet doomed at last to wake a lexicographer.' Johnson did not abandon 'the dreams of a poet,' however, and Robert DeMaria, Jr, has shown recently the extent to which Johnson realized his original design. Beginning with Umberto Eco's observation that a dictionary with its 'potentially unordered and unrestricted galaxy of pieces of world knowledge' is in fact *'a disguised encyclopedia,'*[10] DeMaria goes on to show, in a book-length study, how the quotations Johnson chooses treat 'an identifiable cluster of concerns: knowledge and ignorance, truth and probability, learning and education, language, religion and morality' (x). For Johnson, 'as for many of his literary predecessors, the dictionary was both a word book and a combination of all other literary kinds, a quintessential book of books designed to perform all the tasks of entertainment and instruction germane to writing of any sort' (4). It was, in short, 'a world of words.'

That phrase comes from book 11 of *The Ring and the Book*. Guido speaks, almost at the end of his second monologue:

Sirs, have I spoken one word all this while
Out of the world of words I had to say?
Not one word! All was folly; I laughed and mocked!

Sirs, my first true word, all truth and no lie,
Is –   (11.2415–19)

The phrase appears in the context of choices Guido has made in speaking, moral choices that manifest themselves in truth and lying. To make such choices is to use a feature of language which bothers Locke and certainly bothers Johnson: many words are not only equivocal but multiple in meaning.

The most obvious feature of the entries in the *Dictionary* is Johnson's attempt to give all the meanings of a word as it is actually used or has been used, and to supply quotations to illustrate all those meanings. When he defends the 'multiplicity' of his examples, he says that 'those quotations which to careless or unskilful perusers appear only to repeat the same sense, will often exhibit, to a more accurate examiner, diversities of signification, or, at least, afford different shades of the same meaning.' The overwhelming impression of any reader of the *Dictionary* is that words are equivocal in their signification,[11] and that, for all Johnson's powers of accumulating and illustrating and 'reduc[ing] to method,' the language remains, as he himself says near the beginning of his Preface, 'copious without order, and energetick without rules.' Even the commonest words are not univocal. John Collard, a logician whom Browning's father admired, uses the word 'pound' as an example of an equivocal word, but he adds a note of warning: 'Doctor Watts has set down *book* and *house*, as univocal words, yet Dr Samuel Johnson attributes *five* different meanings to the word *book*, and *seven* to the word *house*.'[12] Locke had attacked '*Inconstancy*' as an abuse of language – "tis plain cheat and abuse, when I make [words] stand sometimes for one thing, and sometimes for another'[13] – and yet equivocation is an inescapable feature of the language. Johnson himself despairs when he comes to many of the ordinary verbs in the language, words like 'break' and 'get' and 'make': 'while our language is yet living, and variable by the caprice of every one that speaks it, these words are hourly shifting their relations, and can no more be ascertained in a dictionary, than a grove, in the agitation of a storm, can be accurately delineated from its picture in the water.' The Victorians still praised Johnson, as Carlyle did in 'The Hero as Man of Letters' (1840), for the 'general solidity, honesty, insight and successful method,' for the 'architectural nobleness' of the dictionary, and Maurice, who was a Coleridgian, spoke in 1838 of Johnson's wonderful power of 'collecting and accumulating,' but Maurice also asks, in the light of the historical and comparative studies of the new philology that was making its mark in England by the 1830s, 'Is there no common meaning, not even a bead-string to hang the different meanings upon?'[14] Johnson does not neglect etymology, and he does distinguish between 'primitives' and 'derivatives,' but the distinction is more backward-looking than it is anticipatory: the 'primitives' look back to Lockeian epistemology, where words are the signs of ideas derived from the five senses. Then 'the original sense of words is often driven out of use by their metaphorical acceptations,' Johnson points out, and 'the metaphorical will become the current sense.' Johnson thus explains equivocation in Lockeian terms. As Elizabeth Hedrick observes in her 1987 essay on Johnson's debt to Locke's theory of language, 'he turns Locke's suggestion in Book III of the *Essay*, that abstruse applications of words are ultimately derived from meanings that pertain to objects and experiences in the material world, into a functioning lexicographic principle' (424). Browning, who seems not to have been influenced by the new philology championed in England by Coleridgians like Trench and Maurice,[15] and who told Mrs Orr 'that he knew neither the German philosophers nor their reflection in Coleridge, who would have seemed a likely medium between them and him' (Orr 108), would gain from Johnson a sense of language as a living form which is modified, subtly but inevitably, by every speaker of it, the changes being the result not so much of broad historical or social or cultural forces as of individual decisions, 'the free choice of the Mind' (in Locke's words) 'pursuing its own ends' (*Essay* 3.5.6). Though Johnson complains of the way in which multiple senses make his task difficult, he uses a phrase – 'the exuberance of signification' – which sums up the attraction of words for a young poet like Browning. The extent to which Browning absorbed the lesson of the *Dictionary* as he read it – that words shift and change in meaning because they represent the choices of the individual mind, and so are intimately bound up with human knowledge and human psychology – is perhaps indicated by a comment made by James Murray, the first editor of the dictionary based on the new philology: 'Browning constantly used words without regard to their proper meaning,' Murray complained; 'he has added greatly to the difficulties of the Dictionary.'[16]

The reader may find helpful a brief summary of Locke's theory of language, particularly as it came to Browning through Johnson's *Dictionary*. There was a copy of Locke's *Essay* among Browning's books – it was the third edition of 1695 – and it was given to Browning, like so many of the books important to him, by his father (this book is item A1468 in Kelley and Coley's catalogue of the Brownings' books in *The Browning Collec-*

tions). Book 3 of the *Essay* is called 'Of Words,' and in it Locke sets out his theory. Its essence is that words are the signs of ideas, and that the connection of word and idea is an arbitrary one. Sensations, the data provided by our senses, crowd in upon our minds where, in ways that Locke explains, they become ideas, those generalizations from experience that make up our knowledge. To these ideas we attach sounds – the spoken rather than the written word is primary for Locke – but there is no natural or inevitable connection between sound and idea. Words are 'voluntary Signs' (3.2.2), and we link them with our ideas 'by a voluntary Imposition, whereby such a Word is made arbitrarily the Mark of such an *Idea*' (3.2.1). Through 'common use' and 'tacit Consent' (3.2.8) on signification we are able to communicate with others. Except for proper names, words are general and abstract, 'For the multiplication of Words would have perplexed their Use, had every particular thing need of a distinct name to be signified by' (3.1.3). Nonetheless, words depend upon 'common sensible *Ideas*' (3.1.5), and Locke, as Hans Aarsleff points out in his seminal study of 1967, provides 'the unquestioned rationale for all etymological searching'[17] when he writes that names 'for Actions and Notions quite removed from sense' have in fact 'had their first rise from sensible *Ideas*' (3.1.5). The names of simple ideas – cold, hard, sweet, scarlet – cannot be defined, since they depend upon the actual experience of one of our five senses, but the names of 'mixed Modes and Relations' can be analysed, since for them the mind chooses a certain number of ideas and 'ties them together by a Name' (3.5.4). Again and again Locke makes the point that such naming is a choice made by the mind, reflecting human concerns and serving human purposes. The general terms we use for swift and economical communication, for example, are 'only Creatures of our own making' (3.3.11), since all things in nature are particulars. The sorting out of things into classes and species is 'the Workmanship of the Understanding' (3.3.12), and naming itself, especially of 'mixed Modes and Relations,' is not a capricious act but an arbitrary one; that is, it represents (as the etymology of the word indicates) a judgment made by the understanding, 'the free choice of the Mind, pursuing its own ends' (3.5.6).

In the Preface to his *Dictionary*, Johnson reiterates some of these key Lockeian ideas. The best-known statement is the one in which he insists on language as a human construct. 'I am not yet so lost in lexicography, as to forget that *words are the daughters of earth, and that things are the sons of heaven*. Language is only the instrument of science, and words are but the signs of ideas.' These sentences are so familiar that it is easy to let their implications slip by us. Locke's language theory, grounded as it is in 'common sensible *Ideas*,' seems to be tied firmly to the world of things, so that words can be (from the perspective of naïve empiricism) largely settled in their meaning. Locke is much more complex and problematic than the person who insists, simply, that words mean what they say. God may have created things, but he did not give human beings names for them, so that words are the immediate signs not of things but of our ideas of things. 'Words,' Locke says, 'as they are used by Men, can properly and immediately signify nothing but the *Ideas*, that are in the Mind of the Speaker' (3.2.4), and there is no guarantee that those ideas will be the same as those in the mind of the individual who listens. Human beings '*suppose their Words to be Marks of the* Ideas *in the Minds also of other Men, with whom they communicate*' (3.2.4), and use and consent make communication possible, but the supposition of shared understanding is a supposition only. Every speech act is a potential source of equivocation, that feature of our language Johnson tried to make manageable through clear and careful arrangement of the multiple meanings of words. Elizabeth Hedrick, in her account of Johnson's indebtedness to Locke's theory, argues that Johnson uses two methods for explaining multiple meanings. One method is clearly Lockeian: 'Johnson's impulse, at least initially, is to associate the radical meanings of words with ideas that are closer to the world of sense than those that follow, and to write definitions that move from primitiveness to complication in a way that imitates the action of the mind as it abstracts, then recombines, ideas to form more rarified notions than those with which it begins' (434). The other method is one Locke would deplore: 'Johnson saw that human passions and interests can appropriate, and even supplant, radical senses' (425), and he recognized 'that the authority of the lexicographer is ultimately no match for the irrational forces governing linguistic change' (440). 'Human passion can carry the meanings of words in directions never suggested by their etymons, subordinating their radical senses to human attitudes and interests' (442).

Locke's theory, and Johnson's use of it, provide us with some crucial elements of Browning's understanding of language. In the *Dictionary* Browning encountered what Johnson called, ruefully perhaps, 'exuberance of signification,' each shade of meaning representing a choice made by the mind of the individual speaker, and coloured by his or her passions and emotions. Words, then, are the uttering of the private life of the mind, and they are the expression of the passions and emotions that are bound up with the judgments made by the understanding. Language, in short, is the outering of the inner life – that is its essential nature – and to study human psychology Browning needed only to start with the study of the dictionary.

Since human nature is depraved as a result of the fall, human psychology is largely an account of human foolishness. Because Adam and Eve disobeyed God, 'they fell from their original righteousness and communion with God,' in the words of the Westminster Confession of Faith[18] – 'that excellent compendium of sound doctrine' to which members of the Brownings' church were 'expected cordially to ... assent'[19] – 'and so became dead in sin, and wholly defiled in all the faculties and parts of soul and body.' 'And we in them,' the Congregationalists added.[20] As a result of our sinful state, our ideas of the world are limited and distorted, and our passions and emotions are often in conflict with our judgments, or in control of them. The language which reflects the disorder of our inner lives is, as a consequence, foolish. Browning often uses that adjective to describe words in the love letters, when he and Elizabeth are (in her phrases) 'talking upon paper' and using 'a sphinxine idiom' (*Correspondence* 10:50 and 10:188) so that there are misunderstandings: 'Have I your meaning here?' Robert asks at one point (*Correspondence* 11:75). He tries to explain *his* meaning: 'How I never say what I sit down to say! How saying the little makes me want to say the more! How the least of little things, once taken up as a thing to be imparted to you, seems to need explanations and commentaries, – all is of importance to me – every breath you breathe, every little fact (like this) you are to know!' (*Correspondence* 11:309). The fault, as Robert presents it, lies sometimes in the speaker or writer, sometimes in the nature of language itself. 'As for words, written or spoken – I, who sin forty times a day by light words, and untrue to the thought, I am certainly not used to be easily offended by other people's words, people in the world' (*Correspondence* 12:95–6). Words are not only 'light' but 'foolish.' 'I send you some even more than usual hasty, foolish words' (*Correspondence* 12:214), Robert writes in April 1846, while in July he begins a letter breathlessly with 'Dearest Ba, the love *was* as you admit, beneath all the foolish words.'[21] Even though Robert the lover gallantly excepts Elizabeth's words – 'a word, a simple word from you, is not as a word is counted in the world: the word between us is different' (Kintner 1024) – he condemns language itself in a letter of 25 March 1846: 'Foolish, as all words are' (*Correspondence* 12:177).

The word 'fool' is derived from the Latin *follis*, which means bellows, but it is also, as the *OED* points out, 'in late popular Latin employed in the sense of "wind-bag," empty-headed person, fool.' The etymology gives us a cluster of images which recur throughout Browning's poetry and which indicate that in a fallen world 'words are,' as Clara says at one point in *Red Cotton Night-Cap Country*, 'but words and wind' (2329). The bellows itself turns up in 'Of Pacchiarotto, and How He Worked in Distemper,' for instance, and elsewhere the bladder and the bubble are variations on the windbag. All swell up as people breathe and blow and puff (a favourite verb of Browning's),[22] and all eventually break to reveal vacuity within. 'Soon, the late puffed bladder, pricked, shows lank and skinny' ('Pietro of Abano' 107). The pricking of the bubble may also be a messy business, as when Browning's Aristophanes uses it as a metaphor for the demagogue:

'(Noisome air-bubble, buoyed up, borne along
By kindred breath of knave and fool below,
Whose hearts swell proudly as each puffing face
Grows big, reflected in that glassy ball,
Vacuity, just bellied out to break
And righteously bespatter friends the first)'

(*Aristophanes' Apology* 1696–1701)

The breaking is, as this passage indicates, a deflating of human pride, the agent of the collapse being either truth or 'some clear word of God.' Truth has a beneficial effect on man, says Don Juan in *Fifine at the Fair*: it 'Neither plumes up his will nor puffs him out with pride' (2256) – this from a man who characterizes all that he has said of Elvire as 'word-bubbles' (2315). God is truth, and his word pricks the bubble of human words or clears away their haze. It is Bishop Blougram who uses the phrase 'some clear word of God' (463) as a contrast for the 'puff of hazy instinct, idle talk' (465) of Napoleon. The effect of 'idle talk' is summed up in the French proverb *se payer de mots*, which Browning uses in the Epilogue to *Pacchiarotto and How He Worked in Distemper*: 'If I paid myself with words / (As the French say well) I were dupe indeed!' (73–4).

One of Quarles's *Emblemes* ('my childhood's pet book,' Robert told Elizabeth in 1846; Kintner 978) makes use of the etymology of the word 'fool' and is a probable source for the tropes Browning uses. It is the first emblem in the second book (see illustration), and it pictures a figure in cap and bells trying to blow out the sun with a bellows. His companion, described as 'silly Cupid,' lights a candle on top of an orb (the world),

Sic Lumine Lumen ademptum.

The fool trying to blow out the light of the sun with a bellows. Emblem 1 of book 2 of Francis Quarles's *Emblems Divine and Moral: Together with Hieroglyphics of the Life of Man* (London, 1777). This particular edition was in Browning's library, the poet's copy having belonged to his grandfather. See item A1913 in Kelley and Coley's *The Browning Collections*.

but his is a 'false' and 'feeble' light which is 'self-consuming.' *Sic Lumine Lumen ademptum*, 'thus light is taken away by light,' is the motto. The verb *adimo*, when used of a person, refers to death, and the consequences of the actions of these two fools are, as the explanatory poem makes clear, death and 'perpetual night.' Here is the sixth and last stanza of the *explicatio*:

> Deluded mortals, tell me, when
>   Your daring breath has blown
> Heav'n's taper out, and you have spent your own,
>   What fire shall warm you then?
>   Ah, fools! perpetual night
>   Shall haunt your souls with Stygian fright,
> Where they shall boil in flames, but flames shall bring no light.

The epigram summarizes the moral:

> Thou blow'st heav'n's fire, the whilst thou go'st about,
> Rebellious fool, in vain, to blow it out:
> Thy folly adds confusion to thy death;
> Heav'n's fire confounds, when fann'd with folly's breath.

'Folly's breath' may be an accurate description of human speech after the fall, but it is, like the vanities condemned by the preacher in Ecclesiastes, double in nature: it may be empty, but it is also of immense significance. Just as Qoheleth, conscious that 'God shall bring every work into judgment,' 'still taught the people knowledge' and 'sought to find out acceptable words' (Ecclesiastes 12:14, 9, 10), so human beings speak with purpose, however foolish, and God can use such speech for his own purposes. Our understanding of God's use of human speech may be clearer if we turn to the Westminster Confession. As a result of the fall, human beings are (in the view of the Calvinist theology which lies behind the Confession) 'wholly defiled,' and man, being 'dead in sin, is not able by his own strength to convert himself, or to prepare himself thereunto.' Therefore God has made a 'Covenant of Grace,' a second undertaking replacing the first, the Covenant of Works, which required the obedience of Adam and Eve. In this second covenant, God 'freely offereth unto sinners life and salvation by Jesus Christ, requiring of them faith in him that they may be saved, and promising to give unto all those that are ordained unto life, his holy Spirit, to make them willing and able to believe' (32–43). The action of the Holy Spirit is crucial. It operates not in extraordinary ways but through our ordinary human faculties, especially the understanding, where it enables us to interpret the Word and to reach a 'full perswasion and assurance of the infallible Truth and Divine Authority thereof' (19). 'We acknowledge,' say the authors of the Confession, 'the inward illumination of the Spirit of God to be necessary for the saving understanding of such things as are revealed in the Word' (20). The 'inward work of the holy Spirit' (19) manifests itself not only in reading and interpreting but in speaking and writing, and because it does not forestall 'that natural liberty' (42) – that 'power of acting upon choice,' the Congregationalists added (Walker 377) – which characterizes the will of all human beings, it works in subtle and mysterious ways. Human speech, so ostensibly foolish, is also the means by which the Spirit operates, and human breath, so apparently material and empty, may also be one with that divine breath. Browning is fascinated with the ironic conjunction of those two kinds of breath, and with the riddle which appears as soon as one tries to distinguish them. This is the kind of riddle which has no definitive answer, at least among human beings, though God has the answer and will, we trust, ultimately bring light out of darkness, and replace the obscurity of the glass through which we now see darkly with the clarity of face-to-face contact.

A good example of Browning's posing of such a riddle is 'An Epistle Containing the Strange Medical Experience of Karshish, the Arab Physician.' The poet positions his nineteenth-century reader in such a way that it is relatively easy for him or her to recognize the folly of Karshish: the medical knowledge which the Arab physician gathers and values ('there's a spider here' 45) the reader knows to be worthless; and the judgment he makes about the death and resurrection of Lazarus ("Tis but a case of mania' 79) the reader knows to be wrong. Moreover, Karshish's dismissal of Lazarus as 'stark mad' (264) cannot stand up against the reader's recognition that Lazarus interprets and judges all things in human life correctly, in terms of their ultimate import. 'Should his child sicken unto death, – why, look / For scarce abatement of his cheerfulness, / Or pretermission of the daily craft!' (159–61) – because Lazarus knows that immortality is a sure thing. So Lazarus looks like the wise man, and Karshish looks like the fool. Moreover, it is the fool who speaks – or rather writes – and if his words are the expression of his soul, they are, in the materialist terms Karshish himself uses, 'that puff of vapour from his mouth' (6). Yet we note that Karshish is curiously attracted to

Lazarus and unwilling, in spite of all the better knowledge that he professes, to abandon the riddle of the 'case.' Nor can Karshish provide 'Good cause for the peculiar interest / And awe indeed this man has touched me with' (287–8), and he cannot explain his motive for writing: 'An itch I had, a sting to write, a tang!' (67). We note that the nouns Karshish uses all name physical sensations, and yet we suspect that these suggestions of irritation and appetite are not a full account of what propels him. The idea which in fact propels him – 'This man so cured regards the curer, then, / As – God forgive me! who but God himself' (267–8) – he dismisses as evidence of the madness of Lazarus, and he apologizes for repeating it, excusing himself because 'in writing to a leech / 'Tis well to keep back nothing of a case' (265–6). Yet that is the idea to which he returns in the sudden outpouring in the postscript: 'The very God! think, Abib, dost thou think?' (304). The idea is, of course, the Incarnation, and we suspect that, through all the folly of Karshish's interpretations and judgments, the Holy Spirit is inwardly at work, making it possible for Karshish to interpret the 'case' which so puzzles him, manifesting itself in the fascination Karshish feels for Lazarus, and moving Karshish towards (what the Westminster Confession calls) 'the saving understanding' by irritating him into writing. The prodding may be that of the Holy Spirit, but its presence is by no means certain, and we can only guess at it (in the words of the critic Browning quoted to Isabella Blagden in 1863) 'in details' and see it 'only by reflexion.' So the text for us (and Lazarus for Karshish) is like 'the whole creation' as described by Barrett Browning's Romney Leigh: it 'perplexes us with questions' (*Aurora Leigh* 4.1175–6).[23] The poem provides a metaphor for the process of answering the questions, and it is the pilgrimage, the journey where disparate and apparently miscellaneous experiences all take their place in a single comprehensive and comprehensible pattern. 'I reach Jerusalem at morn,' Karshish writes, 'There set in order my experiences' (52–3).

To set in order one's experiences is to interpret them, and interpretation is, in Browning's view, the crucial human activity, as we shall see. We must now look at a number of models for reading and interpreting. These models are related to each other, and they come from several sources: Browning's upbringing in the Congregational church and the church's way of reading and interpreting the Bible; Locke's account of the way in which we judge phenomena and so arrive at opinion (particularly when knowledge based on the evidence of the senses is limited or incomplete); and the way in which the emblem, with its picture, motto, and explanatory poem, answers the question Bunyan's pilgrim poses in the House of the Interpreter: 'What means this?' We begin with Congregationalism.

The Browning forebears belonged to the Church of England, but when Robert Browning Senior married, he followed his wife to an independent congregation, the York Street Chapel, Walworth, where the minister was the Reverend George Clayton. The document which Clayton signed on accepting the pastoral charge specifies the beliefs and order of the church: the 'Doctrinal truth' it professes is 'for the sake of distinction ... called *Calvinistic*'; its beliefs are stated in 'that excellent compendium of sound doctrine,' the Westminster Confession of Faith, and in the 'larger and smaller Catechisms'; its discipline and order are 'those usually observed by Protestant Dissenters of the Congregational Denomination.'[24]

The poet-to-be was probably not much moved by the structure of a Clayton sermon. Like Browning's father when he was reading a book, Clayton is fond of numbering the main points and the subdivisions of his argument, but such clarity of organization must have seemed mechanical to the young Browning, and it does not do justice to the complexity and depth of Clayton's understanding of Congregationalism and of the theology which defined it. After he has read his biblical text and provided a brief introduction, Clayton typically outlines his main points, 'first,' 'secondly,' and 'thirdly'; then he elaborates each of those points, carefully numbering the points in each subdivision; finally, with some formula such as 'I call upon you' or 'I beseech you,' he appeals directly to his congregation to apply the lesson of his text, since, as he says in a sermon of 1838, there are 'things to be believed, and things to be done; or, as it has been expressed by some, the credenda, and the agenda, of Christianity.'[25] The young Browning may have been bored with Clayton's numbering of his points (the speaker in *Christmas-Eve* sleeps through 'the heads of the sermon, nine in number, / And woke up now at the tenth and lastly' 1256–7), but because Clayton's practice is for the purpose of conveying his understanding to others and not part of the effort and striving and attention which, he insists, are due to every biblical text, his practice masks his way of wrestling with the words of the Bible. That way Clayton defines in his Introductory Sermon to his 1838–9 *A Course of Sermons on Faith and Practice*, a series of discourses on the Apostles' Creed, clause by clause, and on each of the Ten Commandments. 'How is the word of God to be read?' is a question in the 'larger catechism' (which the York Street Chapel had specified as one statement of its accepted doctrine), and the answer identifies the understanding as the chief faculty acting on the scriptures, which are to be approached 'with diligence, and attention to the matter and scope of them; with meditation, application, self-denial, and prayer.'[26] Clayton's Introductory Sermon is an elaboration of that answer.

Clayton's text is 2 Timothy 1:13: 'Hold fast the form of sound words, which thou hast heard of me, in faith and love which is in Christ Jesus.' In his usual systematic way, Clayton explores the possible meanings of 'the form of sound words,' but our concern at the moment is with the way in which we approach them, and that way is indicated in the imperative 'Hold fast.' Clayton's focus is upon the understanding (though he notes that 'there are certain limits to rational investigation where the truth of God is concerned. There are points which we shall never be able, in the present imperfect state, to fathom or explain'). Here is his account of the understanding at work:

> The understanding must be employed in ascertaining the sense and meaning of Holy Scripture; in comparing evidence; in deducing just conclusions from authentic premises; in tracing the harmony, the connexion, and the bearing of one truth upon another; so that the various links of the chain may be held in their unbroken connexion. This is the work of an enlightened understanding, which must be employed in investigating, comparing, establishing, and deriving improvement from, the truth presented to our notice. (8)

Why is so much mental effort necessary? Because 'you can never hold fast that which you have never considered, and received, and understood, and of which you have not the rational grounds for a satisfactory conviction' (9). All that mental effort, however, is not unsupported, and in the Puritan tradition out of which Congregationalism came, the one great support is the Holy Spirit, the Interpreter who not only sustains the operations of the understanding but carries the truth of its conclusions into the heart. Here is Clayton on the 'witness by the powerful operations of the Holy Spirit within':

> It is a very easy thing to maintain an opinion as an opinion – an orthodox tenet – because we may be able clearly to define it, and abundantly to substantiate it by rational evidence. That is one thing. But it is another thing to receive the truth into the heart, and to experience all its bland and blessed effects in transforming the character, and in renewing the soul. Then we have a witness which is more valuable, in point of fact, than ten thousand

theories, or ten thousand merely speculative arguments. This is the inward evidence which every real Christian derives from his own state of mind, his feeling, his character, his conduct; and by which he is able to demonstrate the truth of the blessed Gospel.   (12)

Clayton is, in short, defining the kind of reader response where the interpretation of a text is not a matter of intellectual assent alone, but a recreation of the text in the mind, feelings, character, and conduct. The text becomes living truth. Whatever Browning's specific beliefs, he seems to require both of himself and of his readers the essential activities in the interpretation of biblical texts: 'comparing evidence,' 'deducing just conclusions from authentic premises,' and 'tracing ... the connexion, and the bearing of one truth upon another'; moreover, he does not hesitate to suggest, as he does with a secular text like *The Ring and the Book*, that such interpretation will 'save the soul.' The question Browning asks at the beginning of that poem – 'Do you see this . . . Book'? (1.33) – is in effect the question he asks of all his texts, and while the seeing may initially only be that of the physical eye, that verb soon expands to embrace the hermeneutics with which we are at the moment concerned. Exegesis alone is not enough: the text must become a living power – an uncomfortable and disconcerting one – within us, and in the drama of our inner lives the text plays the role of antagonist. We can see that aspect of interpretation more clearly if we turn to a work with which Browning grew up. It is *The Pilgrim's Progress* and it begins, significantly, with a man reading a book.

The Pilgrim's Progress was a 'favourite childhood book,' and John Maynard in *Browning's Youth* retells the story of the young Browning shocking a visitor, 'a certain Mrs Cole,' by fetching '"from the library a carved head which he called, 'Christian' & stroked affectionately saying he was 'very fond of old Christian.'"'[27] 'Old Christian,' the reader of Bunyan will remember, first appears in rags, '*a Book in his hand, and a great burden upon his Back.*'[28] Bunyan in his dream 'looked, and saw him open the Book, and Read therein; and as he read, he wept and trembled: and not being able longer to contain, he brake out with a lamentable cry; saying, *what shall I do?*' (8). The book is, of course, the Bible, and for fallen humanity, depraved as a result of the disobedience of Adam and Eve, its text is an indictment, bringing human beings to a conviction of their sinful state. The book spurs Christian to action, and its words will ultimately comfort and save him as he engages with them, and comes to realize, gradually, their full function and power. The biblical passage defining that power – a text quoted frequently in sermons of Browning's day – is 2 Timothy 3:16 and 17: 'All scripture is given by inspiration of God, and is profitable for doctrine, for reproof, for correction, for instruction in righteousness: That the man of God may be perfect, thoroughly furnished unto all good works.' 'Perfect,' one perhaps needs to point out, means 'complete,' and the use of that adjective suggests a progress from the partial and limited to the full and finished. Such progress is part of Clayton's view of the 'two great objects' of 'every Christian pastor': one is conversion, which Clayton likens to birth, and the other is 'establishment and edification,' which he compares to 'the progressive stages of growth, in childhood, and in youth, till it shall reach maturity and perfection' (2). Such progress depends upon texts, which begin as a challenge (and sometimes as an accuser) and end as a comforter and the means of salvation. Yet another book that was in Browning's library fills out our understanding of that moral and spiritual progress.

The book is by an author whose emblems were favourites of Browning's: Francis Quarles. This particular volume is not an emblem book but a collection called *Judgment and Mercy for Afflicted Souls; or, Meditations, Soliloquies and Prayers* (first published in 1646, but Browning's copy was published in London in 1837). Here we see the experience of conversion dramatized in a series of characters (I am using the word in the seventeenth-century sense, as a label for a literary genre), and in each section the interaction of character and text is the substance of the drama. The work is in two parts and (in the words of the anonymous nineteenth-century editor),

> in the first part, we see the wicked man glorying in his iniquity; but whilst he is defending, by the most plausible reasoning, his evil course, a scripture judgment presents itself to his conscience, drives him to meditation, and from thence to prayer. In the second part, the sinner is represented as under the hiding of God's countenance – not exulting in his strength, but deploring his weakness and insufficiency: he is comforted by a scripture promise, is led to meditation, and strengthened by prayer.   (xi–xii)

Each character in this work is an internalized drama, with the biblical text bringing about the peripeteia: conviction of sin in part 1, comfort and conversion in part 2.

The pattern of the internal dramatic action is the same in both parts. 'The Sensual Man,' the first character in part 1, begins with 'Come, let us be merry, and rejoice our souls in frolic and in fresh delights' (1). Then there is a turn, signalled by the conjunction 'But' ('But, my soul, when those evil days shall come') and leading to the biblical text: *'God will bring thee to judgment.* Eccles. xi. 9.' This is followed by three longer biblical texts, one from Proverbs and two from Ecclesiastes, and then by three quotations from church fathers. The texts (like the Ten Commandments for the sinful person) accuse the speaker, and bring about a conviction of sin. Following the texts is 'His Soliloquy,' which begins, 'What hast thou now to say, O my soul, why this judgment, seconded with divine proofs, and backed with the harmony of holy men, should not proceed against thee?' (2). A conviction of sin leads to conversion, and 'His Soliloquy' ends with 'Prostrate thyself before Him who delights not in the death of a sinner, and present thy petitions to Him who can deny thee nothing in the name of a Saviour.' There follows 'His Prayer,' which includes contrition and confession ('I am impure and vile, and have wallowed in the puddle of mine own corruptions'), and finally a petition for conversion: 'Make me a new creature, O my God, and destroy the old man within me' (3). The pattern in part 2 is parallel. The first section in part 2 is called 'The Weary Man's Burden,' where the speaker begins by lamenting, 'I have lost the favour of my God' (69). The turn leads immediately to the biblical passage: 'Put thy trust in God, who hath said – *Come unto me all you that are heavy laden, and I will give you rest.* Matt. xi. 28' (69–70). There are three more biblical passages and one from a church father. Then comes 'His Soliloquy,' which begins, 'True, my soul – if thou only cast an eye upon the letter of the law, that letter would soon cast thee and condemn thee' (70). (In the words of one of Isaac Watts's hymns, also among Browning's books, 'to convince and to condemn / Is all the law can do.') In this part, however, the biblical text is a comfort: 'But, O my soul, there is a Gospel to mitigate the rigor of that law' (70). This fact leads to 'His Prayer,' also with its contrition and confession ('acknowledging my grievous sins') and its petition: 'Let thy Word comfort me, let thy truth conduct me, and let thy Spirit counsel me' (71). At each point in these meditations or internalized dramas, the quotation from the Bible interrupts the reader's own thoughts and initiates a parleying with the interjecting text; that dialectic leads to a struggle of understanding, and finally to the comfort of the biblical promise of salvation. One remembers that a conversion is etymologically a turn, and in these meditations and soliloquies, the text, and the Holy Spirit within it, turn the sinner and effect his or her salvation.

We note, in passing, how closely conversion is linked with troping.

Both are turns, and both involve the transformation of one thing into something else. Since conversion is a turn from sin to salvation, that something else is the opposite of the state or point where we start, and in this context troping is not just the allying of unlike things but the metamorphosis of one thing into something which is just the reverse of its nature or character. The biblical verse which defines conversion also uses similes where the image is reversed or inverted. It is Isaiah 1:18, and the prophet exhorts his listeners to repentance: 'Come now, and let us reason together, saith the LORD: though your sins be as scarlet, they shall be as white as snow; though they be red like crimson, they shall be as wool.' Browning quotes this verse in *Red Cotton Night-Cap Country* as the 'march-tune' (401) for his verbal battle with Annie Thackeray, and he quotes it again in 'Ned Bratts,' the poem from the 1879 *Dramatic Idyls* which, of all Browning's poems, makes the fullest use of *The Pilgrim's Progress*. Bunyan repeats the verse to Ned Bratts's wife:

> '"Look unto me and be ye saved!" saith God:
> "I strike the rock, outstreats the life-stream at my rod!
> Be your sins scarlet, wool shall they seem like, – although
> As crimson red, yet turn white as the driven snow!"'
> (179–82)

Browning's Bunyan links the prophet's troping with a popular emblem for a miraculous and saving transformation. That emblem comes out of the miracle at Meribah (Exodus 17:1–7), where Moses strikes the rock and brings forth living water. The transformation of rock into water is yet another instance of the radical change that we are linking with troping, and Browning himself makes the link explicit in the third book of *Sordello*, when he breaks off his narrative and contemplates his own present situation 'on a ruined palace-step' (3.676) in Venice. There Moses becomes the type of the 'Metaphysic Poet' (3:829), the model for Browning himself, though the miracle as performed by the poet takes courage and though the results may be meagre: 'Mark ye the dim first oozings? Meribah!' (3:830). In 'One Word More,' 'He who smites the rock and spreads the water' (74) is identified with the poet who is both prophet and mage. Eleanor Cook has explored these connections in her 1974 book, *Browning's Lyrics*, and George Landow has shown how Moses striking the rock was (in large part because of Paul's typological interpretation of the act in 1 Corinthians 10:4) a commonplace type for Victorian readers.[29] We shall return to these connections, but our concern at the moment is with a divinely inspired transformation for which the verbal equivalent is troping. Inspired as that act may be, poet – and sinner – are not simply passive when filled with the power of the Holy Spirit. Nor is the change the result of a sudden and irresistible illumination. Instead, it is more likely to come, slowly and even painfully, out of the understanding and its typical work of interpretation and application, application manifesting itself primarily in the making of choices.

Choice is the crucial action in bringing about the transformations we are examining, and it is the chief expression of Christian liberty, that concept so central to Milton and to Puritan theology, and to Congregationalism, which belongs to the Puritan tradition. Christian liberty was the basis of the Congregational understanding of church order: each 'gathered' church was independent and 'particular,' and 'Besides these particular churches' (in the words of the Savoy Declaration (1658), which added to the Westminster Confession (1646–8) a 'platform of church polity' defining the institution and order of the Congregational churches) 'there is not instituted by Christ any Church more extensive or Catholique entrusted with power for the administration of his Ordinances, or the execution of any authority in his name' (Walker 404). The Congregationalists extended such liberty to the verbal formulations of their faith, and while the essence of their faith is unchanging, the words in which it is expressed may – and almost certainly will – vary from person to person and from group to group. The preface which the Congregationalists added in 1658 to the Westminster Confession is the first indication of that freedom.

On matters of doctrine, the Congregationalists tolerated diversity of opinion while celebrating 'the substance of the same *common salvation, or unity of their faith*' (354). Their preface asserts that the text which follows (the Westminster Confession, with some changes, omissions, and additions), while an expression of 'their *common faith and salvation*,' is not a test of faith, nor an exaction: it is 'no way to be made use of as an *imposition* upon any.' 'The *Spirit of Christ* is in himself too *free*, great and generous a Spirit,' the preface continues, 'to suffer himself to be used by any humane arm, to whip men into belief; he drives not, but *gently leads into all truth*, and *perswades* men to *dwell in the tents* of *like precious Faith*; which would lose of its preciousness and value, if that sparkle of freeness shone not in it: The character of his people is to be a *willing people*' (Walker 355). 'And as this great Spirit is in himself free, when, and how far, and in whom to work, so where and when he doth work, he carrieth it with the same freedom, and is said to be a *free Spirit*, as he both is, and works in us: And where this *Spirit of the Lord is, there is Liberty'* (Walker 356). When George Clayton preaches on such Christian liberty, in an 1836 sermon called *Christian Unity,* he repeats the essential points of this preface. 'A firm and steadfast adherence to "the truth as it is in Jesus," must be regarded as indispensable to the preservation of Christian unity,' but 'The matters which God has not insisted on, in his written word, as essential to salvation, let no man magnify into paramount importance.'[30] 'Give me,' Clayton says, 'entire concord in essentials, and entire liberty in things indifferent; and I can fully understand how all real Christians, in despite of the differences, which have too widely separated them, may be perfectly joined together in the same mind and in the same judgment' (10). Moreover, even for essential matters, there is no need that the words in which they are expressed should be the same for all believers. 'The free exercise of private judgment' (10) means that there will be different ways of expressing the same beliefs, and words themselves are less important than their sense. Here is how Clayton champions the varying verbal witness of individual believers (the reference at the beginning of this quotation is to his text, 1 Corinthians 1:10, 'that ye all speak the same thing'):

> It is to be noted that the apostle desires that they would speak the same THING, though not always the same precise words. We must not be too rigidly exact in tying men to our theological vocabulary. Words may be either ill or well chosen, to convey any particular idea or conception; but let me not quarrel with my brother for the lack of good taste, or good judgment, in the structure of his phraseology, or for an infelicitous selection of his terms, if he really mean the same thing. In my turn I may require the same candid indulgence, and should deem myself hardly dealt by, to be made an offender for a word. The tranquillity of the church has been too often disturbed by the 'strife of words,' and abundantly too much stress has been laid on 'the shibboleth' of party, when imposed and forced upon others, whether their organs have been framed to pronounce it or not. *Things*, not words, are to be regarded – 'That ye all speak the same thing.'   (12)

The chief manifestation of liberty is the immediacy of the relation between the individual soul and God. In addition to the freedom from sin and death that Christ 'purchased' for believers, the Westminster Confession states, Christian liberty includes believers' 'free access to God, and their yielding obedience unto him, not out of slavish fear, but a childe-like love and willing minde' (68–9) – rather like the unfallen

Adam's 'true filial freedom' (4.294) in *Paradise Lost*. According to Mrs Orr, Browning's 'conviction of direct relations with the Creator' was 'the central fact of his theology' (Orr, 373), and it is a persuasion which comes directly out of his Congregationalist upbringing. So central is this focus on 'the salvation of individual souls' that Richard J. Helmstadter has argued, in a 1979 essay, that such individual effort is the defining idea of nonconformist thinking from the 1830s to the 1880s.[31] 'In keeping with their very strong tendency to treat men as individuals rather than as members of a larger corporation such as the church or the state, Evangelicals accorded to each individual a heavy weight of responsibility for his own salvation,' Helmstadter argues (142). His thesis has been criticized, by David Bebbington and others, for not giving sufficient weight to a sense of communal responsibility, in the family, in business, and in politics,[32] but nonetheless the emphasis on individual salvation and on individual responsibility for it is at the centre of nonconformist thinking. Section 9 of the Westminster Confession is entitled 'Of Free-will,' and it begins, 'God hath endued the Will of man with that natural liberty and power of acting upon choice, that it is neither forced, nor by any absolute necessity of Nature determined to do good or evil' (Walker 377). The phrase 'and power of acting upon choice' is the Congregationalists' addition to the Westminster Confession, and that addition emphasizes the centrality of choice in one's moral and spiritual life.

Christian liberty was the chief aspect of Congregationalism admired by Elizabeth Barrett. Six months into Robert's courtship of her, and in the midst of a discussion about schismatics ('hating as I do from the roots of my heart, all that rending of the garment of Christ'), Elizabeth suddenly confesses, 'I used to go with my father always, when I was able, to the nearest dissenting chapel of the congregationalists – from liking the simplicity of that praying & speaking without books – & a little too from disliking the theory of state churches.' She criticizes the Congregationalists – 'There is a narrowness among the dissenters which is wonderful, – an arid, grey Puritanism in the clefts of their souls' – but is attracted by their sense of freedom under God: 'but it seems to me clear that they know what the "liberty of Christ" *means*, far better than those do who call themselves "churchmen"' (*Correspondence* 11:10). Robert is delighted by Elizabeth's confession: 'Can it be you, my own you past putting away, *you* are a schismatic and frequenter of Independent Dissenting Chapels? And you confess this to *me* – whose father and mother went this morning to the very Independent Chapel where they took me, all those years back, to be baptized – and where they heard, this morning, a sermon preached by the very minister who officiated on that other occasion!' (*Correspondence* 11:15).[33]

Choice is possible only if one's knowledge is incomplete – a univocal text would leave no room for interpretation – and the Westminster Confession defines the limitations on our knowledge and provides a guide to interpretation. While God's scheme of salvation may be clear enough, much must be deduced from Scripture: 'All things in Scripture are not alike plain in themselves, nor alike clear unto all: yet those things which are necessary to be known, believed and observed for Salvation, are so clearly propounded and opened in some place of Scripture or other, that not onely the learned, but the unlearned, in a due sense of the ordinary means, may attain unto a sufficient understanding of them' (20). Sufficient, but not complete. Interpretation is always necessary – judgments must be made about the meaning of texts and about their applicability to one's life – and interpretation is fraught with difficulties. There is only one rule of which we can be certain: 'The infallible Rule of Interpretation of Scripture, is the Scripture it self' (21). That rule means that 'when there is a question about the true and full sense of any Scripture (which is not manifold, but one) it must be searched and known by other places, that speak more clearly' (21). Such searching obviously involves choices, and when there is choice, there is always the possibility of error. Interpreters, however, have a guiding light and a source of authority in the Holy Spirit. 'We acknowledge,' say the writers of the confession of faith in a statement I have quoted already, 'the inward illumination of the Spirit of God to be necessary for the saving understanding of such things as are revealed in the Word' (20).

The secular source of the interpretive process which leads to choice is Locke's *An Essay Concerning Human Understanding*, and in spite of all the charges against Locke in the first half of the nineteenth century that he had undermined religious belief – and Hans Aarsleff in his essay 'Locke's Reputation in Nineteenth-Century England' gives a detailed account of all those charges[34] – the *Essay* is in fact a guide to judgment where knowledge is limited or uncertain. The *Essay*, as we shall see, is not at all incompatible with Christian liberty as understood by the Congregationalists, and it only seemed incompatible to those who knew Locke by reputation, or who had read only parts of the *Essay*. Most people were aware of Locke's epistemology – that, in the words of John Stuart Mill, 'all knowledge consists of generalizations from experience'[35] – and most people knew that Locke had rejected innate ideas, but few read the whole *Essay* or were aware of its total shape and purpose.

Locke does indeed reject innate ideas in book 1, and he does set out the epistemology for which he was best known in book 2, but in the third book, as we have seen, he adds the language theory which goes along with that epistemology, and in book 4 – the climactic part of the *Essay* – he brings those concerns together and relates them to conduct: the exercise of judgment and the making of choices on which to base our actions. The epistemology for which Locke is remembered suggests, to the naïve empiricist, that we can be certain only of those things for which we have the evidence of our five senses, and it is easy to assume, as some did, that such evidence is a sufficient guide to life. Locke, however, is not nearly so sanguine and much more realistic. Knowledge is limited, he keeps insisting, and is inadequate as a guide for conduct. Here is a crucial passage from book 4:

> The Understanding Faculties being given to Man, not barely for Speculation, but also for the Conduct of his Life, Man would be at a great loss, if he had nothing to direct him, but what has the Certainty of true *Knowledge*. For that being very short and scanty, as we have seen, he would be often utterly in the dark, and in most of the Actions of his Life, perfectly at a stand, had he nothing to guide him in the absence of clear and certain Knowledge. He that will not eat, till he has Demonstration that it will nourish him; he that will not stir, till he infallibly knows the Business he goes about will succeed, will have little else to do, but sit still and perish.   (4.14.1)

But we do not, in fact, 'sit still and perish'; we go about our daily business without the aid of proof, and on the basis of our judging probabilities. Judgment is 'the Faculty, which God has given Man to supply the want of clear and certain Knowledge in Cases where that cannot be had' (4.14.3); it is our guide in this 'State of Mediocrity and Probationership' (4.14.2), so that we may 'spend the days of this our Pilgrimage with Industry and Care, in the search, and following of that way, which might lead us to a State of greater Perfection' (4.14.2).

Locke's reason for writing the *Essay* is to set out the grounds for the making of choices and to guide us in the degrees of trust we can put in those decisions. Hence, in book 4 he defines a scale of interpretations, from most certain to least probable. Intuitive Knowledge, where the Mind 'perceives the Truth, as the Eye doth light, only by being directed toward it' (4.2.1), and Demonstrative Knowledge, which requires intervening ideas or proofs, both provide certainty. Much more problematic are the various kinds of opinion, '*the several degrees and grounds of Proba-*

bility, and Assent or Faith' (4.15.2). The highest degree of probability is based on 'the conformity of any thing with our own Knowledge, Observation, and Experience' (4.15.4), and is our ordinary attitude towards 'all the stated Constitutions and Properties of Bodies, and the regular proceedings of Causes and Effects in the ordinary course of Nature' (4.16.6). The next degree of probability is based on the testimony of others, 'when I find by my own Experience, and the Agreement of all others that mention it, a thing to be, for the most part, so; and that the particular instance of it is attested by many and undoubted Witnesses' (4.16.7). 'Thus far the matter goes easy enough' (4.16.9), so long as testimony squares with common experience; but when testimony questions the validity of such experience, or contradicts it, we are, after the mind has examined all such matters, in the realm of *'Belief, Conjecture, Guess, Doubt, Wavering, Distrust, Disbelief,* etc.' (4.16.9). In this realm, the grounds for giving or withholding assent are, when judged by the criterion of knowledge, shaky or insubstantial. But in many matters which are of concern to us, we must interpret, judge, choose, and act, though knowledge is either partial or unattainable.

I summarize Locke at some length, not because there is any evidence that Browning read the *Essay* itself, but because book 4 lies behind a system of logic championed by Browning's father and certainly known by the poet, though he clearly had reservations about this enthusiasm of his parent, and joked about logic-books during his courtship of Elizabeth. She teases Robert about his supposed fiancée, 'Miss Campbell,' and his conduct with her: 'No wonder that your father should give you books of logic to study, books on the "right use of reason," if you do not understand that I am not better than she.' Robert replies gallantly, 'Ah, you reconcile all extremes, destroy the force of all logic-books, my father's or mine' (Kintner 1013, 1016). Nonetheless, the system is one which attempts to show us how to reason under the actual and limited conditions of our lives, and it moves finally in a direction not envisioned by Locke and probably not much attended to by Browning Senior, though it certainly attracted the interest of Browning Junior, who borrowed its terms to explain his actual use of language in poetry. That direction is a subversion of 'system' entirely, and the substitution of 'method.' The language of 'method' attempts to reflect the actual movements of the mind in thinking and interpreting; moreover, 'method' typically distinguishes between such language and the language we use to teach our discoveries and conclusions to others.

The logic is the work of a John Collard, and Browning's father thought so highly of him that he bought all of his books, as well as the text of another thinker who acknowledges his indebtedness to Collard. Collard published his first book under a pseudonym – he reversed his surname to Dralloc – in 1795. It is *An Epitome of Logic*, and on the flyleaf Browning wrote, in a note dated 4 June 1873, 'My father estimated this book highly: he mentioned it to Archbishop Whately, who had never heard of *Dralloc* – i.e. Collard.'[36] In 1796, Collard published, under his own name, an expanded edition of the *Epitome*. He called it *The Essentials of Logic: being a second edition of Dralloc's Epitome Improved, comprising an Universal System of Practical Reasoning; illustrated by familiar examples, from approved authors*. Browning's father's copy is in the Armstrong Browning Library, and is marked and annotated in his characteristically systematic way: he underlines key words of the argument, he marks the stages of the argument in the margins with letters ('a,' 'b,' 'c,' etc.) or with numbers, and he uses vertical lines or slanting parallel lines in the margins beside passages that seem to him important.[37] This particular copy is marked from beginning to end. The parent's way of reading a book may account for Robert's telling Elizabeth, in August of 1846, that he and his father 'have not one taste in common, one artistic taste,' and 'the sympathy has not been an intellectual one' (Kintner 960). The son certainly would not have gone on as the father did, buying Collard's reworking of his material into a school text (*A Praxis of Logic, for the Use of Schools*, London, 1799), and purchasing yet another book, Levi Hedge's *Elements of Logick: or A Summary of the General Principles and Different Modes of Reasoning* (Cambridge, Mass., 1816); Hedge was a Harvard philosopher who names Collard approvingly as one of his predecessors. Collard's work, and Hedge's, are so heavily indebted to Locke that both read like compendiums of the *Essay*. They summarize Locke's epistemology and his theory of language. More important, however, they represent a move (initiated by Locke) towards ways of thinking where the procedures and arrangements grow directly and organically out of the matter and the situation.

Collard's work, and Hedge's, belong to the 'new logic' of the eighteenth century – I am using Wilbur Samuel Howell's label – as opposed to the 'old logic,' Aristotelian in origin, with its emphasis on 'the deductive examination of accepted truths as its main procedure of enquiry' and on the syllogism as its 'master implement.'[38] The 'new logic,' in contrast, had its origins in Bacon and Locke, 'stressed observation and experiment as the main procedures of inquiry,' and 'regarded induction as the most basic instrument in logic' (Howell 696). In his chapter 'John

Locke and the New Logic,' Howell shows how quickly Locke's *An Essay Concerning Human Understanding* was being read as a treatise on logic, initially by scholars at Dublin and Oxford, and how Locke himself prepared a text on logic, entitled *The Conduct of the Understanding*; it and its parent work, the *Essay*, 'were without question the most popular, the most widely read, the most frequently reprinted, and the most influential, of all English books of the eighteenth century' (277). The 'new logic' would push outwards to new truths and new knowledge, in contrast to the 'old logic' and the syllogism, which Locke attacks because 'this way of reasoning discovers no new Proofs, but is the Art of marshalling, and ranging the old ones we already have' (4.17.6). Nor can the syllogism deal adequately with probability or opinion. Locke, recognizing the limitations of sure and certain knowledge, places at the centre of thinking '*Illation* or *Inference*,' 'the Perception of the connexion there is between the *Ideas*, in each step of the deduction, whereby the Mind comes to see, either the certain Agreement or Disagreement of any two *Ideas*, as in Demonstration, in which it arrives at Knowledge; or their probable connexion, on which it gives or with-holds its Assent, as in Opinion' (4.17.2). Both Collard and Hedge locate themselves in the 'new logic' of Locke. In his Preface to his *Elements of Logick*, for instance, Hedge attacks previous texts for focusing on the syllogism: 'They contain no elements nor rules to assist us in reasoning on subjects of probability, or on the ordinary events of human life' (iii). Demonstrative reasoning, Hedge goes on to say,

> is of little importance in regulating our judgments and conclusions concerning events, which are irregular in their occurrence, and which depend on contingent circumstances. To reason on subjects of this kind, it is necessary to understand the nature of moral evidence, and the grounds of probability. It is by moral evidence alone, that we reason on historical facts, and the casual occurrences of life. It is also this evidence, which influences our conclusions on the important and interesting subjects of government, morals, and religion.   (vi–vii)

Collard goes even further in the concluding chapter of his *The Essentials of Logic* by asserting that 'the analytic and synthetic methods, though beautiful piles of mental structure, have no real existence in the practical world'; they are 'imaginary models' and 'standards of perfection' (252). 'Complicated subjects unfold themselves to the mind in [a] very irregular manner' (252), and 'it is indeed certain, that, in matters of enquiry, the mind, without regarding any rules whatever, pursues, to obtain its information, the best method which presents itself to its view, and, perhaps, never proceeds twice in the same way' (251).

The chapter from which I have just been quoting – there is no corresponding chapter in Hedge – is called 'Of Method,' and it is concerned not with the marshalling and ordering of our knowledge but with 'how discoveries are made' and with 'the best means of communicating them to others' (247–8). 'Method,' Collard writes, 'is divided into *analytic, synthetic*, and *arbitrary*' (248); the first two terms are used by Browning, as we shall see shortly, and the third is of great importance in our understanding of Browning's methods. Collard's account of the first two is predictable: 'In the analytic method, which is also called the method of *resolution*, we are taught to begin with a composition, and reduce it gradually into its first principles' (248). Collard's first example is from chemistry, but 'this is also the method recommended to define a complex term, or a combination of ideas; and, if it were possible to reduce all the parts of the composition into simple perceptions of sensation and reflection, the analysis would be complete' (248). (We note, in passing, that analysis is based on Locke's epistemology and, in so far as it is concerned with language, on his understanding of etymology.) The synthetic method proceeds in the opposite way: it 'is that wherein we begin with the simple parts, and put them together in an orderly manner, till we have completed the composition' (248). The actual experience of thinking and discovering, however, is not nearly so neat and systematic as analysis and synthesis would suggest, and the two, though 'universal guides,' are 'ingenious fabrications of the mind' (249). Our actual thinking, by which we discover new things, Collard calls the 'arbitrary' method, a term he borrows from Watts's logic. (This is the same Watts, Isaac Watts, whose hymns and songs Browning knew as a child, and whose hymns he sometimes quotes to Elizabeth in the letters of 1845–6. Watts's *Logick: or the right use of reason in the enquiry after truth*, belongs to the 'new logic' of Locke's followers; it was first published in 1725, and went through numerous editions in the eighteenth century. The passage Collard quotes below appears in the fourth and last part.) Because this method brings us close to Browning's typical way of proceeding, I quote the whole of the passage Collard quotes from his predecessor:

> '*Arbitrary method*,' says Dr Watts, 'leaves the order of nature, and accommodates itself to many purposes; such as, to treasure up things, and retain them in memory; to harangue and persuade mankind to any practice in the religious or the civil life; or to delight, amuse, or entertain the mind.'
> Those writers and speakers whose chief business is to amuse or delight,

to allure, terrify, or persuade mankind, do not confine themselves to any *natural order*, but in a *cryptical* or *hidden method*, adapt everything to their designed ends. Sometimes they *omit* those things which might injure their design, or grow tedious to their hearers, though they seem to have a necessary relation to the point in hand: sometimes they *add* those things which have no great reference to the subject, but are suited to allure or refresh the mind and the ear. They *dilate* sometimes, and flourish long upon little incidents; and they skip over, and but lightly touch the drier parts of their theme. They *place the first* things *last*, and the *last* things *first*, with wondrous art; and yet so manage it as to conceal their artifice, and lead the senses and passions of their hearers into a pleasing and powerful captivity.' – A beautiful description [Collard continues in his own voice] of the effects which the native ingenuity of the mind might produce, by shaking off the trammels of general rules.   (250–1)

Omissions, additions, dilations, reversals – 'Why, he writes *Sordello!*' says Browning in his 1863 revision of that poem (5.620). For readers of Browning will recognize that the terms Collard uses and the methods he defines are those Browning appropriates for his running-titles for the poem in 1863, for that portion of book 5 where Sordello reviews his progress as poet: 'He asserts the poet's rank and right, / basing these on their proper ground, / recognizing true dignity in service, / whether successively that of epoist, / dramatist, or, so to call him, analyst, / who turns in due course synthetist.' Both methods fail Sordello, and the arbitrary method failed Browning himself in that poem. Nonetheless, his distinction (maintained throughout most of his career) between discovery and communication has its source in the 'new logic' championed by his father, and ultimately in Locke's *Essay,* for Locke had insisted on the need to 'distinguish between the Method of acquiring knowledge, and of communicating it; between the Method of raising any Science, and that of teaching it to others' (4.7.3). Browning does consider himself a teacher, and Watts's account of the 'arbitrary' method of communication as a *'cryptical* or *hidden'* one parallels the words of the reviewer whom Browning quoted approvingly to Isabella Blagden (and whom I quoted in the Introduction to this book): 'one central meaning, seen only by reflexion in details.' The 'one central meaning' is hidden, and 'reflexion in details' is a riddle designed not only to teach but to carry the truth of the teaching into the heart of every Oedipus.

It is Browning's Paracelsus who reflects the concerns of his creator when he discovers the difference between thinking (the province of logic) and communication (the province of rhetoric):

only then I found
Such teaching was an art requiring cares
And qualities peculiar to itself:
That to possess was one thing – to display
Another. (3.651–5)

The display is not a manifesting of the obvious but a presenting of the cryptic and riddling. 'I *know* that I don't make out my conception by my language,' Browning tells Ruskin in a letter of 1855 – the statement is not an admission of failure but exasperation at Ruskin's failure to see that not making out his conception is his method – and anyway, he asks Ruskin, 'Do you think poetry was ever generally understood – or can be?'[39] Browning insists in this same letter that it is the function of poetry to push its readers towards new knowledge, not 'to tell people what they know already, as they know it.' Poetry 'is all teaching ... and the people hate to be taught.' The hatred stems from the effort needed to understand. Browning would not simply 'paint it all plain out,' as Ruskin wanted him to, and if one thing is to be deduced from another, one would not, Robert told Elizabeth in 1845, give both things, showing 'half by half like a cut orange' (*Correspondence* 11:3). Instead, Browning told Ruskin, 'I try to make shift with touches and bits of outlines which *succeed* if they bear the conception from me to you.' Browning's aim was to make the created text itself not only something of a riddle, but a compelling one, so that its effect would be like that Elizabeth experienced when she read the unfinished 'Saul' in 1845: 'I cannot tell you how the poem holds me & will not let me go untill it blesses me' (*Correspondence* 11:49). The word 'bless,' etymologically related to the Old English word for 'blood' and hence associated with the bestowing of well-being, vigour, and power, is an accurate one for the effect Browning hoped for if only the reader would wrestle with his text, so that it becomes the site of combat between poet and reader, and a stage in the development of the reader's soul.

Solving a riddle is yet another model of interpretation, the riddle being for Browning of the kind that Eleanor Cook, in her outline of 'a proposed anatomy of the enigma or riddle,' calls 'Pauline.' 'By Pauline riddling I mean riddle as in "For now we see through a glass darkly; but then face to face."' 'The text is so familiar,' she continues, 'I hardly need observe that this is the kind of riddle that will end in revelation, in light, in the dispersal of cloud, in the clarifying of the obscure, in the answering of the inexplicable, in the straightening of the labyrinthine, and so on through many a well-known trope for enigma.'[40] The particular kind of riddle with which Browning was most familiar was the emblem.

From childhood on, Browning was fascinated with the emblem tradition, and knowledgeable about it. In *The Browning Collections* there are six books by Francis Quarles, including two copies of the *Emblemes*, 'the most important and most successful English emblem book.'[41] One copy – the one now preserved in the Balliol College Library – was given to Browning by his mother when he was a child, and what he says later to Elizabeth about a legend of King Lud might also be said about that volume: it 'delighted my infancy, and now instruct[s] my maturer years' (*Correspondence* 11:26). 'Quarles' Emblems, my childhood's pet book' (Kintner 978), he tells Elizabeth when he is describing in detail one of the pictures from it. That Browning should have received the book from his mother is not surprising. It survived, as Karl Josef Höltgen points out, 'as a devotional work and found a new reading public among nineteenth century Evangelicals and Nonconformists, when the emblem tradition itself was long forgotten' (31). Not, however, by Browning. His father gave him a copy of Andrea Alciato's *Emblemata* (Paris, 1589) – Alciato's *Emblematum Liber* of 1531 was the prototype of European emblem books – and Browning owned a copy of Hermannus Hugo's *Pia Desideria* (Antwerp, 1659), one of Quarles's major sources (both of these volumes are in the Armstrong Browning Library at Baylor University). Browning may also have known Wither's emblems, if he is indeed referring to the 1635 *A Collection of Emblemes* in a letter (about 1843) to a Mr Powell, saying he may 'venture to beg a single day's loan of your priceless old Withers [*sic*], – to refresh the fading memories of my very earliest youth' (*Correspondence* 6:256). The emblem tradition is also prominent in another favourite childhood book of Browning's, Gerard de Lairesse's *The Art of Painting*. 'I remember,' Lairesse writes in his chapter 'Of the Ordonnance of hierogylphic [*sic*] Figures,' 'that when I was under my father's instructions, and studying design, my gusto was for emblems, which I collected from his and other masters' works, and then made intire compositions of them.'[42] His father, he says, 'diverted' him, but he persisted. At the beginning of his book, Lairesse provides the reader with 'An Emblematic Table of the Art of Painting,' and in Browning's copy of the book preserved in the Beinecke Library at Yale University, there is an asterisk in pencil beside the table, and double vertical lines in the margin beside the first two lines of the text. The 'table' is in fact a description of a picture which is clearly emblematic, as Lairesse's 'Explanation' shows, and the images and the explanation together make a picture and an interpretation, but, curiously enough, there is no actual picture, though other parts of the book are filled with illustrations. On the flyleaf of this copy, Browning wrote in 1874: 'I read this book more often and with greater delight, when I was a child, than any other: and still remember the main of it most gratefully for the good I seem to have got by the prints, and wondrous text.'

Andrea Alciato introduced emblems into European literature, using what Peter M. Daly refers to as a 'tight three-part form.'[43] The three parts are the motto or word, the actual picture (usually a woodcut or engraving), and the explanation and application of the idea expressed in word and picture together. Motto and *explicatio* are clearly interpretations of images which are wordless and therefore cryptic, so it is not surprising that Rosemary Freeman, in her standard account of the genre in her 1948 *English Emblem Books*, should speak of the motto as 'interpreting and completing' the picture and of the *explicatio* as that 'in which the picture and motto are interpreted and a moral or religious lesson is drawn.'[44] The relation among picture, motto, and *explicatio* is the central issue in criticism of the emblem. Browning's understanding of that relationship is to make the motto and the *explicatio* the solution to the riddle posed by the picture, the relation of word and picture being an arbitrary one because it is a matter of human judgment, but also (paradoxically) a necessary one because the interpretation is to be found rather than made.

We might begin our exploration of this tangled issue by pointing out the obvious: that the emblem is a linking of two arts, one visual, one verbal, and that it belongs in the context of the long-standing view that poetry, like painting, should present concrete and precise images. I have already cited the Horatian tag *ut pictura poesis*, but the *Princeton Encyclopedia of Poetry and Poetics* refers to 'the more explicit earlier statement of Simonides of Keos (first recorded by Plutarch, *De Gloria Atheniensum*, 3.347a, more than a century after *Ars Poetica*): "Poema pictura loquens, pictura poema silens" (poetry is a speaking picture, painting a silent [mute] poetry).'[45] But what exactly is the relation between the visual image and the word? The answer to that question parallels the debate in language theory over the relation between sign and signifier: is that relation natural and inevitable, or is it arbitrary and conventional? Plato raised the issue in his *Cratylus*, and it has bedevilled language theory ever since. In the criticism of the emblem there is a parallel binary pattern. On the one hand, the relation between motto and *pictura* can be seen as natural and 'hieroglyphic'; on the other, it can be seen as rhetorical and 'fanciful.' Freeman, for instance, quotes Henri Estienne and his handbook of 1645. 'He distinguishes,' she writes, 'between two kinds of resemblances between things – the "intrinsicall, occult, naturall and essentiall" on the one side, and on the other the "extrinsicall, manifest, artificiall, knowne and accidentall."' Where the symbol is 'of the accidental kind,' 'the relation between the image and its significance is purely arbitrary' (24–5). In Barbara Lewalski's view, 'The primary tradition behind most Renaissance emblem books was probably rhetorical, finding the essence of the emblem not in a natural, mysterious, divine corrrespondence but in a contrived rhetorical similitude or conceit, with close affinities to epigram,'[46] but she notes, of Estienne, Giovio, and Puttenham, that 'these theorists did, however, reinforce the view of emblems as grounded in the divine order of things rather than simply in the conceits of human wit – that is, as symbols or allegories found, not made' (185). Quarles expresses the same view in his address 'To the Reader' prefixed to his *Emblems*: 'Before the knowledge of letters, GOD was known by Hieroglyphics. And indeed what are the heavens, the earth, nay, every creature, but Hieroglyphics and Emblems of his glory?'[47]

The understanding of the emblem as a rhetorical conceit which is nonetheless grounded in the divine order of things is also, I think, Browning's view of the genre, a view fostered by the Congregationalist understanding of the role of language in making sense of creation. The Congregationalists insist on the need for language to make the world intelligible – not in any Kantian sense, but in so far as language enables people to read creation properly and find in it the working of Providence and the scheme of salvation. Without the word, creation would be only a puzzle; without language, the world would have little – or no – meaning. The most extreme statement of this view is in Calvin himself. 'Whenever God offered any sign to the holy Patriarchs,' Calvin writes in the *Institutes of the Christian Religion*, 'it was inseparably attached to the doctrine, without which our senses would gaze bewildered on an unmeaning object.'[48] The Westminster Confession is far more moderate, but it begins by insisting on the need for the word: 'Although the Light of Nature, and the Works of Creation and Providence, do so far manifest the Goodness, Wisdom and Power of God, as to leave men unexcusable; yet they are not sufficient to give that knowledge of God and of his Will, which is necessary unto salvation' (17), and hence God reveals himself in his word, 'the holy Scripture.' In a chapter which is wholly an addition to the Westminster Confession ('Of the Gospel, and of the extent of the Grace thereof'), the Congregationalists make the point again: 'This promise of Christ, and salvation by him, is revealed onely in and by the Word of God; neither do the works of Creation or Providence, with the Light of Nature, make discovery of Christ, or of Grace by him, so much as in a general or obscure way; much less that men destitute of the revelation of him by the Promise or Gospel, should be enabled thereby to attain saving Faith or Repentance' (Walker 388). In this context, Browning's question in book 1 of *The Ring and the Book*, 'For how else know we save by worth of word?' (1.837), takes on a broader and more urgent meaning. For him, as for the Congregationalists among whom he was brought up, creation could be known, without language, only in 'a general or obscure way.' The word makes possible the discovery of creation's meaning. Discovery is the key word in this context. Just as Locke distrusted the fancy, the Congregationalists distrusted the imagination; both make fiction, while the meaning of creation is not to be invented but to be found. 'This world's no blot for us, / Nor blank,' says Fra Lippo Lippi; 'it means intensely, and means good: / To find its meaning is my meat and drink' (313–15). Find, not make. Language is thus the human response to creation, and while words may be a human invention and arbitrary in relation to the ideas of which they are the signs, they become a heuristic when the mind is illuminated by the Holy Spirit.

The Holy Spirit as the solver of riddles appears most memorably in the first episode of Christian's journey in *The Pilgrim's Progress*, when Christian comes to the House of the Interpreter. In that house, which is, in Peter M. Daly's words, 'virtually an emblem theatre,'[49] Christian's host shows him a number of pictures in different rooms, and Christian, confronted with each picture or scene, asks the same question: 'What means this?' The Interpreter answers, and the lesson in hermeneutics which he provides to Christian is best described by Milo Kaufmann: 'The House is the Word; and, in keeping with Puritan belief about its perspicuity, in it dwells its own sure interpreter, the Holy Spirit. Christian may be exposed to dark riddles in his exploration of the Word, but single authoritative interpretation is ever at his elbow in the person of his host.' The lighting of the candle (glossed by Bunyan himself as illumination) and the taking of Christian's hand (explained by Kaufmann as a conventional Puritan metaphor for faith) suggest 'that the way is dark, and that Christian may stumble.' 'The Word, while it may be trusted to yield its secrets to the humblest in grace, is obscure and dark in the sense that its truths must be searched out, emptied from riddles and mysteries, drawn up from the deeps, and in every case sought in pureness of intention' (62–3).

Responding to an emblem begins with a reader confronting a picture or image. The picture is non-verbal, so its meaning is hidden, and it presents itself to the human eye as a riddle. The eye must discover the meaning which is inherent in the image, and to become intelligible the picture needs the agency of human language. Interpretation is the process of translating the picture or image into words. The syntactical form of that translation is the statement of identity: the observer names the image (a lantern, for instance), and identifies it (through the use of the copula verb 'is') either with another image (a beacon, say) or with an abstraction (illumination, perhaps, or the word of God) or with both. The statement of identity – the subject, the copula or linking verb, and the subject complement – is the syntactical form of interpretation of the riddle. One notes that syntax divides image and idea – picture is separated from meaning as the parts of speech follow one another in a linear sequence – but the subject and its complement are to be understood as one. The statement of identity which is the basic form of interpretation is also the basic form of metaphor, and that word in Greek means a carrying across or translation, understood by Browning as an inner drama which is not simply an idle or fanciful exercise, but rather the essential human activity. The drama can be seen at its simplest in a late love poem from *Ferishtah's Fancies* (1884), the most emblematic of all Browning's volumes of poetry. Here is the lyric:

You groped your way across my room i' the dear dark dead of night;
At each fresh step a stumble was: but, once your lamp alight,
Easy and plain you walked again: so soon all wrong grew right!

What lay on floor to trip your foot? Each object, late awry,
Looked fitly placed, nor proved offence to footing free – for why?
The lamp showed all, discordant late, grown simple symmetry.

Be love your light and trust your guide, with these explore my heart!
No obstacle to trip you then, strike hands and souls apart!
Since rooms and hearts are furnished so, – light shows you, – needs love start?

The movement of this poem is typical of the emblem. There is no motto (or it is perhaps embedded in the poem, as 'Be love your light'), but there is a *pictura* (presented in verbal images) and an *explicatio*. The picture is of a lover groping her way across a darkened room, every object apparently awry, as opposed to walking across a lighted room, where she can clearly see that everything is in its right place. The *explicatio* begins with the line, 'Be love your light and trust your guide, with these explore my heart.' The metaphor is a double one: the speaker carries an image across to an image (room to heart) and he carries an image across to an abstract idea (light to love). The controlling metaphor for the movement of the lyric, from darkness to light, is also one of the conventional tropes for solving a riddle; so too is the move from a miscellany ('Each object ... awry') to an intelligible order ('simple symmetry').

There is yet another model for the kind of interpretation which is the solving of riddles, and it is to be found in the sermons of a different preacher – different from George Clayton, that is – whom Browning admired. He was the minister not of an independent congregation but of the established church, and he was Canon Henry Melvill, who was at Camden Chapel, Camberwell, in the 1830s. Browning's admiration was apparently lifelong, for his daughter-in-law remembers his coming to her, on 'the Sunday afternoon before the last one of his life,' saying he 'would read aloud if I wanted him to do so, suggesting one of Canon Melville's [*sic*] sermons.'[50] There were five volumes of Melvill's sermons in the Browning library sold at Sotheby's in 1913, including the volume of *Sermons* published in London in 1833, the Browning copy of which is now in the Armstrong Browning Library. The editor of Melvill's collected sermons, C.P. M'Illvaine, praises them as 'expository' rather than 'inventive': 'There cannot be anything new in the preacher's message,' M'Illvaine points out, since he is 'to "know nothing among men but Jesus Christ and him crucified."' 'The truth as it is in Jesus' is the subject of all preaching, the phrase itself coming from Paul's epistle to the Ephesians (4:21) and appearing both as the title of a Melvill sermon and as the way in which the Congregationalists characterize themselves in the preface they added to the Westminster Confession: they are those who '*love the truth as it is in Jesus*' (Walker 355). Paradoxically, 'the truth as it is in Jesus' is not a limiting truth but leads rather to the variety and abundance M'Illvaine praises in Mevill: 'Distinct *objects* in the preacher's message, like the letters in his alphabet, are few ... [b]ut their combinations, like those of the letters of the alphabet, are innumerable.'[51] Melvill was especially good at taking unlikely biblical texts and showing the scheme of salvation in them. Apparently unimportant details, and historical facts that seemed only incidental, Melvill treated as riddles, and the excitement and appeal of his sermons lay in his progressive unfolding of the mysterious and obscure. Melvill's chief interpretive tool in solving the riddle of his texts is typology.

My example is from his *Sermons on Certain of the Less Prominent Facts and References in Sacred Story* (London, 1845), the second volume of which was in the Browning collections sold at Sotheby's in 1913, the title page inscribed with the name of Browning's sister. The first sermon in the second volume is entitled 'The Young Man in the Linen Cloth,' and its text is Mark 14:51, 52: 'And there followed him a certain young man, having a linen cloth cast about his naked body; and the young men laid hold on him: and he left the linen cloth, and fled from them naked.' The incident occurs after the scenes in the garden of Gethsemane and before Jesus appears in front of the high priest. 'St. Mark is the only Evangelist who mentions this occurrence' (2:135), Melvill begins, and in spite of all the limited information in the passage – limitations which make the facts seem 'most improbable' and the reasons for them 'quite insufficient' (2:137) – the story is not to be set aside, but to be considered carefully, attentively, and intensely. The opening sections of the sermon contain reiterated exhortations to focus our attention. 'If we have only this single account, it goes sufficiently into detail to afford much scope for thought and inquiry; the facts would not have been related at all, and much less with such careful accuracy, had they not been facts which it was important for us to know; and they would have been related, we may venture to believe, more than once, had not their single statement sufficed for information and instruction' (2:135). The uniqueness of the passage, its concreteness, and its brevity, are all indications of its claim upon us: 'This very abruptness, this very mysteriousness, should obtain for the facts our serious attention' (2:136). The improbability of the facts and the lack of explanation are signs of the riddle: 'There is good ground for our searching for some deeper interpretation, for our concluding that the Evangelist designed to convey some more important intimations than have yet been derived, when he brought so strangely into his story this unknown young man, and as strangely dismissed him' (2:137). Melvill solves the riddle with a way of proceeding which is typical of his sermons, and with an appeal to an authority – the Holy Spirit – which guarantees the truth of his interpretation.

Melvill's sermons usually have three movements. Having read the biblical text he has chosen, Melvill first undertakes a careful, vivid, and precise recreation of the historical facts: 'Let us then, without further preface, apply ourselves to the examination of the facts which St. Mark sets before us in the words of our text' (2:136). Though he allows himself the occasional supposition, the occasional filling out of the historical picture with details not in the written record, he is careful to distinguish such material from the facts themselves. In this particular text, he focuses on the one concrete detail we are given: the word 'linen' to describe the 'cloth cast about his naked body.' Melvill draws upon philology in dealing with that word, giving his listeners its Greek form and arguing that it is a word designating a cloak or outer garment often used as a shroud, and also used for religious purposes: it was 'indicative of special strictness, of a rigid adherence to the law of God, or the traditions of the elders' (2:138). From these facts, Melvill infers that the motivation of the crowd in laying hold of the young man was the same as its motivation for the seizure of Christ.

The second movement of a Melvill sermon is the act of interpretation. In those historical facts which he has so carefully and concretely presented, Melvill finds 'a yet deeper meaning' (2:140), a meaning which is 'symbolical or figurative' (2:140). 'The facts would not have been written, except for our admonition and instruction: we are, therefore, to study them with all care,' Melvill says, 'with caution,' 'with prayer' (2:143), with 'striving of the mind' and 'intenseness of the gaze' (2:150). He always insists that his interpretation lies *in* the facts, rather than being a generalization or abstraction from them; that it is a discovery rather than an invention. In the second sermon in this collection – it is the one called 'The Fire on the Shore' – Melvill uses the label 'figurative facts' (2:148), and it indicates that there is a doubleness in all facts, if only we would come to understand them fully. The evangelist himself 'gives nothing but the facts' (2:143), but the reader responding to the historical record must ask, as Melvill does of the 'fire of coals' image in the text of his second sermon, 'what truths did these symbolically teach, when taken, as they must be, in immediate connection with the other figurative facts?' (2:148). By insisting on the identity of fact and interpretation, Melvill allies himself with Carlyle, Ruskin (who also admired Melvill's sermons), and the Pre-Raphaelites in their 'aesthetic of the factual.'[52] The phrase is Herbert Sussman's, and is from his 1979 book, suggestively entitled *Fact into Figure*:

> From their common grounding in typological exegesis and religious science, Carlyle and Ruskin developed an aesthetic in which the facts of nature, of history, even of contemporary life can become through the intensity of their representation radiant with transcendent meaning. Within this view, realism and symbolism are not opposed but inter-dependent. In the-

ory, at least, the more intense the power of observation, the more extensive the awareness of the symbolic meaning; the more accurately each minute fact of the phenomenal world is reproduced, the more forcefully the spiritual significance will shine through. Such an aesthetic depends upon faith in a sacramental universe ... (7)

Art thus approaches the condition of scripture. The model for symbol 'is Jesus, the Word made Flesh, the transcendent manifested in historical time' (9).

Jesus Christ is at the centre of Melvill's interpretation of the incident with the young man in the linen cloth. 'We believe,' he says again about the historical facts, 'that a yet deeper meaning attaches to the incidents in question; that these incidents were symbolical or figurative: in other words, that they were designed to shadow forth the facts of our Redeemer's final triumph over death' (2:140). He then proceeds to a typological reading of the facts. The precedent for the placing side by side of two figures like the young man and Christ is the law's prescription 'that the high priest should take two goats, and present them before the Lord at the door of the tabernacle of the congregation' (2:140). One was to be killed 'as a sin-offering,' one burdened with sins and 'let go into the wilderness.' 'These goats, taken together, constituted a type of the Redeemer' and together 'furnished a sufficient and accurate figure' (2:140). In this 'double representation' (2:141) we see 'the two grand facts, that Christ died for our sins, and that he rose for our justification'; in the same way in the incident under examination, Christ and the young man show 'the tragedy of the crucifixion, and the triumph of the resurrection' (2:141). Thus typology compels us, Melvill asserts, to assign to this text 'a prophetic or typical character, in place of passing it over as an incident from which little can be learned' (2:141). He imagines in the crowd who witnessed the incident 'a devout and aged Jew, like Simeon ... searching ... for notices of the scheme of redemption, for types or figures of the deliverance promised, from the earliest time, to the fallen race of men' (2:141). Such a man sees a figure who is to die, and longs for 'something to correspond to the goat escaping as well as to the goat dying' (2:141) – and finds, after 'a moment of intense anxiety,' a sign in the young man. 'And thus the incident which has engaged our attention, is made to fill an important place as symbolical, or prophetic, of Christ's triumph over his enemies' because of 'an exactness of correspondence with the types of the law' (2:142).

In his second sermon in this series, the one called 'The Fire on the

Shore,' Melvill comments on typology as a method of interpretation, and gives us some of its essential characteristics:

the Jewish and the Christian dispensations are not so truly distinct and detached economies, as component parts of one great plan and arrangement. There have never been two ways in which sinners might be saved: in the Old Testament, as in the New, 'everlasting life is offered to mankind by Christ, who is the only Mediator between God and man, being both God and man.' In the New Testament, indeed, we have the clearer exposition of the great scheme of mercy: God's wondrous purpose of saving the Church through the sacrifice of His only-begotten Son is there set forth with a fulness and precision, which it were vain to seek in the writings of the Old. Nevertheless, there is no difference whatsoever in the doctrine propounded, but only in the measure of its revelation ... The process was but continued, though with less of vail and obscurity ... (2:148)

Melvill also gives the criteria for a typological interpretation: completeness (it must include all the facts) and consistency (consistent, that is, with the types embodying the scheme of salvation God has provided for fallen man). He does make some allowances, however, and cautions against too neat an account and too ingenious a reading: 'different ends were subserved by the same series of facts' (2:149), he notes, and 'it is never required, in the interpretation of a parable, whether delivered in word or by action, that every minute particular should be made to shadow forth a truth' (2:149). Interpretation, in short, requires good judgment.

George Landow's study of biblical typology in his 1980 book, *Victorian Types Victorian Shadows*, confirms the account of it given by Melvill. 'Typology connects two times,' Landow writes in his introduction, 'the second of which is said to "complete" or "fulfill" the first, and therefore it provides a meaningful structure to human history.'[53] At the centre of that history is Jesus Christ, and 'a type is an anticipation of Christ' (22), who is the antitype. Landow, paraphrasing Newman, points out 'the essential incompleteness of such types and their essential inadequacy to save man' (25). We might borrow a phrase from Browning himself to make the same point: 'Type needs antitype,' says the poet in his 'Parleying with Francis Furini' (483, though we note that Browning is talking about binary opposites in this passage and not about a pattern of promise and fulfilment). Landow continues: 'Essentially Moses, like all other types, functions as an elaborate trope that permits man to begin to understand something otherwise too great for his comprehension by first providing an historical analogy to make that truth accessible and then emphasizing that the true reality vastly surpasses its historical image' (26). Reading typologically is thus like solving a riddle, since economy is the principle with which the materials are first presented to us, and since our wrestling with them brings 'progressive revelation' (31). 'Christ is the central reality of human history' (39), and one might expect that, with the Incarnation, types could be discarded, since 'their function would have ceased and they would now have become mere historical facts' (38). But types, and the puzzles they present to human understanding, retain their efficacy precisely because they were 'originally created by God to accommodate truth to man's limited post-lapsarian faculties' (39) – that is the principle of economy – and, moreover, there was a 'widespread belief that scriptural types could be fulfilled in the individual's own life' (50) and not just in Jesus Christ. A type thus opens to the believer 'the meaning of the universe' and 'the central meaning of history,' and places the believer 'in a completely ordered world' (40). So Melvill comments on 'the first prophecy' (it is Genesis 3:15) in his discourse of that title, the first in his collected *Sermons* of 1833: 'a wonderful passage, spreading itself over the whole of time, and giving outlines of the history of this world from the beginning to the final consummation' (1:10–11). One could hardly ask for greater illumination from a riddle.

Not surprisingly, then, the third part of a Melvill sermon is a 'personal application' of the text: 'it is both lawful and useful to search for some personal application, that we may feel our own interest, and find our own profit, in the passage reviewed' (2:150). Melvill labels such an application an 'allegory' (2:150), and the label indicates that he is going beyond interpretation, where fact and figure are one and the same, to application, where the teaching is other than the literal fact. In 'The Young Man in the Linen Cloth,' for instance, Melvill places his listeners in the position of an observer of the mob scene, an observer who sees the coming death of Jesus but not the sign of his resurrection: 'Oh, how often with ourselves may there be something of the like missing, as by a moment or a hairbreadth, of a gracious communication which would scatter our doubts, disperse our fears, and fill us with joyful expectation ... Let us take this lesson from the symbolical occurrence which has been under review – a lesson as to perseverance in duty, though in the face of dangers and difficulties' (2:142). So the sermon ends with an exhortation to attentiveness and alertness, for God everywhere provides signs of his scheme of salvation, if only we would open our eyes.

There is one further point to be made about typology as a riddle-solving technique, and that has to do with its relations with troping. We saw how, in the emblem, interpretation becomes metaphor through the statement of identity, when 'this means that' becomes 'this is that.' Typology takes 'this means that' and ultimately identifies everything with Christ, since all types find their antitype in him. He is not only the one Man who is also the one God, but the rose, the dove, the lamb, the stone rejected by the builders, the rebuilt temple, the bread and wine, the vine, the tree of life, the word, and so on through a catalogue of conventional Christian metaphors. The antitype is the completion of the type, and it is not, as the name suggests, the binary opposite of the type, but the final turn in a divine economy, the unifying and identifying trope of the Christian view of the world. The ontological basis for the turning, and ultimately the identifying, of all things is suggested in a note which Browning wrote in his copy of Donne. This particular copy – the *Poetical Works* published in Edinburgh in 1779, three volumes bound in one – is marked extensively by Browning, and there is one passage in satire 5 which he both underlines and marks with an 'x.' The lines are these:

> If all things be in all,
> As I think, since all which were, are, and shall
> Be, be made of the same elements,
> Each thing each thing implies or represents;
> Then man is a world ...

Browning repeats the 'x' at the bottom of the page, and writes the following note: 'x) qu: "The key to the *conceits* of Donne, & his admirers?"'[54] So the kind of troping which is (in the words of Dr Johnson) the yoking 'by violence together' of 'the most heterogeneous ideas' is not just a human fancy or fiction but an appropriating of the power of nature and a manifesting of the essential character of creation: 'Each thing each thing implies or represents.' Browning would have met with this idea elsewhere, in Plato's *Timaeus*, for instance, but more likely in Paracelsus, for whom, as Jolande Jacobi points out, the four elements are 'the four fundamental forms of matter, which are potentially and sometimes invisibly contained in all perceptible things, even if they no longer manifest themselves outwardly in their typical original form.'[55] Human beings, who share the makeup of creation ('man is a world'), are not confined to its external appearances, but share in its unseen powers; that sharing manifests itself in the ability to relate everything to everything else, or to turn everything into everything else.

The three movements of a typical Melvill sermon – a precise and concrete presentation of the historical facts (the precision and concreteness resulting from intensity of gaze and attentiveness of mind), the interpretation of them, and then their application – can be seen to have a place in the long tradition of meditation explored by scholars such as Louis Martz in his 1954 book, *The Poetry of Meditation*, and by Milo Kaufmann in his 1966 book on Bunyan, *'The Pilgrim's Progress' and Traditions in Puritan Meditation*. Kaufmann gives us a detailed account of various and divergent traditions in Puritan meditation, which differs from the Catholic tradition in putting less emphasis on the role of the imagination (which recreates the scene) and more on the understanding, but the pattern of recreation, interpretation, and application remained.[56] It remains, too, in Browning, not so much as a spiritual exercise (though one cannot rule that out with him) but as a habit of mind. If one stands back from *The Ring and the Book*, for instance, one can see a movement parallel to the sequence we have been exploring. First of all, there is the intense focusing on the historical fact, for the poet ('I saw with my own eyes' 1.523) and potentially for the reader ('Do you see this square old yellow Book?' 1.33). And when Browning gives the contents, he says to his readers, 'You know the tale already' (1.377). The problem is its interpretation, and to that task Browning devotes most of the poem. Just as the third movement of the poem – the monologues of the two lawyers and the Pope – is devoted to judgment, so Browning at the end invites each reader to judge for him- or herself the truth of the work, to apply the text to his or her own life.

From time to time, Melvill makes clear the assumptions about language that lie behind his practices as a preacher. Some of these assumptions are in the sermon called 'Idle Words,' the first of the *Sermons Preached at Cambridge* (London, 1840), a volume which was in the Browning library, and others are in 'Truth as it is in Jesus' and 'The Difficulties of Scripture,' the eleventh and twelfth sermons of the 1833 collection, also in the Browning library. In 'Idle Words,' Melvill asserts that language is God-given, that it is the expression of the soul, and that our words are the evidence on which we will be judged or 'justified.' I want to focus on one of these asssumptions – that language is the expression of the soul – because it has a parallel in Browning's thinking. When Melvill talks about the purposes of language as expression and communication, he uses phrases like 'convey[ing] to every one the thoughts which crowd the hidden chambers of my soul' or 'filling [every one] with the images which are passing to and fro in my own spirit' (2.387). He does say that language is 'reason walking abroad,' but he goes on to identify it with the life of the soul: 'it is the soul, not in the secret laboratory, and not in its aerial impalpable mysteriousness; but the soul amid the crowded scenes of life, formed and clothed, submitting itself to the inspection, and influencing the sentiments, of a multitude' (2.388). The sentence could be taken as a description of the chief subject of Browning's poetry, which he defined as 'the development of a soul.' Every reader knows that that phrase comes from Browning's 1863 preface to *Sordello*: 'my stress lay on the incidents in the development of a soul: little else is worth study.'

The word 'soul' has not much entered into critical thinking about Browning, and it remains a vague and insubstantial concept, just as the soul itself remains, in common thinking, a vague and insubstantial thing, a presence which is largely an absence, like the hole in the middle of a doughnut. But the soul was actual and essential for Browning, and he had a precise idea of its relations to mind and to language. We might begin with the gloss on the soul in the colloquy with Charles Avison, the last of the *Parleyings with Certain People of Importance in Their Day* (1887):

> 'Soul' – (accept
> A word which vaguely names what no adept
> In word-use fits and fixes so that still
> Thing shall not slip word's fetter and remain
> Innominate as first, yet, free again,
> Is no less recognized the absolute
> Fact underlying that same other fact
> Concerning which no cavil can dispute
> Our nomenclature when we call it 'Mind' –
> Something not Matter) – 'Soul,' who seeks shall find
> Distinct beneath that something.   (139–49)

The passage describes a problem of naming, and one notes that Browning in part solves that problem by setting aside the vague word 'soul' and replacing it with 'Mind' and 'not Matter.' Mind is easy to name because its operations are discernible through reflection, but the relation of mind and soul is here the crucial thing: because mind is itself an operation of soul, we may know the soul through the way in which we think.

Moreover, the mind, like the soul, survives the physical dissolution of the body. This cluster of ideas turns up in the sermons of George Clayton, not in any systematic way, but simply as assertions which he obviously repeated as part of his faith. In a funeral sermon of 1817 (on the occasion of the death of the Princess of Wales), for instance, Clayton says that man 'is a being compounded of body and soul, of matter and spirit. He has a mind which is immaterial and immortal.' And in another funeral sermon the next year, he rejects a materialist view of the mind and argues for '"a spirit in man," a distinct, an immaterial substance.'[57] The same cluster of ideas turns up in a book in Browning's father's library. The book is Thomas Burnet's *A Treatise concerning the State of Departed Souls, Before, and At, and After the Resurrection* (London, 1739), and Burnet's exploration of the relations of soul, mind, and body is a revealing one for our purposes: the operations of the mind, which are also the operations of the soul, correspond to Locke's account of our mental faculties and to Locke's theory of language, so that names, and then propositions, indicate successive (and progressive) actions of the soul.

Much of what Burnet has to say about the soul is conventional enough: our nature is a dual one (we are 'intirely made up of two Parts, the Soul and the Body' 1–2); the soul is immortal and incorporeal; the soul survives the dissolution of the body and continues in a discarnate state after death. The most interesting part of his book, for our purposes, is his account of the operations of the soul before death. During our life on earth, thinking is the essential operation of the soul. 'We can find nothing at all in the Soul, besides the Power of Thinking, and its various Manners. Now if the Nature of the Soul, or the very Essence of it, as some are us'd to speak, consists entirely in Thought, 'tis essentially Life, and is active or conscious of itself without ceasing; nor can it any otherwise perish than by Annihilation' (19). The soul may have all sorts of powers and attributes, but from the perspective of our limited earthly experience, 'we can never discern or discover, with all our Attention, any Quality in the human Soul, besides Thought, and the Power to think' (19). Burnet calls the attributes of the soul 'this Force of thinking, and this vital Energy' (20), but argues against the soul having 'Extension and Dimension' (20) or anything corporeal; he rejects the materialist view, 'Touches, Impulses, or Dashings against other of corpuscularian Particles,' and insists on 'a Power peculiar to itself, and according to the Laws of a thinking Nature' (37). Those laws correspond closely to Locke's epistemology. The first operation of the soul is 'simple Apprehension' (34), whereby we receive 'ideas' – data from our five senses – from the world around us. 'But there are in us,' Burnet continues, 'besides Ideas or simple Apprehensions, superior and nobler Principles, or Faculties of the Soul, as Judgment, Reason, and a chain of Reasons link'd to one another' (34–5). Finally, there is a 'sovereign Principle' (35), 'the voluntary and spontaneous Force of the Mind' (40), which seems to be something like free will: 'by the Force of this Principle we govern the Body, and command the Spirits which Way we please, to move this or that, or any Part of it: By this Principle we resist the Propensions of the Body, we controul its Appetites, and its Affections, and its external and internal Senses, as often as 'tis our Pleasure' (40).

Burnet then links these various operations with language:

> The Operations of the Soul then, as we said above, following each other in due Order, are divided into simple Perceptions, into Judgments, into Ratiocinations, and, if you please, into Methods, or into a Series of Thoughts that are marshall'd in exact Order; for Method comprehends and disposes of several Ratiocinations. Ratiocination is employ'd in the Connexion of several Judgments, Judgment in comparing and comprehending several Ideas, or several Sensations. Thus if you proceed in Order, the Ideas are the first Elements of Knowledge, and, as it were, the Letters of the Alphabet of which Words are compos'd, and of Words Sentences and Periods, and Discourses of Sentences: And thus the Scale of Thoughts answers, in some Measure, to the several Parts of Speech.   (35)

The sequence which Burnet here describes parallels the account of language which Locke gives in book 3 of his *Essay,* for Locke proceeds from his theory of naming (the arbitrary linking of sound and idea) to his theory of syntax, where 'particles' are used 'to signify the *connexion* that the Mind gives to *Ideas, or Propositions, one with another'* (3.7.1), and where that connection is a true one if the asserted relations correspond to relations actually observed in the world outside us. So the mind does 'connect, not only the parts of Propositions, but whole Sentences one to another, with their several Relations and Dependencies, to make a coherent Discourse' (3.7.1). All those connections require choices and judgments by the mind, and those actions are the central and crucial ones in the earthly life of the soul. Names (which are arbitrary anyway) are less important than syntax, and ideas by themselves or in isolation are neither true nor false. 'Ideas, consider'd separately, are incapable of offering any Truth to us,' Burnet writes, 'and ... they neither conclude, nor affirm, or deny any Thing' (36). Affirming and denying, making statements about relations, all this 'is another Action, another Faculty of the Soul, which by contemplating the Proportions, Regards, and Respects, that there is between these Ideas, (I here take Ideas in the largest Sense,) affirm or deny something concerning them, and consequently concerning the Things which they represent, as they accord or differ, imply or exclude, agree or are oppos'd to each other, and this according to their different Measure and Degrees' (36). So Burnet describes 'the gradual Progress that the human Soul makes in its Operations; in which, from simple Perception it proceeds to Judgments and Arguments; and from thence to a Series and System of Thoughts in the Arts and Sciences' (40).

Browning's own epistemology parallels the cluster of ideas we have been examining in Clayton and Burnet. The mind is immaterial, and beneath it or behind it is the soul, the 'Ruach' which Tsaddik at the end of 'Jochanan Hakkadosh' glosses as 'the imparted Spirit' (781). In her account of Browning's epistemology, Mrs Orr focuses on the mind as immaterial and (she implies) immortal. 'It was the essence of his belief,' she writes, 'that the mind is superior to physical change; that it may be helped or hindered by its temporary alliance with the body, but will none the less outstrip it in their joint course; and as intellect was for him the life of poetry, so was the power of poetry independent of bodily progress and bodily decline. This conviction pervaded his life' (*Life and Letters* 381). Browning himself confirms Mrs Orr's statement in an 1876 letter to Mrs Thomas FitzGerald, where he attributes the idea that mind is an operation of soul not to Clayton or Burnet but to a Baptist minister named Robert Hall. 'The reasoning powers,' Browning says, are the '*eyes* of the soul,' an idea 'momentous to me' and one which he has 'based my whole life upon.' Here is the passage from that letter:

What struck me so much in that life of Schopenhauer which you gave me, was that doctrine which he considered his grand discovery – and which *I* had been persuaded of from my boyhood – and have based my whole life upon: – that the soul is above and *behind* the intellect which is merely its servant. I first met with this doctrine's enunciation in a memoir of Robert Hall the Baptist Minister ... The memoir went on to say that he had a correspondence with some eminent friend on this subject – I believe, Macintosh – who pressed on his consideration that the instrument was not the craftsman, the intelligence – not the soul. The consequences of this doctrine were so momentous to me – so destructive of vanity, on the one hand, – or undue depression at failure, on the other – that I am sure there must be references to and deductions from it throughout the whole of my works ...[58]

The consequences are indeed momentous: every poem is an incident in the development of its creator's soul; the 'imparted spirit' is behind successes and failures both, reminding us that successes are not a matter of human agency alone and that failures are not final but rather 'evidence' (in Abt Vogler's words) 'For the fulness of the days'; that every poem is the setting for an incident in the development of the reader's soul as well as that of the poet, in so far as he or she brings the whole mind to bear upon interpretation of the text.

There is one loose end to be tied up in our weaving together of the threads of Browning's understanding of language, and that end is Horne Tooke. Influential as Tooke was (Hans Aarsleff makes him a pivotal figure in his *The Study of Language in England 1780–1860*), Browning seems to have known him only at second hand, and yet Tooke impinges on Browning through various thinkers and writers, and in ways that, ultimately, reverse the materialism of Tooke's speculations. Tooke had taken Locke's suggestion that all names could be reduced to the names of sensations and had used it as the basis of a powerful (though flawed) study of etymology; and he had taken Locke's defence of the place of abstraction in communication (it is 'for quickness and dispatch sake' 3.3.10), relabelled it 'abbreviation' or 'subaudition,' and extended it into his analysis of the parts of speech and of syntax. Words, says one of the speakers in the dialogue which is *The Diversions of Purley*, are not only 'the signs of things or the signs of ideas,' but also 'the signs of other words,'[59] and so 'subaudition' is a synonym for ellipsis. The primary purpose of ellipsis may be the speed of communication, but it is also a technique for making a text puzzling, since, in Collard's words, it is 'the substituting of one word for one or two others, and, sometimes, a single word for a whole sentence' (*Essentials of Logic* 25), so that the reader is constantly called upon to supply the missing words. Ellipsis certainly characterizes Browning's style, but when, early on in his courtship of Elizabeth, Robert uses the word '*subaudire*,' his reference is not to Tooke but to 'Bos on the art of supplying Ellipses' (*Correspondence* 10:200). Browning's father, so often a conduit for ideas important to the son, had a copy of Tooke – it is Richard Taylor's edition of *The Diversions of Purley*, published in London in 1829 – but he seems to have read only the first fifty pages carefully. His copy, now in the Armstrong Browning Library, has lines under words and in the margins of chapters 1 through 3, but after that there are no pencilled marks, and some of the pages are uncut. Landor, another possible conduit (of whom Browning said that he 'owed more as a writer to [him] than to any contemporary' Orr 230), includes among his dialogues one between 'Johnson and Horne Tooke,' which Browning recommended to Sidney Colvin in 1882, not for the ideas, but for 'the admirably dramatic *ending*.'[60] Browning may have been, early on, aware of Tooke's ideas on etymology from the lectures of the Reverend Thomas Dale, a Cambridge graduate and Anglican clergy-man who was appointed the first professor of the English language and of English literature in the newly established University of London. Browning, whose father enrolled him in the university in 1828, may have heard Dale's lecture 'Introductory to a Course upon the Principles and Practice of English Composition' (delivered 24 October 1828, and printed soon afterwards), which included a bare outline of 'a subject, which,' Dale said, 'I account of peculiar interest' – etymology – and he would have heard Dale refer to Tooke's reducing of the language to 'two essential parts of speech, Noun and Verb.'[61] When Dale is introducing etymology, he makes no reference to the work of William Jones or to that of any of the continental philologists, and the omission helps con-firm Browning's later statement to Mrs Orr, that he knew little of the Germano-Coleridgian line of thought in philosophy, and little, appar-ently, of the Germano-Coleridgian approach to language. Certainly Dale's introductory lecture would leave him with the impression that anyone who wished to understand language should start by reading Locke and Tooke.

There is one more intermediary for Tooke's ideas, and he is, I think, the most important of those I have mentioned: Carlyle. The Browning-Carlyle friendship was a long one, and the facts of it are well known, thanks to the work of Charles Richard Sanders.[62] Carlyle is 'the great teacher of the age,' says Elizabeth to Robert in the early stages of their courtship, and 'also yours & mine' (*Correspondence* 10:101). Carlyle, as G.B. Tennyson has shown, was familiar with the work of Tooke, bor-rowed directly from him, and turned his understanding of language upside down, making etymology 'serve the very reverse of a sensualist philosophy.'[63] In Carlyle's hands, the tracing of abstractions back to their roots in the names of sensible objects or experiences became the means of revealing the spiritual or infinite within all things, since, as he has his Teufelsdröckh say in *Sartor Resartus*, 'all objects are as windows, through which the philosophic eye looks into Infinitude itself.'[64] Browning, to whom Harriet Martineau gave a copy of the American edition of *Sartor Resartus* in the summer of 1837, would there come across Carlyle's argument, derived from Tooke, that all language is metaphorical. The Editor quotes Teufelsdröckh:

> Language is called the Garment of Thought: however, it should rather be, Language is the Flesh-Garment, the Body, of Thought. I said that imagination wove this Flesh-Garment; and does not she? Metaphors are her stuff: examine Language; what, if you except some few primitive elements (of natural sound), what is it all but Metaphors, recognised as such, or no longer recognised; still fluid and florid, or now solid-grown and colourless? If those same primitive elements are the osseous fixtures in the Flesh-Garment, Language, – then are Metaphors its muscles and tissues and living integuments. An unmetaphorical style you shall in vain seek for: is not your very *Attention* a *Stretching-to*? (73)

The 'primitive elements' to which Teufelsdröckh refers are the names of sensations; the 'metaphors' to which he refers are the extensions of those names to meanings other than the original sensation, so that the 'primitive element' is translated or carried across to other things. We remember that metaphor is in Greek a carrying across or a carrying over – its Latin equivalent is translation or transference – and every act of translating or carrying across is an arbitrary one; that is, it is a judgment made by the mind, and it serves some human end or need. In Carlyle's hands, the understanding of language as metaphorical leads him to reverse the act of carrying across and to return to a word's origin in sensible experience which is, rightly viewed, the manifestation of spirit. In Browning's hands, the understanding of language as metaphorical leads him to see the multiple significations of a word as evidence of successive acts of interpretation. Interpretation is the paradigmatic incident in the development of a soul, and such incidents are embedded in language itself. That statement brings us back to the dictionary with which we started this chapter, and to the arrangement of its entries.

In his *Plan* (1747) for the dictionary, Johnson describes how he intends to treat each word: he will give the 'primitive' or 'natural' form of the word first, and then move on to its 'figurative' or 'metaphorical' senses:

> In explaining the general and popular language, it seems necessary to sort the several senses of each word, and to exhibit first its natural and primitive signification, as

To *arrive*, to reach the shore in a voyage. He *arrived* at a safe harbour.

Then to give its consequential meaning, *to arrive*, to reach any place whether by land or sea; as, he *arrived* at his country seat.

Then its metaphorical sense, to obtain any thing desired; as, he *arrived* at a peerage.[65]

Johnson's 'clear and careful attention to arranging significations is,' as Elizabeth Hedrick remarks, 'one of the distinguishing features of his work,' and the arrangement, beginning as it does with meanings 'that are closer to the world of sense than those that follow,' 'move from primitiveness to complication in a way that imitates the action of the mind as it abstracts, then recombines, ideas to form more rarified notions than those with which it begins' (433–4). A dictionary may be the inventory of a language, but in so far as the arrangement of the entries 'imitates the action of the mind' it is also, as Browning read it, a record of judgments and interpretations made by the thinking powers of the soul. For Browning, 'little else is worth study.'

As a coda to the preceding argument, we might turn to one of the emblems in Browning's childhood copy of Quarles. Few of the emblems deal directly with language, but one which does is number 10 in the Fifth Book. Its motto is Psalm 142:7: 'Bring my soul out of prison, that I may praise thy Nature' ('name' rather than 'Nature' is the word in the King James version). The *pictura* (which in fact is missing from Browning's copy, now in Balliol College Library) shows the soul as a human figure in a bird-cage, which an angel with a key kneels to unlock. The *explicatio* tropes the soul as a bird, which hops about 'from sense to reason,' then 'from higher reason down to sense again,' until it 'climbs to Faith' and then, in its restlessness, turns down again. The key to its release is the word, and the historical precedent for the liberating word is in Acts 16, where Paul's release from prison is the result of his praying and singing praises to God. The epigram with which emblem 10 ends uses that episode, and challenges the soul to a singing school:

Paul's midnight voice prevail'd; his musicks thunder
Unhing'd the prison doors, split bolts in sunder:
And sitt'st thou here, and hang'st the feeble wing?
And whin'st to be enlarg'd?

The epigram ends with an imperative that might be the motto for Browning's poetry: 'Soul, learn to sing.'[66]

Chapter Two

Parleying, Troping, and Fragmenting:
Pauline, Paracelsus, and *Sordello*

'A Fragment of a Confession'

'A Fragment of a Confession' is the subtitle of *Pauline,* and it points to the linguistic concerns of Browning's first published poem. A confession is etymologically a speaking with or parleying with, and since 'parleying' is a label Browning will ultimately choose for some of his texts, we can see *Pauline* as his earliest version of such speaking together. The subtitle alerts us to the performative function of a Browning text, which here has three principal aspects: the text is the expression of Browning's own soul and a stage in his soul-making; it is a fiction, being both the dramatic speech of a fictional character who is also shaping his soul, and the edited text of yet another fictional character; finally, it is an actual printed text which presents itself, frequently in a riddling way, to a reader whose struggles with it are a stage in his or her soul-making. Because the words of the text serve multiple purposes, they are layered or equivocal, and hence are a puzzle for the reader, but such layering has a moral and spiritual purpose, in Browning's scheme of things, as the words, already dense with interpretation, invite still further readings.

We begin with the poem as the expression of Browning's own soul. Not in any narrow biographical sense, one hastens to add, in spite of the extent to which Browning was stung by Mill's comment on the writer's 'morbid self-consciousness,'[1] and in spite of his hedging admission, in an 1837 letter to Ripert Monclar, that 'the Abortion in question' was the poet among a host of authors Browning wanted to be, a figure 'who would have been more legitimately "myself" than most of the others' (*Correspondence* 3:265). One turns instead to recurring statements in the letters written to Elizabeth during their courtship, statements where Robert refers to the writing of poetry as a duty, as the service of God, and as the means of saving his own soul. 'I desire in this life,' he writes in a letter of September 1845, '(with very little fluctuation for a man & too weak a one), to live and just write out certain things which are in me, and so save my soul' (*Correspondence* 11:89). Language is thus expressive, but the expression is not limited to the outering or uttering of emotion; it is also the uttering of thinking which leads to choice, and those actions of the soul are, in Browning's view, saving ones. A Congregationalist might object to this apparent secularizing of a religious concern, and insist that saving one's soul means accepting 'the truth as it is in Jesus,' but Browning might well reply (and do so in the spirit of the Westminster Confession) that 'the truth as it is in Jesus' is a final or ultimate truth, and that the process of arriving at that final stage involves many intermediate truths, partial or fragmentary or incomplete, which must be tested and judged and acted upon, and which are just as crucial to the life of the soul as that final turn. The statement I have just quoted from the letter of 1845 is echoed in the final lines of *The Ring and the Book*, where writing a book shall 'save the soul' (12.863), an intent Browning links with duty and service to God in the letters of 1845–6. When Elizabeth proposes writing a poem dealing with the age, 'running into the midst of our conventions, & rushing into drawingrooms & the like' – the poem would be *Aurora Leigh* – Robert writes that 'The poem you propose ... is the *only* Poem to be undertaken now by you or anyone that *is* a Poet at all, – the only reality, only effective piece of service to be rendered God and man – it is what I have been all my life intending to do' (*Correspondence* 10:102–3, 118). Other statements affirm such a momentous purpose. 'A poet's affair is with God, to whom he is accountable, and of whom is his reward,' Browning tells Ruskin in a letter of 1855.[2] 'All our life is some form of religion,' Robert writes to Elizabeth on 25 September 1845, 'and all our action some belief' (*Correspondence* 11:97). 'I have no pleasure in writing myself – none, in the mere act – tho' all pleasure in the sense of fulfilling a duty' (*Correspondence* 10:121), Robert had written earlier, and near the beginning of their exchange of letters he had said that 'I write from a thorough conviction that it is the duty of me' (*Correspondence* 10:70). In that same letter he rejects biography in the poems – 'what I have printed gives *no* knowledge of me' – but goes on to talk about the poems he hopes to write as the making of himself: 'I never have begun, even, what I hope I was born to begin and end, – "R.B. a poem"' (*Correspondence* 10:69). Browning thus anticipates the argument in Wilde's 'The Critic as Artist' (in *Intentions*, 1891), where the 'highest Criticism' is 'the record of one's own soul.' Wilde's speakers are discussing criticism as a creative response to a work of art – 'the primary aim of the critic is to see the object as in itself it really is not,' says Ernest in a half-joking reversal of Arnold's famous dictum – before they go on to discuss interpretation – 'to see the object as in itself it really is' – after supper. For Browning, creation and interpretation are one, and he thinks of the poems he has written and the poems he is to write in the same way as Wilde thinks of the 'highest criticism': 'the only civilised form of autobiography.'[3]

Soul-saving and soul-making, service to God, a sense of duty – these are all motives behind Browning's use of language, and, with Browning's characteristic dislike, or fear, of speaking out with his own voice – a psychological trait for which the best account is still the 1931 book by F.R.G. Duckworth[4] – the speaking out is usually through a mask. In his third letter to Elizabeth, Robert says, in a passage familiar to Browning readers, that 'You speak out, *you*, – I only make men & women speak, – give you truth broken into prismatic hues, and fear the pure white light, even if it is in me' (*Correspondence* 10:22). A month later he uses a lighthouse image to suggest that he provides only glimpses of the hard and busy work behind the intermittent shining forth: 'these scenes and song-scraps *are* such mere and very escapes of my inner power, – which lives in me like the light in those crazy Mediterranean phares' (*Correspondence* 10:70). The artistic results of such a psychological makeup are obvious: 'all my writings are purely *dramatic* as I am always anxious to say' – this to Elizabeth in May of 1845 (*Correspondence* 10:234). But if each text is dramatic, and therefore partial or fragmentary, it is also part of a total effort at soul-making largely hidden from the reader.

The drive towards totality, the desire for a comprehensive mastery of art, is powerful in the young Browning – so powerful that Browning describes it three times and in nearly the same words, first in 1833 in the copy of *Pauline* marked and annotated by John Stuart Mill (the copy subsequently given to Forster and now in the Victoria and Albert Museum), then in an 1837 letter to Ripert Monclar, and again in another copy of *Pauline* now lost to a thief but described in *The Browning Collections* (item B23). Here is the first of those statements:

The following Poem was written in pursuance of a foolish plan which occupied me mightily for a time, and which had for its object the enabling me to assume and realize I know not how many different characters; – meanwhile the world was never to guess that 'Brown, Smith, Jones & Robinson' (as the spelling books have it) the respective authors of this poem, the other novel, such an opera, such a speech, etc. etc. were no other than one and the same individual. The present abortion was the first work of the *Poet* of the batch, who would have been more legitimately myself than most of the others; but I surrounded him with all manner of (to my then notion) poetical accessories, and had planned quite a delightful life for him. Only this crab remains of the shapely Tree of Life in this Fool's paradise of mine.

(Peterson and Stanley, 'Mill Marginalia' 146–7)

I quote this statement in its entirety, because it explains one sense in which *Pauline* is 'a fragment of a confession.' From its creator's point of view, it is only a piece of a mighty plan, but it is nonetheless a speaking or uttering of its creator's soul, however oblique the parleying is. Browning characteristically wanted the obliquity to be opaque. The poem was, he asserted in his preface of 1867, 'my earliest attempt at "poetry always dramatic in principle, and so many utterances of so many imaginary persons, not mine."'

The second linguistic aspect of the text is the one ordinary readers feel most comfortable with: the poem as the dramatic speech of a fictional character, the utterance of an imaginary person. In this context, language again has a performative function. The speech is a confession, and the purpose of confession, in a religious life, is to confirm the change initiated by conviction of sin and contrition, to give outward and communal expression to those inner experiences, and to bring about the conversion which is the final stage of the process of returning to God. Critics of *Pauline* have noted such a process in the speaker, though it is a process emptied, for the most part, of its religious significance. Here the confession has an explicitly artistic purpose: the speaker would 'unlock the sleepless brood / Of fancies from my soul' (6–7) so that he may 'sing' again (17).[5] He has confessed once to Pauline (54–76), and is repeating the experience now in hope of another renewal. In that earlier experience, 'careless words' (63) gave way to careful words ('the feeling rushed / That I was low indeed' 68–9, 'And so I told thee all' 71), and led to Pauline's healing words, which dispelled his despair and 'Bade me look up and be what I had been' (74).

Language as it is employed in confession is contingent, a means to an end, not the end in itself. The end in itself is sometimes imaged as music (as it is in this poem) or silence (as it is here and in Carlyle). The oneness – with God, in religious conversion; with Pauline, in this artistic renewal – has no need for words, so that the language of confession has as its final end its own annihilation.[6] Throughout the poem, the speaker is agonizingly conscious of the fact that he is in a fallen state; images of autumn and of exile, both from himself and from his society, pervade his speech. Language is the means to return to oneness, with Pauline, but that desired state makes language unnecessary.

> I would say much,
> And chiefly, I am glad that I have said
> That love which I have ever felt for thee,
> But seldom told; our hearts so beat together,
> That speech is mockery, but when dark hours come   (863–7)

In 1833, a semicolon follows 'come,' and the line means that speech is mockery, except when dark hours come, when words become necessary for renewal. When Browning revised the poem in 1867, he placed a colon after 'mockery,' and made the next half-line part of the following sentence, in which a series of 'when' clauses leads up to the request to 'Look on this lay I dedicate to thee' (870).

If the confession will, from one point of view, make words unnecessary, it will also, from another point of view, make words possible. His goal, we recall, is to 'sing,' and his confession is, paradoxically, both the means to the end and the end itself. This paradox is bound up with the speaker's desire to embrace the whole of human life, a desire which occurs with enough frequency among Browning's characters to indicate the central place which it has in his thought. When the speaker analyses himself, he finds not just 'consciousness / Of self' (269–70) and 'self-supremacy, / Existing as a centre to all things' (273–4), but also 'a principle of restlessness / Which would be all, have, see, know, taste, feel, all' (277–8). One notes that the desire to embrace everything is defined in terms of ontology and epistemology as well as the experience of the five senses, and so it will inevitably be frustrated. At the end of the passage which most resembles 'Alastor' – lines 729 to 810 – the speaker comes to a sense of his limitations: 'But my soul saddens when it looks beyond; / I cannot be immortal, nor taste all' (809–10). The failure is not, however, without its consolation. If one cannot be everything and know everything and experience everything, words as used by the artist may nonetheless approximate that totality.[7] Pauline urges this view on her lover:

And then thou said'st a perfect bard was one
Who shadowed out the stages of all life,
And so thou badest me tell this my first stage; –
'Tis done: and even now I feel all dim the shift
Of thought.   (883–7)

The verbs 'tell' (which appears only in the 1833 version) and 'chronicle' (which appears only in the 1888 version, as a substitute for 'shadow') both indicate the ability of language to record and communicate experience, but the verb 'shadow' (which appears in both the 1833 and 1888 texts) is even more important in defining the function of language. 'To represent imperfectly' and 'to represent typically' are two of the meanings Johnson assigns to the verb in his *Dictionary,* and both indicate how words, though not themselves 'all life,' may point to it, or suggest it. If we see a representation as imperfect, we must be aware of 'perfection hid' (in Cleon's words, and the root meaning of 'perfect' is 'complete'); and if we see a representation as typical, we must be aware of the antitype lying behind the type. In these ways, what is said paradoxically encompasses what is not said, and the whole may be known through a part.

There is yet another way of grasping the whole of experience. When man lost paradise, he discovered that he could regain it in his beloved, and the *hortus conclusus* passage in the Song of Songs provides the major literary image for this idea. It is only a step from this convention to the feeling that the whole world – fallen as well as paradisal – may be discovered in one woman, or at least in the enclosure which she provides for her lover. Browning's poem begins with an enclosure, Pauline bending over her lover, 'loosened hair, and breathing lips, and arms' making 'a screen / To shut me in with thee' (3–5). Eleanor Cook has explored the importance of this enclosure,[8] and our concern here is with its verbal counterpart: the 'one little word' to which the speaker refers at line 238:

And here am I the scoffer, who have probed
Life's vanity, won by a word again
Into my old life – for one little word
Of this sweet friend, who lives in loving me,
Lives strangely on my thoughts, and looks, and words,
As fathoms down some nameless ocean thing
Its silent course of quietness and joy.   (236–42)

What is the one little word? It might be the title of the poem, Pauline's name, or it might be the name of the speaker, uttered by Pauline. Whatever it is, the function of the word is the same: it effects a turn or conversion, since he is 'won by a word again / Into my old life.' We see here the beginning of a pattern which pervades Browning's poetry: the linking of a turn or conversion, whether spiritual or psychological or moral, with a word which turns – with troping, in short, since a trope is etymologically a turn. Troping, etymology, and Pauline's name converge in the last two lines of the quotation, where the simile for the effect of the presence of the 'one little word' in him turns on the use of 'fathoms' as a verb. Its Old English root means to encircle with extended arms, to embrace – the very image with which this poem begins.

The poem is not just a confession or a parleying with Pauline; it is also a parleying with a library. Like his creator, the speaker grew up in a world of books, as he tells Pauline when he refers to 'my first dawn of life, / Which passed alone with wisest ancient books, / All halo-girt with fancies of my own' (318–20). These books recorded, and transmitted to him, the stories that make up his cultural heritage, and his speech is full of references and allusions to these tales. There are folk-tales, like that of the 'fair witch' who becomes 'an old hag at night' (946; there is a parallel reference at 432), and there is the 'fancy of my own' in which the speaker is himself 'a young witch' drawing down the 'radiant form' of a god (112–23). For 'I myself went with the tale' (321), the speaker tells us, and he identified himself with the heroes of myth and legend:

> a god,
> Wandering after beauty – or a giant,
> Standing vast in the sunset – an old hunter,
> Talking with gods – or a high-crested chief,
> Sailing with troops of friends to Tenedos.   (321–5)

His response to these stories is a vivid recreation of their particulars: 'I tell you, nought has ever been so clear / As the place, the time, the fashion of those lives' (326–7). There are allusions to epic and romance ('I should bring / One branch from the gold forest, like the knight / Of old tales' 526–8), to the *Agamemnon* of Aeschylus and the *Ajax* of Sophocles ('old lore / Loved for itself' 566–7), to the *Antigone* (963–5), and to the conventional journey to the underworld (966–71). This last is an example of 'old stories of dead knights' (962) which he asks Pauline to tell him, or of the 'old lays' (963) which he will read to her. Even the Passion and the Resurrection take their place among these old tales (848–54), and the speaker's response is the same concrete recreation of the events: 'oft have I stood by thee' (849), 'thee' being Christ. His first poetry, we learn without surprise, was a response to these stories: 'I turned to those old times and scenes, where all / That's beautiful had birth for me, and made / Rude verses on them all' (380–2). His inspiration was not nature but books.

In the speaker's immediate past is the poetry of Shelley, inspiring words 'which seemed / A key to a new world' (414–15). Gone now are all references to stories; replacing them are references to ideas and music, to which the speaker responds with as much imaginative vitality as he once did to the old tales:

> I have stood with thee, as on a throne
> With all thy dim creations gathered round
> Like mountains, – and I felt of mould like them,
> And creatures of my own were mixed with them.   (163–6)

The ideas are principally of political and social reform: 'I was vowed to liberty, / Men were to be as gods, and earth as heaven' (425–6). The main image of the initial apostrophe to Shelley – the 'great river' (180) which is 'the pulse of some great country' (189) – suggests the role of the poet as the (tardily) acknowledged legislator of the world, and the sun-treader image perhaps suggests the same role. But it is Shelley's music to which the speaker responds most strongly.

Music, according to the spatial metaphor by which Browning ranks the arts, is a higher art than poetry, and the speaker in *Pauline* again reflects his creator in his response to music and his enthusiasm for it.[9] He constantly associates music with emotions that cannot be expressed in words, and with a higher existence which the notes or melodies reveal to us. In an important parenthesis, the speaker defines music as 'earnest of a heaven, / Seeing we know emotions strange by it, / Not else to be revealed' (365–7), and the association of heaven and emotions with music recurs in the poem, in phrases like 'passion's melodies' (411) and 'music's mystery' (930), for instance. The speaker regularly refers to Shelley's poems as 'songs' rather than tales, and music with all its associations is the essential aspect of Shelley's works. Shelley's words, however, remain crucial. One may hear the music, and one may feel that it is full of emotion and meaning, but without words both the emotion and the meaning remain vague and obscure, felt rather than known. Hence the speaker talks about Shelley's words as intertwined with his music, and as the instrument of revelation: 'And woven with them ['his songs'] there were words, which seemed / A key to a new world' (414–15). Music is thus a metaphor for the origin, ground, and goal of poetry: it rouses emotion, and it is revelatory, being 'earnest of a heaven,' but it needs words to make its meaning clear.

We come now to the last of the three aspects of a Browning text that I outlined in the opening paragraph of this chapter, the text as a challenge to, and riddle for, the reader. *Pauline* presents itself to the reader as an edited text, with epigraph, prefatory quotation (dated at London, with an accompanying riddle, 'V.A. XX'), a footnote by the editor, and a final note giving a place and a date, the date differing from the one attached to the prefatory quotation. The printed poem is, as Clyde de L. Ryals points out (first, tentatively, in his 1976 essay on the genre of the poem, then fully in his 1983 book, *Becoming Browning*), 'a fictional edition,'[10] a text with commentary and editorial apparatus, like *Sartor Resartus*. As such, and in spite of the good will and helpfulness of the editor – Pauline – the whole work is a puzzle for the reader, who must bring to bear on it all his or her intelligence and insight, and whose struggles with its import make the text a part of his or her own life. There is much to puzzle over. In the printed speech itself, there are breakings off, like the one in line 458 (which, in the text of 1833, begins with the words 'Well I remember' and then leaves off with asterisks); there are section breaks, marked sometimes by a line left blank, sometimes by asterisks. And what do the dates signify? What is the relation between the epigraph from Marot and the speech? Or between the quotation from Agrippa and the speech? Critics are right to take up these questions, for the printed text invites an active and interpreting response, of the sort that Henry Kozicki provides, for instance, in his 1990 essay linking Browning and Agrippa.[11] Kozicki argues that Agrippa's occultism is 'a respectable form of Neoplatonism' (in contrast to other Browning critics who have dismissed occultism as 'a shady practice') and that the speaker is 'somehow like a magus.' Agrippa's thought is, in Kozicki's response to the headnote, 'the conceptual underpinning of *Pauline*' and the defining feature of 'the speaker's powers, his original condition, his apostasy, and his redemption' – in short, of the shape of the poem as a whole.

One might add to Kozicki's detailed analysis of the quotation as editorial comment on the speech one further point. The quotation is from the 'Ad Lectorem,' the preface to Agrippa's first and most famous work, the *De Occulta Philosophia*, but the preface is not that of the ambitious young man who wrote the *De Occulta Philosophia* about 1510 or 1511, but that of the older, more experienced scholar who, in 1526, wrote the work to which he refers in a part of the preface not quoted by Browning, the *De incertitudine et vanitate scientiarum et artium*. The whole point of the preface is to draw attention to the earlier book as the work of a young man. Knowing this, the reader faces a puzzle. Is the presence of the quotation to be attributed to the speaker, now standing back and taking an objective look at his own younger self? Or is it to be attributed to Pauline, ready to excuse the speech as adolescent? Or is it to be attributed to the poem's creator, the unnamed author about whom the first readers of *Pauline* could know nothing? The same puzzle is posed by the French epigraph: 'I am no longer what I have been, and can never be.' Trying to solve the puzzle of the Latin epigraph might lead the reader to the texts of Agrippa himself, if one considers the quotation as a clue, and connections with the poem suddenly assert themselves. In addition to all the links so carefully made by Kozicki, one discovers that Agrippa was attempting to embrace all knowledge, that he was dissatisfied with all human endeavours, and that he turned finally to 'one little word.' The *De incertitudine et vanitate scientiarum et artium* is a survey of all the arts and sciences, from poetry to housekeeping. Agrippa argues that all are vanity and ought to be despised: 'there is none whiche is without iuste blame and reprehension, nor that of it selfe deserveth praise, but that which it getteth of his honestie that professeth the same.'[12] All the arts and sciences involve the misuse or abuse of language. Where, then, are we to find the truth? After Agrippa's long catalogue, we come at last to chapter 100, 'Of the Woorde of God.' 'God alone is true, and every man a liar' (373), says Agrippa, echoing Romans 3:4, the text that would become the theme of *The Ring and the Book*; God's word 'alone decerveth everye signification and kinde of woordes' (371). One word in fact unites all the rest, Agrippa had written in an earlier chapter, and it is the name of Jesus, 'in whom all thinges be summed and contained' (137). We can see that the speaker of *Pauline* is like Agrippa when he describes himself as 'the scoffer, who [has] probed / Life's vanity' but who has been 'won by a word again / Into my old life' (236–8). Is that word the name of Jesus? Probably not, but the reader can recognize a habit of mind that is as much that of the Congregationalist as it is of the reader of Agrippa: a crisis brought on by a descent into the world and all that therein is, and a turn and restoration effected by a word.

Pauline is, then, a fragment, and that important genre from the

Romantic period has, in Browning's handling of it, three principal aspects: the text is a historical part of its creator's lifelong effort at soul-making and soul-saving; it is an incident in its fictional speaker's artistic and spiritual life; and the printed text (available in at least two major versions, 1833 and 1888), with all its subsequent editorial accretions, offers itself for understanding and interpretation, so that it becomes an episode in the reader's life and (Browning would hope) a stage in his or her soul-making. The meeting place of all these concerns is the language of the poem itself, a language which serves multiple purposes. In effect, Browning has taken equivocation – that characteristic of language inescapable in Johnson's dictionary – and made it into the operating principle of his art. That principle leads us directly to the dynamic relationship which characterizes the dramatic monologue: the configuration of poet, fictional speaker, and reader. In proposing this configuration, I am going beyond the triangle John Maynard argued for in a brief but important essay published in 1987. 'The essential rhetorical situation of the dramatic monologue,' he wrote, is 'a special form of triangulation in which the reader's position is determined by the relative positions of speaker and listener' (the speaker and listener in the poem, that is).[13] To that triangle we ought to add the poet himself, and to that reader response approach we ought to add expression. Expression and response are both hidden aspects of the text, and yet we feel the pressure of both in every Browning poem.

'Never a senseless gust now man is born'

The title of this section is a quotation from part 5 of *Paracelsus*. The reader will remember that, when Paracelsus is dying, he rises from his couch over the protests of his friend Festus, puts on gown, chain, signet-ring, and sword – the emblems of his authority – and presents a view of creation and of human life that is usually read in the context of the nineteenth-century preoccupation with the themes of evolution and progress. Browning conflates the two, though they are in fact distinct and different, and was insisting on the conflation as late as 1881, when he told Furnivall that 'in reality, all that seems *proved* in Darwin's scheme was a conception familiar to me from the beginning: see in *Paracelsus* the progressive development from senseless matter to organized, until man's appearance (*Part* V.).'[14] Our reading the passage in the context of the debate over evolution and progress, however, has obscured its other concerns, particularly with human language as the essential tool of progress, and with turning or troping as the essential feature of human language. It is with those concerns that this section will deal.

The speech takes its rise from a sudden apprehension of Paracelsus: 'I see all / I know all' (5.543–4). The assertion has its source in Browning himself and in his desire, from the beginning, for an encyclopedic grasp of the world and all that is in it; in the dramatic context of the poem, the assertion is the final stage of Paracelsus's aspirations, voiced in part 1, modified in part 3, but essentially unchanged during his lifetime. He aspires to know. This purpose is expressed in various ways in part 1. Festus gives us one version when he talks about youths 'resolved, like you, / To grasp all, and retain all' (1.244–5), an aim 'so vast / In scope' (1.273–4) that it would comprehend 'the secret of the world, / Of man, and man's true purpose, path and fate' (1.276–7). Paracelsus himself defines his aim in parallel terms: it is 'to comprehend the works of God, / And God himself, and all God's intercourse / With the human mind' (1.533–5). His aim has its parallel in Aprile, who 'would LOVE infinitely' (2.385); that is, he would embrace the whole of 'the loveliness of life' (2.485) by mastering sculpture, painting, poetry, and music. Festus condemns Paracelsus's aspirations as Faustian (Paracelsus has, he says, 'passed the bounds / Prescribed to life' 3.862–3), but Paracelsus himself insists from the beginning that, in pursuing this aim, he is serving God's will (see 1.172–3, 294–5, 363, 359–60). He will confirm that service in the language theory he sets out in part 5. In part 3, however, he protests against easy assertions about God's will:

> one would swear
> Man had but merely to uplift his eye,
> And see the will in question charactered
> On the heaven's vault.   (3.512–15)

Creation is not to be read so easily. Far from having characters or letters that label and explain all in one place, human beings know only scattered words. Lying behind that view is a myth of creation, not as an ordering, a making of a cosmos out of chaos, but as a breaking apart or a fragmenting.

Again and again Paracelsus speaks of gaining knowledge as a gathering of scattered or fragmented pieces. 'I go,' he says at the end of part 1, 'to gather this / The sacred knowledge, here and there dispersed / About the world, long lost or never found' (1.785–7). He repeats the metaphor in part 3, when he is defining 'Two sorts of knowledge'

(3.923), one of which consists of 'a few / Prime principles' and 'many secrets' (3.926–7, 925): 'I must go find them scattered through the world' (3.932). The suggestion of things hidden or secret leads readily enough to the metaphor of creation as a riddle or puzzle, the result of the breaking or fragmenting. 'I betake myself to study again,' Paracelsus says in part 4 of the poem, 'Till patient searchings after hidden lore / Half wring some bright truth from its prison' (4.382–4). 'The primal aggregate' (5.844) is Paracelsus's label for creation understood as a miscellany without a readily grasped order or purpose. The approach to this miscellany as a riddle, however, involves a double perspective: one sees a world where everything lies confusedly, but one intuits wholeness behind the fragments. Such wholeness, with its indwelling purpose and energy and order, is 'the secret of the world' (5.637) which Paracelsus reveals in his last great speech. The linguistic form of this secret is typical of Browning. Here is how Paracelsus expresses it:

I knew, I felt, (perception unexpressed,
Uncomprehended by our narrow thought
But somehow felt and known in every shift
And change in the spirit, – nay, in every pore
Of the body, even,) – what God is, what we are,
What life is ...   (5.638–43)

The noun clauses that are the objects of Paracelsus's verbs – 'what God is, what we are, / What life is' – are the secret, but the syntax circumscribes without revealing. The relative pronoun 'what' points or gestures but lacks antecedents; its only explicit complements are the words 'God' and 'we' and 'life,' which revolve around the linking verb 'is' but remain abstractions opaque from familiar use. More characteristic of Browning's technique of pointing to an answer without actually giving it is his use of parenthesis, that rhetorical device for interrupting syntax. In the quoted passage, Paracelsus twice begins with a subject and verb that clearly require an object ('I knew, I felt'), and then not only puts something in beside the verbs (the literal meaning of parenthesis) but delays the appearance of the object and the promised revelation of the secret. The parenthesis alerts the reader to the fact that, in spite of the promise of the syntax, there will be no revelation. 'Perception unexpressed,' Paracelsus says, undermining the words to come, and 'Uncomprehended by our narrow thought.' Then he repeats the key verbs from the main clause outside the parenthesis – 'felt and known' – but this time with an adverb, 'somehow,' that turns us away from our ordinary understanding of those familiar words, and leaves them a puzzle too. In short, Paracelsus makes the verbs 'shift / And change.' One might think that the effect would be a weakening of them, but in fact it is a strengthening. The lines are a strong appeal not to argument but to actual experience, and in actual experience nothing is fixed. All is 'shift / And change,' but, paradoxically, to know and feel shift and change are to know the unchanging: 'what God is, what we are, / What life is.' The lines are paradigmatic. Browning characteristically fragments syntax because it mirrors a world where knowledge is also in fragments; and he characteristically points towards an answer to the riddle of creation without actually stating it. The myth of creation which underpins such fragmenting and riddling is the one Paracelsus gives at length immediately after the passage I have just quoted.

The spatial metaphors of that myth are obvious enough, and they are the ones critics have seized upon to show how Browning conflates evolution and progress. Paracelsus begins with 'existence in its lowest form' (5.647), regularly uses 'up' as both preposition and adverb, talks about 'inferior natures' and 'the superior race' (5.708, 709), and says that 'all lead up higher' (5.708). Combined with these spatial metaphors, however, is an account of creation as a breaking apart. The emanating of God's power and attributes is a sundering of them, and they become 'dim fragments' (5.687) and 'scattered rays' (5.691). The creation of man is a counter-movement. The 'dim fragments' are 'meant / To be united in some wondrous whole' (5.687–8), and the 'scattered rays should meet / Convergent in the faculties of man' (5.691–2). One needs to draw special attention to the word 'faculties,' because it indicates that the human attributes – they are power, knowledge, and love, as defined by Paracelsus – are also the divine faculties, and the exercise of those faculties is a recreation which reverses the original act of creation. Human beings themselves, in their very nature, are a stage in that recreation. Here is Paracelsus in a passage which combines the spatial and fragmenting metaphors:

Hints and previsions of which faculties,
Are strewn confusedly everywhere about
The inferior natures, and all lead up higher,
All shape out dimly the superior race,
The heir of hopes too fair to turn out false,
And man appears at last.   (5.706–11)

Just as important as the spatial and fragmenting metaphors is the metaphor for re-creation. It is a turning or circular movement, and when that motion is combined with the theme of progress, we have a circling which spirals upwards. Paracelsus does refer explicitly to the circle (at 5.716), but far more extended is his account of the willed human action of turning, which he identifies with that central and essential aspect of all language, the humanizing of creation through the trope of prosopopoeia. A trope, we remember, is literally a turn which typically takes a word and rotates it, so that it points away from its ordinary referent (Hillis Miller writes that the 'most inclusive sense' of the word trope is 'all the turnings of language away from straightforward referential meaning').[15] The crucial turn that human beings give to creation is the animating or personifying of all things. Here is the whole passage as spoken by Paracelsus:

> man, once descried, imprints for ever
> His presence on all lifeless things: the winds
> Are henceforth voices, wailing or a shout,
> A querulous mutter or a quick gay laugh,
> Never a senseless gust now man is born.
> The herded pines commune and have deep thoughts,
> A secret they assemble to discuss
> When the sun drops behind their trunks which glare
> Like grates of hell: the peerless cup afloat
> Of the lake-lily is an urn, some nymph
> Swims bearing high above her head: no bird
> Whistles unseen, but through the gaps above
> That let light in upon the gloomy woods,
> A shape peeps from the breezy forest-top,
> Arch with small puckered mouth and mocking eye.
> The morn has enterprise, deep quiet droops
> With evening, triumph takes the sunset hour,
> Voluptuous transport ripens with the corn
> Beneath a warm moon like a happy face:
> – And this to fill us with regard for man,
> With apprehension of his passing worth,
> Desire to work his proper nature out,
> And ascertain his rank and final place,
> For these things tend still upward, progress is
> The law of life ... (5.719–43)

Prosopopoeia, one notes, is not here the fallacy Ruskin would attack, and it is not the fiction or lying popularly associated with poetry. There is no tension here between troping and truth-telling, because troping is the essential human activity, a turning which Browning daringly identifies with the turning or spiralling upwards which is progress. 'There is no poetry, perhaps no language at all, without prosopopoeia,'[16] says Hillis Miller in the second of two essays on Ruskin and the pathetic fallacy (where Miller shows that Ruskin's argument points to a truth just the opposite of that Ruskin was prepared to admit), and Paracelsus is arguing that there is no progress without language, and without the most characteristic feature of language, prosopopoeia. Its source, Paracelsus argues, is in the divine attributes, scattered at the time of original creation, and then 'convergent in the faculties of man' (5.692).

It is in the context of such an understanding of divine and human faculties that we ought to read an earlier passage in the poem. It is in part 1, where Paracelsus locates truth, not in the world outside us, but within each human being:

Truth is within ourselves; it takes no rise
From outward things, whate'er you may believe.
There is an inmost centre in us all,
Where truth abides in fulness ...   (1.726–9)

The controlling metaphor Paracelsus uses for this truth is light – he uses the word explicitly at 1.736, and adds 'splendour,' 'radiance,' 'ray,' and 'beams' – and the metaphor is both obvious and conventional: God is light, and God is truth. The light may be dimmed or blocked or deflected by 'the gross flesh' (1.730), 'A baffling and perverting carnal mesh' (1.732), but it is divine, and it is the centre of authority in human beings. How that authority works is suggested in a single line from the first part of Paracelsus's account of prosopopoeia, where the winds become voices: 'Never a senseless gust now man is born' (5.723). The adjective 'senseless' is neatly double: it points to the sense or power of feeling that prosopopoeia makes possible in the winds, but it also indicates the sense or meaning that the winds now have as a result of the human wording of them. We are not far from Calvin's assertion, quoted in chapter 1, that without the word of God our senses would 'gaze bewildered' on unmeaning objects.

As words turn creation and gather its fragments into an upward spiral, the troping which drives such progress gradually reveals itself not just as rhetorical figures but as symbols and types. Both those terms appear in Paracelsus's speech:

> But in completed man begins anew
> A tendency to God. Prognostics told
> Man's near approach; so in man's self arise
> August anticipations, symbols, types,
> Of a dim splendour ever on before
> In that eternal circle life pursues.   (5.772–7)

In its widest sense, a symbol is a part of a whole, broken off, but for the specific purpose of being brought together again. Hence the Greek *symbolon* is a mark or token, while the word itself combines a prefix meaning 'one' with a verb that means 'to throw or put together,' so that a symbol is one's contribution to a whole which is to be reconstituted.[17] Symbols are thus the evidence of a past oneness or unity, and the pledge of its renewal. Paracelsus's syntax makes 'symbols' parallel to 'types.' A type, as we saw in chapter 1, is an anticipation, and as such it connects the past and the future, understood as the completion or fulfilment of the present. Hence it is not surprising that, in his 1980 book on the Victorian use of typology, George Landow should connect typology and progress: 'Since typology is essentially a system of progressive revelation, any attempt to apply it to the natural world inevitably leads to some sort of theory of evolution.'[18] The providential shape of human history, then, depends upon language, understood not as the mirror of the world outside us, but as the power within us which turns or tropes that world and brings it back to God.

Language which is simply a reflection of the world outside us is hollow and empty, and Paracelsus sometimes describes that kind of language as an echo, as when he discovers in the 'arch-genethliac's' (2.25) roll the line, 'Time fleets, youth fades, life is an empty dream' (2.43) and labels it 'the echo of time' (2.44). One recalls the myth of Echo who, in John Hollander's words, is 'unable to originate discourse, unable to forbear from reply.'[19] She is imprisoned in a fragmented language, and, being doomed to mere repetition, lacks the freedom to turn the words she hears. Contrast her inability to think and judge with the mental activity of Paracelsus:

> I must review my captured truth, sum up
> Its value, trace what ends to what begins,

Its present power with its eventual bearings,
Latent affinities, the views it opens,
And its full length in perfecting my scheme.   (4. 390–4)

'The best impart the gift of seeing to the rest'

Browning conceived *Sordello* as 'a companion to *Paracelsus*,'[20] he told
Edward Dowden in 1866, and, different as the two poems are (particularly in their accessibility), one can indeed see parallels. In both, we have
men who begin their lives in a 'sequestered nest' (*Paracelsus* 1.36) –
'Goito's mountain-cup / And castle' for Sordello (2.956–7) – and who
aspire to a wholeness and mastery beyond the common lot. The plot of
Paracelsus, which Browning sums up in the verbs 'aspires' and 'attains'
in the titles of the five parts, is like the plot of *Sordello*, a pattern of reaching up first through one course of action and then through another.
F.E.L. Priestley's summary of the shape of *Paracelsus* – 'true aspiration
and ironic attainment followed by ironic or false aspiration and true
attainment'[21] – needs only the last stage ('true attainment') changed to
become a summary of the shape of *Sordello*. Both men die at the end of
their stories, but not before being able to answer the question posed of
every hero of romance: who am I? Paracelsus answers that question, as
we have seen, in the clothing he puts on for his dying speech, and in his
recognition that 'I have been something' (5.593) in aiding the progress of
mankind; Sordello answers that question when he realizes he is Taurello's son (5.741–2) and tramples underfoot the badge which made him
the heir of Taurello's politics as well. The centre of his world is the font
in the castle at Goito, a baptismal font which is also, unknown to him,
his mother's tomb, so that it holds the secret of his birth. His story is the
revelation of that secret and the return to the font which becomes his
own tomb, so that the narrative has a circular structure and ends where
it began. The narrator in fact invites his ghostly audience to link beginning and end: when someone guesses Sordello's fault and the shape of
his life, the narrator advises him to 'Go back to the beginning, rather'
(1.587).

For the nineteenth-century audience of the historical Robert Browning, *Sordello* looks like a very different text from *Paracelsus*, and apparently presents a set of different problems for readers. *Paracelsus* is a
dramatic poem, while *Sordello* is a narrative, modelled on epic and
romance. *Paracelsus* is an edited text with notes, while *Sordello* stands on
its own, without any editorial help. The more one examines the two

texts, however (and especially the subsequent history of the text of *Sordello*), the more the differences dissolve. In the original preface to *Paracelsus*, Browning defines the kind of response he expects from his readers, and does so, characteristically, by talking about filling in gaps and making connections: 'A work like mine depends more immediately on the intelligence and sympathy of the reader for its success – indeed were my scenes stars it must be his co-operating fancy which, supplying all chasms, shall connect the scattered lights into one constellation – a Lyre or a Crown.' The gaps in *Paracelsus* are inherent in the dramatic form of the poem, since drama for Browning is always a matter of showing rather than telling. In the letters of their courtship, Robert objected to the narrative techniques of a writer Elizabeth admired – 'that wonderful woman George Sand' (*Correspondence* 10:292) – because she, with the 'out blurting of a phrase' and 'a scrape of the pen,' could attribute qualities to her characters, while 'a Dramatic poet has to *make* you love or admire his men and women, – they must *do* and *say* all that you are to see and hear – really do it in your face, say it in your ears' (*Correspondence* 11:22). In addition to inferring from the dramatic speeches (and so filling in the gaps in one's understanding of character), the reader must also fill in the gaps in the edited text. The work of the editor is most apparent in the lengthy 'note' which serves as an appendix, where Browning characterizes *Paracelsus*, not as a dramatic poem, but as a 'commentary' on 'any memoir of Paracelsus [the reader] pleases.' Browning's poem, then, is a response to preexisting texts, and Browning insists that the poem is not so much creative as it is interpretative: 'The liberties I have taken with my subject are very trifling.' To prove this claim, he translates a 'popular account' of Paracelsus from the *Biographie Universelle*, and to it he adds 'a few notes, in order to correct those parts which do not bear out my own view of the character of Paracelsus.' His 'own view' is particularly apparent when he claims a number of Reformation figures for his own religious tradition: 'Now, there is no doubt of the Protestantism of Paracelsus, Erasmus, Agrippa, etc., but the nonconformity of Paracelsus was always scandalous.' Browning appends six learned notes to the 'popular account' he gives, and sounds more and more like a critic, claiming the reader's attention ('The reader may remember that ...'), citing parallel passages (about the sword of Paracelsus, for instance: 'I recollect a couple of allusions to it in our own literature'), giving references to other sources ('For a good defence of Paracelsus I refer the reader to ...'), evaluating those sources ('This last, a good book,' he writes parenthetically), clarifying difficulties ('While on the subject of the writings of Paracelsus, I may explain a passage in the third part of the Poem'), and acknowledging different points of view ('for accounts differ'). He is, in short, doing as editor what his readers must do: compare, explain, connect, weigh, and judge. All those critical and editorial activities, formally separated from the poem itself in *Paracelsus*, are incorporated in the role of the narrator in *Sordello*. Like the editor-creator of *Paracelsus*, the narrator claims his listeners' attention, from the first line to the wryly sardonic imperative at the end ('but, friends, / Wake up!' 6.873–4); he suggests that he is only re-presenting his sources ('Yourselves may spell it yet in chronicles' 1.189); he refers to alternative sources ('Many a tale, of this retreat betimes, / Was born,' including that of the 'Chroniclers of Mantua' 6.820–2); and he presents a point of view ('Ah my Sordello, I this once befriend / And speak for you' 6.590–1): instead of '"Thrusting in time eternity's concern"' (1.566), Sordello must learn how to 'Let the employer match the thing employed, / Fit to the finite his infinity' (6.498–9). For the edition of 1863, however, Browning did provide a separate gloss as a guide for the reader: 'the "headlines," or running commentary at the top of the page, is added for the first time,' he told Moncure Conway.[22] The commentary is an interpretation, but it is formally separated from the poem, like Coleridge's prose gloss in *The Rime of the Ancient Mariner*, and the reader is faced with the problem not of making sense of all the connections in the poem, but of bridging the gap between commentary and poem. The very first headline – 'A Quixotic attempt' – raises questions about theme, relations with a prior text (allusion), and the stance, perspective and purpose of the narrator, crucial questions with which the reader must wrestle. *Sordello* thus becomes a paradoxical text, providing the reader with both too much and too little.

Browning's long struggle with the writing of *Sordello* was largely the result of his wrestling with the problem not of gaining insight, but of communicating it. That problem has two sources, one artistic and one rhetorical. The artistic source is Browning's desire to make things new, not by rejecting the conventions of his art, but by turning those conventions to new ends. So he begins *Sordello* by addressing his predecessors, poets and critics, 'friends, / Summoned together from the world's four ends' (1.31–2) – the act of summoning an assembly or coming together is the literal meaning of 'convention' – and then by lecturing those same friends, insisting, as Sordello himself says, that '"my art intends / New structure from the ancient"' (5.642–3). It will not be what his convention expects: conventional. His attitude to his predecessors is anticipated in the preface to *Paracelsus*, where he complains about those who keep the requirements of stage presentation in mind when they are writing a drama designed to be read: 'I do not very well understand what is called a Dramatic Poem, wherein all those restrictions only submitted to on account of compensating good in the original scheme are scrupulously retained, as though for some special fitness in themselves – and all new facilities placed at an author's disposal by the vehicle he selects, as pertinaciously rejected.' When, in the letters during their courtship, Elizabeth chides him for misjudging Horne's poems and thinking them better than in fact they are, Robert defends himself by writing, 'it is a principle with me to begin by welcoming any strangeness, intention of originality in men – the other way of safe copying precedents being *so* safe!' (*Correspondence* 11:292). The rhetorical source for the desire to make things new is the 'new logic' of the eighteenth century, the logic Browning's father knew chiefly through Collard, and whose terms Browning borrowed (I argued in chapter 1) for his commentary on the stages of Sordello's growth. The ultimate method, the one Collard called (using Watts's words) '*cryptical* or *hidden*,' is Browning's own. Though one can define techniques that are common to all texts that use such a method – ellipses, elaborations, reversals, and inversions – the method is at the same time unique to every text. Hence the reader or listener must bring an alert mind and an active imagination to a puzzle which is difficult because conventions are not a sure guide, and the expectations established by them are likely to be frustrated. Our concern, then, is with responses, with the varying relations between poem and listeners, text and readers, that *Sordello* explores. David E. Latané, Jr has pointed out that there are three audiences in the poem – the people and princes of the troubadour Sordello, the ghostly audience of fellow poets summoned by the narrator, and the Victorian readers of the historical Robert Browning[23] – and to that list we can add all subsequent readers of the poem. My concern is primarily with the ghostly audience of fellow poets, and with Victorian and modern readers of *Sordello*.

Sordello begins with an invitation which is also a challenge: 'Who will, may hear Sordello's story told.' It ends with a line which casts responsibility entirely on the listener or reader: 'Who would has heard Sordello's story told.' '"Will,"' Isobel Armstrong has observed, 'is Browning's word for the imagination,'[24] and its use here indicates that, while the teller freely offers his story, he does so conditionally, and relies upon the willing and active response of his listeners. The poet's challenge takes a form which we must now begin to recognize as Browning's masterplot.

(I borrow this word from Eleanor Cook, who in turn borrows it from others.)[25] That plot is the breaking up of things so that they can be put together again, a myth of creation and recreation as a dynamic and ongoing process, always moving towards completion or perfection but never completed (at least from our human perspective). In this plot, the poet imitates God's original act of creation by fragmenting or dividing things, while the reader or listener re-creates by using his or her God-given faculties to connect, restore, and bring together again things that seem only a jumble or miscellany, but are in fact, to use Sordello's own phrase, 'fragments of a whole ordained to be' (3.141). When Browning speaks in his own voice in book 3 of the poem, he focuses, understandably enough, on the role of the poet in providing materials for such a re-creation, and the inclusive pronouns 'we' and 'us' refer to the speaker and his assembled fellows:

The office of ourselves, – nor blind nor dumb,
And seeing somewhat of man's state, – has been,
For the worst of us, to say they so have seen;
For the better, what it was they saw; the best
Impart the gift of seeing to the rest   (3.864–8)

In the forty-five lines or so that follow the definition of these kinds, Browning gives examples of how each proceeds by providing both the poet's words and the listener's responses. The second example clearly corresponds to the middle kind of poets, who say 'what it was they saw,' because the speaker describes Plara the bard's 'youth in a grim town' (3.882), and the imaginary listener agrees that what was seen is accurate: ""'Exact the town, the minster and the street'"' (3.901). The first example is more complex. There the speaker approaches faces as emblems ('there's no face but I can read profound / Disclosures in; this stands for hope, that – fear' 3.870–1), and that beginning suggests saying he 'so has seen,' but (as so often happens in the emblem) the image – the face – speaks; the speech is that of an imprisoned lover, and it evokes a response from the imaginary listener, who judges the speech to be true – true, that is, to the circumstances and situation hinted at in the dramatic text. The third example is the most problematic. There the poet speaks mainly of abstractions – mirth and sadness, lust and love – but insists that "Tis of the mood itself I speak, what tinge / Determines it, else colourless' (3.908–9); the listener affirms his knowledge of the particular: '"'Ay, that's the variation's gist!'"' (3.911).

The poet's response to that ready affirmation is a sceptical '"Indeed?"' For the third kind of poet is different from the other two: they provided content – sights – to which readers responded; he teaches a method – 'the gift of seeing' – which his readers must learn. Browning is making the same distinction that he attributed to Paracelsus, between 'possessing' and 'displaying,' between thought and the communication of thought.

Sordello, like Paracelsus, struggles with 'displaying' or communicating through words, so that he is, as Browning said of Chatterton's creation, Rowley, 'a Man, a Time, a Language, all at once.'[26] The 'Time' was one when 'the most fashionable' language in Italy was Provençal; it was considered polished and suitable to heroic poetry, to 'the fashionable sentiments of ideal honour, and fantastic fortitude.' Hence Dante's master, Brunetto Latini, chose it over 'the inharmonious tongue of his own country.' My quotations come from a little book in Browning's library, Thomas Penrose's A Sketch of the Lives and Writings of Dante and Petrarch (London, 1790), and Browning read it carefully enough to provide, at least for the first twenty pages, an index of names and page references, but he also, on the same blank pages at the back of the volume, lists Sordello and the page (78) where Penrose writes a brief note on him. Penrose says that Sordello 'was particularly well skilled in Provençal poetry' and also that he 'spoke the Italian language with fluency.' Browning picks up neither of these facts, and instead labels Sordello's language as 'Roman.' The 'Time' was one that, we might expect, would interest Browning, for languages were in competition with each other, and one (considered superior) was being usurped by another (more broadly based and associated with political radicalism), yet the narrator sets aside Sordello's part in such change, just as Browning himself seems to have set aside the historical and comparative work of the new philology of his day.

> How he sought
> The cause, conceived a cure, and slow re-wrought
> That Language, – welding words into the crude
> Mass from the new speech round him, till a rude
> Armour was hammered out, in time to be
> Approved beyond the Roman panoply
> Melted to make it, – boots not.   (2.573–9)

Instead, his focus on language is ahistorical, and he considers its adequacy in communication – a questionable adequacy because language fragments and breaks apart:

> Because perceptions whole, like that he sought
> To clothe, reject so pure a work of thought
> As language: thought may take perception's place
> But hardly co-exist in any case,
> Being its mere presentment – of the whole
> By parts, the simultaneous and the sole
> By the successive and the many.   (2.589–95)

'Perceptions' is a troublesome word, but it seems to suggest the many-faceted unity of actual experience. 'Thought' is related to logic, in so far as it attempts a systematic view of the powers of the mind and of the ways in which we order our experience (by analysis and synthesis, for instance). Since language is 'a work of thought,' it is an ordering of experience, but it fragments, in both time and space, the original wholeness of experience. Where experience is 'simultaneous' and 'sole,' language is 'successive' and 'many.' The parts of speech divide experience into the 'many' – a noun or agent, a verb or action, an object or thing acted upon – and syntax is not just the system by which those parts of speech are related to each other, but a sequence in time, normally (in English syntax and in the Aristotelian world view which underlies it) the naming of a thing and the proceeding to predication about it. The passage is a complaint about language when measured by the standard of ideal communication; ideally, words would be unnecessary, and human beings would open into each other, like the angels in *Paradise Lost*, by instant apprehension. In our fallen world, however, the 'mediate word' (*The Ring and the Book* 12.857) is necessary. Language is the instrument by which the poet imitates God and creates by fragmenting; language is also the instrument by which the reader or listener uses God-given powers and re-creates by repairing the breaks. It is for the reader 'to clutch / And reconstruct,' while the poet's 'office' is 'to diffuse, / Destroy' (2.598–600). Sordello, however, would communicate all or nothing. 'Within his soul / Perception brooded unexpressed and whole' (5.435–6), and when he cannot, like Milton's angels, convey all instantaneously, he sees, 'in a tenth part, less and less to strive / About' (2.757–8). When in book 6 the narrator 'befriends and speaks for' his creation, he confirms Sordello's authority (as the 'representative' of 'a Power' above which sounds like God, or like the Neoplatonic One) but distinguishes his knowing from his telling: Sordello is 'for authority the same, / Communication different' (6. 599–600).

The passage on language in book 5 repeats some of the key ideas we have been exploring. In his long speech beginning '"A poet must be earth's essential king"' (5.506), Sordello sets out three stages that reflect the three kinds of poet Browning had defined in book 3: first there is the task of marshalling '"Life's elemental masque"'; its abstractions – evil, good, sinner, saint – parallel the work of poets who 'say they so have seen' (3.866); next there is the act of 'unstationing' the men and women and letting them reveal themselves in their conduct, as in the work of poets who say 'what it was they saw' (3.867); finally, there is a stage Sordello characterizes as a breaking up or fragmenting which will 'unveil' the inner life:

'Man's inmost life shall have yet freer play:
Once more I cast external things away,
And natures composite, so decompose
That' ...   (5.617–20)

Browning interjects in line 620, saying 'but enough!' in the text of 1840, but 'Why, he writes *Sordello*' in the revision of 1863. So Sordello approaches the method of his creator. The kind of communication Sordello aims for he calls 'brother's speech' (5.635), and scholars have usually taken such speech as Browning's ideal too.[27] It clearly relies on a vigorous and imaginative response on the part of the listener or reader:

Yourselves effect what I was fain before
Effect, what I supplied yourselves suggest,
What I leave bare yourselves can now invest.   (5.622–4)

The instrument for such communication is the fragment, for which Sordello's metaphor is the half: 'How we attain to talk as brothers talk, / In half-words, call things by half-names' (5.625–6). The understanding and imagination of the reader supply the other half, but the final stage of such communication is a unity which does indeed resemble that of the angels in *Paradise Lost*: it is the stage where each 'gives each / The other's soul' (5.636–7). Such communication may be Sordello's ideal, but it is not Browning's, at least in so far as his earthly life is concerned. Browning was not about to give his soul to any one of his readers or listeners, and his primary concern, here and elsewhere, is with the workings of the mind, not with its contents; with method, not with materials. His method manifests itself primarily in the fragmenting of syntax and the decomposing of the heroic couplet.

Browning's interrupting and fragmenting of syntax are obvious enough, and account for many of the difficulties readers experience in the poem. Consider the beginning, where the narrator plunges *in medias res* only to break off after two words:

> Appears
> Verona . . . Never, – I should warn you first, –
> Of my own choice had this, if not the worst
> Yet not the best expedient, served to tell
> A story I could body forth so well
> By making speak, myself kept out of view,
> The very man as he was wont to do,
> And leaving you to say the rest for him.   (1.10–17)

There are inversions of ordinary word order (the reversal of subject and verb, for instance); there is the parenthetical 'I should warn you first' which breaks off the first word of the new sentence before any pattern of syntax is established; there is the deictic 'this' separated from its noun ('expedient') by two clauses, and even when we reach the word 'expedient' we do not know the techniques or procedures to which it refers. Inversions, interruptions, and suspensions characterize the style, a defamiliarizing or making strange of syntax[28] that has much to do with Browning's undermining of his verse form, the heroic couplet.

The heroic couplet is primarily a closed form, since the ear waits expectantly for the return of the sound in the rhyme word, and if that sound coincides with end-stopping and with a natural pause in the syntax, the sense of closure is strong. Rhetorical schemes, especially those of balance (such as parallelism and antithesis), make the sense of closure even stronger. Browning is quite capable of writing couplets that use schemes to create a self-contained unit. Consider, for instance, his use of antithesis and parallelism in the following couplet:

> Virtue took form, nor vice refused a shape;
> Here heaven opened, there was hell agape.   (2.527–8)

Or consider this couplet, where end-stopped lines and natural pauses in the syntax are reinforced by the rhyme:

day by day
New pollen on the lily-petal grows,
And still more labyrinthine buds the rose.   (1. 474–6)

Typically, however, Browning frustrates the sense of closure. Though he often uses full or perfect rhymes, the repetition of sound rarely coincides with a natural pause in the syntax or with the strongest of the accents required by the semantics of a clause or phrase; his long syntactical units, fragmented and convoluted, draw attention away from the rhyme; and his constant use of enjambement pushes the sense beyond the limits of the couplet and continuously opens up most of the two-line units. Here is a passage from book 5:

And not a moment did this scorn affect
Sordello: scorn the poet? They, for once,
Asking 'what was,' obtained a full response.
Bid Naddo think at Mantua – he had but
To look into his promptuary, put
Finger on a set thought in a set speech:
But was Sordello fitted thus for each
Conjecture? Nowise; since within his soul
Perception brooded unexpressed and whole.   (5.428–36)

The enjambement of line 428 (the verb pushes on to its object) and the beginning of a new syntactical unit in that line draw attention away from the rhyme ('affect' with 'dialect' in the previous line). In the next two couplets, half-rhymes, enjambement, and the imperfect rhyming of a semantically unimportant word ('but') with the verb 'put' (like the following rhyme of 'each' with the semantically important noun 'speech') weaken the couplet and frustrate the sense of closure, in contrast to lines 435–6, where the full rhyme of the crucial words 'soul' and 'whole' coincides with natural pauses in the syntax and with end-stopping.

The heroic couplet may, as Barbara Herrnstein Smith points out, be a 'force for continuation' as well as a 'force for closure,'[29] and that continuity is particularly apparent when poets use the couplet for narrative poems, as Pope does in his translations of the *Iliad* and the *Odyssey*. Browning, as we know from his late poem 'Development,' read Pope's Homer as a boy, and uses Pope's verse form in *Sordello*. He is entirely capable of telling a story with the vigour, clarity, simplicity, and rapidity readers admired in Pope's handling of the form. Consider, for instance, these lines that bring book 2 to an end:

> – So phrasing, till, his stock of phrases spent,
> The easy-natured soldier smiled assent,
> Settled his portly person, smoothed his chin,
> And nodded that the bull-bait might begin.   (2.1013–16)

Typically, however, Browning frustrates the forward movement of his narrative, and the vigorous nouns and verbs that describe external physical action in Pope are turned towards the complexities of internal action in *Sordello*. The complaint about Sordello's songs, voiced by Squarcialupe and quoted by Naddo, might be turned against Browning himself:

> '"the man can't stoop
> To sing us out," quoth he, "a mere romance;
> He'd fain do better than the best, enhance
> The subjects' rarity, work problems out
> Therewith."'   (2.784–8)

The problems all have to do with the inner life, and it is Sordello who defines them in the pompion-twine image, which he uses as an emblem for his artistic purposes:

> 'Observe a pompion-twine afloat;
> Pluck me one cup from off the castle-moat!
> Along with cup you raise leaf, stalk and root,
> The entire surface of the pool to boot.
> So could I pluck a cup, put in one song
> A single sight, did not my hand, too strong,
> Twitch in the least the root-strings of the whole.
> How should externals satisfy my soul?'   (2.775–82)

Sordello reflects his creator in wanting to comprehend the whole, and he reflects his creator too in being dissatisfied with 'externals' and in wanting to study 'internals.'

There is one further point to be made about the 'brother's speech' to which Sordello aspires, and that is that its ultimate success – 'speech where an accent's change gives each / The other's soul' (5.636–7) –

depends upon the spoken rather than the written word. That 'accent's change' is like the 'one little word' in *Pauline* or the 'sound' in 'By the Fire-Side' that 'shall quicken content to bliss' (193), effecting a turn that embraces everything. Here, the narrator tropes that shift of accent as the 'single touch' that, like troping in *Paracelsus*, may, if it succeeds, turn the past and all its texts upwards into new and greater life, or, if it fails, may turn texts downwards into dead letters:

> a single touch more may enhance,
> A touch less turn to insignificance
> Those structures' symmetry the past has strewed
> The world with, once so bare.   (5.631–4)

To rely on sound for the final and climactic turn is to move spoken language closer to music, and twice in the poem Browning links sound and song to a rising upwards into the realm of angels. In book 3, Browning characterizes his rhymes as sounds

> that spring, dispread,
> Dispart, disperse, lingering overhead
> Like an escape of angels!   (3.593–5)

He had used the same simile, and indeed the same lines, in book 1 (881–3). Both passages link the fragmenting of language with a move towards pure sound that communicates in ways words cannot, and both passages introduce a topic we shall explore in chapter 4: Browning's understanding of the music of poetic language.

'Why need I speak, if you can read my thought?': The Unacted Drama, 'My Last Duchess,' and '"Childe Roland"'

In April of 1876, Browning, fresh from the opening-night performance of *Queen Mary* at the Lyceum Theatre, wrote to Tennyson to congratulate him on the success of the play. The acted version was about half the length of the published one, but, according to the laureate's son Hallam, Tennyson wrote all his plays 'with the intention that actors should edit them for the stage.' Tennyson, however, had misgivings about this practice, since he did not approve of the omission of 'those soliloquies and necessary episodes which reveal the character and, so to say, the mental action of the piece.' He complained 'that the theatric and the dramatic were always being mistaken the one for the other.'[1] Tennyson's view of the relation between the theatrical performance and the dramatic text is part of a long-standing aspect of nineteenth-century culture. Browning had held such a view since the 1830s and 1840s, and it was not new with him, for the distinction between the acted and the unacted drama was well established in the 1820s. In his congratulatory letter, Browning mentions the advantages of reading the play as opposed to watching the production. 'I have more than once,' he tells Tennyson, 'seen a more satisfactory performance of it, to be sure, in what Carlyle calls "the Private Theatre under my own hat" – because there and then not a line nor a word was left out ... whatever was left by the stage-scissors suggested what a quantity of "cuttings" would furnish one with an after-feast.'[2] Browning had long preferred the 'after-feast' to the stage. By the time he had reached the end of his decade-long attempt to be a successful playwright and to satisfy the requirements of the theatre – in the years between 1836 and 1846 – he knew that theatrical performance was incompatible with his interests and aims as a dramatist, and the ideal performance was, for him, the silent reading of a dramatic text in the privacy of one's own study. In May of 1846 he had been invited to a dinner for the Royal Literary Fund, and had been asked to reply to Talfourd's toast, 'To Mr Robert Browning and Dramatic Literature.' Browning, always averse to public speaking, agonized over his task – 'At 8 – eight I conjecture my martyrdom may take place,' he told Elizabeth (*Correspondence* 12:320) – but said that he would 'try and speak for about five minutes on the advantages of the Press over the Stage as a medium of communication of the Drama' (*Correspondence* 12:325). His actual reply was only two sentences long and gave no indication of his views,[3] but Talfourd used the same image as Carlyle when he wished Browning success, 'whether he shall present those works his imagination may vivify, upon the actual scene, to touch our hearts and senses with noble electricity, or only on that ideal stage which all men erect in their own minds.'[4] That contrast is crucial to our understanding of Browning's dramatic poems, especially the ones we now call dramatic monologues, and to our understanding of language which is dramatic but not intended for the theatre. The nature of language in unacted drama is my concern in this chapter: how is the poet using words in such a context? How are we as readers to respond to them in our theatres of the mind?[5] We begin with the historical circumstances.

The term 'dramatic monologue' itself did not come into general use until the end of the nineteenth century, and Browning himself apparently did not use it, but he certainly called other genres 'dramatic' – lyrics and romances, for instance – and he called *Paracelsus* a 'dramatic poem.' The adjective has a psychological motive behind it, as we have already seen: Browning disliked and even feared speaking in his own voice. That personal motive for the dramatic has obscured the fact that making men and women speak in a text to be read silently has 'deep roots' in the culture of the early nineteenth century, as Michael Mason has shown in a seminal but neglected essay of 1974.[6]

The values attached to the unacted drama are entangled with the legal arrangements of the London theatres, the licensing of only two houses – the 'Theatres-Royal,' Covent Garden and Drury Lane – as 'legitimate' (that is, they had, as a result of patents issued by Charles II, a monopoly on the production of the nation's theatrical legacy, the plays from the Elizabethan period on), while all other theatres were licensed only for 'burlettas' and melodrama (literally, drama with musical accompaniment). 'The major theatres continued to think of themselves as guardians of legitimate drama and of culture, the minor to think of themselves as the true home of popular entertainment.'[7] The division between the 'patent' theatres and the 'minor' ones (whose productions were legalized by the Theatre Regulation Act of 1843) was not, however, so sharp, and the 'patent' theatres and their managers (as we know from Macready's diary) could not survive without appealing to popular taste. F.G. Tomlins, the man who campaigned for an end to the monopoly of the 'patent' theatres, uses that difficulty as his principal argument against them. The 'patent' theatres, he writes, do not actually perform the plays for which they are licensed – 'it does not pay "to *do* them"' – and 'the bills display a miserable struggle for popularity.'[8] The pamphlet in which these sentences appear, A Brief View of the English Drama (1840), has a political agenda, and Tomlins sent a copy to Browning,[9] perhaps hoping for his support. Tomlins had been agitating for reform of the theatres since 1832, and he wanted legislation which would introduce free competition among all theatres, since, as he said confidently in his 1839 pamphlet, The Past and Present State of Dramatic Art and Literature, 'free competition will alone produce excellence and quantity.'[10] Edward Mayhew set out parallel views in his Stage Effect: or, the principles which command Dramatic Success in the Theatre (1840), arguing for 'the extending the licence to "all theatres to perform the best dramas they can obtain."'[11] Changing the legislation regulating the theatres, however, could not so easily dispel the anti-theatrical bias of the age, the sense that the unacted drama was superior to the acted drama, however well done.

That view rested upon the assumption that the 'action' required in stage production distorts or obscures the 'poetry' of a dramatic text. Sir Walter Scott in his 1819 essay on the drama wonders, mildly, 'whether, with all these means and appliances [in the theatre], minds of a high poetic temperature may not receive a more lively impression from the solitary perusal, than from the representation of one of Shakespeare's plays.'[12] By the early 1840s, when a theatre reformer like Tomlins could refer to the 'recognition of the division of the Drama of our time, into the Acted and the Unacted' as 'universal,'[13] attitudes had hardened. In R.H. Horne's A New Spirit of the Age (1844), we find assertions that 'the Theatrical Spirit is the most undramatic that can be,' and that 'the press gave to the world what the corrupted stages were too sunken in their own earthly ruins to be able to believe in, or even recognize as having any affinity with their own existence.'[14] Elizabeth Barrett makes the same distinction between theatre and press early in her exchange of letters with Browning. In February 1845, when she is expressing her love for Shakespeare and 'our old dramatists,' she writes, 'But the theatre in those days, was a better medium between the people & the poet; and the press in those days was a less sufficient medium than now' (*Correspondence* 10:80). Now, she says in another letter ten days later, the theatre 'vulgarizes' the drama (*Correspondence* 10:101). That same view shapes her Aurora Leigh (1856), who, considering a number of genres before choosing epic, rejects drama because of 'the modern stage' (*Aurora Leigh* 5.300). Aurora honours the 'worth' of drama, and would therefore not 'keep it down / To the level of the footlights' (5.318–19); she hopes the drama may outgrow 'the painted scene, / Boards, actors, prompters, gaslight, and costume' and 'take for a worthier stage the soul itself' (5.338–40). We can best understand that bias if we turn to an essay used by Mason: Charles Lamb's 'On the Tragedies of Shakspeare, Considered with Reference to their Fitness for Stage Representation' (1811). (We note, in passing, that when Horne imagines someone asking, 'Who *are* those unacted dramatists?,' the answer is 'Shakspere,' Jonson, Beaumont and Fletcher, Ford, Webster, Marlowe, 'in fact all the rest of the Elizabethan dramatists,' and in modern drama, 'Nearly all the best authors' (Horne 100–1). Shakespeare is Lamb's chief example: his plays 'are less calculated for performance on a stage, than those of almost any other dramatist whatever.')[15]

Lamb begins by contrasting 'that absolute mastery over the heart and soul of man, which a great dramatic poet possesses,' with 'those low tricks upon the eye and ear' which are the stock-in-trade of the actor (1:97–8). 'The things aimed at in theatrical representation, are to arrest the spectator's eye upon the form and the gesture, and so to gain a more favourable hearing to what is spoken: it is not what the character is, but how he looks; not what he says, but how he speaks it' (1:101). This arrest of the spectator's eye and ear blocks the kind of communication that a 'dramatic poet' aims at: to put 'the reader or spectator into possession of that knowledge of the inner structure and workings of mind in a character' (1:99). Not the signs of passion, not the looks and gestures and tones of voice, but 'the motives and grounds of the passion' (1:98); not the appearance of characters, but 'the internal workings and movements of a great mind, of an Othello or a Hamlet, for instance' (1:98) – these are the concerns of the 'dramatic poet':

Why, nine parts in ten of what Hamlet does, are transactions between himself and his moral sense, they are the effusions of his solitary musings, which he retires to holes and corners and the most sequestered parts of the palace to pour forth; or rather, they are the silent meditations with which his bosom is bursting, reduced to *words* for the sake of the reader, who must else remain ignorant of what is passing there.   (1:100)

So, too, with Othello, for whom Shakespeare's text gives us 'the grounds of the passion, its correspondences to a great or heroic nature, which is the only worthy object of tragedy' (1:102). The words give us 'the texture of Othello's mind, the inward construction marvellously laid open with all its strengths and weaknesses, its heroic confidences and its human misgivings, its agonies of hate springing from the depths of love' (1:102). 'The truth is,' Lamb says by way of summary, 'the Characters of Shakspeare are ... the objects of meditation' rather than 'curiosity as to their actions,' and the words of the text take us directly into their minds. 'But when we see these things represented [on the stage], the acts which they do are comparatively every thing, their impulses nothing' (1:106). 'What we see upon a stage is body and bodily action; what we are conscious of in reading is almost exclusively the mind, and its movements' (1:108).

The key, both to the reader's experience of a dramatic text and to the way in which language works in such a text, is the concept of abstraction. 'The reading of a tragedy is a fine abstraction,' Lamb says at the end of his essay (1:111), and the exact meaning of that word is of some importance. Literally a drawing away, abstraction is first of all a disengaging of the character in the dramatic text from the actor representing that character. Scott was to say in his essay on the drama that the English theatre-goer 'does not wish to see Hamlet in the abstract, so much as to see how Kemble performs that character, and to compare him perhaps with his own recollections of Garrick in the same part' (21), but Lamb had already complained of the theatre-goer identifying the actor with the character he or she represents: 'It is difficult for a frequent playgoer to disembarrass the idea of Hamlet from the person and voice of Mr K. We speak of Lady Macbeth, while we are in reality thinking of Mrs S.' (1:98). 'I am not arguing that Hamlet should not be acted,' Lamb says later, 'but how much Hamlet is made another thing by being acted' (1:101). He does not care for that other thing, insisting instead on 'that vantage-ground of abstraction which reading possesses over seeing' (1:106). Abstraction, then, means a detaching of a dramatic character from the face, voice, and gestures of the actor representing him or her; ideally, it means a detaching of the character from any particular appearance which appeals to the senses, and a direct apprehension of the mind and soul of the character. 'In the reading of [*Othello*],' says Lamb, 'we see with Desdemona's eyes; in the seeing of it, we are forced to look with our own' (1:108n). So too with *King Lear*, which, Lamb says in a famous assertion, 'cannot be acted' : 'while we read it, we see not Lear, but we are Lear,– we are in his mind' (1:107). Abstraction, then, is bound up with a particular kind of communication, the direct speaking of mind to mind, of soul to soul. Browning's lines in *Sordello* can be read as a summary of Lamb's argument, for after the poet would 'show' men and women and then 'unstation' them 'in the world,' he comes to a third stage: 'Man's inmost life shall have yet freer play: / Once more I cast external things away,' – this line is in effect a definition of abstraction – 'And natures composite so decompose / That ...' (5.617–20).

The title of this chapter is a quotation from *The Return of the Druses* (3.87). In its contrasting of speaking and reading, it sums up the issue we are exploring in the drama, and in its suggestion of unmediated communication, it sums up the ideal for which the dramatic poet aims. Anael, the heroine of the play, is addressing Djabal, whom she, like the other initiated Druses, considers to be 'man in semblance, but our God' (1.135) and hence capable of informing without speaking: 'When the command passed from thy soul to mine,' Anael says to him in act 4, 'I went ...' (4.35–6). Anael uses the verb 'read' as a metaphor for unmediated communication, but the figure undermines her meaning. Reading supposes a medium, and while we may 'read' faces and gestures, we rely primarily upon words for both precision and subtlety in communication, and as our primary access to the thoughts of another.

The language theory which lies behind such reading can be traced back to Locke. For him, words are the signs, not of external things, but of ideas within the mind. The popular understanding of empiricism would make words the signs of things, as the women of Bleeding Heart Yard do when they are teaching Mr Cavalletto English in Dickens's *Little Dorrit*: 'household objects were brought into requisition for his instruction in a copious vocabulary, and whenever he appeared in the Yard, ladies would fly out at their doors crying, "Mr Baptist – teapot!" "Mr Baptist – dust pan!"'[16] Swift, we remember, satirizes the view that 'Words are only Names for *Things*' in one of the scenes in the Academy of Lagado, where two men carry on a conversation by showing each other objects from bundles they carry on their backs. In Locke's language theory, however, words – 'articulate Sounds' – are '*Signs of internal Conceptions*' (3.1.2). These ideas are all 'invisible, and hidden from others, nor can of themselves be made to appear' (3.2.1), except in so far as they are (to quote again from Lamb) 'reduced to *words* for the sake of the reader, who must else remain ignorant of what is passing there' (1.100). Words are, in Locke's definition, 'external sensible Signs, whereby those invisible *Ideas*, which [man's] thoughts are made up of, might be made known to others' (3.2.1).

There are, in Locke's language theory, two kinds of 'invisible *Ideas*,' and hence two classes of words: first, our generalizations from experience (the sensations which come to us through our five senses) and the names we attach to those generalizations, and secondly, the connections which the mind itself gives to generalizations, and the linking words which express those relations. When we are considering the first kind of words (the names which we attach to our generalizations from experience), Locke's theory may seem, at first glance, to allow little access to the mind of an individual character, since he insists on names as conventional, and since he also insists that to use a name as a sign of anything other than a clear and distinct idea (or cluster of ideas) is an abuse of language. But how do we know that the precise meaning we attach to a word is the exact sense of it in the minds of others? Stephen K. Land, in his history of the philosophy of language in Britain, notes that 'the contradiction inherent in the Lockeian view of communication was addressed neither by Locke himself nor by any of his eighteenth-century successors in the theory of language. The difficulty of holding that ideas are both private and yet comparable is simply not noticed in the period.'[17] That difficulty, however, is opportune for the writer of the unacted drama, since the reader must not only know the conventional significance of a word, but also puzzle over the exact sense or senses of it as used by the dramatic character. In a theatrical performance, the tones and gestures of the actor limit the meaning, since an actor can voice a word or line in only one way at a time, and since an actor's gesture or look is an interpretation which reduces the range and possibilities of meanings of the printed text. For in the unacted drama, the reader can do what a member of a theatre audience cannot: he or she can pause, scan and review, proceed quickly or slowly, and move backwards and forwards in the text in the discursive manner which typifies the activity of the mind. The result is a keen awareness of the text as context, the nouns and verbs of the text being connected by the words which signify the links made by the mind. Locke calls such linking words 'particles': they include conjunctions, prepositions, and (most important) the copula 'is,' all of which make possible affirmations and denials, propositions and assertions. Particles 'are not truly, by themselves, the names of any *Ideas*' (3.7.2), but are 'all *marks of some Action, or Intimation of the Mind*' (3.7.4). Through them we can study 'the several views, postures, stands, turns, limitations, and exceptions, and several other Thoughts of the Mind' (3.7.4). James Engell has shown how Locke's assertion that 'the mind has a power' to consider ideas 'not only as they are united in external Objects, but as it self has join'd them' (2.12.1) prepares the way for the Romantic understanding of the imagination.[18] It also prepares the way for the unacted drama. The language of such drama may have a linear thrust in so far as it moves the action forwards, but its primary purpose is to express the inner life of the characters, and to allow the reader to move around in the text as if he or she were inside the mind itself. Language is the medium of such exploration. Locke's understanding of both names and syntax is the philosophical foundation of the unacted drama, and of its development, in Browning's hands, into the dramatic monologue.

There is yet another dimension to that fruitful difficulty in Locke's language theory, and it involves the extent to which the reader not only discovers the meaning(s) of a dramatic character's words, but himself or herself participates in making the meaning. Readers may assume that words give them direct access to the ideas in the mind of someone else, but there is no guarantee that the image attached to the idea in the mind of the reader is exactly the same, or even generally the same, as that in the mind of the speaker. Words in themselves are general and not particular, since they are abstracted from one time and place and set of circumstances, and are 'made to mark a multitude of particular existences' (3.1.3). While Locke insists, when he is trying to remedy the abuses of language, that one should use no word without a clear and distinct and determinate idea of which the word is a sign, such clarity and distinctness are likely to be possible only if one attaches the word to a particular time and place and set of circumstances. When Burke, for instance, deals with language in his *A Philosophical Enquiry into the Origin of our Ideas of the Sublime and Beautiful* (1757), he points out that words fail to raise precise images:

> If I say, 'I shall go to Italy next summer,' I am well understood. Yet I believe no body has by this painted in his imagination the exact figure of the speaker passing by land or by water, or both; sometimes on horse-back, sometimes in a carriage; with all the particulars of the journey. Still less has he any idea of Italy ...[19]

So one may ask what images Browning's readers might have when Luria, for instance, talks about 'My land, our Florence all about the hills, / The fields and gardens, vineyards, olive-grounds' (*Luria* 4.304–5) or sums up 'Beautiful Florence' with 'her domes and towers and palaces' (4.259–60). Few of Browning's readers would actually have been to Florence, and even if they had, they might well ask: what fields exactly? which towers? In Charles Lamb's view, the lack of a precise image is an advantage. When he is dealing with costume on stage, he talks about a Macbeth he has seen, in 'the coronation robe of the Scottish monarch':

> But in reading, what robe are we conscious of? Some dim images of royalty – a crown and sceptre, may float before our eyes, but who shall describe the fashion of it? Do we see in our mind's eye what Webb or any other robe-maker could pattern? ... Whereas the reading of a tragedy is a fine abstraction. It presents to the fancy just so much of external appearances as to make us feel that we are among flesh and blood, while by far the greater and better part of our imagination is employed upon the thoughts and internal machinery of the character.   (1:111)

Words may not raise a precise image, let alone the particular image in the mind of the speaker, yet each reader is likely to have an idea evoked by the word (since language is conventional and since meaning rests upon common usage), and each reader is likely to attach a concrete picture to that idea, a picture derived from his or her own experience. That image is the reader's interpretation of the word, and so a linguistic sign which began as a choice made in the mind of a speaker becomes, in the mind of a listener or reader, another choice, both like and unlike the original. There is no communication without interpretation. So we begin to glimpse the way in which the reading of a dramatic text of the kind Browning wanted to write can be both direct access to the mind of a character and an event in the development of the reader's soul.

There is a problem in the dramatic poet's push towards abstraction: his language relies heavily on general terms for recurring or universal human emotions and passions, instead of images that would tie those emotions and passions to the particular and the concrete. That move towards abstraction is clearest in a passage I have already quoted from book 3 of *Sordello*: Browning defines three kinds of poets, beginning with the one who reads 'profound / Disclosures' (3.870–1) in every face, and ending with the one who speaks 'of the mood itself' (3.908). Here is the language of that third kind of poet:

'As all mirth triumphs, sadness means defeat:
Lust triumphs and is gay, Love's triumphed o'er
And sad: but Lucio's sad. I said before,
Love's sad, not Lucio; one who loves may be
As gay his love has leave to hope, as he
Downcast that lusts' desire escapes the springe ...'   (3.902–7)

Lucio all but disappears in the flurry of abstractions – a logical result of the push to portray, like Wordsworth, 'the primary laws of our nature,' 'the essential passions of the heart,' and 'our elementary feelings.' Horne in his chapter on the drama uses parallel terms to contrast the 'poet' (that is, the writer of dramas to be read) with the 'poetaster' or popular playwright: 'The poet deals with eternal nature, and the eternal effects of nature. The poetaster deals with the tastes of men as formed by their circumstances, and fashioned by convention and association; the poet with the passions of men and the qualities of things' (2:102). The aim was certainly noble – Horne speaks of the poet extending 'our knowledge and experience, making the soul wise' (2:102), and Tomlins talks about imparting a 'motion' to the reader's soul 'that impels it to a better and nobler aim' ('Relative Value of the Acted and the Unacted Drama' 337) – but the general and abstract language was a weakness in the theory of the unacted drama, and one which was potentially fatal to it. Browning, however, learned to avoid that weakness. Dwight Culler's remark about the Browning monologues is the right one: 'the thing that happened with Browning and the dramatic monologue is not so much a matter of the poet's projecting himself into another being as of the generalized passions being made specific.'[20] How Browning made the passions specific is now our concern.

Michael Mason identifies one technique: 'the giving of virtually *all* the facts within the versified text' (251). Browning was already moving towards this technique in *Strafford*, as Mason points out, when in act 4 scene 2 'a group of spectators specify not only Pym's actions but also those of the King, Strafford, and some nearby curtains' (245) – specifications that might have appeared in the text only as stage directions, or that might have been left to the art of the director. One could point to other scenes in the plays: to act 1 scene 1 of *A Blot in the 'Scutcheon*, for instance, where again Browning has spectators describing action – it is the pageantry of the arrival of Tresham and Mertoun – and so usurps the roles of both director and designer. This gathering of circumstantial detail within the dramatic text is strongest in Browning's best-known dramatic monologues – one has only to contrast the effectiveness of 'My Last Duchess' in 1842 with the unsuccessful plays of that period – but the source of that technique is not primarily the theatre, and usurping the role of director and designer cannot wholly account for the extraordinary sense which the best Browning monologues give us, of being inside the mind of a particular character and of seeing things from his or her perspective. There are two non-theatrical sources for this effect: the prose genre called the character, and the emblem. Of these two, the emblem is the more important for Browning, as we saw in chapter 1, but we begin with the character.

In 1837, Browning's father gave him a copy of *The Characters of Theophrastus*, published in London in 1824, and 'illustrated by Physiognomical Sketches' – contemporary ones – that give each character of the Greek original the appearance of an emblem, since there is a title (such as 'The Dissembler'), a picture (usually a shoulder-length portrait of the type), and a text. This particular copy is now in the Armstrong Browning Library at Baylor University, and the markings in it are, according to John Maynard, 'probably by both father and son.'[21] Many of these markings are in the notes by the editor and translator, Francis Howell, and those notes draw attention to the degree to which Theophrastus, unlike his mentor, Aristotle, is both particular and dramatic in his exploration of human nature: 'the one created his own world of abstractions,' says Howell, while 'the other was an observer and describer of individual facts.'[22] (The sentence in which these clauses appear is marked with a curved line in the margin, and the words 'one' and 'other' are underlined in the systematic way characteristic of Browning's father.) Though Theophrastus was presenting types abstracted from particular people in a particular time and place, and though his organizing idea is based on Aristotle's scheme for the ethical judgment of character (the mean, which has both an excess and a defect), nonetheless 'in the definition of abstract terms, he employed himself in the collection of facts' (166) and relied on 'the extensive observation of individual character' (165). Browning (father or son) also marks two sentences by Theophrastus himself, in the preface addressed to Polycles, and both sentences deal with the individualizing of the abstract. In the first, Theophrastus defines his plan: 'I shall first briefly define the term; and then pourtray the manners of the supposed individual to whom the character is attributed' (5). He defines manners more fully in an earlier paragraph, as 'the domestic conduct, and, what may be termed, the *besetting practices* of various characters' (4). Such a way of proceeding becomes the model for the seventeenth-century character, with its initial defining sentence, its details of conduct, manners, and appearance, and its concluding sentence, a summary which may be witty or admonitory or aphoristic. Along with all this particularizing detail is another aspect of the Theophrastian characters which is important for our purposes but of which Howell disapproves: 'Theophrastus has been called, – not, I think, with strict propriety, the father of the dramatic style' (xiii). Since Howell wants to claim Theophrastus for science and not for the drama, and since he is cautiously interested in physiognomy and even phrenology – 'the correspondence between external forms and the qualities of mind' (xix) – he has little to say about the dramatic, but we can see that making a character speak is a logical step in the particularizing of the genre. Hence Theophrastus gives typical words and sayings and sometimes speeches of his characters. In the second character, 'The Adulator,' for instance, about half the text is direct speech. Half is an unusually high proportion, however, and other characters have few or no words attributed to the type being pictured. Nevertheless, it is an easy step from the mixed form of the Theophrastian character to a completely dramatic character, where the particularizing details of circumstance and conduct are internalized, given in the speech of the character and from his or her point of view.

Quarles as a writer of characters takes us a step farther: not only are we given particularizing details from the point of view of a certain type, but we are given a dramatic action – an action which has a beginning, complications, peripeteia, and dénouement – which takes place entirely within the soul of the speaker. I have already (in chapter 1) referred to a book which Browning owned, Quarles's *Judgment and Mercy for Afflicted Souls* (London, 1837), which is not an emblem book at all, but a book of characters. There are 'The Sensual Man' and 'The Weary Man,' 'The Presumptuous Man' and 'The Good Man,' and each character is a play in miniature, an internalized action which is the same for all: it is the drama of conversion, beginning with an expression of the character's attitudes that typically arise out of his particular vice, and proceeding through peripeteia to a conviction of sin, contrition, confession, and a final turning away from sin and back to God. Browning would call such internalized drama 'Action in Character' – the phrase comes from the 1837 preface to *Strafford* – and, while he is not referring specifically to conversion when he says he wants to portray 'incidents in the development of a soul,' those incidents can be seen as parts or fragments of that more comprehensive Christian experience, in so far as the incidents involve a struggle of understanding, the making of a choice, and another struggle with the consequences of that decision. The incidents may be particular, as they usually are in Browning, but conversion is abstract and universal, and so the characters of Quarles anticipate the monodrama, that genre which appeared in a variety of ways both in Britain and in Europe in the nineteenth century. Dwight Culler, whose 1975 essay 'Monodrama and the Dramatic Monologue' is the chief account of the form, shows how much the genre lent itself to abstraction: 'In pure monodrama,' he writes, 'character is little more than a formal thread on which the beads of passion are strung' (380). 'The passions explored in the monodrama are universal and abstract; those in the dramatic monologue are so connected with the particular acts and circumstances of an individual, with his deeds and situation, that we can hardly avoid partly sympathizing with and partly judging him' (382). We do enter into the mind of a character, and we do assess him or her, largely because we enter into the process by which a character assesses and interprets sights and actions. Those particularizing details are frequently summed up in one image – a painting, a tomb, a fellow monk – which counteracts the universal and abstract nature of the experience of the mind or soul. Browning's fascination with the emblem is, I think, the main source of this individualizing and particularizing technique.

William Allingham gives in his diary for 6 April 1876 an account of a visit from Browning, who 'took down Quarles's *Emblems* from the shelf' and, saying '"Quarles did a great deal for me – he was a man of great genius,"' proceeded to read passages aloud. He read 'with especial relish the close of the dialogue of Eve and the Serpent,' where Eve says, 'fruit's made for food: / I'll pull, and taste, and tempt my Adam too / To know the secrets of this dainty.' The Serpent says, 'Do.' Browning's response to this exchange, according to Allingham: '"That's exquisite!"'[23] 'Do,' used in another context in a letter of 1884 to Katharine Bronson, immediately reminded Browning of this same emblem: 'By the way, what is the most emphatic close of any verse I ever read, if not this which *you* shall read. It occurs at the end of the first of Quarles' Emblems – a beloved book of my boyhood.'[24] Browning then proceeds to quote (inaccurately) the lines I have just quoted. Much earlier in his life he had responded to the *pictura* in this same emblem when he wrote a cryptic rhyme underneath it: ' – are such / – to touch / – did not God inspire / – fire.'[25] The particularizing technique is obvious: in the poem itself, Eve responds to the sight of the apple and to the temptation of the serpent; outside the poem, the reader responds to the *pictura* and to the dramatic scene. For both Eve and the reader, the beginning of the dramatic action is an image to be interpreted, and the image checks any tendency towards abstraction. How such an emblematic way of proceeding works can be most easily seen in a familiar poem, 'My Last Duchess.'

It is difficult for a teacher and critic to see 'My Last Duchess' in a fresh way, just as Lamb found it difficult 'to appreciate that celebrated soliloquy in Hamlet, beginning "To be or not to be,"' because it had been 'so handled and pawed about by declamatory boys and men' (1:99). Nonetheless, we can perhaps renew our experience of the poem if we see that both dramatic characters and we as readers begin with a picture. The Duke and the envoy are looking at a painting which the Duke interprets for his guest. The reader of this dramatic poem does not have a precise image of that painting, in spite of R.J. Berman's printing of one specific Renaissance portrait that Browning may have seen in reproduction,[26] and must conjure up for himself or herself the mantle and wrist, the 'spot of joy' on the cheek, and the '"faint / Half-flush that dies along her throat."' The reader, in short, attaches his or her own particular images to those nouns and adjectives, rather than responding to a painting he or she can actually see, and so the reading of the poem is, as Lamb said of the reading of *Macbeth*, 'a fine abstraction' which allows us to see the painting as the Duke sees it, and to interpret his interpretation. In spite of the many theatrical details in the poem, details which, in a drama not designed to be read, would be left to the stage directions or to the director (the drawing of the curtain, the gesture towards the painting, the sitting and looking, the rising, the going together down past the bronze sculpture of Neptune), the 'Action in Character' and the corresponding action in the mind of both the envoy and the reader can be seen as belonging to the emblem. The Duke's first four words – 'That's my last Duchess' – are in effect the motto of the poem, and that motto is a statement of identity typical of the translating that makes up the action of an emblem. Here a painting is translated into a woman. The deictic 'That,' with its performative function and accompanying gesture (not in the poem but played out in the private theatre of the reader's mind) is made one with 'my last Duchess,' words which (in our initial understanding of them) name, in a conventional way, the subject of the painting and which (in our final understanding) state its ominously admonitory meaning. Such a growth in understanding the Duke's thoughts, on the part of both envoy and reader, depends upon two words in that motto: the copula 'is' and the adjective 'last.' The rest of the poem is the *explicatio* of those words.

The envoy knows from the outset that 'last' means 'subsequent to another,' but for readers (at least in our first linear move through the text) that meaning is only one of several possibilities. For us, 'last' seems most likely to mean 'most recent,' and we may at this point associate 'last' with 'late' (an adjective the Duke pointedly does not use). Both we and the envoy learn, as we listen to the Duke, just how equivocal his 'last' is, for in fact his speech makes the word embrace four of the five meanings Johnson gives in his *Dictionary*. We listen to the Duke's criticism of the Duchess's lack of discrimination ('her looks went everywhere,' and all sorts of things drew from her 'the approving speech') and we realize that she is, in his judgment, the least satisfactory of all the duchesses of Ferrara; she is, in Johnson's words, 'hindmost; which follows in order of place.' All her predecessors are implied in the Duke's reference to his 'nine-hundred-years-old name,' so the Duchess is also 'latest; that which follows all the rest in time.' Then come the ominous lines, 'I gave commands; / Then all smiles stopped together,' and 'last' becomes 'Beyond which there is no more.' Finally come the lines where the Duke refers to the negotiations for a marriage to the 'fair daughter' of the Count, the envoy's master, and so 'last' ultimately means 'next before the present.' We, like the envoy, gradually come to realize that all four senses of 'last' are operative, and that all are intertwined. Moreover, those senses lead us back to the painting and to the copula ('is') which holds together picture and woman. That copula is no simple statement of identity; instead, it indicates (to borrow nouns from Locke) a stand, a turn, a limitation, and an exception in the mind of the Duke. The stand is the statement of identity, which has connotations of control ('since none puts by / The curtain I have drawn for you, but I'); the turn is the painting as warning – if the Count's 'fair daughter' does not behave as the Duke wishes, she too will end up as a painting; the limitation is the reducing of the last Duchess to a picture; and the exception is the implication that the Duke will not have another Duchess like his last one. Thus the 'particle' 'is' and the equivocal 'last' are the keys to the mind of the central character: the Duke carefully and calculatedly reveals the multiple meanings of the words (while saying he has no 'skill / In speech'), and the envoy – and we as readers – gradually realize that the meanings, so carefully distinguished and separated by Johnson, are all ominously related.

Although 'My Last Duchess' is a fragment of an unacted drama, we can see clearly in it some of the essential elements of Browning's use of language in the dramatic monologue. The starting point is an image, usually visual but sometimes (as we shall see) aural; the speaker then translates that image into words, the translation being a statement of the meaning of the image and hence an interpretation of it. The paradigmatic form of that statement is the subject/copula verb/subject complement pattern, where the copula indicates both the turn which marks the metaphor and the translation which reveals the meaning. The conventional senses of the words will be readily apparent, but understanding the exact sense or senses in which the speaker is using them will require the reader to move backwards and forwards within a text which is also the context for the crucial words. There is one further aspect of the language of the monologue which is not apparent in 'My Last Duchess,' and that is the extent to which it gives the reader access to a complete dramatic action within the mind of the character. The paradigm for that complete dramatic action, as Browning treats it, is conversion, and it can be studied in another familiar monologue, '"Childe Roland to the Dark Tower Came."'

Although '"Childe Roland"' was first published in the *Men and Women* volumes of 1855, it became one of the *Dramatic Romances* in Browning's 1863 rearrangement of his shorter poems, and there it remained, through successive editions, as the final poem in a group of some two dozen. The text is (to use Browning's statement from the preface to *Strafford*) 'one of Action in Character, rather than Character in Action.' The outward events one would expect in romance are here limited: there is certainly a perilous journey, but the poem ends just at the point when Childe Roland is about to fight the crucial fight, against a foe who has not yet appeared. In contrast to the physical quest, which is incomplete, the action within Childe Roland himself is a complete action, with a beginning, middle, and end, and one can see it, at least initially, in romance terms: Roland undertakes a journey into himself, has a crucial struggle with the guilt and evil that he finds there, and triumphs over them, apparently achieving an inner fitness for the physical battle to come. That statement is, however, too bald and optimistic an account of the inner action where, as Harold Bloom says, 'nearly every figuration ... reduces to ruin,' and 'yet the poem, as all of us obscurely sense, appears to end in something like triumph.'[27] That sense depends, I think, on Browning's playing off the inner action against the outer action. The poem itself gives us a clue to this manner of proceeding when Childe Roland says, 'Think first, fight afterwards – the soldier's art' (89). 'Thinking first' is bound up with the question of his mental and spiritual preparedness for the coming battle: 'And all the doubt was now – should I be fit?' (42).

The inner action is essentially interpretation. In Harold Bloom's powerful argument about the 'map of misprision,' 'Roland rides with us as interpreter,' and 'his every interpretation is a powerful misreading'; his 'trial by landscape' nonetheless enables him both to accept destruction and to come to a 'triumphant realization' about the nature of his experience.[28] The poem, Bloom argues, falls into three parts: stanzas 1 to 8 'are the induction, during which an initial contraction or withdrawal of meaning is gradually redressed by a substitution or representation of the quest' (109); the second movement (stanzas 9 to 29) is the 'ordeal-by-landscape' (110); the last five stanzas 'alternate between an *askesis* of defeated metaphor and a magnificent, perhaps triumphant metaleptic return of earlier powers' (112). I would like to suggest a somewhat different reading of that 'Action in Character.' Each visual image and Roland's reaction to it are like the *pictura* and *explicatio* of an emblem, the interpretations turning the images in progressively perceptive ways. The temporal sequence of these emblems makes up the 'Action in Character,' the climactic image being the dark tower itself. Roland's interpretation of the tower is the moment when he casts off his blind self (labelled the 'fool') and proceeds with his seeing self. That conversion leads to the motto, the last line (and title) of the poem. There, for the first time in the dramatic action, Roland names himself; he also names the chief image which stimulates the change in him, and he designates the action which brings him to the climactic moment: he 'came.' The 'Action in Character' is summed up in that word.

The sequence begins with the 'hoary cripple.' The untrustworthy guide is a conventional figure in romance, just as someone who is old and deformed is a conventional figure in the waste land. Childe Roland's response to him – 'My first thought was, he lied in every word' (1) – is certainly a misreading, since Roland admits in the third stanza, as critics from Mrs Orr to Harold Bloom have pointed out, that the cripple is not lying: the 'ominous tract' to which the cripple directs him is the one 'which, all agree, / Hides the Dark Tower' (14–15).[29] Roland's reaction indicates his paranoia, and the 'hoary cripple' appears to the reader of this text not only as a character in his own right but as a projection from within Roland, the figure of his crippled understanding. Roland's sorry state is confirmed in the stanzas which follow, where he comments on the quest itself. He examines his motives, and finds little pride or hope, but rather 'gladness that some end might be' (18). He can see nothing beyond the waste land, and he conceives of the end of his quest, not as a renewal, but simply as the end of his present state. Just as (in the simile in stanzas 5 and 6) the sick man's friends act as if he were dead before he has actually died, so all things around Childe Roland seem to indicate failure before he has actually failed.

To be in a fallen state is to be 'dead in sin,' in the words of the Westminster Confession, 'and wholly defiled in all the faculties and parts of soul and body.'[30] That defiling in this particular poem involves a dulling and distorting of the senses, and the deprivation of the ability to interpret images. Much, in fact, is not seen at all. When Roland first contemplates the waste land, it is a 'gray plain' (52) without any distinguishing features. Roland will eventually see that the landscape is in fact full of things whose meaning he struggles to understand, but at this stage nature is only 'starved,' 'ignoble' (56), and sterile: 'a burr had been a treasure-trove' (60). The time is sunset, and the 'red leer' (48) of the dying day suggests a sadistic delight in pain and misery. As often happens in the emblem tradition, the interpreter makes the *pictura* speak, as (in stanza 11) Roland attributes words to nature. The crucial line is '"It nothing skills: I cannot help my case"' (64) – words which reflect Roland's own passivity. We remember that he, for all his distrust of the 'hoary cripple,' nonetheless followed his directions 'acquiescingly' (15). 'Quiet as despair' (43), he resigned himself to failure. 'Despair' is a word that belongs in a theological context: it is the giving up of all hope in God's scheme of salvation, and can be seen as passivity twisted into sin. The poem thus begins with a mental and spiritual state that could be seen as universal and abstract, but Browning particularizes that state, largely through the images to which Childe Roland responds. To free oneself from such a state requires mental effort, but it is effort which, as understood by the Congregationalists, is not without support. Conversion is possible because of the 'Covenant of Grace,' wherein God 'freely offereth unto sinners life and salvation by Jesus Christ' (35), an offer which is, however, contingent upon 'that natural liberty and power of acting upon choice'[31] in each person. Browning, as always, is interested in the nature of such choice and the precise way in which it comes about, perhaps because he suspects that the motions of the mind in interpretation are not to be wholly distinguished from the motions of the Holy Spirit, the interpreter. Such effort, with its hidden support, leads to the 'saving understanding' of all things visible in this world.

Roland's conversion begins with the sight of the 'stiff blind horse.' He names the details of the animal's appearance, and then proceeds from such images to interpretation: 'He must be wicked to deserve such pain' (84). That interpretation leads Roland to a conviction of sin, the first stage in conversion. 'I shut my eyes and turned them on my heart' (85), and his memory, with its promise of 'earlier, happier sights' (87), seems to offer an escape from the sight of the horse, but the actual memories of Cuthbert and Giles are not happy ones – the past is full of sin and crime – and Roland's disappointment forces him back: 'Better this present than a past like that' (103). He returns to the present, however, with a consciousness of sin, though the sin is in his fellows and perhaps in his society rather than in him (at least so far as his present understanding goes). The result is a shift from passive to active in his sense of sight. The kind of active perception to which he now comes is analogous to Carlyle's teaching about 'Descendentalism' in *Sartor Resartus*: 'The beginning of all Wisdom,' says Teufelsdröckh, 'is to look fixedly on Clothes ... till they become *transparent.*'[32] Hence, in stanza 18, when Roland returns resolutely to the present and 'my darkening path' (104), his senses are clearly alert and his seeing is intense: 'No sound, no sight as far as eye could strain,' he reports initially, until 'something' 'Came to arrest my thoughts and change their train' (108). The 'something' is the 'sudden little river,' and the change is from a 'train' of thoughts – a sequence of linear associations, perhaps – to the beginnings of a narrative, with the river as antagonist and the alders and the willows as its victims. As with the 'hoary cripple' and the 'stiff blind horse,' Roland still attributes malice and crime to the river ('which had done them all the wrong') but does not define the act, referring to it only as 'Whate'er that was' (120). With the next *pictura*, the 'fell cirque' (133), Roland is less ready to make statements or attributions, and more ready to question and to explore possibilities. In fact, he asks four questions about the cirque (129–31), and it is only after such exploration that he arrives at an answer which 'no doubt' (137) is the most likely. His desire to see things as in themselves they really are is even more apparent when he confronts the instrument of torture in stanza 24. He uses and rejects three nouns ('that wheel / Or brake, not wheel – that harrow' 140–1) before coming to a fourth noun – 'Tophet's tool' (143) – that defines not the physical nature of the object but its moral character. The next step for this questing interpreter of images is to connect seer and thing seen, to discover that all seeing is interpretation and leads back to the interpreter himself. When Childe Roland had happened on the 'fell cirque,' he looked on this scene of madness and imprisonment as an outsider. In stanzas 28 and 29, where he finds himself trapped by the mountains, imprisonment becomes part of his own experience. The moment Childe Roland realizes that he is the prisoner, that same moment he realizes that he has found the place he has been searching for, 'the Tower itself' (181).

The tower is the central image or *pictura*, the earlier images being only (in Harold Bloom's words) 'process' or 'one-thing-after-another' (*Map of Misreading* 110). As Childe Roland treats it, it is the image which makes sense of all the others – or, to be more accurate, of his interpretation of all the others – and the syntactic form of this sense-making is (as we should now expect) the statement of identity: 'This was the place!' (176). Again there is the deictic 'This,' a performative word and an abstraction, carried across to a noun, 'place,' also an abstraction, but both abstractions mean intensely for Roland, and that intensity he conveys in the adverb 'burningly': 'Burningly it came on me all at once' (175). Is it going too far to suggest that that adverb points to the Holy Spirit? Flame is, after all, a conventional metaphor for the Spirit, and the poem will end with a picture illuminated by fire: 'in a sheet of flame / I saw them and I knew them all' (201–2).

The phrases Childe Roland uses to describe the tower are the *explicatio* of this climactic *pictura*. 'Built of brown stone' (183) gives us only the conventional colour of the waste land; far more important are the two preceding phrases, 'The round squat turret, blind as the fool's heart' (182). Both parts of that line tell us something about perception. The tower is 'squat' – low and close to the ground – rather than high and commanding; towers conventionally are associated with range and comprehensiveness of sight, like the 'open watch-tower' in Browning's essay on Shelley, but here is a tower which seems to have dwindled and shrunk – a parody of a watch tower – and hence it is associated with limited perception. The phrase 'blind as the fool's heart' is crucial. The poem itself defines the word 'fool' in the parenthesis in stanza 25:

> (so a fool finds mirth,
> Makes a thing and then mars it, till his mood
> Changes and off he goes!)   (147–9)

The fool is changeable in mood, making and lightly discarding images without grasping their significance; the wise man (as in Carlyle) stares fixedly at the thing until its meaning reveals itself. No one can hand such wisdom to anyone else; it must be gained through each individual's experience, and that is why Roland insists on the tower's uniqueness: 'without a counterpart / In the whole world' (183–4). In recognizing his own blindness, Childe Roland comes to see, and so the wise man is born out of the fool. This new life is confirmed in the last three stanzas of the poem, which indicate a perception which is now intensely alert. The moment when he sees his predecessors 'in a sheet of flame' is like a 'baphometic fire-baptism,' as Susan Hardy Aiken has argued: 'His horn blast, like Teufelsdröckh's defiance of the Everlasting No, is the climax of an initiation; and Roland too is saying, in effect, "Then it was that I began to be a Man": his repetition of his own name is the final symbolic affirmation of his new identity.'[33] The last line of the poem condenses all Roland's interpretations and focuses them on a few words that mean intensely.

The line is not Browning's, and it predates Shakespeare, who uses it in *King Lear*. For the reader to interpret this poem, Browning provides editorial assistance: after the title there is a parenthesis, '(See Edgar's song in *Lear*).' The imperative prods the reader to remember that Edgar speaks the line when he is in disguise and has lost his true name; later, as the nameless champion, he appears when the trumpet is blown, fights Edmund, and regains his name. The reader may also remember that the discovery of one's identity is a conventional part of the romance quest, the quester usually being able, at the end, to answer the question 'Who am I?' The answer, one notes, is not simply a name, but a condensed story, the suggestion being that one's experience forges one's identity. Another antecedent is the reply the Ancient Mariner gives to the Hermit's question, 'What manner of man art thou?,' the answer being the 'ghastly tale' to which he is condemned to return again and again. There is no such question in Browning's poem, but Roland identifies himself by giving a condensed version of the action of the whole poem. His story, unlike that of the Ancient Mariner, is not a curse, and its telling is liberating. By naming the hero, specifying the central action, and giving the climactic setting, Roland draws the 'Action in Character' into one motto or slogan. The crucial word is the verb 'came,' and it is, we can now see, equivocal in meaning. Our first understanding of the verb is the primary or 'primitive' sense Johnson gives in his *Dictionary*: Roland travels from some distance, and arrives at his destination. But as we trace the metaphorical senses of the verb in Johnson's *Dictionary*, we discover that it encompasses the inner action of the poem as well as the outer. One metaphorical sense is 'to attain any condition or character,' and since Roland identifies the dark tower with his own blindness, it is the condition to which in the past he 'came.' Now that he is 'burningly' aware of his own state, the verb refers to a change, and 'to change condition either for better or worse' is one of the senses Johnson gives. We feel, as Bloom points out, that the change is a positive one, a conversion or turn which is in fact a spiral upwards. The fifth meaning Johnson gives for the verb defines such a movement: 'To advance from one stage or condition to another.' So '"Childe Roland to the Dark Tower Came"' is a motto which is also a challenge or slogan for every reader of this monologue.

I use the word 'slogan' deliberately because (as the *OED* indicates) 'slug-horn' is the earlier form of 'slogan,' a word of Gaelic origin meaning a battle-cry, 'usually consisting of a personal surname or the name of a gathering-place.' Browning apparently misuses the word, making it a horn or trumpet that Childe Roland blows, and he had no guidance from Johnson, since neither 'slogan' nor 'slug-horn' appears in the *Dictionary*. Nonetheless, the sound is clearly a summons or challenge to battle. Even more suggestive is the link with parleying. Clyde Ryals points out (drawing on the *OED*) that 'the phrase "to beat or sound a parley" means to call for a parley by sounding a drum or trumpet.'[34] The challenge Childe Roland is issuing is also his creator's challenge to the readers of this unacted drama, and for them (as for Roland) the struggle to interpret is a battle within, a civil war. To this struggle Carlyle's comments in *The French Revolution* are applicable. There are two kinds of civil war, Carlyle writes, 'the modern *lingual* or Parliamentary-logical kind, and the ancient or *manual* kind in the steel battlefield,' but there is 'one great difference between' them:

> In the manual kind, where you front your foe with drawn weapon, one right stroke is final; for, physically speaking, when the brains are out the man does honestly die, and trouble you no more. But how different when it is with arguments you fight! Here no victory yet definable can be considered as final.[35]

The poem, then, is open-ended, and the slogan at the end is a challenge to the reader to engage in a dialogue with the poem, to interpret it. Of that parleying, as the subsequent criticism of the poem and subsequent allusions to it in fiction and poetry show, there is no end.

A return to this chapter's title, and a summary of the meaning and technique of 'reading a thought,' may be useful, since we are, in effect, defining how to read a dramatic monologue. To begin with, there is (at least in the primary way in which the poem presents itself to us) no actual speaking voice reading the poem aloud, even though (as we shall see in the next chapter) Browning himself did read his monologues aloud to family and friends. Such a voice, with its particular tones and inflexions, might stand between the listener and the words of these dramas not written to be acted. Instead, the silent reading of the text allows us to attend to the words themselves, as the point of entry into the dramatic character's thoughts and the movements of his or her mind. For the purposes of practical criticism, the reader must bring to the words of the text the understanding that embedded in them are the multiple meanings that represent choices or judgments made by the speakers of the language, some or all of which may be reiterated by the dramatic character. How is the reader to judge which meanings are operative and which are not? By setting key words in the context of the monologue as a whole, understood as the *explicatio* of a character's interpretation of an image or images. Such a reading of a monologue is primarily synchronic; that is, the various meanings as given by Johnson are all in play. The status of words as obsolete or archaic or dialect, for instance – their history, in short, as opposed to current use – seems less important for Browning, though sometimes the diction of a monologue does require a diachronic reading. One such occasion is Andrea del Sarto's reference to 'such frank French eyes' (160), a phrase which is, as David Shaw notes, 'a specimen of living philology.'[36] More important than 'frank' as a key to Andrea's mind is the word 'still' in the concluding lines, where Andrea contrasts himself with 'Leonard, Rafael, Agnolo': 'So – still they overcome / Because there's still Lucrezia, – as I choose' (265–6). The repetition of the word in conjunction with a crucial (if repeated) choice indicates that its multiple meanings (both as adjective and adverb) are a record of the development of Andrea's soul, those meanings being played out in the monologue, from the silencing of Lucrezia at the beginning, and their sitting 'Quietly, quietly' (17) as if motionless in a picture, through to the 'till now' and 'continually' and even 'in an increasing degree' of the adverb. Trench in his 1851 lectures *On the Study of Words* had used Emerson's characterization of language as 'fossil poetry' as part of his argument for reading diachronically.[37] For Browning, that which is stored up in language is the record of spiritual development, upon which every speaker draws in making his or her own choices.

'I kept time to the wondrous chime': Rhyme's Reason, 'Love among the Ruins,' *The Inn Album*, and 'Of Pacchiarotto'

'Am I not a rhymester?' Robert asked Elizabeth in April of 1846, when he was defending his use of the word 'gadge': 'who knows but one may want to use such a word in a couplet with *"badge"* – which, if one reject the old & obsolete *"fadge,"* is rhymeless' (*Correspondence* 12:241). For in spite of Browning's success with blank verse, he is primarily a rhymer, and thought of himself as a virtuoso in the art of sound repetition. 'Everybody knows *I* beat the world that way – can tie and untie English as a Roman girl a tame serpent's tail,' he boasted to Fanny Haworth in 1839 (*Correspondence* 4:138). When a critic annoyed him in 1845, he told Edward Moxon that 'I'll be hanged if I don't rhyme him to death like an Irish Rat!' (*Correspondence* 11:178) – a threat he made good on more than thirty years later in his 'Of Pacchiarotto, and How He Worked in Distemper.' In 1887, when he was describing for the benefit of Furnivall his new poem, 'a number of confabulations with certain people dead and gone ... whose personalities serve to strike out some sort of spark from myself,' he reminded Furnivall of the crucial fact of the poem's style: 'all in rhyme, as you know.'[1] We note that, in addition to the *Parleyings* among the late poems, the other most personal and intensely felt text – *La Saisiaz* – is also in rhyme.

When Browning instructs others in the art of reading his poetry – and he characteristically avoids such advice – the instruction usually has to do with pronunciation and rhyme. For instance, he tells Palgrave, in a letter of 1869, how to pronounce 'metamorphosis' (with the accent on the penultimate syllable) and he provides a rhyme for it ('diagnosis').[2] In 1884 he wrote a limerick to instruct Mrs FitzGerald on the rhyme for 'Folkestone':

As to the rhyme for Folkestone, I am forced to say there is an *l.* in that word which sounds in the ear and should appear to the eye, – and it is absent from 'joke's tone': my example would therefore run thus –

There was a sky-painter at Folkestone
Whose tone for the sky was egg-yolk's tone:
    This fanciful fellow
    Mistook blue for yellow
So – small was his fame out of Folkestone![3]

Browning claimed for himself not only immense facility in finding rhymes but unusually acute hearing, so that he spurned easy and obvious rhymes and rejoiced in difficult and grotesque ones. The English language is not so rich in rhyme words as Italian, for instance, particularly when the rhyming syllables are not just one but two or three. Byron in *Don Juan* had exploited double or triple rhymes for comic effect, and Browning does so too, though he extends the range of effects from the playful to the satiric. The playful may include a game called 'crambo,' which is (in the words of Johnson's *Dictionary*) 'A play at which one gives a word, to which another finds a rhyme.' That game lies behind the entries in the inn album in the poem of that name, and Browning uses the word itself for the rhymes in the concluding poem in the *Jocoseria* volume: it is 'a grave tale told in crambo.' The term is a censorious one (it is used in that way by one of the two poets of Croisic at line 669 in the poem of that name), since its root – the Latin word for cabbage – has come, in its metaphorical application, to mean 'any distasteful repetition' (*OED*); the word indicates that, in Browning's view, there is good rhyming and bad rhyming. In Browning's scheme of things, bad rhyming has a clinching effect, as when he says of a verse in 'Pambo' (the last poem in *Jocoseria*) that 'The smooth line hath an end knot!' (20), or when he criticizes the rhymes of the odes and sonnets of Maillard: 'welded lines with clinch / Of ending word and word' (*The Two Poets of Croisic* 563–4). Good rhyming, for Browning, is part of the music of poetry, and repetition of sound is an essential feature of 'true *melos*' ('Of Pacchiarotto, and How He Worked in Distemper' 548). Our concern in this chapter is the nature of 'true *melos*,' which is bound up with the relation of 'chime' or correspondence of sound – a conventional metaphor for rhyme – and keeping time; in short, with the relation of rhyme and music in poetry.

Browning seems to have been exploiting some features of spoken

English which his knowledge of music helped make apparent to him: stress and segmentation. I borrow these terms from Ian Gordon, who identifies them as part of the permanent structure of the language, and as features continuing from its Germanic sources. Stress refers to the practice – so familiar and natural that it is not taught – of accenting one syllable in a word or one syllable in a word-group, so that the rhythm of English speech has 'moments of maximum emphasis,' 'secondary and tertiary stresses,' and 'bundles of unstressed syllables.' Segmentation refers to the practice – also natural – of marking word-groups with a pause, such as the dot in a line of Old English poetry or the comma, colon, and period of modern punctuation.[4] Both stress and segmentation indicate a sense which seems to be native to speakers of English: the fitting of varying numbers of syllables into units of time which, to our ears, are equal. When we recite 'Three blind mice,' for instance, and come to the second line, 'See how they run,' we know, without even thinking about it, that each syllable of 'how they' has half the duration of 'See,' and that there is a pause after 'run' which fills out the unit of time. Keeping time, then, is an essential and defining feature of our language, as crucial to it as it is to music. Browning, who prided himself on his knowledge of music[5] – 'I can write music,' he boasts to Elizabeth in 1845 (*Correspondence* 10:264) – made the most of the native rhythm of the language. We might begin our exploration of Browning's prosody by looking at accounts of his reading aloud.

His manner of reading his poems seems to be related, as E.A.W. StGeorge has recently argued,[6] to his conversation, which was, according to Sidney Colvin, 'straightforward, plain, emphatic, heartily and agreeably voluble.'[7] Though he characteristically avoided speaking in public, he 'read often to our own little family circle,' his daughter-in-law remembered,[8] and when he quoted from memory, he liked 'odds and ends of rhyme and doggerel,' according to Anne Thackeray: 'A doggerel always had a curious fascination for him, and he preferred to quote the very worst poetry in his talks.'[9] It is Mrs Jameson who likens Browning's reading aloud to music. In a letter of 12 May 1846, Elizabeth tells Robert about a visit of Mrs Jameson, who 'told me how you had recited "in a voice & manner as good as singing," my "Catarina"' (*Correspondence* 12:321).

We can best understand the word 'musical' as a description of Browning's reading aloud if we examine the accounts of ear-witnesses who heard both him and Tennyson. The best-known occasion was the night of 27 September 1855, when the Tennysons visited the Brownings, then living temporarily in London: Tennyson read *Maud*, Browning read 'Fra Lippo Lippi,' Dante Gabriel Rossetti sketched the laureate as he sat with open book on the end of a sofa, and William Michael Rossetti stored up impressions he would later record: Browning, he writes, read 'with as much sprightly variation as there was in Tennyson of sustained continuity.'[10] 'Sustained continuity' is a reference to Tennyson's habit of lengthening the vowels in his verses and thus slowing the tempo, so that his reading gave the impression of chanting. Browning's reading seems to have been more like his conversation: boisterous, genial, emphatic, and rather loud. Rossetti was not the only listener to contrast the styles of the two poets. Sidney Colvin in his *Memories and Notes* remembers Browning as 'always ready' to read to a group 'where he could count on intelligent sypmathy': 'His utterance was flexible and dramatic, very different from that of Tennyson or Rossetti and such other poets as have preferred in reading their own verses to adopt and sustain one key or another of chanting monotone' (83–4). And Max Müller, for whom Browning read aloud 'Andrea del Sarto,' remembered that

> his delivery was most simple and yet most telling. He was a far better reader than Tennyson. His voice was natural, sonorous, and full of delicate shades; while Tennyson read in so deep a tone, that it was like the rumbling and rolling sound of the sea rather than like a human voice. His admirers, both gentlemen and ladies, who thought that everything he did must be perfect, encouraged him in that kind of delivery; and while it seemed to me that he had smothered and murdered some of the poems I liked best, they sighed and groaned and poured out strange interjections, meant to be indicative of rapture.[11]

Colvin (who, like Müller, preferred Browning's manner of reading) remembers hearing Browning 'coming out once with a long, crabbedly fine screed from John Donne,' reciting 'the thundering final stanzas from the *Song of David* of Christopher Smart,' and reading 'the Pompilia section of *The Ring and the Book*' with 'such tenderness' that 'at certain points ... he could control neither his voice nor his tears, and had nearly all his audience in tears with him' (82–4). An especially interesting memory, for our purposes, is Colvin's account of Browning's reading 'his Greek battle-poem, *Echetlos*,' 'with the long tramping measures, duly stressed by his foot stamping vigorously in time' (84).

Keeping time is the most characteristic feature of Browning's prosody, and it is bound up with his understanding of the music of poetry. William Irvine, in a modern comment on that same September 1855 evening that William Michael Rossetti wrote about, remarks that Browning 'responded to *Maud* by reading "Fra Lippo Lippi" in a manner as dramatic as Tennyson's had been musical.'[12] The adjectives ought to be reversed. It was Tennyson who was being 'dramatic' while Browning was 'musical' – as Northrop Frye, reacting against 'the sentimental fashion of calling any poetry musical if it sounds nice,'[13] argues in the *Anatomy of Criticism* when he is contrasting the two poets. As a technical rather than a sentimental term, 'musical' refers to the division of syllables into units or measures of equal time. The number of syllables in the measures may vary, but the interval of time does not. As in a bar of music, the unit begins with a strong accent or beat, and includes pauses and rests as well as the sounds actually pronounced. Browning's poetry is 'musical' in this technical sense. The only book-length study of Browning's prosody – Harlan Hatcher's *The Versification of Robert Browning* (1928) – proceeds on this theory: 'that the fundamental characteristic of verse, which distinguishes it from prose, is that verse is regularly divided into measures of approximately equal time intervals by a succession of blows, or accents. These measures, or time parts, by their regular recurrence, give the ear the sense of rhythm. In this respect at least verse and music are analogous.'[14] Hatcher describes Browning as 'an aggressive timer; one whose subjective sense of rhythm is so alert and robust that it arranges into sensibly equal time parts which are experienced as rhythmic any series or succession of sounds' (24). That sense, as we have already seen, is native to speakers of English, so that Browning's 'energetic observance of time' (Hatcher 25–6) is the renewing for poetry of a vitality inherent in the language.

The title of this chapter is a quotation from 'The Flight of the Duchess.' The retainer who tells the story, himself caught up in the words of the Gypsy crone, hears them as a combination of speech and music to which he responds, like the Duchess herself, by beating time. Of the sounds he hears he asks,

> was it singing, or was it saying,
> Or a strange musical instrument playing
> In the chamber?   (512–14)

The reference to instrumental music is of some importance: John Neubauer has shown how the gradual growth of instrumental music in the eighteenth century 'forced an aesthetic revaluation of major import' of music without words, from entertainment to 'the purest, most essential form of music.'[15] The crone's recitation is music with words, however, and without the words the music would not have a meaning (just as, as we have seen earlier, an image without words would be unmeaning). Hence the retainer says, 'Word took word as hand takes hand, / I could hear at last, and understand' (563–4). The music, in the metaphor used by the retainer, 'props' the words (561) – stands under them, that is, and holds them up – and that metaphor seems unremarkable enough until we remember that understanding is, from an idealist perspective, liter- ally standing under, so that the words hold up the music, in a reciprocal relationship. That reciprocity is distilled in the word 'chime.' Etymologi- cally related to 'cymbal,' chiming is the rhythmic striking of an instru- ment; in so far as it is associated with bells, chiming is a series of combined musical sounds which come under the heading of harmony ('As ... a continued Succession of *single* musical Sounds produces *Melody*, so does a continued *Combination* of these produce *Harmony*,' says Charles Avison in defining his terms at the beginning of his *An Essay on Musical Expression*);[16] and in so far as chiming is a term for harmony, it comes figuratively to stand for harmony of various kinds, particularly rhyme. In the old Gypsy's 'chime,' the retainer hears a number of things: 'And I kept time to the wondrous chime, / Making out words and prose and rhyme' (557–8). The second and third nouns are especially interest- ing. Why should 'prose' be a feature of poetry which seems so close to music? Not because (as Hatcher thought) units of equal time distinguish poetry from prose, but because such units are common to both, and nat- ural in the language. Rhyme, as we shall see, far from being merely ornament or doggerel (as Browning's far-fetched rhymes often seemed to his listeners) reveals the music of our language by marking its meas- ures. Sometimes the rhyme marks the strong beat at the beginning of a bar; sometimes it marks the final note in a cadence.

With such an understanding of the music of poetry, Browning is an- ticipating the theory of prosody set out by Coventry Patmore in his 1857 essay in the *North British Review*, the essay then called 'English Metrical Critics,' subsequently titled 'Essay on English Metrical Law,' and later recognized, most recently by Dennis Taylor, as a 'landmark article' which inaugurated 'the new era of Victorian metrical theory.'[17] As usu- ally happens in such revolutions, the new was in fact a turn to the old. Patmore argues for 'the true view of metre, as being primarily based upon isochronous division by ictuses or accents';[18] 'metre, in the pri- mary degree of a simple series of isochronous intervals, marked by accents, is as natural to spoken language as an even pace is natural to walking'; hence 'verse is but an additional degree of that metre which is inherent in prose speaking' (132), a heightening which creates 'the two indispensable conditions of metre':

> first, that the sequence of vocal utterance, represented by written verse, shall be divided into equal or proportionate spaces; secondly, *that the fact of that division shall be made manifest* by an 'ictus' or 'beat,' actual or mental, which, like a post in a chain railing, shall mark the end of one space, and the commencement of another.   (136)

Rhyme as the marker of such spaces has a metrical function: 'far from being extra-metrical and merely "ornamental," as most persons imagine it to be ... it is the quality to which nearly all our metres owe their very existence' (154). Rhyme supplies 'the limits of the verse' and is hence a 'time-beater' (154). 'Pace them in rhyme' is the phrase Browning supplies for the speaker in 'The Last Ride Together' (1855). 'Well,' says the speaker addressing the poet,

> Your brains beat into rhythm, you tell
> What we felt only; you expressed
> You hold things beautiful the best,
>   And pace them in rhyme so, side by side.   (67–71)

The last line links rhyme with measured time, as in walking, and Browning thus anticipates Patmore's simile, 'as an even pace is natural to walking.' Elizabeth, however, had already linked rhythm and walking in her 1845 comments on 'The Flight of the Duchess.' Its rhythm, she writes to Robert, 'does more & more strike me as a new thing; something like (if like anything) what the Greeks called *pedestrian metre*, – between metre and prose.' She does not quite connect the rhyme and the rhythm, saying only that 'the difficult rhymes combin[e] too quite curiously with the easy looseness of the general measure' (*Correspondence* 11:167).

The 'isochronous intervals,' analogous to bars in music, do not, Patmore argues, coincide necessarily with feet. 'In modern verse, those collocations of accented and unaccented syllables which we call "feet," are not true measures' (139), and 'the common notion of an exact proportion inherent in syllables themselves seems to us to be quite untenable' (140). The time value of any syllable, Patmore argues, depends entirely upon its relation to the other syllables with which it is combined, 'so that the monosyllables, a, as, ask, asks, ask'st, though requiring five degrees of time for their articulation, may have precisely the same temporal value in verse' (140). Patmore's remarks point to a neglected aspect of Browning's prosody (and, I suspect, of that of other Victorian poets as well): the playing off of the accentual-syllabic metre against the isochronous intervals and the quantity or duration of the syllables. In 'A Toccata of Galuppi's,' for instance, Browning's stanzas are triplets with unusually long lines, the effect of which depends upon the difference between conventional metrical scansion of them and our sense of the isochronous intervals which make up the music of the piece. If one scans the lines in the conventional way, they are, as Browning himself told Furnivall, 'purely Trochaic' (*Browning's Trumpeter* 24), and, as so often happens when the trochee is used in English, the final foot is catalectic, so that the lines consist of eight feet but fifteen syllables. Our musical experience of reading the poem is quite different. We do not hear trochees, and we certainly do not hear eight feet in each verse. Instead, we hear a four-stress line with a strong caesura in the middle, a musical time-beating which preserves the pattern of Old and Middle English alliterative verse, without the alliteration. The first stanza, for instance, begins with an anacrusis, and the first isochronous interval begins with the accented syllable 'lup.' The four accents (marking the beginning of four bars) fall as follows:

      /   /   /   /
Oh Galuppi, Baldassaro, this is very sad to find!

The fourth bar includes the pause at the end of the line and the two syllables at the beginning of the next line:

      /   /   /   /
I can hardly misconceive you; it would prove me deaf and blind;
      /   /   /   /
But although I take your meaning, 'tis with such a heavy mind!

With this kind of scansion, we can see clearly the function of rhyme as a time-beater.[19] In each verse, the accented syllable which is the rhyme word marks the beginning of an interval or bar. The usual number of syllables in each isochronous interval is four (or, in every fourth interval, three plus a rest), but the duration of the syllables and the pauses varies a great deal, so that there is a tension between the accentual metre and the musical time. Consider, for instance, the first line in the seventh stanza: 'What? Those lesser thirds so plaintive, sixths diminished, sigh on sigh.' The musical accents fall on 'less,' 'plain,' 'mi,' and 'sigh,' but 'What' and 'those' are so clearly accented that we hear strongly the trochaic words 'lesser' and 'plaintive,' and the trochee, which is (in Hopkins's description of it) a falling foot, fits with the meaning of the words 'lesser' and 'diminished.' Moreover, the pauses (commas) stretch the intervals of musical time, and lead to the words of the next line – 'suspensions,' 'solutions' – nouns which name the breaking of the pattern and the return to it in the cadence.[20]

We might examine the music of Browning's poetry by looking at a familiar lyric, 'Love among the Ruins,' which stood first in the *Men and Women* volumes of 1855. I choose this lyric because Paul Fussell, to whose *Poetic Meter and Poetic Form* (1965) every teacher of prosody must be indebted, singles out this poem as an example of 'appliquéd metrical regularity,' because the metre overwhelms the sense instead of giving 'the illusion of having risen intrinsically and subtly from within the uniqueness of the poetic occasion.'[21] The reader will remember that in this lyric Browning uses a twelve-line stanza with alternating hexameter and dimeter lines, each long line rhyming with the following short line. The rhyme marks the limits of the measures, so that the dominant effect is one of contrast between an extended unit and a curt or abrupt one:

> Where the quiet-coloured end of evening smiles,
>   Miles and miles
> On the solitary pastures where our sheep
>   Half-asleep
> Tinkle homeward through the twilight, stray or stop
>   As they crop –
> Was the site once of a city great and gay,
>   (So they say)
> Of our country's very capital, its prince
>   Ages since
> Held his court in, gathered councils, wielding far
>   Peace or war.

Fussell's response – 'Dancing, anyone?' – is an unsympathetic recognition of the music of the poem, which is (to borrow Patmore's 'great general law') dipodal. 'All verse, like all music,' says Patmore, 'is either in triple or common cadence; or, in classical phraseology, comes under either the dactylic or trochaic category' (143). 'Love among the Ruins' is in the latter category – its time signature would be 2/4 or 4/4 – and as is so often the practice when the trochee is used in English, the lines are catalectic, the rest at the end (signalled by the masculine rhyme) filling out the measure.[22] Moreover, the words with which the poem begins – 'Where the' – make up an anacrusis which, in Patmore's words, is the 'unaccented portion of a foot or bar, which generally commences a verse or a strain of melody,' and 'is always less than the isochronous metrical or musical spaces which succeed it' (150). We note, in passing, that *anacrusis* is a Greek word meaning 'the striking up of a tune' and that, as the *Princeton Encyclopedia of Poetry and Poetics* says, the 'one or more initial syllables which are not part of a regular metrical scheme' are often seen as analogous to 'a note or notes occur[ring] before the first actual bar of the melody.'[23]

Once we have given a technical account of the music of 'Love among the Ruins,' we confront a much more difficult question: what does the music mean? We have been conditioned by Pope's dictum to expect that 'the sound must seem an echo to the sense,' and we know that Browning does not spurn such an alliance elsewhere. In 'Andrea del Sarto,' for instance, there is the clogged metre of the line, 'In their vexed beating stuffed and stopped-up brain' (80), where the spondee in the fifth foot (in combination with the pushing apart of the plosives 'p' and 'b') brings the tempo to a near standstill, or the steady movement of 'This low-pulsed forthright craftsman's hand of mine' (82), where the trochaic compounds cutting across the iambic feet provide a 'low-pulsed' rhythm. (Browning probably heard 'low-pulsed,' 'forthright,' and 'craftsman' all as trochees. When Ruskin challenged him on his pronunciation, Browning shot back, '*Foldskirts* not a trochee?' and went on with a barrage of examples: we are 'accustomed from the nipple to say lord and landlord, bridge and Cambridge, Gog and Magog, man and woman, house and workhouse, coal and charcoal, cloth and broadcloth, skirts and fold-skirts, more and once more.' The trochees, writes Browning, are not 'exactly as I like' but 'exactly as the language likes.')[24] There is no such coalescing of sound and sense in 'Love among the Ruins,' and so we must look elsewhere for the meaning of the music. 'Suit / Measure to subject, first,' says Browning in the 'Parleying with Charles Avison' (333–4), thus giving the first principle of the function of all isochronous units of sound – and so we turn to the theme of the poem. The lyric is concerned with time, specifically past and present, here juxtaposed: the urban energy of the landscape's past is contrasted by the speaker with the pastoral quiet of its present, and that contrast lies behind the title, where something living enacts itself amid something dead. The speaker extends the contrast to include present and future, for in the present the lovers are apart, while in the future he will come to the 'girl with eager eyes and yellow hair' in the 'little turret,' and they will rush together in an embrace which will 'extinguish sight and speech,' even though speech seems to be a goal of his arrival, since the girl is 'dumb / Till I come.' The relation among past, present, and future is problematic, as critics have noted: the speaker's agitation over the city, its ambitious energy and epic action, undermines his choice at the end, which seems too abrupt, too smugly moral, too much an avoiding of or suppressing of the past to which he seems guiltily attracted.[25] That decision, we note, coincides with the short line of the couplet which, because the rhyme returns too soon after the hexameter, gives the effect of imbalance or disproportion. Time as theme and time as music thus coincide, but the sound is not imitating the sense. The measures, rather, are the speaker's mode of perception itself.

Browning knew Carlyle's teaching that time is a mode of human perception or, as Carlyle calls it in 'Natural Supernaturalism,' the climactic chapter of *Sartor Resartus*, a 'Thought-form,' one of the 'two grand fundamental world-enveloping Appearances,' the other one being space.[26] (In a letter written a little more than a month after Carlyle's death in February 1881, Browning reminisced about him and mentions only one work: 'He wrote *Sartor* – and such letters to me in those old days!')[27] 'Time and space,' Browning told Furnivall in October 1881, are 'purely conceptions of our own.' Moreover, Browning goes on, time and space are 'wholly inapplicable to intelligence of another kind – with whom, as I made Luria say, there is an "everlasting moment of creation," if one at all, – past, present, and future, one and the same state' (*Browning's Trumpeter* 34). Time is thus both the means of making sense of our experience and the way of approaching the 'everlasting moment.' Nor is such an approach an illusion. Teufelsdröckh argues:

'Or thinkest thou it were impossible, unimaginable? Is the Past annihilated, then, or only past; is the Future non-extant, or only future? Those mystic faculties of thine, Memory and Hope, already answer: already through those mystic avenues, thou the Earth-blinded summonest both Past and Future, and communest with them, though as yet darkly, and with mute beckonings.' (261)

Memory and hope are the two faculties which enable us to make a start on escaping from the 'illusory Appearance' which is time. In poetry, the aural embodiment of time is the isochronous interval marked by strong accents and by rhyme which, says Patmore (perhaps echoing Carlyle), 'has been said to appeal to memory and hope' (147), and which therefore both keeps time and transcends it. We must now explore the way in which rhyme embodies memory and hope.

Once a sound has been established in the memory by a strong accent, we wait, for varying lengths of time, for the same sound to recur, and in that wait we are bringing together past experience and future expectations, so that our sense of intervening sounds and measures is a tense one: we beat time until chiming sound and accent bring our agitation to resolution. Rhyme as a 'time-beater' is thus neatly double: it embodies our sense of duration and of a continuum which make up our ordinary experience of time – it 'beats' time by striking at measured intervals – and it also 'beats' or overcomes time by giving it a shape. That shape, Patmore argues in a fashion parallel to Carlyle's idealism, is not objective, and a regularly recurring beat is not something we hear, but something we think we hear. The beat, in fact, *'has no material and external existence at all*, but has its place in the mind, which craves measure in everything' (136). Our hearing of a clock is instructive. 'The ticking of a clock [tick tick tick tick] is truly monotonous; but when we listen to it, we hear, or rather seem to hear, two distinct tones [tick tock tick tock], upon the imaginary distinction of which, and the equally imaginary emphasis of one, depends what we call its rhythm' (137).

The dipodal rhythm and the rhyme of 'Love among the Ruins,' then, are the embodiment of the speaker's perception of time. Instead of linking past and future, he wishes to separate them: of the 'whole centuries of folly, noise, and sin' that make up the past, he says, 'Shut them in.' The result is a curtailing or attenuation of the future and a present characterized by irreconcilable opposites which he feels in that part of him that is an emblem of his vitality, both physical and imaginative: 'oh blood that freezes, blood that burns!' The next lines label these opposites as 'Earth's returns / For whole centuries of folly, noise and sin!' The returns are not only retaliation for sin or the consequences of it, but also the rhyme, where sounds recur; we actually hear that repetition when 'returns' comes quickly after 'burns.' This crucial rhyme – as crucial as exactly the same words in *The Rime of the Ancient Mariner* – sums up the speaker's perception and the state of his soul. Like Coleridge's voyager, cursed by Life-in-Death, the siren 'Who thicks man's blood with cold'

(193–4), the speaker experiences as one 'return' of his obsession with the ruined city 'blood that freezes.' Also like the Ancient Mariner, for whom

> at an uncertain hour,
> That agony returns:
> And till my ghastly tale is told,
> This heart within me burns   (582–5)

the speaker here must rhyme quickly and obsessively when he speaks of the past.[28] The 'burns' - 'returns' rhyme gives the dramatic and psychological action central to the poem, and makes us hear the time-beating of a man imprisoned in time. No wonder the final line – 'Love is best' – and its motto-like appeal to a general truth with which all would agree are no more satisfactory than the Ancient Mariner's extolling the virtues of family and community life – and of love – while preventing the Wedding Guest from taking part in a ceremony central to those virtues.

The speaker's rhyming is very different from that of the crone in 'The Flight of the Duchess,' whose music is liberating both for the Duchess (whose 'hands' slow fanning ... moved to measure' 532, 534) and for the retainer (who 'kept time to the wondrous chime' 557). The crone's theme is the same as that of the speaker in 'Love among the Ruins': it is 'How love is the only good in the world' (615). The crone's speech moves, however, towards sound without signification ('There grew more of the music and less of the words' 691), and of the repeated sounds the retainer can give only 'this poor version' (697), for which he blames

> those who had the hammering
> Of prosody into me and syntax,
> And did it, not with hobnails but tintacks!   (699–701)

The double rhyme ('syntax,' 'tintacks') might in another context be labelled strained or forced, but here the effect is a sense of imperfection, a comic sense of inadequacy when measured against a mean or standard. That imperfection is summed up in the nails metaphor: tintacks are short and light, while hobnails, though also short, have a big head, and are used on heavy boots and shoes. Hobnails, like boots, are made for walking, for the natural rhythm that makes possible the romance journey, the 'great deliverance' (611) that claims the Duchess and ultimately the retainer. 'As natural to spoken language as an even pace is to walking' is also Patmore's simile for the music – the isochronous intervals – of both poetry and prose.

I have been dealing with the music of 'Love among the Ruins' as the mode of perception of the speaker, and hence I have been defining its dramatic function, but we must turn now to the reader and his or her experience of the poem. One might think that, from the perspective of music, the printed text is analogous to a musical score, coming alive only when it is performed or read aloud. Patmore, however, argues that poetry, like the unacted drama, is to be abstracted from the voice of any one reciter, and to be read silently: 'few lovers of good poetry care to hear it read or acted; for, although themselves, in all likelihood, quite unable to give such poetry a true and full vocal interpretation, their unexpressed imagination of its music is much higher than their own or any ordinary reading of it would be' (138). One notes that Patmore calls reading aloud an 'interpretation,' and it is limited, whereas silent reading makes possible our awareness of metre, rhythm, and music all at the same time.

The nature of the reader's experience, his or her 'unexpressed imagination' of a poem's music in the silent reading of it, can be guessed at in the one poem for which Browning composes a tune. It is 'Pietro of Abano' in the 1880 volume, *Dramatic Idyls: Second Series*. The poem is written in units of eight lines (one hesitates to call the units 'stanzas' because Browning often runs the units together in longer sections). The trochee is the dominant foot, and the lines, each with a strong caesura, vary in a regular pattern from six to eight feet: a hexameter first, then an octometer, a hypercatalectic hexameter, and a heptameter; the next four lines repeat that sequence. The rhyme scheme is a combination of quickly recurring sounds and delayed repetition: *a b a c d b d c*. Criticism faces the task of relating this accentual-syllabic poetic form to the legend which is the content of the poem, and there is no obvious or persuasive way of defining that relationship. Then, in a comment added at the very end of the poem, Browning indicates that there is another way of hearing the poem, a way which does not displace or replace the accentual-syllabic reading, but which is to be heard at the same time: 'I have,' says the poet, ' – oh, not sung! but lilted (as – between us – / Grows my lazy custom) this its legend. What the lilt?' (443–4). He then prints eight bars of music of his own making. We remember that 'legend' is derived from the Latin *legenda*, things to be read, and to 'lilt' a 'legend' seems to suggest that we are to fuse the actions of ear and eye, a fusion possible only in the silent perusal of the text. A 'lilt' (as *Grove's Dictionary* makes clear) is not a song, but a melody without words which is designed for the beating of time. 'Whenever,' the *Dictionary* says, 'in the absence of a musical instrument to play for dancing, the Irish peasant girls sing lively airs to the customary syllables la-la-la, it is called "lilting."' Browning's 'lilt' in 'Pietro of Abano' is eight bars of music, in 4/4 time, with a melody that consists of a combination of quarter and eighth notes. Each bar corresponds to a half-line in the poem, and the lines of varying lengths resolve themselves into bars of equal time but unequal numbers of syllables. One might try this 'lilt' by singing the melody with only the syllables la-la-la, until the time is firmly fixed in mind and the beat becomes something one cannot get rid of, like a child's song; then turn to the poem itself and replace la-la-la with the words of Browning's text. Here, for instance, is a typical four-line unit (lines 389–92). I have marked both the notes and their corresponding syllables with the typical beats of a bar of 4/4 time: strong (s), weak (w), medium (m), weak (w):

S   W   M   W | S   W   M
Scholar's debt discharged in full, be | 'Thanks' my latest breath!

The effect of the 'lilt' is to make us hear the quantity of the syllables as well as their accent, but the 'lilt,' which consists entirely of quarter and eighth notes, also forces us to hear a quantity which is often at odds with the duration we would, in our ordinary voicing of the lines, give each syllable. For instance, in the lines above we hear the rhyme words '[sur]vival' and 'rival' as trochees in accentual-syllabic scansion but as spondees in the quantitative scansion of the 'lilt,' and the rhyme itself marks, not the beat at the beginning of a bar, but the end of a musical phrase. The rush of the eighth notes towards the cadence in the last two bars of the 'lilt' seems to coincide with a delayed satisfaction, our hearing at last of the long-suspended rhyme which ties together the eighth and the fourth lines in the eight-line unit.

What is a critic to make of this 'lilt'? What is its relation to the 'legend'? What does it express? What is its effect? Browning himself tells us what the 'lilt' expresses: it is 'for love of that dear land which I so oft in dreams revisit' (442), and so its presence is like light in a painting, the artist's expression of his love for his subject. Such a feeling is related to theme and content primarily as their opposite. Love is absent in the 'legend' itself, the story of the relationship between Pietro and the Greek 'stranger' (169) who becomes pope. Love is also absent from the poem's other subject, Browning's reading of the 'legend' and his judgment of its subject. He has read Pietro's 'big book' (419), and his response is a lament: 'O Peter, still thy taste of love's to come!' (424). But the love which is so conspicuously absent both from the story and from the poet's judgment of it is present in the poet's telling of both matters, and its presence manifests itself, not in explicit statement or in semantics, but in pure sound. Three years before this poem was published, Pater had made his well-known statement that 'All art constantly aspires towards the condition of music,' and in poetry the 'handling' is everything and the 'mere matter' nothing, or at least 'nothing without the form.' Art, Pater had argued, is always striving 'to get rid of its responsibilities to its subject or material,' and the form 'should become an end in itself, should penetrate every part of the matter.'[29] In this poem Browning moves towards that aesthetic ideal, but he would never entirely divorce form from content or from meaning (he does, after all, allegorize the 'lilt' as love of Italy), and the music is for him 'motions of the soul.'

The phrase appears in *Paracelsus*, in the words of Aprile. While this over-reacher would in the other arts express, according to the capabilities of each, 'all passions, / All soft emotions' (2.466–7), he would finally turn to music as the most satisfactory:

I would supply all chasms with music, breathing
Mysterious motions of the soul, no way
To be defined save in strange melodies.   (2.477–9)

This passage comes after Aprile defines the other arts as imitative and expressive. In sculpture, for instance, 'Every passion sprung from man, conceived by man, / Would I express and clothe in its right form' (2.433–4); in oratory and literature he would express 'all passions, / All soft emotions': 'no thought which ever stirred / A human breast should be untold' (2.465–6). Music, however, goes beyond the expression of passions and emotions to 'motions of the soul.' Browning makes the same connection again much later in his career, in the 1887 'Parleying with Charles Avison.' There he makes the well-known statement that 'There is no truer truth obtainable / By Man than comes of music' (138–9), and he does so in the context of a lengthy passage where he explores the relation of mind and soul; soul 'lets emerge, / In flower and foam, Feeling from out the deeps / Mind arrogates no mastery upon' (162–4), and music, 'by sound, thy master-net' (236), catches (but cannot hold) the movements in 'Soul's profound' (249).

The passage in *Paracelsus* raises an issue central to the aesthetics of music in the eighteenth century, an issue Browning was familiar with through an essay which, primarily because of its title, has been 'singled out as the key document' of the history of the term 'expression,' even though, in John Neubauer's estimation, 'the essay barely departs from a conventional and somewhat vague theory of imitation' (152). The work is Charles Avison's *Essay on Musical Expression* (first published in 1752). For Avison, imitation in music is the echoing of the sounds of nature or the mimicking of movements in the world outside us; expression is the outering of passions within, and accounts for the affective function of music, 'the peculiar Quality' of which is 'to raise the *sociable and happy Passions*, and to *subdue* the *contrary ones*' (4). Imitation in music is limited, Avison argues, and 'Music as an imitative Art has *very confined Powers*' (60). 'Music can only imitate Motions and Sounds, and the *Motions* only imperfectly; it will follow, that musical Imitation ought never to be employed in representing Objects, of which Motion or Sound are not the principal Constituents' (66):

> Thus the gradual rising or falling of the Notes in a long Succession, is often used to denote Ascent or Descent, broken Intervals, to denote an interrupted Motion, a Number of Quick Divisions, to describe Swiftness or Flying, Sounds resembling Laughter, to describe Laughter; with a number of other Contrivances of a parallel Kind, which it is needless here to mention. Now all these I should chuse to stile Imitation, rather than Expression; because, it seems to me, that their Tendency is rather to fix the Hearers Attention on the Similitude between the Sounds and the Things which they describe, and thereby to excite a reflex Act of the Understanding, than to affect the Heart and raise the Passions of the Soul.   (57–8)

Because those passions spring from within, and because they embody themselves in melody and harmony, Avison calls music 'expressive,' but in fact, as John Neubauer and Kevin Barry have pointed out, Avison's understanding of 'expression' is a variant of the concept of mimesis, and 'expression,' as Avison and his contemporaries used the word, is 'a systematic *imitation* of specific internal states of feeling,'[30] the imitation being systematic because it depends upon the use of the elements of music as codes for various passions and feelings. 'Various Modes, or Keys, (besides the various Instruments themselves) ... are very expressive of the different Passions' (73):

> Thus the *sharp* or *flat Key*; slow or lively Movements; the *Staccato*; the *Softenute*, or smooth-drawn Bow; the striking *Diesis*; all the Variety of Intervals, from a Semitone to a Tenth, &c; the various Mixtures of Harmonies, the Preparation of Discords, and their Resolution into Concords, the sweet Succession of Melodies; and several other Circumstances besides these, do all tend to give that Variety of Expression which elevates the Soul to Joy or Courage, melts it into Tenderness or Pity, fixes it in a rational Serenity, or raises it to the Raptures of Devotion.   (74–5)

To treat the elements of music as a code for raising and soothing the passions is to treat music as rhetoric. Avison, however, suggests something beyond rhetoric when he makes the link between the passions and the elements of music less specific and less definable than one might expect. Ultimately, the affective power of music is 'beyond the Power of Words to express' (3). 'In Avison's defense of harmony and counterpoint,' John Neubauer argues, 'is a glimpse of a genuine departure from mimesis' (153).

The nature of that departure can be better understood if we follow Avison in contrasting music and painting, and think about the kind of sign we have in each art. 'During the eighteenth century, at least until the final discourses of Sir Joshua Reynolds, ' writes Kevin Barry, 'painting stands as the type of the "full" sign, and holds first place in any theory of representation' (2). So too in Aprile's speech on the hierarchy of the arts in *Paracelsus*. Sculpture and painting come first: 'I would carve in stone, or cast in brass, / The forms of earth' (2.421–2); 'I would contrive and paint / Woods, valleys, rocks and plains, dells, sands and wastes' (2.450–1) as well as 'Bronze labyrinth, palace, pyramid and crypt, / Baths, galleries, courts, temples and terraces' (2.458–9). By apparent contrast, Aprile describes oratory and literature as the expression of the passions, but his expression, like much of Avison's, is the coding of passions in words, 'in language as the need should be' (2.472), he says. Even when he comes to music, he describes it as an imitative art, 'breathing / Mysterious motions of the soul,' but the word 'mysterious' and the link between breath and inspiration and between breathing and equal intervals of time all suggest something else. Since that something else often seems vague or insubstantial or difficult to define, we start moving towards a concept of music, in contrast to painting, as an empty sign. Music seems to point to something beyond itself, but one cannot say what that something is. As James Beattie remarks in 'On Poetry and Music, as they affect the Mind' (written in 1762 but not published until 1776), without words 'a piece of the best music, heard for the first time, might be said to mean something, but we should not be able to say what.'[31]

To talk about a sign as empty, however, is to bring to it a theory of representation. Occasionally in Avison and more frequently in Browning, one can sense another way of understanding music as a sign. This way is bound up with Browning's myth of creation as a breaking apart or fragmenting. The result, for language, is a gap between sign and referent. In Locke's theory of language, there is no necessary connection between articulate sound and the idea of which it is the sign, and words are metonymic, a substitute for ideas which are private and insensible. Locke's diction indicates the metonymic nature of language, particularly his use of the word 'stand' in phrases such as 'stand as' or 'stand for': a human being makes sounds 'stand as marks for the Ideas within his own Mind' (3.1.2); or 'the Ideas [words] stand for, are their proper and immediate Signification' (3.2.1). Musical sounds, however, do not 'stand for' anything but themselves. In music there is no gap between sign and referent, because sign and referent are one. Music is, as the speaker of Pauline says, 'an earnest of a heaven' (365) because it prefigures the ultimate unity of all things. (I am taking the phrase from Pauline out of context, since the speaker goes on to treat music as representation, by which we know 'emotions strange ... Not else to be revealed.') In Browning, the idea of music as 'whole' and 'sole' (the adjectives are from Sordello 2.593, 594) is often figured by music as play.

One of Browning's earliest metaphors for 'my rhymes' is the transcendental platan in Sordello:

My transcendental platan! mounting gay
(An archimage so courts a novice-queen)
With tremulous silvered trunk, whence branches sheen
Laugh out, thick-foliaged next, a-shiver soon
With coloured buds, then glowing like the moon
One mild flame, – last a pause, a burst, and all
Her ivory limbs are smothered by a fall,
Bloom-flinders and fruit-sparkles and leaf-dust,
Ending the weird work prosecuted just
For her amusement ...   (3.596–605)

The rhymes, like the tree, are to amuse, and we assume that something designed to amuse is something to be taken lightly. Browning does not dispel that assumption, either here or elsewhere, but, as we shall see, play and amusement are finally, for him, serious activities. Not for nothing did he call his last volume Asolando and explain in the dedication to Mrs Bronson that asolare was a verb meaning 'to disport in the open air, amuse oneself at random.' Play has no purpose beyond itself. It is not a sign of anything else. It is 'whole' and 'sole.'

I started this book with a consideration of language in relation to sight and to the visual arts, and in that context interpretation ('this means that') and troping ('this is that') are the chief linguistic acts. Language in relation to the ear and to music leads us in a different direction, where 'this is this' and nothing else. Music thus brings us, as it brought Browning, to explore an idealist understanding of language, which is the subject of the next chapter, but before we turn to that topic, we must see how Browning links music to character and uses rhyme for the purposes of satire.

In some of his later poetry, Browning makes rhyme and time-beating indicators of moral and intellectual worth. He contrasts unskilful or merely conventional rhymes, and the thumping rhythms that go along with them, with the complex (though not smooth and melodious) music and virtuoso rhyming which he calls (borrowing, he says, from Pindar) 'the true *melos*' ('Of Pacchiarotto' 548). Browning had much earlier used such a contrast in *Pippa Passes*: the students in the second scene provide bad rhymed couplets for Phene to read to reveal their tricking of Jules, and their authority in such matters is Bluphocks, the schemer and manipulator who would undermine all things, including poetry, with couplets like '*How to Jonah sounded harshish, Get thee up and go to Tarshish*' (350–1) or with a satirical epitaph like '*Here a mammoth-poem lies, Fouled to death by butterflies*' (296–7). *Melos* is not unrelated to such obvious rhymes and time-beating. It is one of the six elements of poetry listed by Aristotle in his *Poetics*, and, as Gerald Else has pointed out, originally meant a 'limb' or 'member,' and so 'the application of the word to song must refer in some way to its division into members' or units of equal time.[32] Such a division is the essence of the music of poetry, but 'the true *melos*' avoids unvaried repetition and beats that are merely regular, like a Strauss waltz played without the grace notes and the hesitations at the beginning of each bar. 'True *melos*' also avoids the clumsiness of characters like 'our lump of learning, Brother Clout, / And Father Slouch, our piece of piety,' who 'clump-clumped' to Rome, with 'beads and book in hand' but no music in their heads, we may infer from the satire of Caponsacchi's bishop in *The Ring and the Book* (6.373–4, 376). Browning associates moral and intellectual authority with 'the true *melos*,' his standard as a satirist, and he attacks conventional or obvious music and the rhymes that mark its time.

In 'The Householder,' the epilogue to *Fifine at the Fair*, for instance, the speaker, a widower, mocks the rhymes and diction of the conventional epitaph ('Affliction sore long time he bore,' or 'Till God did please to grant him ease' 30–1) and contrasts such a style with his own. His is an eight-line stanza, where the rhyme and the rhyming words are conventional enough (the scheme is *a b a b c d c d*) but the metre is not. Browning constructs lines where he plays off metrical feet against musical bars or units of equal time, and while the lines have five or six feet, the units of equal time are invariably four, the rhyme words marking the strong beat at the beginning of every fourth bar (which consists of one beat and then rests). The resulting tensions are appropriate to a dramatic situation where the speaker, the man, is full of conflicting emotions, centred on the woman who returns unexpectedly from the dead. The accentual metre (considered by itself) reflects those tensions, for the drive forward of the trochees and dactyls is retarded by the spondees, as in the first line:

```
/  x | / x | / x   | x  x  / |  /   /
```
Savage I was sitting in my house, late, lone

The fourth line neatly ties the retarding spondees to the sense (in 'Tongue-tied now, now') while the remaining iambs ('blaspheming like a Turk') speed up the tempo when his words flood out. Behind all such metrical conflicts is a steady four-beat line, where rests fill out the units of equal time. Browning himself provided a quantitative scansion of the poem for Furnivall in 1881 – a one-sentence answer to a question from his 'trumpeter': 'I think the metre / - - - - / - - - - / - - / - // is continued throught [sic] the savage-soliloquy' (*Browning's Trumpeter* 29). The slashes I take to be the divisions of the bars, and the macrons an indication of quarter notes, thus:

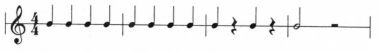

Savage I was   sitting in my house, late,   lone

We notice that the strong beats sometimes coincide with alliterating words, and some lines, such as 3 and 4, make full use of alliteration: 'Head of me, heart of me, stupid as a stone: / Tongue-tied now, now blaspheming like a Turk.' The alliteration indicates Browning's return to the music of earlier poetry in English, and his recognition that a four-stress line seems to be natural to poetry in English. The four-stress line is capable of fitting varying numbers of syllables into its bars, and so it has a rough vigour that contrasts with the smooth and polished rhythm that is the result of syllable-counting. The conventional epitaphs Browning quotes are smooth and easily scanned ('*Affliction sore long time he bore*'), but consider the line with which he contrasts such a snippet: 'What i' the way of final flourish? Prose, verse? Try!' (29). Browning's apostrophes mark elided consonants and usually indicate an extra syllable to be fitted into a unit of equal time, but such an elision hardly helps us in line 29, where one has to hurry through a flurry of syllables in the first bar ('What i' the way of') and then struggle to mouth clustered consonants in the next two bars ('final flourish? Prose, verse?') and somehow cope at the same time with the strong pauses. 'Try!' says the 'I' of the poem, and the imperative is as much a challenge to the reader as it is to his dead wife. The closure or 'end' to which the poem comes depends largely on the contrasting of syllable-counting with the genuine music or *melos* of poetry. 'Do end!' says the 'I,' proposing the lines of the conventional epitaph. The wife's reply counters his diction and metre: '"I end with – Love is all and Death is naught!" quoth She.' The strong beats of the four musical bars fall on 'I' (the beat causing the pronoun to contrast strongly with the 'I' at the end of the previous line), 'all,' 'naught,' and 'She,' the semantically important words in the line, while 'She,' the rhyme word, is the final tonic chord that resolves the sequence of discords in the rhythm and in the dramatic tensions of the dialogue. 'She' has been the focus of the 'I's' attention throughout, and 'She' is both wife and muse, offering release from his 'savage' self-pitying state and inspiring genuine music in his poetic speech.

There is the same possibility of genuine music at the end of *The Inn Album*. There Browning signals the turn towards comedy (the conventional suggestion at the end of a tragedy) with the appearance of the 'girl' (1095), the 'very young' (1087) woman in the story, just at the moment when the 'young' woman dies and completes the catastrophe of a plot Browning calls 'a tragedy in a new style.'[33] Here is how Browning counterpoints the death of one character with the promise of new life in another:

> As she dies,
> Begins outside a voice that sounds like song,
> And is indeed half song though meant for speech
> Muttered in time to motion – stir of heart
> That unsubduably must bubble forth
> To match the fawn-step as it mounts the stair.   (3048–53)

'Half-song though meant for speech / Muttered in time to motion' – the conjunction of song, speech, time-beating, and rhythmic bodily movements suggests a restoration of harmony, an integration of things which, in the preceding tragedy, had been pulling apart. The emblem of that pulling apart is the Inn Album itself, a miscellany with its 'album-language' (261): its inflated or merely conventional diction, its easy or forced rhymes, and its inscriptions urged by others ('Add to the Album!' 435, or 'Each of us must contribute' 2401). The inflated diction is obvious in 'the oft-quoted, much-laughed-over line – / "Hail, calm acclivity, salubrious spot!"' (3077–8), a line which is the ironic motif of the poem. The too-easy rhymes appear in a number of contexts. The younger man, for instance, is a 'ready rhymer' (2406), and the older man would outdo him:

> 'I'm confident I beat the bard, – for why?
> My young friend owns me an Iago – him
> Confessed, among the other qualities,
> A ready rhymer. Oh, he rhymed! Here goes!
> – Something to end with '*horsewhip!*' No, that rhyme
> Beats me; there's '*cowslip,*' '*boltsprit,*' nothing else!
> So, Tennyson take my benison, – verse for bard,
> Prose suits the gambler's book best! Dared and done!'   (2403–10)

(One notes, in passing, the final three words of the quotation, yet another of Browning's allusions – here used ironically – to Smart's 'wonderful poem,' which we will consider in relation to the idealist goal of language in the next chapter.) When the older man proposes rhymes to go with the 'oft-quoted, long-laughed-over line,' he calls upon a muse for whom the finding of rhyme words is more important than the musical function of rhyme:

> '"*Hail, calm acclivity, salubrious spot*"
> You begin – *place aux dames*! I'll prompt you then!
> "*Here do I take the good the gods allot!*"
> Next you, Sir! What, still sulky? Sing, O Muse!
> "*Here does my lord in full discharge his shot!*"
> Now for the crowning flourish! mine shall be ...'   (2949–54)

We note that the rhyming verses here are not those actually composed by the 'young' woman (2951) and the younger man (2953) but verses proposed for them by the older man, who has just been bullying the woman and attempting (what she later calls) 'mastery / Over my body and my soul!' (2639–40) as well as mastery over the dénouement of the action. Such manipulation is characteristic of the speeches that make up the tragic action, where each character attempts to impose speech on others. In his recent analysis of the poem, E.A.W. StGeorge has shown how 'Browning casts a desire for control over the situation as the desire to control what is said' (94). When a character proposes a speech for another, he or she is interpreting the opinions and feelings of that other person, and precluding the struggle for meaning which each individual must undertake. In this poem, bad rhyming is associated with such preëmptive speech. Rhyme establishes boundaries and creates enclosures. In the tragic action of this poem, such a function of rhyme is associated not with the temporal and the aural (as it is at the end of the poem) but with the spatial and the visual. At the beginning of the poem, the older man, looking for paper on which to total his losses, is happy to find the Inn Album itself, because its inscriptions – 'page on page of gratitude / For breakfast, dinner, supper, and the view!' (2–3) – are all poetry, and the rhymes leave blanks on the page:

> I praise these poets: they leave margin-space;
> Each stanza seems to gather skirts around,
> And primly, trimly, keep the foot's confine,
> Modest and maidlike; lubber prose o'ersprawls
> And straddling stops the path from left to right.
> Since I want space to do my cipher-work,
> Which poem spares a corner?   (4–10)

Rhyme establishes a visible boundary for each stanza, a boundary which (as the 'maidlike' simile suggests) is not to be transgressed; moreover, it bounds a regular syllabic metre where the 'foot's confine' is as inviolable an enclosure as the stanza itself. The older man's prime concern, however, is the distinction between poetry and prose, a distinction which, for him, has nothing more than a utilitarian value. He distinguishes between the two in the same way Bentham did,[34] by pointing to the lineation: in prose, the lines run all the way from the left-hand to the right-hand margins, while in poetry they don't. The observation is simple-minded, and it has no purpose beyond the older man's looking for space to write on, but it also introduces the main pattern of the plot, which involves being out of bounds and the divisive and ultimately fatal consequences of such acts.

Even the 'very young' woman, whose return at the end is the promise of renewal, uses rhyme to interpret and bound the thoughts of another. The scene in which she asks the 'young' woman to assess the cousin whom she – the 'girl' – is planning to marry is typical of rhyme's place in the language of the poem. As so often happens in Browning, there is a visual image – an elm-tree with a crow in it, seen through a frame, the window of the inn-parlour – and both interpret that image as if it were a *pictura* in an emblem. The 'girl,' however, does the interpreting for her friend, and claims the ability to 'read' her thoughts. Surely, the 'girl' says, the cousin – the young man to whom she is engaged – is

> 'as worth your pains
> To study as my elm-tree, crow and all,
> You still keep staring at.'   (1319–21)

Then the 'girl' insists, '"I read your thoughts"' (1321), and her reading is rhyming:

> '"Would, tree, a-top of thee
> *I wingèd were, like crow perched moveless there,*
> *And so could straightway soar, escape this bore,*
> *Back to my nest where broods whom I love best –*
> *The parson o'er his parish – garish – rarish –"*
> Oh I could bring the rhyme in if I tried:
> The Album here inspires me! Quite apart
> From lyrical expression, have I read
> The stare aright, and sings not soul just so?'   (1322–30)

The verses, we note, use not only end-rhyme but internal rhyme; the internal rhyme shifts between the second and third feet in the verses, and the shifts upset our expectations, our sense of the timing of the recurring sound, even as the end-rhymes bound the verses. The 'young' woman rejects the 'girl's' reading and effects a peripeteia which foreshadows the end of the tragic action. Where the 'girl' ended with '"sings not soul just so?"' the 'young' woman begins with a reversal:

> 'Or rather *so*? *"Cool comfortable elm*
> *That men make coffins out of, – none for me*
> *At thy expense, so thou permit I glide*
> *Under thy ferny feet, and there sleep, sleep,*
> *Nor dread awaking though in heaven itself!"'*   (1331–5)

The 'girl's' expression is the visual image of the peripeteia: 'The younger looks with face struck sudden white' (1336). We note that the 'young' woman avoids end-rhyme in her reading and that her lines are not easily scanned. We note, too, that, while the 'girl' talks about soaring and escape and love even while limiting such a sense of freedom with conventional rhymes, the 'young' woman talks about the final enclosure, the elm-wood coffin and the grave, while suggesting a genuine escape by avoiding rhymes proposed by others. Here is how she apostrophizes the elm and asks to be buried under it:

> '"so thou permit I glide
> Under thy ferny feet, and there sleep, sleep,
> Nor dread awaking though in heaven itself!"'   (1333–5)

The internal sound repetitions in these lines are not full rhymes ('feet' and 'sleep,' 'dread' and 'heaven') but they embody the meaning fully. The *rallentando* of line 1334 depends upon the long 'e's' and the rests or pauses, and such a slowing down makes possible the calm iambic regularity of line 1335, its steady beat coinciding with a tone of quiet confidence.

The rhymes of 'Of Pacchiarotto, and How He Worked in Distemper,' like those of *The Inn Album*, distinguish one kind of character from another, and serve a satiric purpose. In a comprehensive review of Browning's poetry in the *Temple Bar* for 1869, Alfred Austin had charged Browning with being unmusical: 'Poor Mr Browning is both muddy and unmusical to the last degree. In fact, his style may fairly be described as the very incarnation of discordant obscurity.'[35] In 1876, Browning finally answered Austin and others of 'those nicely-eared, my critics,'[36] and the satire of 'Of Pacchiarotto' turns on the question of 'true *melos*' (548). Browning contrasts the measures demanded by his critics with the measures of his own poetry, and he does so in rhymed trimeter couplets where the rhymes are often double or triple, so that there is no mistaking the beat. The story, Browning says, was 'begun with a chuckle, / And throughout timed by raps of the knuckle' (537–8) – a neatly double-edged claim in which Browning both defends his own time-keeping and suggests the satirist's conventional beating of sense – time, that is – into his enemies. His enemies he tropes as chimney-sweeps, who can be seen as a parody of the satirist, since they sweep away soot and dirt, and the 'measure' (467) to which they dance is a parody of 'true *melos*.' For 'my visionary dance of chimney-sweeps' (so Browning describes this part of the poem to Gosse, Hood 175), the poet proposes various instruments to beat that parodic measure: '"So, saltbox and tongs, tongs and bellows," / (I threw up the window) "your pleasure?"' (465–6). Saltbox, tongs, and bellows are all instruments used to beat time, bellows being (as in Quarles) the emblem of the fool, while the saltbox and tongs are used for popular and simple rhythmic effects (in their notes, Pettigrew and Collins cite the *OED*, which in turn cites Webster: 'In burlesque music, the salt-box has been used like the marrow-bones and cleaver, tongs and poker, etc.'). Browning also proposes other common objects: 'Bang drum and blow fife – ay, and rattle / Your brushes, for that's half the battle!' (482–3). Drum and fife he proposes tongue-in-cheek, for he well knew that the obvious and repetitive rhythm of both had satisfied the speaker of 'Up at a Villa – Down in the City': '*Bang-whang-whang* goes the drum, *tootle-de-tootle* the fife; / No keeping one's haunches still: it's the greatest pleasure in life' (53–4). He knew, too, that some readers thought that all of his poetry could be characterized by those two lines. 'Do you see the "Edinburg,"' he asked Isabella Blagden in a letter of October 1864, 'that says all my poetry is summed up in "Bang whang, whang, goes the Drum?"'[37] Browning does not dismiss such time-beating out-of-hand. On the contrary, he says to the sweeps,

> what with your rattling and tinkling,
> Who knows but you give me an inkling
> How music sounds, thanks to the jangle
> Of regular drum and triangle?   (486–9)

What he objects to is the reducing of poetry to time-beating only, to something simple and instantly grasped, to uncomplicated grammar and '"clearness of words which convey thought"' (559). His own 'harsh analytics' (457) require something more difficult, the 'thought-tormented music' that Joyce's Gabriel Conroy heard in Browning:

> But had you to put in one small line
> Some thought big and bouncing – as noddle
> Of goose, born to cackle and waddle
> And bite at man's heel as goose-wont is,
> Never felt plague its puny *os frontis* –
> You'd know, as you hissed, spat and sputtered,
> Clear cackle is easily uttered!   (564–70)

Browning's own instrument for 'true *melos*' is very different from the saltbox and tongs, the drum and the fife of his opponents. It is an arrow, an instrument of measured length because it is an extension of a part of the human body (as McLuhan has taught us to understand technology); in this instance, the arrow is an extension of the arm, and so it is related to the etymological base of *melos*. Browning draws upon Pindar for the specific kind of arrow he is talking about. It is

> that arrow
> Of song, *karterotaton belos*,
> (Which Pindar declares the true *melos*)
> I was forging and filing and finishing.   (546–9)

The *karterotaton belos* is 'a shaft most mighty in strength,' and it is strong because of the time and skill that went into its making. 'Forging and filing and finishing' are the verbs which identify Browning as the skilled artificer, and the poetry is strong, not because it is smooth and regular in its beat, but because its beat and measured length encompass so much that its power lies in its roughness, in breaking rules (491) rather than being bound by them. So he instructs his readers in scansion, for instance, which simply overrides the usual pronunciation of an Italian town. The couplet is as follows: 'I leave ye to fancy, our Siena's / Beast-litter of sloths and hyenas' (268–9). Neither the rhyme nor the timing is regular, but Browning solves the problem: '(Whoever to scan this is ill able / Forgets the town's name a dissyllable)' (270–1). For such a couplet our hearing must be double: we are aware of both the full rhyme and the actual imperfect rhyme, and we hear both the time disruption of the extra syllable in 'Siena' and the elision which smooths out the measure. Browning's critics would claim he has 'No ear!' Browning himself would claim the subtlety and complexity of 'true *melos*.'

'Knack of rhyme' (*The Two Poets of Croisic* 170) is, by itself, not enough to guarantee 'true *melos*' – one of the major points Browning seems to be making in telling the story of the two poets from the Breton town where he vacationed. The first poet is René Gentilhomme, who wrote for the Prince of Condé 'songs and sonnets, madrigals, and much / Rhyming thought poetry and praised as such' (231–2), though in fact it is 'Rubbish unutterable (bear in mind!)' (233). If René does not succeed with his ear, however, he does with his eye. When lightning blasts the ducal crown from the top of a marble pillar and the Prince asks (like the conventional reader of emblems) '"What may this mean?"' (326), it is René who – poet turned prophet – says that the Prince will not, as expected, succeed to the throne of France. The prophecy comes true, and René enjoys a 'burst of fame' (393) which leads to 'Nothing!' (396): 'No doubt his soul became at once aware / That, after prophecy, the rhyming-trick / Is poor employment' (524–6). The second poet, Paul Desforges Maillard, is also a ready rhymer. 'Have people time / And patience nowadays for thought in rhyme?' (559–60), asks the narrator, echoing, no doubt, a concern of his creator. At any rate, Maillard writes 'Verses of society' (553) – odes, quatrains, sonnets – all 'welded lines with clinch / Of ending word and word' (563–4). 'Clinch' indicates something fastened and secured rather than something giving order to movement, and it is one of the effects of the concluding couplet of the *ottava rima* form Browning chooses for this poem. Our concern, however, is with Maillard, who attacks the poetry in the *Paris Mercury* with an allusion which could be turned back on his own rhymes. 'Crambo,' he calls the pieces in 'the Journal's [poetry] corner' (669). I have already explored the meaning of the word, but it is time now to expand on the image – cabbage – which is its root. Browning's nineteenth-century readers might remember Juvenal's seventh satire and the line, 'Occidit miseros crambe repetita magistros.' In that line, cabbage twice-chewed or served up again ('crambe repetita') becomes a metaphor for easy sound repetition, to which the only appropriate response is gastric upset. Maillard is deaf to his own crambo and immune to the dyspepsia it causes. Browning in his own rhyme in 'Pambo' both defines the fault and indicates the need for self-criticism: 'The smooth line hath an end knot!' (20), Browning says, and 'end knot' is the rhyme for 'offend not,' the concluding words of the first verse of the thirty-ninth Psalm: '*I said I will look to my ways / That I with my tongue offend not*' (17–18).

The narrator who tells the stories of the two poets is a satirist, and he proposes both a test for poets and a standard for poetry. The 'simple test' used when 'people take on them to weigh / The worth of poets' (1233–4) seems, at first glance, to have no explicit connection with poetry: '"Which one led a happy life?"' (1240). But in the lyric appended to *The Two Poets*, the woman who speaks tells the poet that rough music succeeds – and leads to a happy life – where merely regular verse does not. 'All I care for,' she says after she has charged him with not knowing music,

> Is – to tell him that a girl's
> 'Love' comes aptly in when gruff
> Grows his singing. (There, enough!)   (105–8)

The standard for poetry, in the view of the narrator of *The Two Poets*, was set by Donne:

Better and truer verse none ever wrote
(Despite the antique outstretched *a-i-on*)
Than thou, revered and magisterial Donne!   (910–12)

Donne, we remember, was, like Browning, charged with being unmusical, and Browning would probably not have been unhappy to join his favourite seventeenth-century poet as the target of Ben Jonson's famous complaint, that Donne, for not keeping of the accent, deserved hanging.

The reason for the complexity of Browning's rhymes and the roughness of his measures is suggested in 'Apollo and the Fates,' the prologue to the *Parleyings* of 1887, and the reason is that the music is an attempt to hold together the 'whole round of creation,' and to move all things upwards towards primal unity. In the prologue, the characters seem opposed in every way: Apollo is 'Day's god,' the Fates 'queens Night-crowned!' (42); they are old and he is young, a 'boy-thing' confronting 'crones'; he is associated with hope, they with fear; and so on. Yet both are concerned with measures. They 'kindle,' 'mete out,' and 'cut asunder'; he glows with light which is troped as 'shafts.' When he offers them wine, then, the result is a dance in which opposites circle round as he joins hands with them: 'Drive we a dance, three and one, reconcilingly' (203). Mrs Orr's comment in her *Handbook* that the wine is 'imagination as supplement to and interpreter of fact'[38] has set the direction of most subsequent criticism, and has obscured the possibility that wine is the quickening spirit which manifests itself in the ability to beat time skilfully and to hold opposites together in verses which are not smooth but complex. Consider, for instance, the stanza where the circling round of time with which the Fates are concerned becomes the spiralling upwards of human possibility:

Manhood – the actual? Nay, praise the potential!
  (Bound upon bound, foot it around!)
What *is*? No, what *may* be – sing! that's Man's essential!
  (Ramp, tramp, stamp and compound
Fancy with fact – the lost secret is found!)   (211–15)

The diction suggests an energetic and awkward dance – 'ramp, tramp, stamp' – to the rough music, the 'true *melos*,' which holds together all things in a 'compound' and dynamic pattern.

'Adjust Real vision to right language': The Idealist Goal of Language, 'Parleying with Christopher Smart,' 'Abt Vogler,' and 'Saul'

The 'Parleying with Christopher Smart' from Browning's 1887 volume is a late exploration of the idealist view of language. That view is bound up with Browning's reading of Smart's great 'Song to David,' a poem Browning had in his head 'after nearly fifty years,' he told Furnivall in 1887, and one which he repeated, from memory, 'to people of authority enough – Tennyson, the present Bishop of London – and – last year to Wendell Holmes, who had asked me innocently at Oxford, "whether I knew the wonderful poem."'[1] The 'wonderful poem' is a song of praise to one who is 'Servant of God's holiest charge, / The minister of praise at large' (13–14), and David's ability to name and bless everything in creation is inspired by 'His Muse, bright angel of his verse' (97), who is troped both as healer and as 'Blessed light' (100). Smart's own muse is suggested in the final stanza, and it is Christ. We note that the song has a double perspective: David is presented as praising all of creation, and Smart, praising David, repeats his praise of creation, but Smart writes as one enjoying the benefits of the Christian dispensation. David is, in a familiar pattern from typology, the type of Christ, and the climax of Smart's song is the stanza glorifying the Incarnation and the Redemption. David only believed in the Messiah; Smart knows Christ as historical and his actions as real. 'Thou' (Smart says, addressing David) 'at stupendous truth believed, / And now the matchless deed's achieved, / Determined, Dared, and Done' (514–16). 'Dared and done' are the words with which Browning begins *La Saisiaz*, and they indicate that he is, like every Congregationalist, repeating in his own life the life of Christ. Smart's climactic reference to Christ indicates the source of his inspiration for the song – he too has dared and done because of the example and through the grace of God – and so he is able to write his master-piece. In the 'Parleying,' Browning interprets that act of composition as the recovery of the identity of sign and signified, a recovery made possible (as Boehme and Swedenborg had suggested) in Christ.

Browning begins the parleying, not with an exploration of music and song, as one might expect, but with painting. He pictures himself proceeding through Smart's works as if he were 'exploring some huge house, had gone / Through room and room complacently' (17–18), just as Christian in *The Pilgrim's Progress* proceeds from room to room in the House of the Interpreter. In this particular house, however, only one room stands out, and it is the chapel with its Raphael madonna, Browning's analogy for the 'Song to David,' the masterpiece in the midst of 'Safe mediocrity' (26). Browning's question is not the usual one about interpretation – what does this mean? – but is rather a question about the significance of the master work. There are, in fact, two questions:

Now, what I fáin would know is – could it be
That he ...
...
... was found but once combining so
The elder and the younger, taking stand
On Art's supreme?   (87–8; 91–3)

And 'Did you ... resume the void and null, / Subside to insignificance, – live, die' (99–100)? The questions are misleading because they draw attention away from Browning's central concern: the nature of the 'Song to David' itself, and the kind of language which Browning heard in it. As Browning describes that language in the parleying, it is language which, at least for this one time, repairs the divisions brought about by the fall, and makes sign and signifier, soul and speech, one. 'Smart,' Browning says, of all poets writing between Milton and Keats, 'solely of such songmen, pierced the screen / 'Twixt thing and word, lit language straight from soul' (113–14). The energy which enabled Smart to recover such unity Browning tropes as 'fire-flame' (126), a metaphor derived from God's appearance to Moses in the burning bush and associated with the hidden but powerful name of God. The recovery of such unity is also a recovery of the power Adam had in naming the beasts: the names are not arbitrary and conventional but natural and necessary, since they participate in the essential being of each thing named. In the parleying, Browning links such naming with unmediated sight: Smart was able (like Boehme) to see not just the appearances of nature but the essences: 'there fell / Disguise from Nature, so that Truth remained / Naked' (140–2):

> Sense, penetrating as through rind to pith
> Each object, thoroughly revealed might view
> And comprehend the old things thus made new,
> So that while eye saw, soul to tongue could trust
> Thing which struck word out, and once more adjust
> Real vision to right language ...   (146–51)

'Adjust / Real vision to right language' – the phrase neatly sums up the idealist goal, which Browning explicitly associates with Adam's naming of the beasts, an act which he hears repeated, if only once, in Smart's song:

> heaven's vault
> Pompous with sunset, storm-stirred sea's assault
> On the swilled rock-ridge, earth's embosomed brood
> Of tree and flower and weed, with all the life
> That flies or swims or crawls, in peace or strife,
> Above, below, –each had its note and name
> For Man to know by, – Man who, now – the same
> As erst in Eden, needs that all he sees
> Be named him ere he note by what degrees
> Of strength and beauty to its end Design
> Ever thus operates – (your thought and mine,
> No matter for the many dissident) –
> So did you sing your Song, so truth found vent
> In words for once with you?   (151–64)

Once the moment of unity is passed, however, language lapses into its fallen state, and sign separates itself from signified. Names are arbitrarily attached to the appearances of things rather than their essences. Here is how Browning tells of the return to a clothed rather than a naked world:

> Then – back was furled
> The robe thus thrown aside, and straight the world
> Darkened into the old oft-catalogued
> Repository of things that sky, wave, land,
> Or show or hide, clear late, accretion-clogged
> Now ...   (164–9)

In the final section of the parleying, Browning tries to account for Smart's return to mediocrity. Twice he asks, 'Was it because' (185, 201). The first 'was it because' suggests that Smart was really an empiricist at heart, using his judgment (the crucial faculty in Locke's scheme of things) and cataloguing the world in the hope that the names, arbitrarily given, would at least suggest the power within things. Here is Browning's first question:

Was it because you judged (I know full well
You never had the fancy) – judged – as some –
That who makes poetry must reproduce
Thus ever and thus only, as they come,
Each strength, each beauty, everywhere diffuse
Throughout creation, so that eye and ear,
Seeing and hearing, straight shall recognize,
At touch of just a trait, the strength appear, –
Suggested by a line's lapse see arise
All evident the beauty, – fresh surprise
Startling at fresh achievement?   (185–95)

The second 'was it because' suggests that Smart resigned himself to the transitory nature of divine inspiration:

– Was it because you judged – when fugitive
Was glory found, and wholly gone and spent
Such power of startling up deaf ear, blind eye,
At truth's appearance, – that you humbly bent
The head and, bidding vivid work good-bye,
Doffed lyric dress and trod the world once more
A drab-clothed decent proseman as before?   (201–7)

Nonetheless, Browning argues, the 'Song to David,' unique as it is and a one-time act, is 'effectual service' (209). The song he characterizes (using the same metaphor as he uses for Miranda in *Red Cotton Night-Cap Country*) as 'one word's flash,' and that phrase occurs three times (at lines 208, 213, and 222). While the 'fire-flame' metaphor troped the source of the poet's energy and inspiration, the 'flash' tropes the effect of the song on the reader.

At this point, when he considers reader response, Browning becomes critical of Smart's method and of the idealist understanding of language.

Smart may have judged that his 'one word's flash' was 'effectual service' (209), but Browning asks,

> What comes next?
> Why all the strength and beauty? – to be shown
> Thus in one word's flash, thenceforth let alone
> By Man who needs must deal with aught that's known
> Never so lately and so little?   (211–15)

The 'strength and beauty' to which Browning refers in these lines are attributes of Nature, and they provide both enjoyment and instruction, which are also the conventional effects of poetry. The poet is 'instructor' (228) and he does 'Please' (232) – but 'Please simply,' Browning says to Smart, 'when your function is to rule – / By thought incite to deed' (232–3). Browning criticizes the 'flash' of Smart's poem because it preempts the responsibility of each human being to 'learn life's lesson' (239) for himself or herself, and because it anticipates the method 'favoured in our day' (240):

> The end ere the beginning: as you may,
> Master the heavens before you study earth,
> Make you familiar with the meteor's birth
> Ere you descend to scrutinize the rose!   (241–4)

The verb 'descends' suggests that Browning is advocating a response something like Carlyle's descendentalism, where one examines with intense scrutiny every minute particular of the appearances of this world. Such scrutiny will ultimately be revelatory (and hence, in Carlyle, the terms 'descendentalism' and 'transcendentalism' are paradoxically synonyms). For that experience Browning provides a motto – 'learn earth first' (255) – and an image from Neoplatonism, the ladder:

> I say, o'erstep no least one of the rows
> That lead man from the bottom where he plants
> Foot first of all, to life's last ladder-top.   (246–7)

'"Live and learn,"' Browning says in the final lines of the parleying, '"Not first learn and then live, is our concern"' (264–5). For the purposes of living and learning, the Lockeian theory of language, where human beings must use their judgment, is more useful than the idealist theory which, in its paradigmatic form (as Adamic language), provides, without any struggle, full knowledge of the essences of things.

The same attitude towards revelation – wonder and appreciation when it happens, apprehension at its forestalling of growth – is apparent in Browning's discussion of the word 'symbol' in the 'Parleying with Bernard de Mandeville.' Browning revives Mandeville to answer Carlyle, who knew something about symbols, and while Browning does not reject the Carlylean view that a symbol is revelatory as well as concealing, and that every symbol is a manifestation of spirit, he instructs his friend in the proper use of symbols in human life. Browning presents Carlyle as arguing that '"Man, with the narrow mind, must cram inside / His finite God's infinitude"' (151–2), and when that attempt fails, as it inevitably must, Carlyle rejects symbols altogether: '"Abjure each fond attempt to represent / The formless, the illimitable!"' (167–8). Browning would not go to such extremes. He would retain the symbol as a heuristic, but he would be only tentative and suggestive in affirming the ontological identity of sign and thing signified. The symbol is a 'guess at truth' (171), and such a guess is sufficient for the purposes of human life. His example of a symbol is the ground-plan of Goethe's estate in Weimar. The plan is a 'tracing' (170) which is obviously not the estate itself.

> Do you look beyond
> The algebraic signs, and captious say
> 'Is A. the House? But where's the roof to A.,
> Where's Door, where's Window? Needs must House have such!'
> Ay, that were folly. Why so very much
> More foolish than our moral purblind way
> Of seeking in the symbol no mere point
> To guide our gaze through what were else inane,
> But things – their solid selves?   (180–8)

So we would 'Look through the sign to the thing signified' (192), but to look for the essence of both signifier and signified will instantly be shown as foolish if we but turn the sign. The turning here is literal, the physical act of rotating something by hand, but, as we have already seen, the turning may also be verbal, in the form of troping. At any rate, the attempt to 'Look through the sign to the thing signified' will only show that the 'thing signified' is in fact just a 'point,'

Each an orb's topmost sparkle: all beside
Its shine is shadow: turn the orb one jot –
Up flies the new flash to reveal 'twas not
The whole sphere late flamboyant in your ken!   (194–7)

At the end of the parleying, however, Browning affirms the ontological identity, in a symbol, of sign and thing signified, and he does so through the myth of Prometheus. Prometheus brought fire down from heaven,

The very Sun in little: made fire burn
And henceforth do Man service – glass-conglobed
Though to a pin-point circle – all the same
Comprising the Sun's self, but Sun disrobed
Of that else-unconceived essential flame
Borne by no naked sight.   (304–9)

Then Browning instructs Carlyle in the proper use of such a symbol. If the 'mind's eye' (309) strives 'To follow beam and beam upon their way / Hand-breadth by hand-breadth, till sense faint' (312–13), the attempt is an 'Idle quest!' (315). If, however, one uses the symbol for the purposes of human life, 'In little, light, warmth, life are blessed' (317), and sensible perception followed by inference is sufficient for our present situation: 'Sense, descry / The spectrum – mind, infer immensity!' (315–16).

Again in the Prologue to *Asolando* Browning explores the doubtful effects of revelation on ordinary human lives. The poem, which critics rightly compare with Wordsworth's 'Ode: Intimations of Immortality,' lacks the elegiac tone of its predecessor, because the clouds of glory that invest everything in creation preclude language itself. When the poet first came to Asolo, he writes,

I found you, loved yet feared you so –
    For natural objects seemed to stand
Palpably fire-clothed!   (23–5)

Browning's simile for such flaming garments links 'natural objects' with the burning bush in which God manifested himself to Moses. In that episode, God and Moses at least spoke to each other, and God at least provided a riddling form of his name; in Browning's repetition of the episode in his experience of Asolo, words are simply unnecessary. The 'fire-clothed' objects evoke

Terror with beauty, like the Bush
Burning but unconsumed. Bend knees,
   Drop eyes to earthward! Language? Tush!
Silence 'tis awe decrees.   (27–30)

In the poet's old age, however, the 'lambent flame,' like Wordsworth's clouds of glory, has disappeared, and 'The Bush is bare' (35). The poet then needs language, and its purpose is 'to know and name' (37) each thing in creation: 'Hill, vale, tree, flower' (36). The verbs 'know and name' suggest the Lockeian theory, where generalizations from sense perception make up our knowledge, and where names are articulate sounds arbitrarily attached to those generalizations. The adverb 'arbitrarily' indicates that the attachment is a matter of human judgment, and the name itself is an invention of the mind, a 'fancy' having no necessary connection with the thing it names. What authority can such acts of invention and judgment claim? Browning's answer to that question in this lyric involves a shift from the eye to the ear. Like Moses, who sees the burning bush but hears the voice which reveals its meaning, the poet hears 'A Voice' (38), and while his eye had been 'dazed' (42), his ear is 'purged' (41). The Voice, Browning says, 'Straight unlinked / Fancy from fact' (38–9). To break the link of something with its opposite is to make it possible for human beings to know that thing in itself, without the need for its opposite. Here 'Fancy,' associated by Locke with the fictions created by the mind – dangerous things when propositions do not coincide with the actual relations of things – becomes a faculty which reflects the creative power of God, the ultimate artificer, who here instructs the poet in troping: '"Call my works thy friends!"' (43). Such 'calling' might in another context be an arbitrary turning; Browning, with considerable daring, here gives the turning divine authority and the force of revelation.

Browning's exploration of the idealist goal in language nearly always involves three matters which he sees as related: the cataloguing of the world by naming it (an interest which comes out of the encyclopedic ambitions he had from his beginnings as a poet), the identifying of the whole of creation with the Word who is Christ, and the manifesting of that ultimate unity of all things in music. The relations of those three matters Browning had examined in a number of earlier poems, and I want to look at two of them in detail: 'Abt Vogler' and 'Saul.'

The meaning of Abt Vogler's music is bound up with the attempt to contain within a single structure the whole of human knowledge and experience. The recurring image for such an encyclopedic view is the palace of art, and the most familiar version of that structure is Tennyson's poem of 1833, where the art is visual – painting and mosaics – matching every mood and every legend, and presenting every myth as part of one great myth which is circular in structure ('cycles of the human tale / Of this wide world, the times of every land' 146–7). Less familiar is the 'magic dome' (106) in which Constance in Browning's 'In a Balcony' imagines the Queen existing; it also is a palace for the eye, since it houses 'Pictures all round her,' and it too is encyclopedic, the paintings representing 'the whole earth's display' (111). In 'Abt Vogler,' however, the palace is a palace of music – Vogler actually uses that phrase at line 57 – and the phrase indicates the fusing of an art which is spatial (architecture) with an art which is temporal (music).

The immediate antecedent for both Tennyson's palace of art and Browning's palace of music is Coleridge's 'Kubla Khan.'[2] Tennyson describes his palace as a 'lordly pleasure-house,' and the label echoes Coleridge's 'stately pleasure-dome':

> In Xanadu did Kubla Khan
> A stately pleasure-dome decree:
> Where Alph, the sacred river, ran
> Through caverns measureless to man
> Down to a sunless sea.   (1–5)

The dome may not be built until the poet revives within himself the song of the 'damsel with a dulcimer'; if he can remember that song, he will become the divinely insane poet: 'And all should cry, Beware! Beware! / His flashing eyes, his floating hair!' Coleridge's poem makes three links which are of great importance for Browning's poem: the link between memory and architecture, between music and architecture, and finally between language and architecture.

First of all, memory. We are so plagued in our own time with the careless assumption that the goal of education is to make people creative that we sometimes forget that inspiration is useless unless it has some materials to breathe life into, and those materials are supplied by the memory. It was no accident that the ancients made memory the mother of the Muses, and in this, as in so many matters, the ancients knew what they were about. (Convincing contemporary educators of the value of what used to be called 'memory work' is another matter.) There is a very old tradition in which memory is linked to architecture, the link being made by the classical rhetoricians. They developed an interesting and, perhaps, still workable system of improving one's memory by recognizing that the basis of a good memory is orderly arrangement, and by discovering the model for such order in architecture. The rhetoricians taught orators to remember long speeches by memorizing places in a real building, and by attaching images representing the various topics of their speeches to these places. As one walked through the building in one's imagination, the various images or objects would come into view, and hence, through this arrangement, one was able to contain the whole of one's speech in one's mind. This 'science of mnemonics' is usually attributed to the Greek rhetorician Simonides, who is known primarily through the story that Cicero tells about him in book 2 of the *De oratore*. Having by good fortune escaped harm when the roof of a banqueting hall collapsed, Simonides was able to help relatives identify the bodies of the dead because he remembered the part of the hall in which each person was sitting. The story illustrates the art of memory which was advocated by Cicero, Quintilian, and the unknown writer of the treatise called the *Ad Herennium*. All these writers give us a picture of a building containing images that represent aspects of human experiences, and that picture is of considerable importance for later ages, especially for the English Renaissance and the nineteenth century. As Frances Yates has shown, that picture is the basis of our understanding of the idea of the Renaissance theatre, particularly Shakespeare's Globe, since its ground-plan realizes in a precise way the oft-quoted line about all the world being a stage.[3] For the nineteenth century that picture is also the basis of our understanding of the palace of art. Like the Globe theatre, the palace of art gives us, within the boundaries of a single structure, a reflection or representation of the whole world, and of the place of human beings in it. It is (to use Renaissance terms) a microcosm or 'little world' which sums up the 'great world.'

Why undertake such a representation at all? The chief answer to that question is not a statement of the meaning of the palace, but rather that such a representation is an end in itself, like play, and gives us pleasure. Hence Coleridge and Tennyson refer to the palace as a 'pleasure-dome' or 'pleasure-house,' and Solomon, invoked by Abt Vogler as his predecessor in 'piling' a palace, does so to 'to pleasure the princess he loved!' But what pleases us is what satisfies our human desires, and human desires, as we know from literature and our own experience, are notoriously difficult to satisfy because we are always conceiving more than we are capable of getting. Hence, the palace of art is also an emblem of human aspiration, and as such it suggests an upward striving, an attempt to gain the kind of comprehensive knowledge and power usually reserved for God alone. The attempt must necessarily end in failure, but it is a failure that is not without its compensations. For the artist typically claims (as Browning did) that his is a special power which is at least analogous to that of God. The chief tool of the artist is his song, and in myth and legend the song is linked with architecture.

The link lies in the chant or charm, the word 'charm' having as its root the Latin *carmen*, song. In a charm, articulate sounds and music work together to build a structure, just as in myth and legend a building comes into being while music is being played. The classical precedents for this pattern are the building of Troy by the music of Apollo and the building of Thebes by the music of Amphion. Carlyle refers to the latter in *Sartor Resartus*, and goes on to insist in the climactic chapter that 'not only was Thebes built by the music of an Orpheus; but without the music of some inspired Orpheus was no city ever built; no work that man glories in ever done.'⁴ Tennyson has a poem on Amphion and alludes to Apollo's building of Troy in 'Œnone' (where Œnone will 'speak, and build up all / My sorrow with my song, as yonder walls / Rose to a music slowly breathed' 38–40) and in 'Ilion, Ilion' (which was unpublished during Tennyson's lifetime); his Camelot in *Idylls of the Kind* is a city '"built / To music, therefore never built at all, / And therefore built for ever"' ('Gareth and Lynette' 272–4). The pleasure-dome in Coleridge's 'Kubla Khan' will be built only if the poet remembers the song of the Abyssinian maid:

> Could I revive within me
> Her symphony and song,
> To such a deep delight 'twould win me,
> That with music loud and long,
> I would build that dome in air,
> That sunny dome!   (42–7).

All of these precedents suggest that the ordering of time and the ordering of space are linked in an essential way; that they are both, as Carlyle taught, 'Thought-forms'; and that while, for many, these forms may be a veil or prison, for some (such as musicians, the 'few of us whom [God] whispers in the ear' 87) they are liberating and revelatory. They find their ultimate unity in the name of God.

The name of God is at the centre of an idealist understanding of language. To focus on 'the ineffable name' is to make grammar the defining feature of language, and grammar is concerned with the relations of words (all of which have both their origin and end in the Word) rather than with the naming of discrete ideas. The chief and most influential spokesman for such a view in the nineteenth century was Coleridge. Browning seems not to have known Coleridge's prose, and there is no evidence that he read, for instance, *Aids to Reflection*, where Coleridge's language theory is most accessible. Instead, Browning seems to have derived an understanding of the idealist position from older writers, particularly Boehme and probably Swedenborg. Nonetheless, because Coleridge makes so clear the relation of grammar (the architecture of language) and 'the ineffable name,' and because such relations have a parallel in 'Abt Vogler,' a brief account of Coleridge's language theory may be useful.

In a diagram Coleridge calls 'the Noetic Pentad,' which appears not only in *Aids to Reflection* but in his *Table Talk* and *Logic* as well, he presents grammar as a pattern of opposites that are in fact expressions of unity. There are seven parts of speech, says Coleridge, the primary one being neither a noun nor a verb but a fusion of both, the 'verb substantive' which Coleridge identifies with the name of God, 'the INEFFABLE NAME, to which no Image can be attached,' and of this name all language is the expression. The name is the tetragrammaton, God's answer to Moses out of the burning bush, and, as biblical commentators point out, the name is not the static thing the King James translation suggests ('I am that I am') but an ongoing, active, creative power in the process of working out its divine purpose (Coleridge's translation is 'I am in that I will to be').[5] Coleridge treats the tetragrammaton in Kantian fashion, as that which stands under all appearances, a standing under which makes (through etymology) substance and understanding one. The ineffable name also stands under all grammar. Out of the 'verb substantive' come noun and verb, which Coleridge presents as opposites (he labels them 'thesis' and 'antithesis'), and adjective and adverb, modifiers of these opposites, while the infinitive and the participle unite these opposites when they act as gerunds (he labels the participle a 'synthesis,' the infinitive a 'mesothesis').[6]

The first stanza of 'Abt Vogler' establishes in this same idealist way the links among music, words, palace, and 'the ineffable Name':

Would that the structure brave, the manifold music I build,
  Bidding my organ obey, calling its keys to their work,

> Claiming each slave of the sound, at a touch, as when Solomon willed
>   Armies of angels that soar, legions of demons that lurk,
> Man, brute, reptile, fly, – alien of end and of aim,
>   Adverse, each from the other heaven-high, hell-deep removed, –
> Should rush into sight at once as he named the ineffable Name,
>   And pile him a palace straight, to pleasure the princess he loved!

One notes, to begin with, that Vogler tropes his 'touch' on the keys as verbal and performative ('Bidding,' 'calling'). The stanza as whole is a wish, and it is analogous to God's creating word, though with differences that distinguish the Creator from his creature, who, as Browning says in *The Ring and the Book* 1.717, 'Repeats God's process in man's due degree.' God's creating word is an imperative – 'Let there be light' – which instantly brings light into being. The artist's creating word is a wish – 'Would that' – and although it is a wish for instantaneous creation ('Would that the structure ... Should rush into sight at once'), Vogler expresses it 'after he has been extemporizing,' and in a medium – language – which is subject to time. Desiring to beat time, he can only keep time. In this world, music is 'manifold' and language (as in *Sordello*) separated into parts, 'the simultaneous and the sole' divided into 'the successive and the many' (2.594–5). Nonetheless, the analogy with Solomon makes all the parts emanations of 'the ineffable Name' that stands under creation and under the grammar of this stanza, which can be read as a version of Coleridge's 'Noetic Pentad.' The stanza is rich in nouns and verbs – the chief opposites in Coleridge – and they develop into rhetorical patterns such as the antitheses of lines 4 ('Armies of angels that soar, legions of demons that lurk') and 6 ('heaven-high, hell-deep'). All these opposites are held together by the stanza's periodic structure. The eight lines make up a single sentence, with the main verb delayed until the seventh line. The suspending of the completion of the syntax forces the reader to keep in mind all the intervening clauses and phrases, to fit them into a sentence under construction and to 'build' it just as Vogler 'builds' his music, until the pile becomes the completed palace in line 8. The periodicity, then, enacts in time a creation which, if it were the subject of divine fiat, would be instant. The music of the poem – the metre and rhyme – does the same thing. Browning uses dactylic hexameters with a strong caesura in the third foot and catalexis in the sixth; the indentation marks the rhyme, the first line rhyming with the third, the second with the fourth, and so on. The rhyme, which falls on the accented syllable – the first syllable – of the sixth foot, beats the time, which is triple; dactyls, trochaic variations, and pauses make up the iso-chronous intervals or bars.

Abt Vogler's concern with music is not with its beating time, however, but with harmony. He contrasts music with painting and poetry, and in that contrast we can sense that something in music goes beyond both imitation and expression. 'Had I painted the whole,' he says, 'Why, there it had stood, to see, nor the process so wonderful' (43–4). 'Had I written the same, made verse,' he goes on, the poetry might be 'triumphant art, but art in obedience to laws' (45, 48). Music, in contrast to these arts, reveals the creative power 'Existent behind all laws,' and he tropes that power, as Browning himself does in his letters to Elizabeth and in *The Ring and the Book*, as 'the finger of God.' That power reveals itself neither in imitation nor in expression, in both of which the sign points to something beyond itself, but in harmony where the sign and its power are one. Harmony, moreover, is a pattern of relationships in which, as in syntax, the whole is greater than the sum of its parts.

Rousseau's treatment of harmony in his *Dictionnaire de Musique* (Paris, 1768) is a helpful commentary on stanza 7 of 'Abt Vogler.' There was a copy of the *Dictionnaire* in Browning's library – it is item A1975 in Kelley and Coley's *The Browning Collections* – and Browning may also have known Rousseau's comments on music in his *Essay on the Origin of Languages*. First, here is the whole of stanza 7:

> But here is the finger of God, a flash of the will that can,
>   Existent behind all laws, that made them and lo, they are!
> And I know not if, save in this, such gift be allowed to man,
>   That out of three sounds he frame, not a fourth sound, but a star.
> Consider it well: each tone of our scale in itself is naught;
>   It is everywhere in the world – loud, soft, and all is said:
> Give it to me to use! I mix it with two in my thought:
>   And, there! Ye have heard and seen: consider and bow the head!

'Each tone of our scale in itself is naught' can be more fully understood in the light of Rousseau's contrasting of music and painting in his *Essay*. 'Colours last, sounds vanish,' writes Rousseau (in Victor Gourevitch's translation):

> Moreover, every colour is absolute, independent, whereas every sound is for us only relative, and distinct only by contrast. By itself a sound has no absolute character by which it might be recognized; it is high or low, loud

or soft in relation to another sound; in itself it is none of these. Nor is a given sound by nature anything within the harmonic system; it is neither tonic, nor dominant, nor harmonic, nor fundamental; for all of these properties are only relationships ...[7]

Here music is not a sign of anything, but is rather a system of relationships which, in the poem, emanate (like grammar in the Coleridgian and idealist view) from God, who is one. That system of relationships is the focus of one aspect of music, harmony or *accord*. Under the latter heading in the *Dictionnaire*, Rousseau writes that 'L'Harmonie naturelle ... est composée de trois Sons différens' – they are the 'Son fondamental,' and its third and fifth – and that these three sounds 'forment entr'eux l'*Accord* le plus agréable & le plus parfait que l'on puisse entendre: d'où on l'appelle par excellence *Accord parfait*.'[8] Browning tropes such *Accord parfait* as a star, but in doing so he rejects the words 'fourth sound' as a label for the chord. In Rousseau the 'fourth sound' is a dissonance: 'l'addition de la Dissonnance produisant un quatrième Son ajoûté à l'*accord* parfait, c'est une nécessité, si l'on veut remplir l'*accord*, d'avoir une quatrième Partie pour exprimer cette Dissonnance' (*Dictionnaire* 16). Moreover, harmony is not complete without this fourth part: 'Ainsi la suite des *accords* ne peut être complette & liée qu'au moyen de quatre Parties' (16). Vogler makes the same point: 'Why rushed the discords in but that harmony should be prized?' (84). In his entry on *harmonie* itself, Rousseau treats harmony as inferior to melody and measure, because it does not imitate anything, and hence is not 'dramatic': 'l'*Harmonie* ne fournit aucun principe d'imitation par lequel la Musique formant des images ou exprimant des sentimens se puisse élever au genre Dramatique or imitatif, qui est la partie de l'Art le plus noble, & la seule énergique' (*Dictionnaire* 242). Harmony is not natural – 'qu'aucun animal, qu'aucun oiseau, qu'aucun être dans la Nature ne produit d'autre Accord que l'Unisson, ni d'autre Musique que la Mélodie' (242) – and as it is used only by Europeans and 'Peuples du Nord,' it is only 'une invention gothique & barbare dont nous ne nous fussions jamais avisés, si nous eussions été plus sensibles aux véritables beautés de l'Art, & à la Musique vraiment naturelle' (242). The fact that harmony does not imitate anything, that it is not a sign of anything, is precisely why Vogler values it. He may interpret it, as indeed he does, but he is fully aware that the music is itself and, like the name of God, not a sign of something essentially different from itself.

Just as Solomon began with the name of God, so Abt Vogler as interpreter uses that powerful word as the ground of the meaning he finds in the music: 'Therefore to whom turn I but to thee, the ineffable Name?' (65). The parallel between building the palace of music and building the house of his life is the chief pattern of the interpretation, and it is based on Paul's distinction, in 2 Corinthians 5:1, between 'our earthly house' and the 'building of God ... eternal in the heavens.' So Vogler addresses God as 'Builder and maker, thou, of houses not made with hands!' (66). The statements of faith that follow are some of Browning's familiar ideas: love provides insight into God's plan for the world; desires to realize the good and the beautiful are witnesses of God's intention to fulfil such dreams; imperfection on earth is the promise of perfection in heaven. Implicit in the analogy is the parallel between music and speech: both are discourses – a parallel Rousseau makes in his *Diction-naire* when he remarks, in the entry on *harmonie*, that 'la Musique, étant un discours, doit avoir comme lui ses périodes, ses phrases, ses suspensions, ses repos, sa ponctuation de toute espèce' (238). If music has its periods and pauses, speech has its harmony, and its harmony is its grammar and syntax, a system of relationships that are not simply arbitrary but are rather the creative and ordering energy of the ineffable Name itself. Stanza 12 – the final stanza in the poem – defines the nature of discourse, both musical and spoken. The musical discourse is a succession of harmonies with modulation and dissonance:

> I feel for the common chord again,
> Sliding by semitones, till I sink to the minor, – yes,
> And I blunt it into a ninth, and I stand on alien ground,
> Surveying awhile the heights I rolled from into the deep;
> Which, hark, I have dared and done, for my resting-place is found,
> The C Major of this life: so, now I will try to sleep.   (91–6)

From the perspective of rhetoric, the structure is that of the loose sentence, in contrast to the periodicity of the first stanza. The periodic wound up to the palace; the loose unravels to 'my resting-place.' His 'resting-place' is the pause, signalled by the period at the end of the poem, so far as speech is concerned; so far as music is concerned, it is 'the C Major of this life,' which is not 'the ultimate simplicity, the ultimate truth,' as Nachum Schoffman says in his book on Browning and music,[9] but rather the spatial arrangements 'of this life' in which both musician and man operate. Vogler has been playing with the opposites of space and time, those 'Thought-forms' which, like the noun and verb, the antithetical divisions of the ineffable Name, are the result of God-head projecting itself by division. Now Vogler, like Smart's David, has 'dared and done,' and the allusion links the ineffable Name and the whole round of creation in a moment of unity where words and notes, primarily through their relationships, reach towards the idealist goal.

That same reaching makes up both the theme and structure of 'Saul,' where Browning uses not only music but the visual arts to arrive at speech which is prophetic. The sights that David sees are material for interpretation, but his saying that 'this means that' relies on typology, so that 'the whole round of creation,' praised by Browning's David as it was by Smart's David, ultimately finds its antitype in Christ. Music, too, turns out to be revelatory, but the sequence of 'The Flight of the Duch-ess,' where words gave way to pure sound, is here reversed, and pure sound finally gives way to prophetic speech. We begin with the music of the poem.

David is a singer, and the purpose of his music is an affective one, a purpose conventional enough at first glance but more problematic when we consider the nature of Saul's affliction. In the biblical account, Saul is described as possessed of an evil spirit (1 Samuel 16), and Abner in the poem refers to 'Saul and the Spirit' and the 'strife' between them (9), but Saul's affliction is in fact *accidia*, a loss of purpose, of faith, and of a taste for life, the result of his disobedience, so that he matches David's later description of him as 'Saul the mistake, / Saul the failure, the ruin he seems now' (279–80). Music which rouses and soothes the passions is clearly inadequate for the restoration Saul needs. Hence David moves from instrumental music through songs with words to words alone. He begins by tuning his harp (34) and playing various pieces he calls 'tunes,' such as the pastoral one – 'the tune all our sheep know, as, one after one, / So docile they come to the pen-door till folding be done' (36–7) – and moves on to tunes that, in the manner of the music of Orpheus, affect various creatures and charm them so that they, like the quails, 'fly after the player' (43) or are elated or quickened in some way. Then 'tunes' give way to 'song,' where words and music combine: the wine song, the funeral song, the 'glad chaunt / Of the marriage' (55–6), the 'great march' (57), and 'the chorus intoned / As the Levites go up to the altar in glory enthroned' (59–60). As in Paracelsus's great speech and Smart's 'wonderful poem,' there is a canvassing of the whole cycle of both natural and human life – 'I have gone the whole round of creation,' David says at the beginning of section 17 – with the result that the cycle turns out to be a spiral and the way round the way up, a result appropriate to the typological structure of the poem, since typology is a pattern of progressive revelation. The progress depends upon words. By the time David comes to the climactic part of his restoration of Saul, he is speaking, but with 'No harp more – no song more!' (237). The music instead becomes an integral part of his speech, and the reader hears it in Browning's prosody. The metre is anapestic, with many variations (iambs, spondees, bacchics, and cretics). When Browning published the first and fragmentary version of the poem in 1845, the lineation consisted of a trimeter followed by a dimeter, the indentation of the dimeters signalling the rhyme; when he published the complete poem in 1855, he changed the lineation, printing the lines as pentameters and in rhyming couplets, so that the rhyme is more clearly a time-beater. The unusually long lines – fifteen syllables – vary considerably in their tempo, movement, and syntax, but the variations are possible and effective only because one is aware of the steady beat, and so music and words become one. Our concern at the moment, however, is with the shift in David's efforts, from instrumental music through song with words to words which are musical. The significance of that shift, and its implications for our understanding of David's language in sections 17 and 18 of the poem, become apparent only when we turn to typology, which is clearest in those aspects of the poem which draw upon painting rather than music.

The poem begins with a picture which, as critics such as Suzanne Edwards have pointed out,[10] has the characteristics of a Pre-Raphaelite painting: the visual details are carefully and accurately given, and the lighting, also carefully specified, is dramatic, since the 'sunbeam, that burst through the tent roof' and illuminates Saul contrasts so strongly with the surrounding darkness:

> He stood as erect as that tent-prop, both arms stretched out wide
> On the great cross-support in the centre, that goes to each side;
> He relaxed not a muscle, but hung there ...   (28–30)

The costuming, later described, is precise also: there are the jewels in Saul's turban ('All its lordly male-sapphires, and rubies courageous at heart' 65), 'the armlets of price, with the clasp set before' (212), and 'the pile / Of his armour and war-cloak and garments' (217–18). But the initial scene is the crucial one, and just as a Pre-Raphaelite painting often pictures a moment of intense meaning or a moment when an entire story is summed up in the naturalistic details, so the moment when

David first sees Saul is full of meaning for him and even fuller in its meaning for us. Everything depends upon Saul's posture. David, lacking the revelation which is to come, interprets the posture in terms of the natural world which he knows. Saul

> hung there as, caught in his pangs
> And waiting his change, the king-serpent all heavily hangs,
> Far away from his kind, in the pine, till deliverance come
> With the spring-time ...   (30–3)

For the reader, whom Browning expects to be versed in biblical typology, the picture and David's interpretation of it mean more than David knows. Saul's posture makes him a type of Christ on the cross, but because Saul is only a type, we know that the posture may prefigure but that it lacks both the meaning and the efficacy of its antitype. David's simile links a physical change – the serpent shedding its skin – with a psychological and spiritual change which he sees Saul's posture as (he hopes) prefiguring. David, caught up in the Old Testament dispensation, does not allude to the incident in Numbers 21:4–9 where Moses, charged with delivering the children of Israel from a plague of serpents, makes a serpent of brass and sets it upon a pole, so that 'if a serpent had bitten any man, when he beheld the serpent of brass, he lived.' Only the reader can know that the typological interpretation of that incident was sanctioned by Christ himself when he told Nicodemus, 'And as Moses lifted up the serpent in the wilderness, even so must the Son of man be lifted up' (John 3:14). Here is Christ as interpreter, his reading setting the example and providing the authority for ours, which must as a result of Christ's words be a strong one, since the type is 'innate' – one 'which Scripture itself has expressly asserted to possess a typical character' – and not 'inferred' – one 'not specially noticed or explained in Scripture, [but] yet, on probable grounds, inferred by interpreters as conformable to the analogy of faith, and the practice of the inspired writers in regard to similar examples.'[11] The poem, however, turns upon an inferred type, for which the picture is in section 15. As Glenn Everett has pointed out, 'the structurally important situation in the poem is Saul's suffering and David's attempt to alleviate it: Saul's punishment and David's love.'[12] Everett does not point out that the picture with which the poem begins is matched by a complementary picture, introduced in stanza 10 (the first of the stanzas added in 1855 to complete the poem) and given fully in stanza 15. The poem began with David gazing at Saul, and its continuation begins with David looking up and gazing at Saul's eyes (122). The complementary picture is one of Saul looking at David's face in an attempt to read its meaning, and looking into his eyes. The reader will remember that David is sitting 'with my head just above his vast knees, / Which were thrust out on each side around me' (223–4), and that Saul puts his hand on David's head and pushes his fingers through his hair:

> and he bent back my head, with kind power –
> All my face back, intent to peruse it, as men do a flower.
> Thus held he me there with his great eyes that scrutinized mine.   (229–31)

(We note, in passing, how the inverted syntax of 'held he me there' and the sequence of accented syllables 'holds' the tempo of the line by slowing it.) The painterly placing of the two figures and the painterly gesture of Saul are both, we are conditioned to think, filled with meaning, and while we know that David is a familiar type of Christ (a type suggested by his passing reference to himself as a lamb in line 225), we do not know the exact typological function of countenance and gesture. The gesture is a search for meaning on Saul's part, but David's countenance and answering look find their meaning in David's sudden outburst: 'And oh, all my heart how it loved him!' (232). David's love, limited in its ability to do, finds its antitype in the sacrificial love of Christ who through death does provide the 'new life altogether' (235) David can only wish for Saul. '"See the Christ stand!"' completes and fulfils the picture of David's face, a completing to which David himself draws attention just before the moment of revelation: 'O Saul, it shall be / A Face like my face that receives thee' (309–10). The human face analogy makes clear the precise nature of the typological relationship: the face into which Saul looks is a prefiguring of the Incarnation. David's language at the moment of revelation is precise. 'See,' he says, and the seeing is possible only because 'the Christ' appears in human form. The definite article distances Christ and makes him sound unfamiliar, and the verb 'stand' (contrasting with the crucified posture of the despondent Saul) indicates that Christ is the antitype, himself and no one else: he does not 'stand for' anything. He it is who makes sense of the types, which are analogous to each other and in their relation to the antitype.

In the context of such a typological structure, language is both providential and prophetic. Just as David's face is a type of the Incarnation, so his words are types of the Word. David's words are incomplete and inadequate, restoring Saul in part but falling short of his desires for Saul. 'What spell or what charm'? David asks; 'what next should I urge / To sustain him where song had restored him?' (127–9). The only match for such a desire is the Word, Christ himself, 'The great Word which makes all things new,' says the speaker in 'By the Fire-Side' (132), alluding to the Christ who presides over the 'new heaven' and 'new earth' in Revelation 21:5. Browning attempts something very daring indeed in the last parts of 'Saul,' when 'the truth came upon me' and there is 'No harp more – no song more!' (237): he gives words which are meant to be expressions of the Word. Such a daring attempt and its inevitable failure may account for Browning's unwillingness to finish the poem in 1845. And though the attempt is a failure, we need to define carefully David's way of proceeding in sections 17 and 18, and contrast his language there with his language – or at least his conception of language – in earlier parts of the poem. Section 9 of the poem, culminating in the words 'King Saul,' is the type; sections 17 and 18, culminating in the words 'See the Christ stand!' are the antitype.

In those earlier parts, language is first of all a response to nature. David describes his words in a Lockeian way, as a naming and cataloguing of the world as perceived by his senses. At this stage, David is like the poet in 'How It Strikes a Contemporary,' a 'recording chief-inquisitor': 'I have gone the whole round of creation,' he says; 'I saw and I spoke' (238). He also judged. We remember that Locke makes language the embodiment of human concerns and human judgment, judgment being necessary because our propositions may not all be based on the full evidence of our senses and must inevitably slide from knowledge into varying degrees of opinion. David pictures himself as judging creation and returning to God 'His creation's approval or censure' (241), but his central proposition, 'I report, as a man may of God's work – all's love, yet all's law' (242), is opinion or 'report,' and does not yet have the force of revelation. That comes when David says, 'Now I lay down the judgeship he lent me' (243), and turns to the kind of language which is the antitype of his Lockeian words and propositions: the language of prophecy and revelation.

Browning draws attention to the shift from 'reporting' to prophecy in the single line which makes up section 16 of the poem: 'Then the truth came upon me. No harp more – no song more! outbroke – ' (237). We might expect that when David speaks as prophet, God is speaking through him, but in fact David keeps talking of 'I' and keeps giving authority to his witnessing of revelation ('Would it ever have entered my mind' 271). Moreover, he proceeds by analogy, arguing from his own faculties to the nature of God, from 'man's nothing-perfect to God's all-complete' (253). Analogy works well enough as a mode of argument in the context of revelation and of typology, since, as Coleridge taught his age in *Aids to Reflection*, 'language is analogous, wherever a thing, power, or principle in a higher dignity is expressed by the same thing, power, or principle in a lower but more known form'[13] – a statement parallel to Patrick Fairbairn's definition of typology when he is distinguishing it from allegory: typical interpretations require 'that the same truth or principle be embodied alike in the type and the antitype. *The typical is not properly a different or higher sense, but a different or higher application of the same sense*' (1.3). A type thus parallels the Coleridgian theory of the symbol, and it is not to be invented but to be discovered. Type and antitype must not only resemble one another, but must have been designed to resemble each other; there must, says Fairbairn (quoting Bishop Marsh), be *'previous design'* and *'pre-ordained* connection' (1.46). Hence the language of section 9 and of sections 17 and 18 is the same, but in the latter two sections David claims for his words an authority they did not have in the first part of the poem. His words are a type of the incarnate Word, as manifest to Saul's ear as his face is to Saul's eyes. As such, his words have a place in an analogy defined by Melvill and derived from Paul (Colossians 1:15): 'What speech is to thought, that is the Incarnate Son to the invisible Father.'[14]

The words of the poem mediate between the two other arts – painting and music – which have their emblem in the lilies twined round the harp strings when David first arrives in Saul's tent. The mediation takes the form of the discovery of meaning which is neither explicit nor fully intelligible in either painting or music, without the agency of words, and finally without the Word. So David takes the picture of Saul in his crucified posture and invents its meaning – a limited one, for him – in the king-serpent simile. Then he takes his own face, into which Saul looks so intently, and discovers its meaning, thanks to the power of love which, so often for Browning, is a power of insight and revelation. Browning refers to such mediation in the last lines of *The Ring and the Book*, where he comments on 'Art': 'So may you paint your picture' (12.858), he says, and 'So, note by note, bring music from your mind' (12.860). The third art is poetry – 'So write a book' – and that act 'shall mean' in ways only words can manage. In our ordinary experience, words mean something because we have arbitrarily assigned a meaning to articulate sounds, and that meaning is sustained by convention and habit. In our experience of typology, however, words mean something because they are types of the Word which gives shape and purpose to the whole of creation. Because types are essentially incomplete (they make truth accessible in a fallen world and to limited human faculties), they are also essentially related to their antitype, who is ultimately Christ, 'the central reality of human history' (Landow 39), the one who unites all opposites and repairs all divisions. Browning often tropes the relation between type and antitype in spatial terms, with the type imaged as reaching up, and the antitype as leaning down. The animating spirit of the type is human desire, and its reaching up is answered by a 'yearning down,' as in stanza 4 of 'Abt Vogler':

> In sight? Not half! for it seemed, it was certain, to match man's birth,
>   Nature in turn conceived, obeying an impulse as I;
> And the emulous heaven yearned down, made effort to reach the earth,
>   As the earth had done her best, in my passion, to scale the sky   (25–8)

This reciprocal relation of type and antitype can be seen as Browning's version of Coleridge's 'Noetic Pentad,' where language hangs together because all the parts of speech emanate from the Word, and where all human words are ultimately grounded in the incarnate Word, the 'Truth as it is in Jesus.' If human words are types of the Word, then creation is essentially verbal, and prosopopoeia, the trope which animates nature, is not a human attribution (or, as Ruskin called it, a 'pathetic fallacy') but a discovery of the true character of the created universe. Browning uses prosopopoeia at the end of 'Saul,' where the brooks speak: 'And the little brooks witnessing murmured, persistent and low, / With their obstinate, all but hushed voices – "E'en so, it is so!"' (334–5).

Browning's chief source for this divine language topos is Boehme, who turns up in a poem which is parallel to 'Saul' in a number of ways: '"Transcendentalism: A Poem in Twelve Books."' The speaker – a poet – addresses a brother poet, pictured as a singer with a harp, like David, and also like David, a boy-poet, a figure who, as Eleanor Cook points out, appears frequently in Browning's early work.[15] Here the boy-poet is at fault, speaking 'naked thoughts / Instead of draping them in sights and sounds' (3–4). The speaker corrects his practice with some familiar ideas: one does not reject 'sights and sounds' or 'images and melody' (17), but neither does one return to a time when our senses apprehend many objects but (perhaps through habit) do not consider them as riddles and do not attempt to state their meaning:

> Objects throng our youth, 'tis true;
> We see and hear and do not wonder much:
> If you could tell us what they mean, indeed!   (19–21)

Here, the meaning (the human comprehension of which depends upon words) is not to be arrived at through human judgment, but to be revealed. The model for such revelation is the illumination experienced by Jacob Boehme in 1600, an experience Browning recounts in the poem:

> As German Boehme never cared for plants
> Until it happed, a-walking in the fields,
> He noticed all at once that plants could speak,
> Nay, turned with loosened tongue to talk with him.
> That day the daisy had an eye indeed –
> Colloquized with the cowslip on such themes!   (22–7)

Browning (who told Edward Dowden in 1866 that 'I knew something of Boehme, and his autobiography, and how he lived mainly, and died in the Goerlitz where he was born')[16] is here using an incident recounted by the Reverend William Law in his 'The Life of Jacob Boehme, The Teutonic Theosopher,' prefixed to the four-volume English translation of Boehme's *Works* published between 1764 and 1781. Law's narrative makes clear the fact that the language of plants Boehme heard was a language where the words were not arbitrary but necessary, and participated in the nature and essence of the things named. 'About the Year 1600, in the twenty-fifth Year of his Age,' Law writes, Boehme 'was again surrounded by the divine Light, and replenished with the heavenly Knowledge; insomuch, as going abroad into the Fields, to a Green before *Neys-Gate*, at *Gorlitz*. he there sat down, and viewing the Herbs and Grass of the Field, in his inward Light he saw into their Essences, Use and Properties, which were discovered to him by their Lineaments, Figures, and Signatures.'[17] Law attributes Boehme's book *De Signatura Rerum* to this experience, and it is to that book that we must turn for an understanding of that key word, 'signature.' The essence or 'innate genuine form' or 'signature' of each thing, animate and inanimate, is verbal, and the verbal is 'the receptacle, container, or cabinet of the spirit, wherein it lies': 'if the spirit opens to him [each human being] the *signature*, then he understands the speech of another; and further, he understands how the spirit has manifested and revealed itself ... in the sound with the voice.'[18] 'Everything has its mouth to manifestation,' Boehme says at the end of the first chapter of the *Signatura Rerum*; 'and this is the language of nature, whence everything speaks out of its property, and continually manifests, declares, and sets forth itself for what is good or profitable' (12). We are not far from Hopkins's paired notions of inscape and instress, though here it is not just a matter of each thing finding 'tongue to fling out broad its name'; instead, each thing has the ability to carry on a discourse. 'So come,' the brother poet says to the boy-poet in Browning's poem, 'the harp back to your heart again! / You are a poem' (46–7); by that he seems to mean that the boy, like everything else in creation, must speak out the truth or essence within him. That essence is 'the word of God, or the divine voice,' according to Boehme, and speech is music, since Boehme describes one's physical being as 'the instrument, which the inward, living, powerful word, or divine voice uses, wherewith it forms and works' (90). In one of the autobiographical passages in the *Signatura Rerum*, Boehme defines himself as God's musical instrument: 'I shall be the manifestation of the spiritual divine world, and an instrument of God's Spirit, wherein he makes melody with himself, with this voice, which I myself am, as with his signature' (154). The boy-poet as God's instrument (not yet fully sounding) appears in the emblem with which the poem ends:

> The best of all you showed before, believe,
> Was your own boy-face o'er the finer chords
> Bent, following the cherub at the top
> That points to God with his paired half-moon wings.   (48–51)

This emblem lacks both motto and *explicatio*, though we as readers may infer a good deal about immaturity, aspiration, incompleteness, and (to make the riddle even more enigmatic) parentheses in those 'paired half-moon wings.' The main point, however, is this: the essence of creation is verbal, and each creature must learn to speak out the divinity – the words – within him or her. To do so is to repair the break between sign and signified which came about as a result of the fall.

In his *Mysterium Magnum: Or, an Explanation of the First Book of Moses called Genesis*, Boehme presents a myth of the loss and recovery of verbal identity in which Adam by his sin divides sign and signifier while Christ forges a new unity of the two in the Incarnation. Adam named each beast with its natural and necessary name because, as Boehme writes, 'he knew the Property of all Creatures, *and gave Names to all Creatures* from their Essence, Form, and Property. He understood the Language of

Nature, *viz.* the manifested and formed Word in every one's Essence, for thence the *Name of every Creature* is risen.'[19] With Babel, however, came the separation of name and essence. 'Mankind had framed the sensual Language of the *holy Spirit* into a *dumb* Form, and used the formed Word of the human Understanding *only* in a Form, as in a contrived Vessel or *Vehiculum*; they spoke only with the *outward* contrived Vessel, and understood not the *Word* in its own proper Language of *Sense*; they understood not that God was *in* the speaking Word of the Understanding' (*Works* 3.197). The way in which God may be '*in* the speaking word' becomes apparent when Boehme talks about Christ's recovery of the identity of sense and spirit. The language of sense alone Boehme identifies with the consonants in a language; the spirit, he says, is the vowels, which breathe life into those dead letters, and vowels do so because (with some licence) Boehme identifies the five of them with the tetragrammaton Moses heard out of the burning bush. Vowels, breath, spirit, and the name of Jesus – all are essentially one – revive and quicken the letters of a language which are dead because they are only letters, separated from the Word of which they ought to be part, and which alone can 'introduce the *holy Sense* again into the Sensual tongue' (*Works* 3.204). Such a cluster of ideas seems to lie behind the lines in '"Transcendentalism"' where Browning describes another mage, John of Halberstadt:

> Or some stout Mage like him of Halberstadt,
> John, who made things Boehme wrote thoughts about?
> He with a 'look you!' vents a brace of rhymes,
> And in there breaks the sudden rose herself,
> Over us, under, round us every side,
> Nay, in and out the tables and the chairs
> And musty volumes, Boehme's book and all, –
> Buries us with a glory, young once more,
> Pouring heaven into this shut house of life.   (37–45)

Here Browning images the dead world of sense as 'the tables and the chairs / And musty volumes,' while the living spirit is 'a brace of rhymes.' Rhyme, we remember, depends primarily on the repetition of vowel sounds, which are here 'vented' – expressed or exhaled. A 'brace' is anything which clasps or connects or fastens, and it may here be simply a pair of rhyming words, but the effect is the recovery of primal unity: heaven and 'this shut house of life' become one again. 'Who helps more, pray, to repair our loss' (34), Browning asks of John of Halberstadt.

He asks the same question of 'Another Boehme with a tougher book / And subtler meanings of what roses say' (35–6). Who is this other Boehme? A clue may lie in the fact that 'German Boehme' of line 22 was originally 'Swedish Boehme,' and Browning may simply have blundered, as he insisted to Dowden (Hood 103–4), or he may, as Richard Lines has recently argued, conflated Boehme with Emmanuel Swedenborg.[20] Certainly Browning would have found in Swedenborg a myth of language parallel to the one he found in Boehme. The speech of the angels, Swedenborg argues, is natural, 'flowing spontaneously from their affections and thoughts,' and 'the first language of the human race here on earth was of the like kind.'[21] 'But Man since that time cut himself off successively more and more from these heavenly communications, by transferring his affections from the Lord and from Heaven, to himself and the world, and so brought himself to relish no other delights, but what proceeded from the love of self and of the world, upon which his internal faculties, before open to Heaven, became shut, and his external faculties wide open to the world; and where this is the case, man is in light with regard to the things of this World, and in darkness with regard to the things of Heaven' (144). God, however, has not left human beings without compensation, and it is the Word. 'For when a Man reads the Word, and understands it in it's [sic] literal or external meaning, the Angels receive it according to it's internal or spiritual sense; for the Angels think spiritually, as Men think naturally; and though these two ways of thinking appear widely different, yet they come to the same by Correspondency. Thus it came to pass, that after Man had broken off his connection with Heaven, the Lord substituted the Word as a medium, whereby to restore that connection' (184–5).

In Boehme, then, and perhaps in Swedenborg, Browning encountered a myth of language which made rhyming and the breathing which creates it both a metaphor for the action of a quickening spirit – a conventional troping of breath – and the means whereby separate sounds are brought together in a single pattern, which restores the primal unity of letter and spirit, of sign and signified. No wonder the speaker in 'The Flight of the Duchess' refers to the 'chime' as 'wondrous.' To 'vent a brace of rhymes' is, in this context, to move language towards an idealist position to which Browning is attracted, and which seems to lie behind his fascination with doggerel, with repetitions of not just one but two or three syllables, and with unexpected or complex rhymes. The more difficult the search for a rhyme, the closer its finding brings us to the Word in which all things chime.

Chapter Six

'For how else know we save by worth of word?': *The Ring and the Book*

In spite of all that *The Ring and the Book* has to say about the inadequacies of language, the poem does affirm the 'worth of word.' That worth lies in the ability of language to make sense of images that would otherwise be unmeaning; in the ability of language to interpret and give new life to texts that would otherwise be lost; and in the ability of language to present a drama to be played out in the theatre of the reader's mind, where it becomes a stage in the development of the reader's soul. *The Ring and the Book,* in its encyclopedic structure, canvasses most of Browning's concerns with language, which appear in the poem (particularly in the framing books) as critical comment on its structure and way of proceeding. Hence the poem collapses the distinction between creation and criticism and anticipates Wilde's argument in 'The Critic as Artist,' that 'without the critical faculty, there is no artistic creation at all': every text, as one of Wilde's characters says, is an interpretation of an earlier text, itself the 'starting-point for a new creation.'[1] That critical relation between new and old is the main concern of Browning's title.

The poem begins with the words 'Do you see this Ring?,' a question signalling a way of proceeding which is that of the emblem: there is first of all a picture or a visual image. We note, however, that there is no guiding motto, and the *explicatio* we expect is no explanation at all but an account of the making of the ring. As a result of that opening question, we may picture a ring in our mind's eye, and we may even manage the embossed lily-flowers and the 'lilied loveliness' of the gold, but in doing so we are taking words which must be abstractions for us and attaching them to images from our own experience. Most readers have not seen the actual historical rings – there are two of them, as A.N. Kincaid has shown us in his 1980 essay sorting out scholarly confusion[2] – and while one of the rings is preserved in Balliol College Library, the other went missing from the British Museum in 1971. The ring Browning asks us to see is an abstraction, then, and the deictic, a gesture which is a dramatic moment between poet and reader, can point literally – the crucial adverb in this context – only to the letters, present in this line and in the title of this book and of the poem as a whole. Such a literal approach becomes, even at this early stage of our response, metaphoric: the reader carries 'this Ring' across to 'this poem,' with the understanding that the poem is circular in structure. Indeed, its circularity is apparent in the title of book 12, which reverses the words of the title of book 1. The rhetorical figure for such a reversal is antimetabole, and that figure, along with repetitions and periodic sentences, makes a ring, as we shall see, of some crucial passages in book 1.

There is one other point to note about this initial picture. When Browning elaborates on the picture by telling how the ring was fashioned, he twice refers to its making as a 'trick' of the 'craftsmen' (1.9) or 'artificer' (1.18). 'Trick' is etymologically linked with 'trifle' – Browning himself links the word with 'toying' and 'trifling' at 1.982–3 – and the link both foreshadows Browning's use of the word 'fancy' and introduces the element of play which, as we have seen in the chapter on Browning and music, indicates something which is 'whole' and 'sole,' itself and nothing else. 'Trick' is the interpretation or response which leads to a new creation. In the thirty lines describing the making of the ring, the 'trick' is the 'gold's alloy' which is mixed with the 'pure gold.' The 'pure gold' he describes as 'slivers,' 'mere oozings from the mine,' which are shaped and tempered by the alloy. The 'trick' – Browning uses the word at line 8, and again in line 18 – is the apparent disappearance of the alloy, its flying 'in fume' with 'a spirt / O' the proper fiery acid' (1.23–4), but one notes that the gold, which was initially only 'slivers' and 'oozings,' is now a ring: 'the shape remains' (1.26). That shape is the language of the poem, the 'alloy' or 'trick' which is both interpretation and creation.

But we are getting ahead of Browning's own interpretation. After he has presented the first of his major images and described the making of the ring in the first thirty lines, his question – anticipating that of the reader – is 'What of it?' (1.31). 'So what?' would be the colloquialism in our day. And colloquial as Browning's words are, they indicate that without interpretation – without words, that is – the picture might be said to mean something, but we cannot say precisely what, and so only words can tell us why we should care about the ring. Before Browning gives us the meaning of the image, however, he gives us the theory of the emblematic procedure he is using. The picture is 'A thing's sign,' he says: 'now for the thing signified' (1.32). The theory involves the two nouns Browning supplies in line 31: "T is a figure, a symbol, say.' That last word 'say' makes the theory tentative, hypothetical, and conditional. Is 'say' a verb in the indicative mood, a statement ('you say' or 'we say'), or is it a verb in the imperative mood, a command to the reader from a poet who knows what he is about; or – a stronger possibility – is it a shared action of poet and reader ('let us say'), an utterance which is conditional, which expresses a common interest, and which establishes a contract? That last possibility is the one I want to explore in Browning's juxtaposing of those two crucial nouns.

As we saw in chapter 1, the relation between the picture and the *explicatio* is the chief critical problem in the emblem. The relation may be, on the one hand, natural and 'hieroglyphic,' or it may be, on the other, rhetorical and 'fanciful.' In the former, the relationship is an essential one and is to be discovered; in the latter, the relationship is an arbitrary one, and is invented. Browning's nouns suggest both possibilities, though the latter is the stronger suggestion. 'Figure' is a rhetorical term, and indicates the action by which the poet takes the image – the ring – and turns it or tropes it, the result of which action is (as here) a metaphor. Browning carries one image across to another image – ring to book – and in doing so creates a riddle. There is no obvious connection between a ring and a book, in shape or in materials or in function, and so the 'thing signified' is no explanation at all, but rather an extension of the puzzle. The word 'symbol' suggests a different relation entirely. One might read the word in a Coleridgian sense, as an ontological term which is the basis of synecdoche because, as Coleridge explains both in *The Statesman's Manual* and in *Aids to Reflection*, the symbol is part of the whole which it represents, but I think Browning is more likely to understand the word in its Greek sense, where it is not primarily an ontological term but the sign of a relationship which has been undertaken and which is to be completed at some future date – a token, in short, which is the sign of a contract. In the words of Marc Shell, 'Before the invention of money in archaic Greece, contracts of exchange required witnesses and/or visible *symbola*. *Symbola* were pledges, pawns, or covenants from an earlier understanding to bring together a part of something that had been divided specifically for the purpose of later comparison.'[3] A ring was one of the usual *symbola*. That convention appears in the poem when Margherita, Pompilia's maid, tempts her to respond to the apparent advances of Caponsacchi: '"Give me a glove, / A ring to show for token!"' (7.1091–2). Richard Chenevix Trench gives a related meaning of the word 'symbol' in his *On Some Deficiencies in Our English Dictionaries* (1857), the papers which set the program for the New English Diction- ary. Though Trench was a Coleridgian, he talks about the meaning the Greek *symbolon* 'sometimes had, namely, the contribution which each person at a pic-nic throws into the common stock.'[4] Here we have a sense of a host of heterogeneous or miscellaneous things brought together, not because they share a common nature, but because their very variety ultimately contributes to a single purpose and pattern. Trench himself uses the word 'symbol' in this particular sense on the penultimate page of *On Some Deficiencies*, when he is talking about the need for volunteer readers in the compiling of the new dictionary, work modelled on pioneering work in Germany. Jacob Grimm used 'no less than eighty-three volunteer coadjutors, who had undertaken each to read for him one or more authors, and who had thrown into the com- mon stock of his great work their several "symbols," the result of their several toils' (56). Trench's use of the word recovers a sense of it obscured by the Coleridgian understanding of the term, and allows us to see that a symbol may be any one of many bits and pieces or frag- ments which one gathers without knowing their full significance or the way in which they fit into the totality of things (although one has faith that they do fit into a totality). Linking the fragments is like the piecing together of a puzzle. After its initial acts of inference and pattern-mak- ing, the mind gradually discovers that the pieces are indeed parts of a whole, as the poet's contract – his ring – promised.

One early verbal imitation of such a process is the extraordinarily long sentence with which Browning confronts the reader in lines 50 through 75. The sentence is a syntactical and rhetorical puzzle, but by the time we reach the end of it, all the disparate words and phrases and clauses – its *symbola* – fall into place in a structure which is circular. Wil- liam E. Baker has already analysed this sentence in his *Syntax in English Poetry 1870–1930* (1967), to show how 'the poet has attempted to distort the sentence mold in order to follow the nimble and intricate move- ments of his mind.'[5] The 'fragmented forms,' 'parenthetical disruptions,' 'labyrinthine structures,' and the 'especially high percentage of elabo- rate elements, many of them composed of three or four subordinate clauses in addition to the main one' (95), all 'illustrate the activity of a mind at once keenly observing and imaginative' (99). While the sentence presents the actual darting hither and thither of a mind active in perception, it also presents a puzzle for the reader, a puzzle which embodies the sense of the word 'symbol' we are exploring. Here is the whole sentence:

This book, – precisely on that palace-step
Which, meant for lounging knaves o' the Medici,
Now serves re-venders to display their ware, –
'Mongst odds and ends of ravage, picture-frames
White through the worn gilt, mirror-sconces chipped,
Bronze angel-heads once knobs attached to chests,
(Handled when ancient dames chose forth brocade)
Modern chalk drawings, studies from the nude,
Samples of stone, jet, breccia, porphyry
Polished and rough, sundry amazing busts
In baked earth, (broken, Providence be praised!)
A wreck of tapestry, proudly-purposed web
When reds and blues were indeed red and blue,
Now offered as a mat to save bare feet
(Since carpets constitute a cruel cost)
Treading the chill scagliola bedward: then
A pile of brown-etched prints, two *crazie* each,
Stopped by a conch a-top from fluttering forth
– Sowing the Square with works of one and the same
Master, the imaginative Sienese
Great in the scenic backgrounds – (name and fame
None of you know, nor does he fare the worse:)
From these ... Oh, with a Lionard going cheap
If it should prove, as promised, that Joconde
Whereof a copy contents the Louvre! – these
I picked this book from.   (1.50–75)

One notes, to begin with, that the poem as a whole has its beginning in the world of ordinary experience, which Browning typically images as a miscellany: the articles for sale in the street market. He does not, like his Romantic predecessors, focus on nature and all its variety, but rather on human artifacts, and those objects, piled haphazardly and varying widely in age, condition, and worth, are all *symbola*, tokens of human relationships. The very listing of them indicates the extent to which they stir Browning's interest and his imagination. One notes, second, that all these tokens of human relationships, heterogeneous as they are, belong within a scheme which (Browning does not blush to suggest) is Providence. 'I found this book,' he says, 'when a Hand, / Always above my shoulder, pushed me once' (1.38, 40–1), and the hand, like the finger Robert refers to in his letters to Elizabeth during their courtship, is his image (derived from the emblem tradition) for God's providential guidance of his life ('every moment of my life,' he told Elizabeth two days after their marriage, 'brings fresh proof to me of the intervention of Providence').[6] In this particular passage in book 1, Browning goes even further: 'Mark the predestination!' he says in a parenthesis in line 40. 'Predestination' is a powerful word from Calvinist theology, and in these lines it makes even stronger the suggestion that the street market, so miscellaneous to the eye of sense, is really, to the eye of the understanding, the scene of relations, not just among human beings, but between human beings and God. The long sentence I have quoted is the verbal representation of a jumble or miscellany, all the parts of which gradually fall into place in one governing syntactical pattern. The syntax is, in our first linear experience of it, labyrinthine. The first two words are 'This book,' and, because we are conditioned by ordinary English word order, we proceed on the assumption that 'This book' is the subject of the sentence. Hence we go on, waiting for the main verb and for the predicate, through a parenthesis with its elaborating phrases and clauses, and then through a series of adjectival phrases beginning with the preposition ''Mongst.' With 'From these' at line 72 we seem to be coming to a sorting out of the syntactical puzzle, but it is only with the last words of the sentence – 'these / I picked this book from' – that we finally have a main clause. It reveals that 'this book,' which we had expected to be the subject, is in fact the object of the sentence. As a result of such a lengthy and riddling suspension of the main clause, the sentence is periodic, a word derived etymologically from *peri*, around, and *hodós*, a way. Hence the conventional metaphor for periodicity is the circle, and the circling round of this sentence from 'This book' to 'this book' is the making of a verbal ring which allows us both to see and to experience the sense of Browning's 'sign' and 'thing signified.' The circular pattern of the sentence I have just been analysing is elsewhere in the early lines of the poem. The account of his finding and buying the book (lines 33 to 83), for instance, is framed by his paying a *lira* : 'Gave a *lira* for it' at line 39, while 'a *lira* made it mine' in line 83. There is another circle in his handling of the book: in lines 33 and 34, he tosses and catches it again, and in line 84 'this I toss and take again.'

One detail of Browning's playing with the book – and it is only a detail – is the action of twirling it about 'By the crumpled vellum covers' (1.35). The action is emblematic. The historical Browning takes the historical book and makes it a circle, a visual image of the artistic action Browning will undertake with the book's contents. That action is a turning or troping of the contents, such turning being the essence of interpretation. One can even see in Browning's twirling about of the book a hint of the progress we found in Paracelsus's great speech. The book is square – 'Do you see this square old yellow Book'? Browning asks – and his artistry is circular, so that he is taking a square and making it into a circle. The circle is an ancient picture of heaven and perfection, the square (in so far as it is associated with the four elements) of earth. 'Squaring the circle' – strictly speaking, the phrase ought to be 'circling the square ' – was one concern of the alchemists, who would thereby make heaven and earth one. 'Putting the infinite within the finite' (the business of all poetry) is Browning's abstract expression of the idea in his 1855 letter to Ruskin.[7] His more concrete aim in making a ring out of a book – to 'save the soul' – is imaged in this same fusion of square and circle.

Browning's great poem, like *The Pilgrim's Progress*, begins with a man reading a book. The book is a challenge to him, and the reading of it is not a casual matter but a crucial act: just as Christian, spurred by the Bible, undertakes a quest for his salvation, so Browning, pushed by a Hand to read the 'old yellow Book,' rewrites it, knowing that the new book 'shall mean, beyond the facts, / Suffice the eye and save the soul beside' (12.862–3). 'And save the soul!' (12.864): Browning's repetition is both an affirmation of the significance of reading and responding for him personally, and a challenge to his readers, for whom Browning's poem is yet another book to be rewritten. We remember that Bunyan also insisted that his book was a challenge to his readers. His metaphors, allegories, and 'Dark Figures,' he says in 'The Author's Apology for his Book,' are all puzzles, but 'My dark and cloudy words they do but hold / The Truth, as Cabinets inclose the Gold.' 'Now Reader, I have told my Dream to thee,' he says in his conclusion: 'See if thou canst Interpret it to me; / Or to thy self, or Neighbour.' The interpretation of a book is the creation of a new book, then, and Browning's telling the story of his act of reading is both an account of his creation of the poem and a puzzle for his readers. He begins with a physical act which is an emblem of translation.

That act is taking the 'old yellow Book' home. Circling may be the governing action of troping and interpreting, but there is a related action, carrying across, which is derived etymologically from 'meta-phor,' and which appears actually and historically here in Browning's reading of the book between San Lorenzo square and Casa Guidi, his arrival marking the moment when 'I had mastered the contents, knew the whole truth' (1.117). He has carried the book across, from market to home, and made it his own. 'Translation' is the Latin version of carrying across, and Browning, presenting the title page of the 'old yellow Book,' begins with its original Latin but quickly drops it: 'nay, / Better trans-late' (1.120–1). Browning insists on the accuracy and literalness of his translation ('Word for word. / So ran the title-page' 1.131–2), just as he will insist on the accuracy of the 'whole truth' he discovers in the story, and so he panders to the ordinary understanding of the word 'fact.' His treatment of that word, however, forces us to see it in a new way and to reevaluate a theory of truth which could be called a picture or a mirror theory: that our words must correspond to something outside us called 'facts.'

Browning was well aware of an assumption among his readers, the 'British Public' whom he addresses directly from time to time, that the material in the 'old yellow Book' is true because it is documented histor-ical fact, and that the material in *The Ring and the Book* is untrue because it is the work of a poet: '"And don't you deal in poetry, make-believe, / And the white lies it sounds like?"' (1.455–6). Browning knows perfectly well that such an assumption is naïve empiricism. A fact is a fact only because it is perceived to be so, and every fact is not only a choice made by the mind out of the welter of our ordinary sensible experience but also an interpretation of that experience. Browning appeals to the naïve empiricism of his readers by calling the materials in the 'old yellow Book' 'pure crude fact' (1.86) and 'the fact untampered with' (1.365) or by saying that 'in this book lay absolutely truth, / Fanciless fact, the doc-uments indeed' (1.143–4), but he nearly always juxtaposes such state-ments with reminders that interpretation is embedded in fact. In one early passage he gives a materialist account of interpretation, saying that the fact is 'Secreted from man's life when hearts beat hard, / And brains, high-blooded, ticked two centuries since' (1.87–8). Later he iden-tifies fact with legal interpretation: the documents are 'Primary lawyer-pleadings for, against, / The aforesaid Five' (1.145–6), 'Pages of proof this way, and that way proof' (1.239). (One notes in passing that the antimetabole of this last line is the embodiment of Browning's ring-mak-ing or circle-making of his materials.) In Lockeian terms, the documents are opinion, which Browning satirizes in his sound patterns: 'Thus wrangled, brangled, jangled they a month' (1.241). Opinion is not the province of the lawyers alone. Of the truth with which he is concerned Browning says, 'Here is it all i' the book at last, as first, / There it was all i' the heads and hearts of Rome' (1.414–15). In short, the 'old yellow Book' is a miscellany of opinions, as various in its views as the wares in the street market, and Browning's poem is not an interpretation of fact but an interpretation of interpretations. The facts which are his materials are 'fancy with fact,' and for every writer who turns to an earlier text, 'Fancy with fact is just one fact the more' (1.464).

The play of opinion is finally not an end in itself, either in Locke or in Browning. Locke explores knowledge and opinion and carefully defines the degrees of each because his final concern is with conduct, a course of action that involves choices having a bearing on our moral, social, and spiritual lives. 'Our Business here,' Locke says in the Introduction to his *Essay*, 'is not to know all things, but those which concern our Conduct. If we can find out those Measures, whereby a rational Creature put in that State, which Man is in, in this World, may, and ought to govern his Opinions, and Actions depending thereon, we need not be troubled, that some other things escape our Knowledge' (1.1.6). Browning too is concerned with conduct, especially the act of choosing, a moral decision that has a bearing on our spiritual lives in so far as it is an incident in the development of our souls. In book 1 Browning keeps making his text challenge his readers:

> I may ask,
> Rather than think to tell you, more thereof, –
> Ask you not merely who were he and she,
> Husband and wife, what manner of mankind,
> But how you hold concerning this and that
> Other yet-unnamed actor in the piece.   (1.377–82).

Of Caponsacchi's conduct, 'was it right or wrong or both?' (1.388); of the conduct of the Comparini, 'What say you to the right or wrong of that' (1.392). When Browning introduces the Pope's monologue in book 1, he reminds his readers that the Pope's is 'the ultimate / Judgment save yours' (1.1220–1) – a reminder reiterated at the beginning of book 12 ('You have seen his [Guido's] act, / By my power – may-be, judged it by your own' 12.9–10).

Browning identifies judgment with the action of his fancy, which is responsible both for the interpretation of the 'old yellow Book' and for the shape of the poem. These ideas he sets out in the djereed simile. After he has asserted that 'Fancy with fact is just one fact the more' (1.464), he explains:

> To-wit, that fancy has informed, transpierced,
> Thridded and so thrown fast the facts else free,
> As right through ring and ring runs the djereed
> And binds the loose, one bar without a break.   (1.465–8)

The lines combine two figures: the javelin hitting the mark (a metaphor for correct judgment) and the javelin threading the rings, 'one bar without a break' (a metaphor for the poet's shaping of the poem).

The holding together of interpretation, judgment, and artistic shaping by the circle metaphor is not without its difficulties and complexities. There is a danger that the endless play of contrary opinions may result in circling round without spiralling upwards, in endless repetition rather than progressive turning. Such repetitive turning is conventionally associated with hell and often imaged as a whirlpool, like that which T.S. Eliot's Phlebas the Phoenician enters in The Waste Land's 'Death by Water,' or that which Margaret Avison's swimmers in 'The Swimmer's Moment' refuse, 'so their bland-blank faces turn and turn / Pale and forever on the rim of suction.' Browning represents such turning in the schemes of antimetabole, which can have a bad sense as well as a good one, and antithesis. At the point where the poet asks whether or not the murderers should be consigned to hell – 'stand or fall?' (1.638) – both schemes appear in the response of 'the world come to judgment': '"I say, the spear should fall – should stand, I say!"' (1.639). Browning continues:

> There prattled they, discoursed the right and wrong,
> Turned wrong to right, proved wolves sheep and sheep wolves,
> So that you scarce distinguished fell from fleece.   (1.645–7)

This sentence proceeds in a loose way, clause hooked to preceding clause, the reversals turning the meaning round and round, until we reach the word 'Till' in line 648, a moment when we realize that the loose structure has become periodic, and that the rhetorical shift corresponds to an advance in judgment: 'Till out spoke the great guardian of the fold' (1.648). The advance represented by the Pope's judgment is a historical fact, but Browning goes on to talk about the shrivelling of fact in memory: it has 'Dwindled into no bigger than a book' (1.671) from whose sensible shape the circle has disappeared entirely:

> and that little, left
> By the roadside 'mid the ordure, shards and weeds.
> Until I haply, wandering that way,
> Kicked it up, turned it over, and recognized,
> For all the crumblement, this abacus,
> This square old yellow book ...   (1.672–7)

The actions are ordinary – 'Kicked it up, turned it over' – but the turning is crucial: it stops the dwindling and starts the circle expanding and reaching upwards again.

Browning's *explicatio* of his opening image, then, is a complex and riddling one. It proceeds by indirection because of Browning's sense of his audience, the 'British Public, ye who like me not' (1.410). Their assumptions about the nature of historical fact and the truth of poetry govern Browning's argument as much as the 'British Reader' governs the Editor's way of proceeding in *Sartor Resartus*. Hence, when Browning at last provides a motto for the ring which is his poem, the lesson seems, in the context of the reports and letters and the sermon of book 12, acceptable enough to a public unsympathetic to language as anything other than a tool for practical life:

> So, British Public, who may like me yet,
> (Marry and amen!) learn one lesson hence
> Of many which whatever lives should teach:
> This lesson, that our human speech is naught,
> Our human testimony false, our fame
> And human estimation words and wind.   (12.831–6).

The motto or lesson – 'our human speech is naught' – is a sweeping indictment of language and, coming from someone whose stock-in-trade is language, is hardly to be taken at face value. For Browning rejects as false 'our human testimony,' the spoken evidence of witnesses which produces facts, and so undermines all human perception; he condemns 'fame,' understood not just as reputation but (as its etymology reveals) that which people say; and he condemns 'human estimation' or judgment which, as Locke taught, is our guide to conduct where sure and certain knowledge is missing, as it often is, so that we could not get along without opinion or 'estimation.' Facts, speech, and opinion are all, according to this 'lesson,' nothing. The alliterative linking of 'words' and 'wind' is also a metaphoric connection, and where wind might be in another context inspiration or the Holy Spirit, here it is simply emptiness, with the suggestion of meaninglessness. There is also, however, a sly characterization of readers who would accept this 'lesson' as fools. The fool, as we saw in chapter 1, is etymologically a windbag, but appears here as an ass, the long-eared 'brother' who is clearly one of Browning's audience. 'How look a brother in the face,' Browning asks,

> and say
> 'Thy right is wrong, eyes hast thou yet art blind,
> Thine ears are stuffed and stopped, despite their length,
> And, oh, the foolishness thou countest faith!'   (12.841–4)

A poet cannot teach directly, and so the explicit lesson of the poem and its sweeping condemnation of language are such that even a long-eared 'brother' must have reservations about it and must think of exceptions – such as his own speech. Moreover, Browning is not simply saying one thing and meaning another. In his experience, words often are foolish, so his lesson is not untrue, but it is to be held in conjunction with its opposite, to which Browning (perhaps conscious of the logical difficulties and contradictions in using speech to say that 'our human speech is naught') immediately turns. Some speech evokes truth, and that speech involves words as they are used in poetry.

'Art may tell a truth / Obliquely' (12.855–6). (How felicitous is that enjambement, which forces the eye to bend – the root meaning of 'oblique' – and turn down and back to the beginning of the next line!) In this motto – the true and long-delayed motto for the emblem with which Browning began the poem as a whole – writing a book 'shall mean, beyond the facts, / Suffice the eye and save the soul beside' (12.862–3). As so often happens when Browning is talking about art, he compares his own art – poetry – with music and painting. Poetry and painting both appeal to the eye through imagery, but poetry is better than painting because one can 'twice show truth, / Beyond mere imagery on the wall' (12.858–9). The imagery is one truth, but words which make its meaning explicit are a second and stronger truth. Poetry is also better than music, better even than Beethoven, whom Browning names explicitly in line 861 in the edition of 1889. The music from one's mind that

Browning mentions in line 860 is, like the imagery of painting, full of meaning, but its meaning is not manifest without words. Hence poetry, which uses both imagery and prosody, is the most effective of the arts because it 'shall mean, beyond the facts.' Like painting, it will 'suffice the eye,' but it also 'save[s] the soul.' Browning is not suggesting a narrow and limited view of the meaning of poetry, where the lesson is stated by the poet and where his voice is accepted as authoritative and final. Instead, Browning's interpretation of that collection of interpretations – the 'old yellow Book' – becomes in turn a fact to be interpreted by every reader. It is the struggle to find meaning which is soul-saving. 'Are means to the end, themselves in part the end?' (1.705), Browning asks in book 1. The answer is clearly yes.

The poem, like all of Browning's works after his experiments with play-writing, is designed to be read silently, and its drama is to be played out in the theatre of the reader's mind. In his account of finding and first responding to his materials, Browning makes clear the fact that he first read the 'old yellow Book' as a dramatic text, major parts of which were written and printed by the prosecution and defence lawyers and never actually spoken in a courtroom – a historical fact specially suited to Browning's purposes. As Richard D. Altick points out in his notes to the Penguin edition of the poem, 'In conformance with Roman practice, there were no "courtroom scenes" in which the two sides confronted each other. The legal arguments were presented to the court in printed form.'[8] Several times in Book 1 Browning refers to this practice: 'Thus wrangled, brangled, jangled they a month, / – Only on paper, pleadings all in print' (1.241–2); and later he refers to 'the pen which simulated tongue / On paper and saved all except the sound / Which never was' (1.1119–21). His reading of legal texts was thus much closer to our reading of a dramatic poem than might at first be apparent. Like his source, he relies on 'the printed voice.' That phrase appears in a passage dealing with Bottini, the public prosecutor who 'only spoke in print,' and it is an oxymoron which provides the title for Eric Griffiths's 1989 book and his important examination of the convention of the speaking voice in printed poetry.[9] 'You miss the very tones o' the voice' (1.1200), Browning says of Bottini's speech, and the printed text is a 'cold black score, mere music for the mind' (1.1216), but such regrets are only minor and generally uncharacteristic notes in a poem in which the purposes and effects depend upon a silent reading. When Browning introduces the poem's mode of presentation, he sounds like a playwright: 'Let this old woe step on the stage again! / Act itself o'er anew for men to judge' (1.824–5). Then, characteristically, he rejects 'the stage' with its sights and sounds: the piece is to 'Act itself o'er anew,' 'Not by the very sense and sight indeed' (1.826) but 'by voices we call evidence' (1.833). In a parenthesis, Browning attacks the sights and sounds of the stage as inadequate access to the inner lives of the dramatis personae: 'the very sense and sight indeed'

> take at best imperfect cognizance,
> Since, how heart moves brain, and how both move hand,
> What mortal ever in entirety saw?   (1.827–9)

The 'voices we call evidence' have their limitations too, since they are a mingling of truth and falsehood,

> Uproar in the echo, live fact deadened down,
> Talked over, bruited abroad, whispered away,
> Yet helping us to all we seem to hear ...   (1.834–6)

Then comes Browning's line defending the printed words of his dramatic characters: 'For how else know we save by worth of word?' (1. 837). That line could be a motto for the dramatic monologue, considered as a genre.

Word proves its worth in interpretation, which is Browning's central concern in the books inside his frame. When in book 1 he introduces the voices which will speak in the body of his poem, he uses a variety of metaphors for the shapings. There is the image of hitting the mark, the usual metaphor for correct judgment, which Half-Rome fails to manage (he 'lets fall wide / O' the mark his finger meant to find, and fix / Truth' 1.856–8); there is 'the web of words' (1.1277) Guido weaves to catch Pompilia; and there is language as clothing: Bottini's argument 'goes as easy as a glove / O'er good and evil, smoothens both to one' (1.1180–1). There are the flowers of rhetoric used by Arcangeli (1.1156) and the extension of that trope to the arguments of both lawyers, 'Truth in a flowery foam' (1.1113). There is the 'divining-rod' (1.1108) for the discovery of truth, and there is the 'recognized machine' (1.1110) of law, 'the patent truth-extracting process' (1.1114). We note, as we proceed through this catalogue, that the one sense which seems to govern all these tropes is sight. A limited or partial or false view is associated with looking obliquely or askance, such as the crowd's 'plague of squint' at 1.879, or the 'swerving' (1.859) of Half-Rome, which Browning defines as a bias that skews one's sight, 'The instinctive theorizing whence a fact / Looks to the eye as the eye likes the look' (1.863–4).

One might think that the opposite of such bent sight would be seeing something straight on (as when, for instance, Childe Roland turns from the hoary cripple and his 'malicious eye / Askance' to face the sights of his present situation, 'as far as eye could strain'), but in *The Ring and the Book* Browning suggests a more complex and comprehensive kind of sight. When Browning says at the end of book 12 that 'Art may tell a truth / Obliquely,' how are we to distinguish the bending or slanting view of art from the squinting and swerving of Browning's characters? One answer to that question is that there is no distinction: all language is interpretation, and every speech comes from a particular mind and gives evidence of the seeing of a particular eye. A second and better answer is that there is a difference, because the artist is aware that any one squinting or swerving is, like the 'rag of flesh, scrap of bone' (1.753) he comes upon as resuscitator, a 'fragment of a whole' (1.752). Browning images that whole as an orb which, at any one time and in any one place, we can see from only one angle. The artist, however, is capable of turning the orb (with the suggestion in that word 'turning' of troping or interpreting) and of presenting another view or perspective. When we look, with the help of the artist, from enough angles, we will, like David, 'have gone the whole round of creation,' and will have discovered that the way round is also the way up. Browning images the way up at the end of book 1 as a ladder and likens it to the 'beanstalk-rungs' by which Jack in the children's story climbed up to heaven (1.1346–7). The orb appears in the 'glass ball' simile at the end of book 1.

The simile comes after a familiar passage on the turning of the seasons and the whirling of colours into white ('The variance now, the eventual unity' 1.1363):

Man, like a glass ball with a spark a-top,
Out of the magic fire that lurks inside,
Shows one tint at a time to take the eye:
Which, let a finger touch the silent sleep,
Shifted a hair's-breadth shoots you dark for bright,
Suffuses bright with dark, and baffles so
Your sentence absolute for shine or shade.
Once set such orbs, – white styled, black stigmatized, –
A-rolling, see them once on the other side
Your good men and your bad men every one,

From Guido Franceschini to Guy Faux,
Oft would you rub your eyes and change your names.   (1.1367–78)

Interpretation makes possible the play of opposites – dark and bright, black and white – and to make one thing into its opposite may be either a lie or a wonderful transformation in which, as we saw in chapter 1, sins that are scarlet become white as snow. Browning calls such a turning both an abuse of language and a miracle. The former appears in a letter to Elizabeth when he is talking about various accounts of Socrates and condemns them with a quotation from Tennyson: 'Yet see how "people" can turn this out of its sense, – "say" their say on the simplest, plainest word or deed, and change it to its opposite! "God's great gift of speech abused" indeed!' (*Correspondence* 12:134). That same act, however, may be a saving one, as in the lines that present the whirling of colours into white: 'The variance now, the eventual unity, / Which make the miracle' (1.1363–4). The 'variance' comes about because man 'shows one tint at a time to take the eye'; that tint is the partial view or squint that characterizes our ordinary sight, but it is the basis nonetheless of unqualified and (apparently) final judgment, the 'sentence absolute for shine or shade.' If a finger shifts the orb – and the finger could be God's, or the artist's – we have a totally different view of the same thing, and 'bright' gives way to its opposite 'dark.' Turning provides an even more comprehensive view: 'Once set such orbs ... / A-rolling, see them once on the other side,' and the result would be such clear and full sight that one is scarce ready to credit it (rubbing one's eyes is a conventional gesture of disbelief). The final clause, 'and change your names,' is the most surprising one of all. Name-changing in the Bible (in the stories of Jacob wrestling with the angel, and Saul becoming Paul after being stricken blind) is the result of a profound change or conversion, after which – if one assumes that there is a connection of some kind between one's name and one's nature – one takes the label which symbolizes the new self. The passage is a remarkable conjunction of Browning's central concerns with language: the seeing from different perspectives which are realized in his dramatic characters; the turning which is the conventional metaphor for troping and interpreting; the expanded sight and new understanding which make engaged reading a soul-saving conversion. Addressing the British Public, 'ye who like me not,' Browning offers his language as the means of that change. 'Whoso runs may read' (1.1381), he says, and though the specific allusion is to Habakkuk 2:2, Browning is drawing upon Paul's metaphor of life as a race to be run (1 Corinthians 9:24), and on the writer of Hebrews ('let us run with patience the race that is set before us' 12:1). Browning, who so often links words with alliteration, here links 'read' and 'run,' and the link is metaphorical as well as alliterative.

The 'words and wind' alliteration, part of the 'one lesson' of the poem, can be taken as a test case for Browning's advice about setting orbs 'a-rolling' and scarcely crediting the result. The very same phrase which characterizes human beings as fools also characterizes words as filled with the Holy Spirit, conventionally troped as wind and associated with sustaining and interpreting. 'God moves in a mysterious way,' says William Cowper in one of the best known of his *Olney Hymns*, and Browning is fascinated with the workings of the Spirit in conjunction with our human faculties, with our human powers of interpreting and making choices. In *The Ring and the Book*, the Holy Spirit pushes Browning to buy the 'old yellow Book' and then sustains him in rewriting it ('The life in me abolished the death of things' 1.520) and in interpreting it. Browning explicitly refers to 'A spirit' when he is talking about his resuscitating of the historical characters:

> A spirit laughs and leaps through every limb,
> And lights my eye, and lifts me by the hair,
> Letting me have my will again with these ...   (1.776–8).

Browning is more circumspect, more ironic, when dealing with his fancy. Appealing as usual to the naïve empiricism of his British readers, he does not provide any other name for this interpretive power within him, and instead challenges the reader to provide one:

> This that I mixed with truth, motions of mine
> That quickened, made the inertness malleolable
> O' the gold was not mine, – what's your name for this?   (1.701–3)

The answer ought to be the Holy Spirit. In the *Correspondence*, it is Elizabeth who takes Robert's talk about inspiration and names the agent of the creative act. When he writes to her that 'the more one sits and thinks over the creative process, the more it confirms itself as "inspiration," nothing more nor less' (*Correspondence* 10:265), she replies:

> Yes, I quite believe as you do that what is called the 'creative process' in works of Art, is just inspiration & no less – which made somebody say to

me not long since, – 'And so, you think that Shakespeare's Othello was of the effluence of the Holy Ghost'? – rather a startling deduction ... only not quite as final as might appear to somebodies perhaps.

Elizabeth then goes on to pursue the idea, which is clearly one she accepts:

At least it does not prevent my going on to agree with the saying of *Spiri-dion* ... do you remember? ... 'Tout ce que l'homme appelle inspiration, je l'appelle aussi révelation,' ... if there is not something too selfevident in it after all – my sole objection! And is it not true that your inability to analyze the mental process in question, is one of the proofs of the fact of inspiration? (*Correspondence* 10:266)

Milton had claimed the Holy Spirit as his inspiration for *Paradise Lost*; Browning, more circumspect, challenges his readers to identify his source of inspiration – and theirs.

We turn now to the concerns with language in the body of the poem. The organization of the framed books is clear enough: there are three groups or rings of books, each ring containing three speakers; one is for Pompilia, one is against her, and one is a 'third something.' Book 11 does not fit into this pattern, but it completes a progression from characters who are not participants in the action to the principals themselves to the lawyers and the ultimate human judge, whose decision is confirmed, perhaps too clearly, in Guido's second monologue, when 'the true words come last' (1.1281). Boyd Litzinger has called the sequence of groups of books the 'Triad of Rumor' (books 2 to 4), the 'Triad of Testimony' (books 5 to 7), and the 'Triad of Judgement' (books 8 to 10),[10] but all the speakers are concerned with interpretation: its nature, its authority, and its bearing upon one's life and one's soul. By the time the reader has reached book 11, he or she has encountered most of Browning's concerns with language, so that the poem is, as one would expect in the epic, encyclopedic in its exploration of the medium of its own existence.

In the first ring of three books, the model for interpretation is the emblem: two speakers begin with a picture or image, while the third (as the 'something' beyond the binary opposition of the first two) does not. The interpretations of Half-Rome and The Other Half-Rome, limited and biased as they are, are nonetheless of some importance in their lives and in the particular circumstances in which they find themselves. Ter-tium Quid, ostensibly detached and objective, interprets without coming to any firm conclusion, and when he says at the end of his monologue, 'only, all this talk, talked, / 'T was not for nothing that we talked, I hope?' (4.1635–6), he and we both realize that the talk has indeed been for nothing. The emblematic procedure is clearest in book 2. The picture at its beginning is that of the bodies of the Comparini laid out in San Lorenzo in Lucina, and Half-Rome (whom we hear as echoing the opening portions of book 1) says to his listener, the cousin of his wife's lover, 'I'll tell you like a book' (2. 4). Like the poet himself in book 1, Half-Rome keeps asking if his listener sees, and seeing is clearly a metaphor for interpretation. 'Sir, do you see?' (2.16), he asks of the sight in the church, and of the altar-step he says, 'For see' (2.52). The seeing is the reading of meaning: the Comparini deserved what they got, and now lie dead on the same spot where they perpetrated the lie about Pompilia's birth: 'Even the blind can see a providence here' (2.87). Half-Rome has his counterpart in Luca Cini, who boasts that he has seen many dead bodies, 'Yet all was poor to this I live and see. / Here the world's wickedness seals up the sum' (2.124–5). 'I'm useful at explaining things,' Luca boasts (2.144), but his explanations are limited: he can give only a physical account of the causes and appearance of the wounds, or shake his head over a wicked world. Half-Rome's reading of the murder is much more focused and urgent. 'Look me in the face!' (2.1469), he says to his listener near the end of his monologue, and he intends his listener to see a wronged husband who is prepared to act, as Guido ought to have acted when he came upon the pair of lovers in the inn at Castelnuovo. Half-Rome brings together seeing, reading, and interpreting in introducing the lesson:

> What, are we blind? How can we fail to see,
> This crowd of miseries make the man a mark,
> Accumulate on one ... devoted head
> For our example, yours and mine who read
> Its lesson thus ...   (2.1479–83)

Like Half-Rome, The Other Half-Rome begins with a picture, 'Little Pompilia ... under the white hospital-array' (3.2, 4) which he then tropes: she is a flower (3.5), a child (3.89), a lamb (3.462 and 642), and a 'lily of a maiden' (3.365). The tropes make Pompilia a type both of the Virgin (Abate Paolo's wooing on Guido's behalf is a parody of the Annunciation) and of Christ. The typology, however, takes a sentimental turn when The Other Half-Rome confesses that 'I ... have no wife, / Being yet sensitive in my degree / As Guido' (3.1678–80). His reading of his initial picture of Pompilia has none of the urgency of Half-Rome's reading of the dead bodies of the Comparini. His listener is a shadowy figure, and though Other Half-Rome alludes, in the last lines of his monologue, to a legal contract or business arrangement of some kind, there seems to be little direct relation between it and his reading of Pompilia. Instead, he refers to a 'lie' (3.1684) and a 'theft' (3.1686) and an affront to his honour, and the sensitive man turns out to be the mercurial man, suddenly threatening and ready to 'deal death around!' (3.1690). Though Guido is the explicit object of his wrath, we know nothing about other persons who might feel it, and so his reading of the case is for us more of a riddle than Half-Rome's.

We turn now to the three central characters in the story – Guido, Caponsacchi, and Pompilia – and to their self-consciousness about their language in their monologues. Their concerns are all related to one major part of language theory, which is naming or (to use the verb which Browning himself uses) 'calling.' Browning's treatment of that theory might be labelled (if we may borrow a phrase which is the title of one of James Reaney's children's plays) 'names and nicknames,' partly because the word 'nickname' turns up in crucial passages in these monologues, and partly because names are, as Locke taught, arbitrary – they are the result, that is, of human judgment. The word 'name,' as the three central characters use it, often indicates correct judgment, while a 'nickname' is, as its etymology ('eke' name) suggests, an addition or substitute for the true 'name.' The motive for nicknames, as Johnson gives it in his *Dictionary,* is a bad one: scoffing, contempt, derision. The motives the three central characters detect in nicknames are more complex, but for all of them 'nicknames' are opposed to true 'names,' and establish a binary pattern of the false and the true, a pattern which must in turn be judged by every reader of these monologues.

In both books 5 and 11, Guido presents himself as a plain-speaker who exposes the 'lies' of others:

I killed Pompilia Franceschini, Sirs;
Killed too the Comparini, husband, wife,
Who called themselves, by a notorious lie,
Her father and her mother to ruin me.
There's the irregular deed: you want no more
Than right interpretation of the same,
And truth so far – am I to understand?   (5.109–15)

His plain-speaking goes along with a contempt for rhetoric (he draws attention to his own way of proceeding at one point as 'a rhetorician's trick' 5.78), and, like Tertium Quid (and Locke), he makes a sharp distinction between rhetoric, which is lying, and plain-speaking, which is truth-telling. Tertium Quid had troped lying as 'decent wrappage' (4.523), and Guido is close to the same trope when he talks about the 'lies' that disguise sexual desires:

> When you chaunt us next
> Epithalamium full to overflow
> With praise and glory of white womanhood,
> The chaste and pure – troll no such lies o'er lip!
> Put in their stead a crudity or two,
> Such short and simple statement of the case
> As youth chalks on our walls at spring of year!   (5.591–7)

Sexual desires are not, however, Guido's main motive, which comes to the fore in his second monologue. 'Then take the word you want!' (11.514), he tells the two priests who are his listeners. The word they want is a confession ('I ought in decency / Confess to you that I deserve my fate, / Am guilty' 11.411–13) and the word they get is not so much a confession as it is a revelation of evil, without any of the conviction of sin or the contrition involved in a confession. The confessional '"word of the man's very self"' (11.512) ought to be part of a profound change, but Guido finally evokes 'something changeless at the heart of me' (11.2392). That something changeless is evil itself, mysterious, ineradicable, and powerful. Hatred is the expression of evil, and it is, as Daniel Karlin argues, 'the source of Guido's creativity, of his aesthetic sense, of his sexual nature.'[11] The philosophical underpinning of Guido's hatred is Benthamite Utilitarianism, with its crude appeal to pleasure and pain as the sole sanctions of human behaviour, but utilitarianism cannot fully account for the hatred Guido expresses. That hatred leads him to undermine much human language as 'nicknaming,' as part of a social contract that sets limits to each person's pursuit of his or her own gain. Hence we

> call things wicked that give too much joy,
> And nickname the reprisal, envy makes,
> Punishment ...   (11.532–4)

A crucial nickname appears at line 1915. 'I think I never was at any time / A Christian,' Guido says, 'as you nickname all the world' (11.1914–15). Instead, he instructs the priests in true nomenclature: 'Name me, a primitive religionist' (11.1917). Guido's synonym for nicknames is 'truth on lip' (11.670), and 'truth on lip' may be useful, so long as one does not deceive oneself into thinking that it is anything other than a 'lie' (11.671).

The deceiving of others through 'truth on lip' appears in Guido's monologue as a parody of the poet's troping. Like the poet imaged as mage or prophet, Guido pictures himself waving a magic wand, so that 'feigning everywhere grows fact' (11.589): 'But, lo, I wave wand, make the false the true!' (11.622). For example, when he considers Pompilia as an animal, he asks, 'How name you the whole beast?' (11.1118). 'You choose to name the body from one head' – the lamb – while Guido insists that he sees a combination of lion and serpent, 'And name the brute, Chimaera, which I slew!' (11.1119, 1125). Or when he tropes his true self as a wolf, he claims the artist's transforming and shape-changing powers, named initially in the verb 'turn':

> Let me turn wolf, be whole, and sate, for once, –
> Wallow in what is now a wolfishness
> Coerced too much by the humanity
> That's half of me as well! Grow out of man,
> Glut the wolf-nature, – what remains but grow
> Into the man again, be man indeed
> And all man? Do I ring the changes right?
> Deformed, transformed, reformed, informed, conformed!   (11.2054–61)

That last line is an extended polyptoton, the rhetorical figure which rings the changes on a single word root, and it is both the verbal embodiment of the act of troping and (because of Guido's evil) a parody of it. 'That's the wolf nature,' Guido says later, and then adds at once, 'do n't mistake my trope!' (11.2316). For him, troping, we realize, is not a divinely inspired power but an empty gesture:

> My fight is figurative, blows i' the air,
> Brain-war with powers and principalities,
> Spirit bravado, no real fisticuffs!   (11.2318–20)

For others, 'Brain-war with powers and principalities' might be a crucial struggle and the 'better fight,' as it is for Milton's Abdiel, whose weapons are words, but 'fisticuffs' are real for Guido and words are finally wind.

When Guido is naming the pagan gods of the 'primitive religionist' he boasts himself to be, he talks about their value in linking 'height to depth' (11.1941), so that we do not 'pry narrowly / Into the nature hid behind the names' (1942–3). In spite of Guido's condemnation of most 'calling' as feigning, he turns suddenly, at the end of his monologue, to names and 'the nature hid behind' them. He cries out to be saved, and the cry is a list of nouns, with titles first, and then proper names: 'Abate, – Cardinal, – Christ, – Maria, – God, ... / Pompilia, will you let them murder me?' (11.2425). Instinctively he turns to an understanding of names that (we may guess) parallels Pompilia's, where name and nature are one, and where the name, therefore, has the power to save. We do not know whether or not Guido is actually saved, but language theory adds another dimension to that topic as it was debated by Browning critics in the 1970s. Guido had begun his monologue by boasting of his control, his command over language, and his clear-sightedness:

> How I live, how I see! so, – how I speak!
> Lucidity of soul unlocks the lips:
> I never had the words at will before,
> How I see all my folly at a glance! (11.158–61)

His cry at the end is not willed but spontaneous, and though the cry is articulate in its naming of names, it is like the *cris naturels* that were, for many thinkers about language in the eighteenth century, the chief origin of human languages. Such cries are not imitative but expressive, and they express human needs, desires, and emotions. Guido does indeed revert to something primitive in human nature, and his devolution may have brought him to the point where a genuine conversion might begin.

Caponsacchi's narrative is, among other things, an account of his struggle with language, with the significance and power of words. When he first becomes a priest, language does not mean a great deal to him, until

> time ran by
> And brought the day when I must read the vows,
> Declare the world renounced and undertake
> To become priest and leave probation ... (6.261–4)

'Just a vow to read!' (6.267), he says, but he is 'awe-struck' (6.268) by it, until the Bishop overcomes his scruples and his 'first / Rough rigid reading' (6.277–8) of the words which will make him a priest. The Bishop suggests an analogy with the Jews and their treatment of the name of God:

> The Jews who needs must, in their synagogue,
> Utter sometimes the holy name of God,
> A thing their superstition bogs at,
> Pronounce aloud the ineffable sacrosanct, –
> How does their shrewdness help them? In this wise;
> Another set of sounds they substitute,
> Jumble so consonants and vowels – how
> Should I know? – that there grows from out the old
> Quite a new word that means the very same –
> And o'er the hard place slide they with a smile.   (6.280–9)

The 'new word' does not, of course, mean 'the very same,' since the name of God is a symbol in the Coleridgian sense, and participates in the Godhead. The Bishop immediately goes on to name his reluctant novitiate – 'Giuseppe Maria Caponsacchi' – and though he slides over the names easily, we realize that they are significant: Joseph and Mary need no comment, but in relation to Caponsacchi – 'Capo-in-Sacco' (6.230), 'old Head-i'-the-Sack' (2.1249) – they are suggestive, the surname indicating the wilful stopping of ears and eyes and a refusal to acknowledge the Christian significance of his given names. Caponsacchi's full name, then, sums up his character at this stage in his experience.

The turning point comes with Caponsacchi's sight of Pompilia, which parallels the *pictura* in an emblem. He sees her first in the theatre, 'A lady, young, tall, beautiful, strange and sad' (6.399), and two parts of her appearance rivet his attention: her 'beautiful sad strange smile' (6.412) and her 'gaze' (6.434). The visual experience is unusually intense:

> That night and next day did the gaze endure,
> Burnt to my brain, as sunbeam thro' shut eyes,
> And not once changed the beautiful sad strange smile.   (6.434–6)

Caponsacchi's task is to interpret that smile, and its meaning, as he approaches the task of interpretation, is not something outside him, to be grasped intellectually, but rather something which has a bearing on his life and on his conduct of it. 'The fact is,' he tells his patron who has noticed a change in him, 'I am troubled in my mind, / Beset and pressed hard by some novel thoughts' (6.475–6). To the patron's expressed fear that he may be 'turning Molinist,' Caponacchi replies, '"Sir, what if I turned Christian?"' (6.473–4). Conversion, then, is the governing pattern of Caponsacchi's experience, and it takes the form of discovering that words are not, as with Guido, 'words and wind,' but rather living powers.

Caponsacchi has plenty of words available when he is contemplating the image of Pompilia, for he is reading Aquinas, and the contrast between the book and the smile, as Caponsacchi treats it, is the contrast between words and silence. He is thinking

How when the page o' the Summa preached its best,
Her smile kept glowing out of it, as to mock
The silence we could break by no one word.   (6.500–2)

The silence to which Caponsacchi refers is, in one sense, the distance between himself and Pompilia (for he thinks 'How utterly dissociated was I / A priest and celibate, from the sad strange wife / Of Guido' 6.492–4), but it is in another sense the infinite which becomes intelligible only when it is finite. Browning would know Carlyle's treatment of silence in *Sartor Resartus*, where in the chapter called 'Symbols' Carlyle has Teufelsdröckh contrast speech and silence: 'Speech too is great, but not the greatest. As the Swiss Inscription says: *Sprechen ist silbern, Schweigen ist golden* (Speech is silvern, Silence is golden); or as I might rather express it: Speech is of Time, Silence is of Eternity.'[12] Silence then is not emptiness but the fullness of primal unity, which can be known only by being broken and fragmented. It is Caponsacchi's task to interpret the riddle of such fragments.

The first breaking of silence is the 'tap' and 'whisper' (6.503, 504) of the go-between (ironically labelled a 'mystery' 6.506) who delivers the first of many letters. Caponsacchi reads the letter and immediately judges it to be a 'transparent trick' (6.537) through which Guido's 'mean soul grins' (6.537). Though the priest cannot yet read the meaning of the smile, its power is already working in him, enabling him to interpret and judge, to 'turn' the letter correctly. In the crucial scene where Caponsacchi first goes and sees Pompilia at the window, the word 'turn,' used in its ordinary physical sense, becomes a metaphor for the movements within Caponsacchi's soul as he struggles with evil and its temptations. He goes because 'I tired of the same black teazing lie /

Obtruded thus at every turn' (6.678–9), and so 'I will to the window, as he tempts' (6.683). The physical journey to the window is not a straight walk but one characterized by crossings and turns: 'So I went: crossed street and street' (6.691); when he has almost reached his goal, he thinks, 'The next street's turn, / I stand beneath the terrace, see, above, / The black of the ambush-window' (6.691–3). An ambush is certainly a turn, and Caponsacchi, expecting to be ambushed, flings a verbal challenge at the Guido who is, he thinks, hiding and ready to pounce: 'take this foulness in your face!' (6.700). The challenge, like that issued by Childe Roland, precipitates the final and crucial turn: 'The words lay living on my lip, I made / The one turn more' (6.701–2). The movement brings him the sight of Pompilia, who 'looked one look and vanished' (6.709), only to reappear on the terrace close above the priest. His response – an intense one – is that of the reader of emblems: 'I stood still as stone, all eye, all ear' (6.724). Caponsacchi has already interpreted the situation, however, in his troping of the anticipated ambush and his response to it: 'Kith, kin, and Count mustered to bite my heel' (6.688), he says, while he will deal a counter-blow, an 'instructive bruise' (6.690). The images – heel and bruise – are those of the first prophecy, God's judgment of the serpent after the fall: 'And I will put enmity between thee and the woman, and between thy seed and her seed: it shall bruise thy head, and thou shalt bruise his heel' (Genesis 3:15). The phrase 'I will put enmity,' as Henry Melvill interprets it in an 1833 sermon called 'The First Prophecy,' is a sign of God's 'converting grace' and an act of Providence, so that Caponsacchi appears as God's champion.

Caponsacchi's physical struggle, arduous and courageous as it is, is less important than his struggle to find words both to communicate with Pompilia and to characterize that communication for his judges. He, like Guido, is concerned with true words, though he wants them for reasons other than Guido's, and the problem of naming for him is a problem that reveals not so much a true-false opposition in words but their inadequacy, particularly in interpreting the sight Caponsacchi struggles to understand – Pompilia's face – and in interpreting the silence (and sometimes the music) that he hears about Pompilia.

Caponsacchi's account of the journey from Arezzo to Rome is the story of how they broke silence. From his point of view, breaking the silence is the finding of words for the true nature of their relationship. 'For the first hour,' he says, 'We were both silent in the night, I know' (6.1176–7). In response to the silence, Caponsacchi speaks to himself, and defends his words to the judges:

You know this is not love, Sirs, – it is faith,
The feeling that there's God, he reigns and rules
Out of this low world ... (6.1193–5)

The silence is broken by a sigh, and then by sounds Caponsacchi hears as music:

At times she drew a soft sigh – music seemed
Always to hover just above her lips
Not settle, – break a silence music too. (6.1196–8)

Music is not meaningless, but without words it is difficult to define its meaning, and Caponsacchi needs an answering word from Pompilia. Twice when she speaks, he finds the words unsatisfactory. When she asks, '"What woman were you used to serve this way, / Be kind to, till I called you and you came?"' (6.1232–3), he says, 'I did not like that word' (6.1234). Then she asks him to read parts of the service. 'I did not like that, neither, but I read' (6.1274). Finally, Pompilia does speak to his approving judgment: 'That I liked, that was the best thing she said' (6.1319). What she says is this:

'Yours is no voice! you speak when you are dumb;
Nor face, I see it in the dark. I want
No face nor voice that change and grow unkind.' (6.1316–18)

Pompilia uses the language of paradox – his voice is no voice, she says – and her trope is the oxymoron: 'you speak when you are dumb.' The trope, which juxtaposes opposites, suggests that they are one in a sense which is a riddle, a mystery – and a comfort. For Pompilia clearly wishes to dispense with ordinary existence – '"Never to see a face nor hear a voice!"' (6.1315) – and with the need to interpret sights and sounds. When speaking and silence are one, there is instantaneous communication, like that of the angels in *Paradise Lost*. The 'best thing' Pompilia says, then, is not about the content of communication but about its nature and means.

The same kind of communication is the goal of reading faces. Caponsacchi is intensely aware of Pompilia's appearance and of her gestures and movements. He remembers everything as his memory 'Recorded motion, breath or look of hers' (6.1159). 'Sometimes I did not see nor understand. / Blackness engulphed me' (6.1178–9):

Then I would break way, breathe through the surprise,
And be aware again, and see who sat
In the dark vest with the white face and hands.   (6.1180–2)

His reading of Pompilia's face, like her interpretation of his voice, fuses opposites, this time the visible and the invisible:

oh, I saw, be sure!
Her brow had not the right line, leaned too much,
Painters would say; they like the straight-up Greek:
This seemed bent somewhat with an invisible crown
Of martyr and saint, not such as art approves.   (6.1988–92)

His mode of interpretation is finally typology, and Pompilia's face, like David's, reveals the Incarnation:

To learn not only by a comet's rush
But a rose's birth, – not by the grandeur, God –
But the comfort, Christ.   (6.2094–6)

Pompilia's monologue turns on the distinction between names and nicknames, but replaces the Benthamite Utilitarianism underlying Guido's monologues with idealism. In her concern with truth, and in her listing of the three truths which have sustained and supported her ('my prayer to God' for deliverance, her deliverer, Caponsacchi, and her pregnancy, the 'promise of my child' 7.617, 623), she appeals to a theory of naming which makes the name symbolic in the Coleridgian (and Cratylian) sense, the name participating in the essential being of the person of whom it is the sign. Nicknames Pompilia associates with lying and with the changes which she has suffered in her brief life on earth. Calling something or someone by the proper name is a crucial matter for her. The verbs she uses for the opposite act – nicknaming – are 'misname' or 'call' or 'style.' Her struggle is first of all a struggle against the silence imposed on her as bride, and then against the false names that confront her at every turn.

Her concern with true names appears at the very beginning of her monologue when she (perhaps because she cannot write) places great importance on names and dates 'writ so in the church's register' (7.3): 'all my names' (7.4), and the name of her son. Her names – Francesca Camilla Vittoria Angela Pompilia – and his – Gaetano – are all names of saints, and they are given for the conventional purpose, to ensure guardianship. The word Pompilia uses for her son in relation to his saint is 'namesake' (7.106), the same name, that is, the repetition guaranteeing the interest, regard, and favour of his patron. Name-giving conventionally occurs at baptism, the initiation into a Christian life, when the name is a sign of one's nature as a Christian. Pompilia hopes that her own name will distinguish her from other girls of seventeen in the future regard of her son:

> my name is not a common name,
> 'Pompilia,' and may help to keep apart
> A little the thing I am from what girls are.   (7.85–7)

The opposite of the true name is the nickname, applied sometimes in sport and sometimes with malice. The former appears when Tisbe and Pompilia play their childish games with the tapestry, where they 'find each other out / Among the figures' (7.187–8): Tisbe becomes Diana and Pompilia Daphne, but 'You know the figures never were ourselves / Though we nicknamed them so' (7.197–8). The latter appears when Pompilia turns to Caponsacchi:

> Then there is ... only let me name one more!
> There is the friend, – men will not ask about,
> But tell untruths of, and give nicknames to,
> And think my lover, most surprise of all!   (7.159–62)

The nickname is not only untrue, but deadly. The defence promised by the rhyme every child has invoked at some time or other – sticks and stones may break my bones but names will never hurt me – is in this story turned upside down, and nicknames not only hurt but kill. The threat, as Pompilia treats it, is both physical and spiritual. One's true name she associates with one's true self, and nicknames, she says in language which anticipates that of Hopkins, unselve: Guido's plot was designed 'To make me and my friend unself ourselves, / Be other man and woman than we were!' (7.707–8). Playful nicknames are another matter, and though Pompilia rejects the nickname given her in her childhood play – Daphne, who becomes a tree – she in fact goes on to trope herself as a plant ('God plants us where we grow' 7.301) and to picture God as putting her 'In soil where I could strike real root, and grow, / And get to be the thing I called myself' (7.331–2). A name is not static, then, but something one grows into, and nicknames and the changes they ring on the self are a genuine threat to such progress.

Pompilia's monologue might also be called the metamorphoses, for change is a central theme, and the shifts and transformations may be good or bad. They make possible the process of selving, but Pompilia also links them with misnaming and silencing. The first major change in her life is her marriage, when the words of the ceremony (though not the results) are unintelligible to her:

> the priest had opened book,
> Read here and there, made me say that and this,
> And after, told me I was now a wife ...   (7.445-7)

The chief result is the silencing of her. Violante tells her that '"Girl-brides never breathe a word!"' (7.460), and Pompilia's growing sense of the duplicity of Violante has the same effect: 'I stood mute' (7.521). Guido's plot and its chief instrument, 'Those feigned false letters' (7.690), are a major threat to her integrity: she realizes, in retrospect, that they were designed 'to bring about a wicked change / Of sport to earnest' (7.696-7), 'To make me and my friend unself ourselves' (7.707). Her experiences in Arezzo are characterized by shifts and changes she can neither control nor understand. Faced with the consummation of her marriage, for instance, she appeals to the Archbishop and to '"the virgin life / You praise in Her you bid me imitate!"', only to be told that 'circumstances make or mar / Virginity, – 't is virtue or 't is vice' (7.753-4, 756-7). Such a shifting and uncertain world is characterized by the misuse of language. Guido's priestly brother Girolamo (who in the patterning of the story is the parody of Caponsacchi) made love to Pompilia and 'taught me what depraved and misnamed love / Means' (7.810-11). When Pompilia considers her biological mother, it is with a sense that the language applied to her is misnaming:

> The rather do I understand her now, –
> From my experience of what hate calls love, –
> Much love might be in what their love called hate.
> If she sold ... what they call, sold ... me her child –
> I shall believe she hoped in her poor heart
> That I at least might try be good and pure ...   (7.875-80)

The opposite of such shifting language is the name which, as in Jacob Boehme's understanding of Adamic language, is the signature of the essential nature and character of the thing or person named. From this perspective, the essence is in the name itself, and so the word has all the power of the person of whom it is the sign. When Pompilia invokes Caponsacchi's name, she affirms that 'Strength comes already with the utterance!' (7.942), and the nature of that strength is defined by the nouns with which she introduces the name itself:

> If God yet have a servant, man a friend,
> The weak a saviour and the vile a foe, –
> Let him be present, by the name invoked,
> Giuseppe-Maria Caponsacchi!   (7.938–41)

She images his nature as a 'glory' and a 'white light' which she interprets as truth:

> That man, you misinterpret and misprise –
> The glory of his nature, I had thought,
> Shot itself out in white light, blazed the truth
> Through every atom of his act with me.   (7.920–3)

To misname Caponsacchi is to 'stain' his nature or to obscure it with 'mist.' Pompilia uses both of those images:

> Yes, my last breath shall wholly spend itself
> In one attempt more to disperse the stain,
> The mist from other breath fond mouths have made,
> About a lustrous and pellucid soul.   (7.932–5)

Pompilia can be so certain about Caponsacchi's name because she has read his face and (like David gazing into the face of Saul) has seen the type of the saviour:

> Thus I know
> All your report of Caponsacchi false,
> Folly or dreaming; I have seen so much
> By that adventure at the spectacle,
> The face I fronted that one first, last time:
> He would belie it by such words and thoughts ...   (7.1179–84)

Hence Pompilia objects to Conti's renaming of Caponsacchi – '"Our Caponsacchi, he's your true Saint George / To slay the monster, set the

Princess free"' (7.1323–4) – because the name suggests love in the context of the kind of romance that Sir Walter Scott had called 'temporal' (the chivalric romance dealing with earthly life, fame, and rewards) rather than 'spiritual' (the lives of saints).[13] Conti's renaming of Caponsacchi has an effect on his actual name, for it suggests the separation of the name and the nature and a consequent change in the name itself, a change which Pompilia tries to define:

> That name had got to take a half-grotesque
> Half-ominous, wholly enigmatic sense,
> Like any bye-word, broken bit of song
> Born with a meaning, changed by mouth and mouth
> That mix it in a sneer or smile, as chance
> Bids, till it now means nought but ugliness
> And perhaps shame.   (7.1329–35)

The name, once the clear manifestation of Caponsacchi's type, changes with the changing tones by which it is pronounced and the changing contexts in which it is uttered, so that it was 'thus made / Into a mockery and disgrace' (7.1339–40). For instance, 'I name his name,' Margherita says (7.1342), and she sees Pompilia 'start and wince' in a way that suggests the guilty lover. That apparent power in the name is a parody of its real power, that of the deliverer whom Pompilia always sees in the priest's face, 'the same / Silent and solemn face' (7.1409–10). In holding by the identity of name and face, Pompilia insists on the identity of verbal sign and signified. The changes she has been struggling with would wrench sign and signified apart, make an ontological distinction between them, and make words into riddles which can be solved only by our knowing the kind of speech act of which they are the sounds. Pompilia would hold by a different understanding of language entirely, where a name cannot be changed if the nature does not change. 'No change / Here,' she says of Caponsacchi's face, 'though all else changed in the changing world!' (7.1414–15). She uses the conventional metaphor – breath or wind – to contrast these two views of language. There are 'foolish words' which are windy and empty, and there are words where the wind is the essence or spirit of the creature uttering them. Hence Pompilia says of the forged letters,

> 'Friend, foolish words were borne from you to me;
> Your soul behind them is the pure strong wind,
> Not dust and feathers which its breath may bear ...   (7.1418–20)

The letters were false and had the potential to kill; the spoken word of Caponsacchi – the first words she hears from him – are the manifestation of a living spirit:

> He replied –
> The first word I ever heard from his lips,
> All himself in it, – an eternity
> Of speech, to match the immeasurable depths
> O' the soul that then broke silence – 'I am yours.'   (7.1442–6)

Towards the end of Pompilia's monologue, there is a passage in which she talks about Caponsacchi's face and the power in it. That power is the power to read 'marks' – Browning seems to be using the word in the same sense as Boehme's 'signatures' – and it is a power which restores the identity of sign and signified which prevailed before the fall. Here is the passage:

> I did think, do think, in the thought shall die,
> That to have Caponsacchi for my guide,
> Ever the face upturned to mine, the hand
> Holding my hand across the world, – a sense
> That reads, as only such can read, the mark
> God sets on woman, signifying so
> She should – shall peradventure – be divine;
> Yet 'ware, the while, how weakness mars the print
> And makes confusion, leaves the thing men see,
> – Not this man, – who from his own soul, re-writes
> The obliterated charter, – love and strength
> Mending what's marred ...   (7.1494–1506)

This passage identifies the power of the face with the power to read and interpret rightly, and we remember that the human face is often for Browning (as Saul's face is for David) a type of the Incarnation, and that reading and interpreting are possible because of the third person of the Trinity. The 'mark' to which Pompilia refers is, in Boehme's term, the 'signature' of woman, the sign which is ontologically one with her essential character, destined (as here) to be divine. In a fallen world, mark and essence separate, leaving 'the thing men see,' the physical sign without its indwelling spirit. To Caponsacchi Pompilia attributes an astonishing power: he reverses the results of the fall and 're-writes / The obliterated charter.' Browning is here using the word 'charter' not as Blake uses it in

'London' where, as E.P. Thompson points out, 'it was a stale counter of the customary libertarian rhetoric' and, in phrases like 'chartered rights' and 'magna carta,' was 'at the centre of Whig ideology.'[14] Instead, Browning is here recovering the original sense of the word, *charta* being not only the paper on which something is written, but (by metonymy) that which is written upon it, the letter, so that a charter is the sign of a relationship, 'written evidence' (as Johnson says in his *Dictionary*) 'of things done between man and man,' but extended here to include things done between human beings and God. In such a charter, words are simple and unequivocal, and are one with the spirit which created them. Pompilia attributes to Caponsacchi the ability to restore that oneness to words, or at least to proper names. To understand names in that way is to have faith, and her faith wavers a bit towards the end of her monologue when she remembers that Guido gained access to the villa by using Caponsacchi's name; in a moment of doubt Pompilia says that 'I know not wherefore the true word / Should fade and fall unuttered at the last' (7.1806–7). Her faith in names remains strong, however, though she suggests that the identity of name and essence may be possible only in heaven. Her example is the word 'marriage.' 'Marriage on earth seems such a counterfeit,' she says, 'Mere imitation of the inimitable' (7.1824–5). An imitation is not ontologically the same as the thing it is like, and perhaps she is, at the very end, suggesting that human language is only an imitation of an ideal language, of which we have (as in the name of Caponsacchi) only vestiges here on earth.

We turn now to the third ring of monologues, the 'Triad of Judgement.' Litzinger's phrase refers primarily to the legal proceedings, since all the speakers have in one way or another been interpreting and judging, but in books 8 and 9 we have the 'machine' of law and the 'patent truth-extracting process' (1.1110, 1114). Browning's metaphors indicate his contempt for the lawyers, which is well known. As he told Julia Wedgwood in a letter of February 1869: 'I hate the lawyers: and confess to tasting something of ... satisfaction, as I emphasize their buffoonery.'[15] The buffoon is a version of the fool, the word being connected etymologically to *buffare*, to puff, so that the buffoon is a puff of wind. Arcangeli's buffoonery takes the form of a layering of language, a mixing that turns out to be like that of a recipe, while Bottini parodies Boehme's idea of signatures, and so empties names of all significance.

From the beginning of book 8, we are aware of Arcangeli juxtaposing two concerns: his son's birthday and the preparations for the feast to mark the occasion, on the one hand, and his outlining of Guido's legal defence on the other. 'Paternity at smiling strife with law' (1.1146) is Browning's phrase in book 1 to describe the monologue, and Arcangeli must constantly discipline himself to turn from the birthday – 'May I lose cause if I vent one word more' (8.126) about it, he says – and to focus on his legal argument. The language of the fond father, full of diminutives and endearments for his son, contrasts strongly with the legal language of the shrewd lawyer. That legal language itself is also layered: throughout the monologue, Arcangeli translates to and from Latin, and the carrying across from English to Latin is an interpretation that is part of the defence. Consider, for instance, Arcangeli's wrestling with the Latin translation of 'Count Guido married':

> Count Guido married – or, in Latin due,
> What? *Duxit in uxorem?* – commonplace!
> *Taedas jugales iniit, subiit,* – ha!
> He underwent the matrimonial torch?
> *Connubio stabili sibi junxit,* – hum!
> In stable bond of marriage bound his own?
> That's clear of any modern taint: and yet ... (8.129–35)

Arcangeli's linguistic act is that of the poet, who takes an abstraction like 'marriage' and tropes it with metaphors like 'torch' and 'bond' ('Come, that's both solid and poetic,' he says later – 8.538 – of a metaphor), but his wrestling with Latin could be labelled 'rhetoric' rather than 'truth.' Style without substance would be another way of describing his way of proceeding.

The layering of English and Latin has a temporal sequence as well as a spatial one: 'Notes alone, to-day,' Arcangeli says, 'The speech tomorrow and the Latin last' (8.146–7). And when his argument is finally done – 'Done! I' the rough, i' the rough! But done!' (8.1728) – he will review and revise, 'Tame here and there undue floridity' (8.1735), and add allusions, 'Poke at them with Scripture' (8.1737):

> To-morrow stick in this, and throw out that,
> And, having first ecclesiasticized,
> Regularize the whole, next emphasize,
> Then latinize and lastly Cicero-ize,
> Giving my Fisc his finish. (8.1741–5)

The buffoonery of Arcangeli becomes apparent when we realize that his rhetoric is in fact a recipe, that all the 'ize' verbs suggest methods of cooking, and that the layering which characterizes his use of language also describes the dishes with which he is obsessed: 'the liver's leathery slice' (8.118) at the beginning and later with its fennel and parsley (8.541–7), the 'lamb's fry' (8.1098), the 'porcupine to barbacue' (8.1378), the rabbit with 'sour-sweet sauce and pine-pips' (8.1380). Hence it is no surprise that, when Arcangeli is finished, he exclaims, 'There's my speech – / And where's my fry'? (8.1745–6). The attitude we are asked to take towards this confusion of mind and stomach is suggested in a remark of Elizabeth's when, in May 1846, she is describing for Robert her sister Henrietta's suitor: 'He is amiable, goodnatured, easy-tempered, of good intentions in the main: but he eats & drinks & sleeps, and *shows* it all when he talks' (*Correspondence* 12:314). That put-down has its dramatic equivalent – an overly obvious one – in Browning's having Arcangeli slip up and say, immediately after his thoughts about the 'porcupine to barbacue,' 'Our stomach ... I mean, our soul – is stirred within, / And we want words' (8.1386–7). That 'want' is as double-edged as the same word in Byron's famous first line in *Don Juan*: there is a need or desire, and there is a lack. With either meaning, words dissolve into the expression of appetite.

Layering is primarily a spatial metaphor, with the suggestion of levels below and above. We have seen (in *Paracelsus*) how troping undertaken in the pursuit of truth leads to ever-higher levels. Here Arcangeli's rhetoric may be a spiralling upwards but his understanding of language is a turning downwards. In his legal argument – 'Honour in us had injury' (8.425) – Arcangeli proceeds upwards through the various levels of creation, beginning 'on the mere natural ground' (8.479), mounting 'from beast to man' (8. 548), and coming to a climax with man as

> creation's master-stroke,
> Nay, intellectual glory, nay, a god,
> Nay, of the nature of my Judges here.   (8.533–5)

When Arcangeli turns to language itself, however, he pictures a descent, and 'translating' means devolution:

> We must translate our motives like our speech
> Into the lower phrase that suits the sense
> O' the limitedly apprehensive.   (8.1498–1500)

Then he goes on to talk specifically in terms of levels and of God-given speech dwindling into animal appetite:

Let
Each level have its language! Heaven speaks first
To the angel, then the angel tames the word
Down to the ear of Tobit: he, in turn,
Diminishes the message to his dog,
And finally that dog finds how the flea
(Which else, importunate, might check his speed)
Shall learn its hunger must have holiday, –
How many varied sorts of language here,
Each following each with pace to match the step,
Haud passibus aequis!   (8.1500–10)

The Virgilian tag – 'with not equal steps' – undermines the matching. The 'not equal steps' are those of the little son of Aeneas, trying to keep up with his father's longer strides as they flee from the sacking of Troy.

Bottini's argument is a reversal of Arcangeli's. He takes his opponent's central theme – 'All means are lawful to a lawful end' (8.1315) – and turns it from the defence of Guido to the defence of Pompilia:

How say you, good my lords?
I hope you heard my adversary ring
The changes on this precept: now, let me
Reverse the peal!   (9.518–21)

In spite of the reversal, however, Bottini is also a buffoon, and where Arcangeli's sin was gluttony, Bottini's is lust. In a gross parody of Pompilia's sense of names as one with the essence of character, and of Boehme's doctrine of the signature of all things, Bottini focuses on the 'intimate essential character' (9.230) of woman, which is certainly not (as Pompilia hopes) ultimately divine but grossly sensual, with 'melting wiles, deliciousest deceits, / The whole redoubted armoury of love' (9.231–2). And where Arcangeli admits the facts and turns them to his legal advantage, Bottini credits few of the facts, and argues that, if one were to admit them, they are excusable on the grounds of woman's 'intimate essential character' and on her need to preserve that essence. His favourite mood is the subjunctive, and his favourite mode of argument is the concession. 'Grant she somewhat plied / Arts that allure' (9.435–6); 'Grant the tale / O' the husband, which is false, for proved and true' (9.443–4); 'Concede she wrote (which were preposterous) / This and the other epistle, – what of it?' (9.473–4).The core of his argument is also a concession, asked for rather than given:

> Concede me, then,
> Whatever friendly fault may interpose
> To save the sex from self-abolishment
> Is three-parts on the way to virtue's rank!   (9.794–7)

'If we believe, – as, while my wit is mine / I cannot' (9.682–3): concession and conditional coalesce in this last quotation, and turn up in characteristic clauses: 'were the thing true / Which is a fable' (9.636–7), 'were the fiction fact' (9.651), 'what and if he gazed rewardedly' (9.741). Concession and the conditional are in Bottini's mouth ways of saying one thing and meaning another, so that words and meaning are at odds with each other. Though Bottini begins with a picture – the Comparini as the Holy Family and Pompilia as the Virgin – the picture has no firm connection with the characterization of Pompilia that follows, and Bottini's digressions, such as the story of Peter, John, and Judas, have the thinnest of links with the legal argument. Here, then, is language where words and meaning separate, because of Bottini's pride and his prurience.

The Pope, whose monologue is 'the ultimate / Judgment' (1.1220–1) save that of the reader, also acts on personal motives, since he is conscious of his approaching death and of God's judgment of all his acts, particularly his most recent, but the personal motive does not obscure his judgment; rather, it sharpens his consciousness of doing 'God's work on earth' (1.1234), particularly of 'bringing his intelligence to bear' (1.1229) on the case and of arriving at a decision which is crucial because five lives – and the fate of his own soul – hang in the balance. The idea of language which stands under his monologue is close to Browning's own: empiricist in its orientation, but with affirmations that the ability to interpret and judge is God-given. When the Pope insists that he finds the truth 'As a mere man may, with no special touch / O' the lynx-gift in each ordinary orb' (10.1243–4), he affirms that the language he is using is the conventional language of human communication, language in which (as Locke taught) the relation between articulate sign and idea is an arbitrary one, and where the truth of most propositions cannot be confirmed by observation of the actual relations of things in the world outside us. Judgment, however, is that faculty 'which God has given Man to supply the want of clear and certain Knowledge in Cases where that cannot be had' (*Essay* 4.14.3). Hence the Pope affirms that, even though his language has no special power or authority, still his judgment (like that of all human beings) is from God: 'Yet my poor spark had for its source, the sun' (10.1284). Moreover, the faculty of judgment, however limited it is, must be exercised, not held in abeyance. The Pope imagines himself confronting Guido's ghost:

> 'God who set me to judge thee, meted out
> So much of judging faculty, no more:
> Ask Him if I was slack in use thereof!' (10.264–6)

What the Pope actually confronts, however, are written documents: 'He reads, notes, lays the papers down at last, / Muses, then takes a turn about the room' (1.1248–9). He is, therefore, in the same position as every reader of *The Ring and the Book*, with nothing to go on but the words on the pages in front of him. And like the reader who has also the Old Yellow Book, the Pope has 'a huge tome in an antique guise' (1.1250), which he also consults. The problems it raises are those of every reader of Browning's poem.

So book 10, like the poem as a whole, begins with a man reading a book, in this instance 'a History ... / Of all my predecessors, Popes of Rome' (10.3, 6). The account of Formosus and his successors is characterized by turns and reversals in judgment, and by still further turns and changes until the Pope asks, 'Which of the judgments was infallible? / Which of my predecessors spoke for God?' (10.150–1). Like the speaker in 'Protus' (from the *Men and Women* volumes of 1855), who puzzles over one scribe's account, then ('two pages' later) the same scribe's history of a 'New reign, same date,' from which account Protus disappears, and finally the note of an 'annotator,' who provides 'hearsay' and 'deduces' that this Protus is the same man who wrote a tract 'On worming dogs,' the Pope in *The Ring and the Book* also finds himself whirled round and round by a text of multiple authors and uncertain history:

> For though mine ancient [the historian of the reign of Formosus] early
>   dropped the pen,
> Yet others picked it up and wrote it dry,
> Since of the making books there is no end. (10.7–9)

The last line is a reference to the (almost) final words of the preacher in Ecclesiastes: 'of making many books there is no end; and much study is a weariness of the flesh' (12:12). The making of books without end is another version of circling round and round, a hellish movement which the Pope will figure as a 'coil / Of statement, comment, query and response' (10.372–3). The texts he has been considering are

> these dismallest of documents
> Which drew night down on me ere eve befell, –
> Pleadings and counter-pleadings, figure of fact
> Beside fact's self, these summaries to-wit ...   (10.213–16)

The Pope knows that his decision, from a human perspective, is only one more turn, but he also knows that the turn he gives to the documents is, in the lives directly affected by it, a crucial matter, since, as the preacher in Ecclesiastes affirms, 'God shall bring every work into judgment' (12:14). 'If I hesitate,' the Pope says,

> It is because I need to breathe awhile,
> Rest, as the human right allows, review
> Intent the little seeds of act, the tree, –
> The thought, to clothe in deed, and give the world
> At chink of bell and push of arrased door.   (10.276–81)

The 'little seeds of act' that he reviews are not only those of the main figures in the case, but his own. His own he can know with some certainty, but those of others he can only infer. He guesses at them in the same way that all readers of Browning's dramatic poems must guess at the motives of his characters, by the silent reading of texts, and on the basis of the written words of those texts. Those words are human and fallible.

The Pope in fact condemns language with the same vigour that Browning does in offering the 'one lesson' of the poem as a whole, and that condemnation, as we have seen, is not to be set aside and dismissed as a simple kind of irony where one thing is said and another meant. In the passage in book 10 which begins at line 346, the Pope describes language as 'barren words' (10.348) and speech as 'filthy rags' (10.372). Truth and lies are inextricably intertwined in human speech, which 'still bursts o'er some lie which lurks inside' (10.351), though the lies in turn are not without some foundation in truth, since 'Out of some core of truth the excrescence comes' (10.355). Such a mixture of truth and lying is the result of the fall and of God's confusion of tongues at Babel, both of which the Pope may be referring to when he uses the word 'curse': the 'barren words ... more than any deed, characterize / Man as made subject to a curse' (10.348–50). The curse, as the Pope goes on to describe it, is the kind of language where words do not correspond to the essential nature of the things they name, as they would if human beings retained Adamic language. So, 'when man walks the garden of this world' (10.360), the Pope says,

> – Why, can he tell you what a rose is like,
> Or how the birds fly, and not slip to false
> Though truth serve better? (10.365–7)

Then the Pope proceeds from naming to communication. If human beings no longer have the Adamic language, then all their names for things are arbitrary, as Locke taught, and statements must all be considered opinion. The Pope tropes opinion as a 'coil' where human beings turn statements and then turn them again:

> Man must tell his mate
> Of you, me and himself, knowing he lies,
> Knowing his fellow knows the same, – will think
> 'He lies, it is the method of a man!'
> And yet will speak for answer 'It is truth'
> To him who shall rejoin 'Again a lie!'
> Therefore this filthy rags of speech, this coil
> Of statement, comment, query and response,
> Tatters all too contaminate for use,
> Have no renewing ... (10.366–75)

The Pope immediately goes on to affirm, however, that this 'coil' is the human way of arriving at truth, and that the 'coil' is not solely a human act.

At one moment in the monologue – it is the one place in the poem where, as Altick and Loucks point out, Browning explicitly says that the 'speech quoted is a product of divine inspiration'[16] – the Pope attributes to the Holy Spirit the ability to turn an argument. That moment occurs in his retelling of the trial of the dead Formosus, when the poor Deacon who is forced to be 'advocate and mouthpiece of the corpse' (10.52) suddenly turns back on the new Pope the charge that Formosus '"Vacate[d] the lesser for the greater see"' (10.60). The Deacon turns the argument because he is 'Emboldened by the Spirit' (10.58). Rarely do we have such an explicit affirmation that responding and arguing are actions made possible by the Holy Spirit, but there are plenty of passages where that idea is suggested. Take, for example, the moment when the Pope, having told the story of Formosus, turns to his own task ('So worked the predecessor: now, my turn!' 10.161) and begins with the words, 'In God's name!' (10.162). The invocation seems only conventional, but we are to take it more seriously than would at first seem necessary. The name of God is, from an idealist perspective, the ultimate ground of all human language, and the guarantee of our ability to speak and judge. A second example is at the end of the Pope's monologue, when the Pope writes the order for execution and affirms as he does so that 'a voice other than yours [society's and civilization's] / Quickens my spirit. "Quis pro Domino?"' (10.2098–9). And there is the affirmation following the Pope's condemnation of human speech as 'filthy rags' : 'He, the Truth, is, too, / The Word' (10.375–6). That statement is conventional Christian doctrine, but coming immediately after the condemnation of human speech, as it does, it asks us to be like the preacher in Ecclesiastes and take a double view of language. Language may be 'filthy rags,' but it is also the means by which we know the truth as much as we are able in this world:

> We men, in our degree, may know
> There, simply, instantaneously, as here
> After long time and amid many lies ...   (10.376–8)

To know 'instantaneously' is to communicate like the angels in *Paradise Lost*, and to dispense with the parts of speech and with syntax, which divides the Word and makes language a temporal sequence; and to know 'simply' is to know things as 'whole' and 'sole' rather than duplicitously, where everything is double and seems to be made up of opposites. The Pope, however, does not deplore his inability to know on earth as he would know 'There': 'be man's method for man's life at least!' (10.381).

The doubleness that I have been exploring is also apparent in the clothing metaphors that the Pope uses for language. These metaphors parallel Carlyle's central trope in *Sartor Resartus*, where Teufelsdröckh says that 'Language is called the Garment of Thought' (73), and indeed the 'filthy rags' metaphor sounds like Carlyle, but its counterpart, which gives the opposite view of language, is biblical and derived from Paul's 'whole armour of God' metaphor in the epistle to the Ephesians. 'Everywhere,' the Pope says,

> I see in the world the intellect of man,
> That sword, the energy his subtle spear,
> The knowledge which defends him like a shield ...   (10.1012–15)

Even when 'armour' replaces 'filthy rags,' however, there is no guarantee that God's champions will fight his battles. Where, the Pope asks, were those who might have helped Caponsacchi?

> Where are the Christians in their panoply?
> The loins we girt about with truth, the breasts
> Righteousness plated round, the shield of faith,
> The helmet of salvation, and that sword
> O' the Spirit, even the word of God, – where these?   (10.1565–9)

Always when the Pope describes a diminishing or falling away from the Word, he affirms as well that the loss is not absolute, and the Word is still 'Appreciable' in however limited a way. For instance, he refers (like Yeats) to heaven as 'There,' and then, in a parenthesis, comments on the adverb as inadequate, probably because it makes a binary out of unity: 'There, (which is nowhere, speech must babble thus!)' (10.1317). So 'the absolute immensity' is

> by the little mind of man, reduced
> To littleness that suits his faculty,
> Appreciable too in the degree ...   (10.1320–2)

Earlier, he had affirmed the authority (however limited) of the faculties of 'mere man':

> all that I do and am
> Comes from the truth, or seen or else surmised,
> Remembered or divined, as mere man may.   (10.1286–8)

The past participles which modify 'truth' in these lines suggest the multiple ways in which human language and judgment are grounded in the Word: witnessed with one's physical eyes (like John in 'A Death in the Desert'); inferred or conjectured without the witness of eye and ear; retained in one's memory; or guessed ('divined') with the help of insight or imagination. The one possibility the Pope explicitly excludes is a materialist understanding of the human mind. 'Mind is not matter nor from matter, but / Above' (10.1352–3), he says, and, as we saw in chapter 1, Browning holds a parallel non-materialist view of the mind. When the Pope tropes 'Man's mind' as a 'convex glass' (10.1310), he insists on its ability to know ultimate truth, though that truth is 'a whole proportioned to our sense' (10.1316). He also insists that our words are related to the Word, though they too are 'proportioned to our sense.' Later he uses the words 'truth reverberate' (10.1390), and such truth is to be understood in a double way: it is 'The same and not the same' (10.1392), for without such doubleness the truth would be 'else unconceived' (10.1392).

The Pope is Browning's model reader: he struggles silently and alone with texts and their meaning; he interprets those texts, arrives at a judgment of them, and acts on that decision; the act has consequences in the world of human affairs, and for him personally, since it is a stage in the development of his soul and may be, for all he knows, the ultimate and crucial deed in his life. Browning's governing trope for reading and interpreting is seeing – insight which is made possible by the Holy Spirit, that is – and John in 'A Death in the Desert' provides lines that could be a motto for all such sight: '"in this word 'I see,'/ Lo, there is recognized the Spirit"' (222–3). The Spirit to which John refers is that of two attributes of God – power and love – and such a Spirit, '"moving o'er the spirit of man, unblinds / His eye and bids him look"' (224–5).

'One thing has many sides': Browning's 'transcripts,' *Balaustion's Adventure* and *Aristophanes' Apology*

'Only a poor creature has just one side to his soul,' Browning told his friends the Skirrows when he was contemplating, with mixed feelings and much uncertainty, his return from Venice to London in December of 1883.[1] The many sides of the human soul guarantee the turning and interpreting of texts, and Browning's multiple turnings of the Old Yellow Book can all be seen as 'the highest criticism,' the kind Oscar Wilde called (in 'The Critic as Artist') 'the record of one's own soul' and 'the only civilised form of autobiography.'[2] A logical development of such a record is to include in one's own poem the text which one is turning, so that one has not just detailed references and allusions as in *The Ring and the Book*, but the complete work which is (again to use Wilde's words) the 'starting-point for a new creation' (143). In *Balaustion's Adventure* and *Aristophanes' Apology*, Browning embeds an entire play in a dramatic speech, and encloses both within his own printed voice (which is explicit in *Balaustion's Adventure* and implicit in its companion piece). Such a technique is related to 'the many experimental genres of framed narration,' in David Shaw's words, which are part of the Victorian revolt against naïve empiricism, the assumption 'that it is ever possible to mirror an unmediated world of primary facts, plain, exposed, and naked to the eye.'[3] Instead, framed narrations are re-presentations of the acts of interpreting, turning, and appropriating, and those concerns Browning focuses on a character he created in the 1870s, Balaustion, who appears in both the major poems which are the subject of this chapter. Balaustion is the figure who both transmits and interprets texts, one a comedy and one a tragedy. In her transmissions we can see how criticism becomes creation, and her responses incidents in her own development. That growth takes the form of turning tragedy into comedy and comedy into tragedy, and though the closed circle might suggest itself as a metaphor for this turning, a more accurate metaphor is the spiral upwards, because its movement is both circular and progressive. The comedy is Euripides' *Alkestis*; the tragedy is his *Herakles* (though, as we shall see, one must qualify the label 'comedy' for the *Alkestis*). Balaustion recites both, but where she interprets the *Alkestis* and makes a new one, she refuses to alter the 'perfect' *Herakles* and is corrected by Aristophanes. Both plays, however, are Englished, turned by Browning himself as his interpretation of the Greek. For that turning, the poet supplies a word: 'transcript.' The word, as he uses it, refers explicitly to the embedded text and obliquely to frames.

The word appears in the subtitle of both *Balaustion's Adventure* and *Aristophanes' Apology.* 'A Transcript from Euripides' is Browning's label for the *Alkestis* and the *Herakles* as they appear in those two poems, and the word turns up again in Browning's preface to his translation, *The Agamemnon of Aeschylus*. In fact, Browning, we think, ought to have used the word 'translation,' and apparently James Murray thought so too. Murray, we remember from chapter 1, had complained that Browning 'constantly used words without regard to their proper meaning,'[4] and the 'proper meaning' of 'transcript' is 'written copy.' In law, a 'transcript' is a copy of a legal document, and if that sense of the word were the sense in Browning's subtitles, then the poet ought to have copied out and printed the Greek of Euripides. He obviously doesn't. The *OED* indicates that a 'transcript' may be an imitation as well as a copy, though imitation is the figurative meaning and includes 'a representation, rendering, interpretation.' Under the primary meaning of the word, however, Murray, sounding the note of the annoyed lexicographer, includes 'a verbal or close translation or rendering,' gives as his example Browning's title for *Balaustion's Adventure*, and labels it '? *nonce-use.*' The word does indeed seem to be used for the nonce. Browning's purpose is to get his readers thinking about translating and to realize that such a carrying across is inescapably double. He wants his word 'transcript' to suggest a copy, partly to appeal to the naïve empiricism of many of his readers, and partly to indicate that there is indeed an original text which he is rendering as faithfully as possible. He also wants to suggest, however, that every rendering is an interpretation, and to replace words in one language with words in another is (as all translators know) to read the original text critically. The act of transcribing is also a quickening of the original text, the bringing it to life, as Balaustion does, in a particular historical context and in a particular moment in one's life, so that the text plays a role and takes on a character that its author could not possibly have anticipated. Balaustion's 'adventure' both keeps the original text alive and makes it look forever different, so that the *Alkestis* is, like the Pope's 'truth' and 'truth reverberate,' both 'The same and not the same' (*The Ring and the Book* 10:1392, 1388). The word 'transcript' both points to and hides that doubleness. Browning may have had in mind an analogy with a musical 'transcription,' the 'arrangement,' in the words of the *OED*, 'or ... modification, of a composition for some voice or instrument other than that for which it was originally written.' My ellipsis indicates a qualification which is characteristic of Murray: the parenthetical comment on this definition is '(less properly).' Browning saw nothing improper about such a 'modification,' and indeed saw it as both desirable and inevitable. The nature of each 'modification' and the relations among the various turnings must be the chief concern of criticism, and hence we must now look at each poem in more detail.

Balaustion's Adventure is, as W.C. DeVane pointed out years ago, 'a play within a play within a play.'[5] The first play is Euripides' *Alkestis*. The second is, in Balaustion's own words, 'our version of the story' (2661), and 'version,' we note in passing, is derived from the Latin for 'turn.' The third is Browning's turning of Euripides and Balaustion both. 'One thing has many sides' (2402), Balaustion says when she is recounting a rumour that Sophocles means to write his own *Alkestis*, and the statement sanctions a fresh telling of every text. 'Since one thing may have so many sides, / I think I see how,' Balaustion says,

> – far from Sophokles, –
> You, I, or anyone might mould a new
> Admetos, new Alkestis.   (2413–16)

To enclose a version within a version within a version, as Browning does, is (to borrow a phrase from 'Saul') to go 'the whole round of creation' and to approach a total or encyclopedic view, so that words which at first seem equivocal (with interpretation pitted against interpretation) are in fact turnings spiralling upwards into a comprehensiveness which holds together in one vast (and usually circular) structure readings and tellings which are at first sharply opposed. How this progressive turning works will be clearer if we sort out the three main plays in this text and examine their relations, each to each.

The innermost play is Euripides' *Alkestis*, recited by Balaustion, and although that play is the base or foundation of the poem as a whole,

Balaustion's repeating of the rumour that Sophocles may write his own *Alkestis* reminds us that Euripides' play is itself only one turning or version of a story which has already been turned by others and will be turned yet again. Euripides' version is in fact the kind of text which is open to varying interpretations, since it is a puzzling work. As the classicist Nathan Greenberg points out, 'the play mingles elements of tragedy and comedy and it is unclear which, if any, of the characters are meant to win our approval.'[6] Is Herakles, for instance, a drunken reveller, an earthy figure, or is he a saviour, 'the instrument' (in Greenberg's words) 'and completer of Apollo's purpose?' (139). The mingling of genres and the mixing of characters invite interpretation and resist closure. Balaustion rises to that challenge: she not only recites but interprets the Euripidean text. Those acts, and the two occasions of them , make up the second of the plays within a play.

The two occasions of this second play differ in historical circumstance but not (we assume) in what is said, so that past and present are one. In the past, Balaustion and her companions from Rhodes are 'at destruction's very edge' (125), with pirates behind them and hostile Syracusans in front ('We ran upon the lion from the wolf' 89). The Syracusans, however, hearing Balaustion sing a song of Aeschylus, 'that song of ours which saved at Salamis' (76), ask '"how about Euripides?"' (132). '"Might you know any of his verses too?"' (137). Balaustion (who, unlike some of her predecessors, has stored 'at brain's edge and tip of tongue' (152) the text of the *Alkestis*) saves herself and her fellows by reciting the play. Her situation has a parallel in that of Sheherazade, who also saves herself by telling stories. The texts are for the story-teller not only life-saving but also liberating and ultimately comic, since they are the means of bringing about the conventional resolution of the comic action, the marriage of lovers who had earlier been threatened with cruel or irrational decrees or even with death. So Sheherazade marries her sultan, and Balaustion attracts the attention of a young man who follows her to Athens where 'We are to marry' (274). There is a fairy-tale quality to Browning's narrative, but the significance which comic romance gives to the reciting of a text is consistent with Browning's views elsewhere: that the assimilation of a text (dare I say, in these perilous educational times, the memorizing of it?) is life-saving, liberating, and life-affirming. The present time of Balaustion's speech is not nearly so exciting. Her listeners are friends ('Petalé, / Phullis, Charopé, Chrusion' 4–5) and the present situation has none of the urgency of the one in the past:

About that strangest, saddest, sweetest song
I, when a girl, heard in Kameiros once,
And, after, saved my life by? Oh, so glad
To tell you the adventure!   (1–4)

In neither past nor present, however, is the reciting of Euripides' text a mere repetition of it, an echo, as it were, for which Balaustion is only the mouthpiece. Even though she says, 'Hear the play itself!' (336), talks about having the courage 'to recite / The main of a whole play from first to last' (218–19), and twice uses the words 'I told the play' (246, 305), her telling is also an interpretation. Her version involves an issue with which her creator struggled from the beginning of his career: the relation between a dramatic text and a theatrical performance.

Balaustion tells her listeners in the present that when in the past she recited the play, she was not only reciting the text she had memorized but also describing the performance of it which she had witnessed:

I saw it, at Kameiros, played the same,
They say, as for the right Lenean feast
In Athens ...   (224–6)

The result is a text which duplicates those which led to Browning's writing of dramatic monologues, for Balaustion includes in her version not only the words of Euripides but the gestures, tones, and appearance of the actors, so that she makes her text encompass the arts of the playwright, director, costume designer, scene designer, and actor. For instance, she indicates the tempo and tone with which lines are to be spoken, as when she says of a line of Admetos, 'slow the words came at last' (967), or gives Alkestis's manner of speaking: 'Word slow pursuing word in monotone' (2002). She notes the spectacle on stage – it is usually a procession – and she blocks in the movements of the actors, as when Herakles discovers the identity of the dead person ('fast, / He plucked the chaplet from his forehead, dashed / The myrtle-sprays down, trod them underfoot!' 1865–7) or when he returns with the veiled figure of Alkestis ('In he strode, / And took his stand before Admetos' 2114–15). The veiled figure of Alkestis is a visual riddle, and Balaustion usurps the roles of both designer and director with the lines describing Herakles in his 'lion-coat' (2130) presenting Admetos with the figure whom he does not recognize as his wife: 'Under the great guard of one arm, there leant / A shrouded something, live and woman-like' (2128–9). So, says

Balaustion, 'plain I told the play, / Just as I saw it; what the actors said, / And what I saw ...' (246–8). To act as the mere recorder of the sights and sounds of the dramatic performance, however, is to act in the same way as simply reciting or echoing the text, and Balaustion's retelling is, in Coleridgian terms, an imitation and not a copy. The ellipsis in my last quotation indicates lines which are in fact crucial in defining the nature of Balaustion's performance. Her telling (or, more exactly, retelling) involves two kinds of repetition.

Those kinds are suggested by the clause I left out of the quotation above:

> and plain I told the play,
> Just as I saw it; what the actors said,
> And what I saw, or thought I saw the while,
> At our Kameiros theatre ...   (246–9)

Those neatly ambiguous clauses, 'what I saw, or thought I saw,' have their origin in the famous episode in the *Aeneid* when Aeneas, not knowing that Dido is dead, catches sight of her in the underworld and, in Virgil's words, 'aut videt aut vidisse putat' (6.454), words which Balaustion translates (with a change of pronoun) in line 248 of the poem. The formula, as J. Hillis Miller has argued in one of his books on the English novel, sums up two kinds of repetition, kinds which he defines as Platonic, where the repetition is a copy and has no effect on the original, and Nietzschean, where the repetition may seem to repeat the original but in fact is different, and gives rise to something ghostly and ungrounded.[7] As Browning uses the formula, it might be more appropriately understood in Lockeian terms. 'What I saw' is the kind of repetition where the relations affirmed in a proposition correspond with the relations actually observed in the world outside the speaker, such correspondence being truth as Locke defines it. 'Thought I saw' is the kind of repetition which does not abandon correspondence, but which recognizes that every act of perception is also an act of attention and selection, the verbal imitation of which is, in Locke's words, 'the free choice of the Mind, pursuing its own ends' (*Essay* 3.5.6), so that 'thinking' takes precedence over 'seeing.' This second kind of repetition is both interpretation and application of the text to one's own life, and Balaustion's speech is not only a recitation of Euripides' text but also a critical reading and appropriating of it.

Balaustion describes both the sights she has actually seen on stage and sights she has not seen but infers or 'thought she saw.' Hence she describes the countenances hidden underneath the masks, '"As she had seen each naked fleshly face, / And not the merely-painted mask it wore!"' (315–16). For this, she tells us, she is taken to task by 'a brisk little somebody, / Critic and whippersnapper' (306–7), who charges her with falsifying her account and making things up:

> 'The girl departs from truth!
> Pretends she saw what was not to be seen,
> Making the mask of the actor move, forsooth!
> "Then a fear flitted o'er the wife's white face," –
> "Then frowned the father," – "then the husband shook," –
> "Then from the festal forehead slipt each spray,
> And the heroic mouth's gay grace was gone"; –
> As she had seen each naked fleshly face,
> And not the merely-painted mask it wore!'   (308–16)

Balaustion's answer to this charge can be read as the theory which underlies her act of interpretation, and it is one which involves a typical Browning concern: the relations of the arts, and particularly of painting and music to poetry. Poetry, she says, 'speaking to one sense, inspires the rest' (319), so that interpretation means the creating of a full picture from sensations that appeal to one sense only. Balaustion begins with painting, and she treats it in a way which suggests the emblem, for she says that if we see a picture, then we want to make it speak; she continues with music and focuses (again, like her creator) on its units of equal time, divisions which appeal to the kinesthetic rhythms in all of us, and particularly the heartbeat, so that music becomes the expression of our common humanity:

> so
> That who sees painting, seems to hear as well
> The speech that's proper for the painted mouth;
> And who hears music, feels his solitude
> Peopled at once – for how count heart-beats plain
> Unless a company, with hearts which beat,
> Come close to the musician, seen or no?   (320–6)

Then Balaustion turns to poetry and its appeal to both sight and hearing. Those senses are not separate and unconnected, linked only

by association (as Berkeley had argued), but are related, like the
Graces:

> And who receives true verse at eye or ear,
> Takes in (with verse) time, place, and person too,
> So, links each sense on to its sister-sense,
> Grace-like ...   (327–30)

There are usually three Graces, and they are the trope for the three
senses Balaustion goes on to specify: hearing, seeing, and feeling. The
simile is richly suggestive. The Graces are sisters, and the blood relation
suggests that the senses, apparently so different in their operations,
share an essence, so that the stimulation of one sense inspires the operation of the others:

> and what if but one sense of three
> Front you at once? The sidelong pair conceive
> Through faintest touch of finest finger-tips, –
> Hear, see and feel, in faith's simplicity,
> Alike, what one was sole recipient of.   (330–4)

Balaustion's lines not only give the idea but evoke the actual experience
of it. Here the 'one sense of three' is sight, and the image evoked by the
visual details is that of the Graces dancing, as in Botticelli's *Primavera*,
moving in a circle which is enclosed by 'faintest touch of finest finger-
tips.' We hear that light touch in the counterpointing of that line, where
the forward movement of the dominant iambic metre is retarded by the
trochaic words cutting across the iambic feet, and we feel that touch
when upper teeth brush lower lip for the 'f' alliteration. Thus three
senses fuse in one, a union indicated by the word 'simplicity,' the root of
which is *sem*, one. The visual image is a dance where the movement is
circular, and the relations of the three figures can be read as an allegory
of troping, where the image of one sense turns to the image of another
sense. That circle will finally be a spiral, as we shall see, but at this point
Balaustion makes a more limited claim for the dance: 'Who hears the
poem, therefore, sees the play' (335). The line brings us back to the issue
we explored in chapter 3, where, the reader will remember, names
which are general and abstract (even though they are signs of concrete
things) come alive only when the hearer supplies images from his or her
own experience. In the theory of interpretation which Balaustion is set-

ting out, words must work in that same way, since Balaustion's listeners, both past and present, have not seen the performance she describes, and must, therefore, create their own images not only for puzzles like the 'shrouded something' who is Alkestis on her return but also for all the visual things Balaustion names as part of the stage and its sights. 'What's poetry except a power that makes?' (318), Balaustion asks. In this context, the making is threefold: it is the providing of images for names which (as Locke taught) are general and abstract; it is the activity of senses other than the one initially stimulated, responding nonetheless to that first prodding; and it is the turning of that first image to other images and ideas in the act of troping.

Just before Balaustion begins to recite the *Alkestis*, she talks explicitly about her words in relation to Euripides', and she does so in ways which seem, on first reading, not consistent with the theory of interpretation we have just explored. In an extended simile, she likens her words to ivy growing in and out of a temple, which is the *Alkestis*:

> Look at Baccheion's beauty opposite,
> The temple with the pillars at the porch!
> See you not something beside masonry?
> What if my words wind in and out the stone
> As yonder ivy, the God's parasite?
> Though they leap all the way the pillar leads,
> Festoon about the marble, foot to frieze,
> And serpentiningly enrich the roof,
> Toy with some few bees and a bird or two, –
> What then? The column holds the cornice up.   (348–57)

Here Balaustion argues that her repetition of the Euripidean text has no effect on the original, which remains what it is whether the ivy is present or not. Moreover, her words, like the ivy, have no essential or organic relation to the original, and the ivy is only a 'parasite' and not an inevitable part of the structure. Balaustion even explicitly rejects an idealist view of language at the end of the passage. In contrast to the Coleridgian argument that 'substance' and 'understanding' are identical because our words 'stand under' and hold up the appearances of things, Balaustion dismisses the view that her words have anything to do with supporting the temple: 'The column holds the cornice up.' In spite of all these obvious meanings in the passage, however, Balaustion asks a crucial question in the midst of it: 'See you not something beside masonry?'

The answer can only be yes, and that affirmation indicates that the temple is not in fact the same as it was originally, that it looks different because of the ivy, which the viewer must incorporate in his or her experience of the temple. Moreover, the relation of parasite and host is a reciprocal one, as J. Hillis Miller has shown in a well-known essay from 1977–9.[8] 'Parasite' in Balaustion's speech appears as 'the God's parasite,' and the god is Dionysus or Bacchus, whose *thyrsus* was a staff or spear encircled with ivy. Dionysus inspired music and poetry, and the conjunction of a god, wine and the arts is one Browning will return to in 'Apollo and the Fates.' In *Balaustion's Adventure* ivy and temple have a double and contradictory relation: the ivy is only a 'poor climber' (347) having no effect on the structure which is its host, and it is the 'something beside masonry' which to the eye of the viewer doubles the lines and shapes of the architecture, on the one hand, and redraws and reshapes them, on the other: the stone is always stone, but the ivy 'wind[s] in and out'; the ivy follows the line of the pillar (it 'leap[s] all the way the pillar leads') but changes it when it 'Festoon[s] about the marble'; and it changes the shape and appearance of the roof, too, when it 'serpentiningly enrich[es]' it. With the ivy present, the temple both is and is not what it always was. So too with Balaustion's words in relation to Euripides'. The *Alkestis* remains the *Alkestis*, and yet it looks different because we are seeing it through and with new words.

The doubleness I have just been exploring is something that Balaustion sums up in this way:

You will expect, no one of all the words
O' the play but is grown part now of my soul,
Since the adventure. 'Tis the poet speaks:
But if I, too, should try and speak at times,
Leading your love to where my love, perchance,
Climbed earlier, found a nest before you knew –
Why, bear with the poor climber, for love's sake!   (341–7)

She insists that she has memorized the *Alkestis* and that, when she recites the words of the play, "'tis the poet speaks,' but at the same time the play has in the experience of Balaustion taken on a life of its own, independent of Euripides, and the text both looks the same and looks different as a result. For those who naïvely expect the original and nothing else, Balaustion asks only for forbearance inspired by love of the speaker. Her request presupposes an original determinate meaning while asking for 'a measure of empathy in each interpreter.' Those are the words of David Shaw who, in *The Lucid Veil* (1987), argues that Jowett's essay 'On the Interpretation of Scripture' (1860) and its five criteria for 'a genuine "science of Hermeneutics"' provide 'the best gloss on Balaustion's own method of interpreting Euripides.'[9] We know that Browning and Jowett discussed the *Alkestis* together, and their 'science of Hermeneutics' adds a crucial dimension to the critical issues we have been exploring: that, in Shaw's words, 'far from being an arid scholarly enterprise, hermeneutics can actually be a life-and-death issue' (198). Balaustion's interpretation of the *Alkestis* in the past literally saved her life. She interprets it again, in the present, to her circle of friends, and this second interpretation, a new 'version' of the play, turns the text upwards in a way which indicates not just the physical survival of the past 'adventure' but moral and spiritual progress.

As Balaustion proceeds through Euripides' text, she is already thinking of the rewriting of it, sometimes by someone other than herself, though in line with her preferences, as when she talks about Sophocles' probable treatment of the Chorus:

> I would the Chorus here had plucked up heart,
> Spoken out boldly and explained the man,
> If not to men, to Gods. That way, I think,
> Sophokles would have led their dance and song.
> Here, they said simply ...   (1520–4)

Moreover, she is constantly explaining the motives behind the words of the characters: 'You see what all this poor pretentious talk / Tried at, – how weakness strove to hide itself' (1433–4), she says, or

>   I think,
> What, through this wretched wrangle, kept the man
> From seeing clear – beside the cause I gave –
> Was ...   (1570–3)

Moreover, she takes images and turns or tropes them, as when Herakles goes 'striding off' (1915) to wrestle with Death. His going, she says, is 'the authentic sign and seal / Of Godship' (1918–19), a sign which she immediately turns to a simile. Here is the whole passage:

> Helper of our world!
> I think this is the authentic sign and seal
> Of Godship, that it ever waxes glad,
> And more glad, until gladness blossoms, bursts
> Into a rage to suffer for mankind,
> And recommence at sorrow: drops like seed
> After the blossom, ultimate of all.   (1917–23)

Having turned the striding into a sign of 'Godship,' Balaustion turns it again ('like seed') and elaborates on that simile:

> Say, does the seed scorn earth and seek the sun?
> Surely it has no other end and aim
> Than to drop, once more die into the ground,
> Taste cold and darkness and oblivion there:
> And thence rise, tree-like grow through pain to joy,
> More joy and most joy, – do man good again.   (1924–9)

The elaboration of the trope neatly combines two ideas: self-sacrificing love, and the organic relations of actions. '"Each deed thou hast done / Dies, revives, goes to work in the world,"' David had said to Saul (163–4), and 'There shall never be one lost good!' said Abt Vogler (69): Balaustion's lines fuse those ideas in the seed, which is 'a rage to suffer for mankind' (1921); it dies and revives, and its progress upwards is imitated in the degrees of comparison ('joy, / More joy and most joy' 1928–9) in Balaustion's language.

Balaustion's interpreting and turning have their climax in a new version altogether of the *Alkestis*. That version has its origin in her complete assimilation of Euripides' text. 'You will expect,' she had said to her listeners in the present, 'no one of all the words / O' the play but is grown part now of my soul, / Since the adventure' (341–3). At the end of her repetition of the play she affirms again her complete absorption of it: 'For I have drunk this poem, quenched my thirst, / Satisfied heart and soul' (2431–2), she says,

> yet more remains!
> Could we too make a poem? Try at least,
> Inside the head, what shape the rose-mists take!   (2432–4)

In an important link to the temple and vine image which preceded the recitation, she uses the vine again, but this time as 'The God's prolific giver of the grape' (2427), which in turn is the source of wine. Though Balaustion is a pagan, and though her references are to the figure of Dionysus or Bacchus, the cluster of images – temple, vine, wine – are central to Christianity too, and each one needs only one more turn to become Christ. It is the Holy Spirit, however, who seems most like the interpretive and creative energy Balaustion describes as being bred by our responses to a poetic text. She begins by praising poets:

> Ah, that brave
> Bounty of poets, the one royal race
> That ever was, or will be, in this world!
> They give no gift that bounds itself and ends
> I' the giving and the taking: theirs so breeds
> I' the heart and soul o' the taker, so transmutes
> The man who only was a man before,
> That he grows godlike in his turn, can give –
> He also: share the poets' privilege,
> Bring forth new good, new beauty, from the old.   (2416–25)

A text, then, is like a deed: it goes to work in the world, dies and revives, raises the person who possesses it from sorrow to joy, and is the instrument of moral and spiritual progress. It is in this context that Balaustion gives her own version of the story, which runs from line 2435 to line 2663 in Browning's text.

Euripides' text had dealt, among other things, with the moral growth of Admetos, though that growth is not without its difficulties and ambiguities, as we see in the climactic scene when Herakles persuades Admetos, determined now to live up to his vow and not betray Alkestis, to take the hand of the 'shrouded something.' In her version, Balaustion too deals with such progress, but where Euripides ended with it, she begins with it, so that her text takes the conclusion of the preceding one and spins it around. In this version, Admetos responds to the music of Apollo (who is, 'for punishment, / A mortal form' (2435–6) and slave to Admetos) and becomes an ideal ruler. Then comes the decree of death, against the injustice of which Admetos cries out: his ancestors were violent and selfish, 'Yet they all lived, nay, lingered to old age' (2485) while he must die. Alkestis pleads with Apollo for the life of Admetos, and the god, arguing that 'should Admetos die, / All, we gods purposed in him, dies as sure' (2527–8), agrees that Admetos will live if Alkestis dies in his place. In a reversal of Euripides' text, Admetos rejects such a proposal, and does so by characterizing his relation with Alkestis as like that of flesh and spirit: "'Tis well that I depart and thou remain,' he says to Alkestis,

Who wast to me as spirit is to flesh:
Let the flesh perish, be perceived no more,
So thou, the spirit that informed the flesh,
Bend yet awhile, a very flame above
The rift I drop into the darkness by.   (2560–5)

Their relationship parallels that of sign and signifier, and that link is not an arbitrary and conventional one, as Locke taught, but a necessary and essential one, since the letters or articulate sounds are dead and without meaning so long as there is no spirit to quicken them and reveal their significance. In Admetos's troping of their marriage, flesh is the sign of spirit, and is essentially related to it; without spirit, flesh becomes 'that abominable show / Of passive death without a quickening life' (2568–9). In the narrative as Balaustion presents it, Alkestis dies, but when she does, 'her whole soul entered into his' (2613), and his life '"Is formidably doubled"' (2635); hence Koré (Persephone), saying such doubling '"is not to die"' (2632), gives up Alkestis and, in a fairy-tale ending, husband and wife live happily ever after. Balaustion qualifies the romance ending by saying she does not know whether or not the pair succeeded in their 'scheme of rule in righteousness, / The bringing back again the Golden Age' (2655–6), but she has clearly raised the story to a higher level by making both husband and wife morally superior and equally self-sacrificing, and by eliminating the agency of a third party, Herakles.

In the second of the nested plays, then, Balaustion both recites the *Alkestis* and makes a new *Alkestis*, and in the play which contains both the other two – this is the third of the plays we must examine – the historical Robert Browning also recites and makes anew, and implicitly issues a challenge to the reader to construct his or her own work. Browning's own turning is threefold: he translates Euripides; he provides a dramatic and narrative frame for the translation; and he sets both in the context of his own life as poet and man. In a 1964 essay, Joseph Friend explored the biographical significance of *Balaustion's Adventure*, arguing that 'the poem reflects the poet's relation with Elizabeth Barrett Browning, both before and after her death.'[10] There is no need to repeat the details of Friend's argument. For our purposes, we should only note that both Euripides' text and Balaustion's story can be read as oblique references to the relations of the historical Robert and Elizabeth, but such a reading is enigmatic and riddling, and much that one might say must remain conjecture, guess, suspicion, or opinion. A few things seem certain. There is, as Friend points out, the meaning of Balaustion's name – 'Wild-pomegranate-flower,' as the text itself gives it (207) – and Elizabeth's use of the pomegranate in 'Lady Geraldine's Courtship' to characterize Robert's poetry, a metaphor 'which led [Robert] to write his first letter to "dear Miss Barrett"' (Friend 181). There is the epigraph from Elizabeth's 'Wine of Cypress' prefixed to the poem and then Robert's use of it again at the end:

> I know the poetess who graved in gold,
> Among her glories that shall never fade,
> This style and title for Euripides,
> *The Human with his droppings of warm tears.*   (2668–71)

Elizabeth's lines introduce the pattern of development or progress with which Robert's text is concerned, for she speaks of Euripides' 'touches of things common / Till they rose to touch the spheres' (the lines Robert uses as his epigraph). The key word in these lines is 'touch,' where the experience of one sense expands, connects with other senses, and rises into comprehension. The epigraph at the beginning and the quotation at the end intertwine Elizabeth's response to Euripides with her response to Robert, and both 'touch' him as he responds to her and to the Greek dramatist by 'transcribing' Euripides and creating Balaustion. Browning also responds to another contemporary work, his friend Sir Frederic Leighton's painting, *Hercules Wrestling with Death for the Body of Alcestis,* which the poet does not simply describe but interprets and judges: 'I pronounce that piece / Worthy to set up in our Poilkilé' (2696–7). All these new texts, new works, 'came of this play that gained no prize' (2704), says the 'I' of the final lines of the poem, a voice which conflates Balaustion's and Browning's, for it refers not only to the 'glory of the golden verse' (2698) – Elizabeth's – from 1844, 'And passion of the picture' (2699) – Leighton's – from 1869–71, but also to the 'Frank outgush of the human gratitude / Which saved our ship and me, in Syracuse' (2700–1). This conflating of the two voices suggests the obvious: that each turning is not separate and distinct, and that readers ought not to make an easy assumption that a text is univocal.

Balaustion's Adventure gives us two major aspects of Browning's understanding of a topic of continuing interest to him: the history and reception of texts. First, the text with which he begins remains itself, like Balaustion's temple, determinate in shape and structure, whatever the additions to it; secondly, the text with which he begins evokes responses and interpretations which give rise to new texts and new works, so that the original text forever afterwards looks different because it has been turned in a new way. Those two aspects of the history of a text are not entirely compatible with each other, and Browning does not attempt to reconcile them, but they do turn up in other poems, such as 'Development' from the *Asolando* volume, and they do account for his interest in the Higher Criticism in an earlier poem such as 'A Death in the Desert.'

First, 'Development,' which is the most accessible of Browning's poems dealing with the reception of a text. Its epigraph might be 'One thing has many sides,' for its subject is the poet's reading of Homer at various stages in his life, and the different ways in which he apprehends the *Iliad* at different stages in his development. Browning defines each stage carefully and vividly. At the age of five, he learns the story of the siege of Troy from his father, who uses fiction to teach the facts of Homer's text: the boy himself is Priam, their cat is Helen, their dogs the Atreidai, and so on. The boy's response is one of 'huge delight' (18) and, in a line which becomes the motif of the poem, he says that 'This taught me who was who and what was what' (16). At the age of seven or eight, he starts learning Greek but in the meantime reads Pope's translation of Homer. Now the earlier game – 'I and playmates playing at Troy's Siege' (25) – is 'make-believe' (26) in contrast to the facts of Pope's text: 'what history so true?' (39). At the age of twelve, he reads Homer in the original Greek. Now Pope seems fiction as 'I learned / Who was who, what was what, from Homer's tongue' (48–9). He has a complacent sense of knowing a first or original text, until it too is called into question by a simple query: '"Who was it wrote the Iliad?"' (52). At the age of twelve, he can answer 'Homer' without hesitation, but later he reads the German critics and Wolf's *Prolegomena ad Homerum* and finds it 'unpleasant work / Their chop and change, unsettling one's belief' (65–6). The idiomatic 'chop and change' refers to Wolf's writing of the history of the Homeric text, his demonstrating that the text had not been fixed for all time, but had itself appeared in many versions as the rhapsodes, revisers, and Alexandrians all made changes, recombining elements and rearranging episodes for varying purposes. Though Wolf argues that the editor's task is to seek out 'the author's true handiwork at every point,' his emphasis is on the need to examine and evaluate 'the witnesses for every reading': 'to examine the properties and individual nature of the sources from which each writer's text is derived; to judge each of the various witnesses, once they are set out by classes and families, by its character; and to learn to follow their voices, and gestures, so to speak, with cunning, but without bias.'[11] This technique of examining 'the testimony of the witnesses,' of those who have read a text and edited it in various ways (by emendations, additions, deletions, and rearrangements), yields ostensibly a history of 'the changes in the transmitted text' (57) but in fact a history of its reception, so that there is, as Browning says in his poem, 'No actual Homer, no authentic text' (71) but rather continuous rereading and reinterpretation, each act of which changes the text while preserving it. We can see that this focus upon the human beings who read texts and who leave evidence of their reading in each recension would be of great interest to a dramatic poet like Browning, who imitates those editorial acts in texts like *The Ring and the Book* and *Balaustion's Adventure*. The question Browning always asks, as he does in 'Development,' is this: what kind of truth can each such reading claim? There is no one answer to that question, and each reading must be judged, as Wolf argues, but in 'Development' Browning provides an answer from his own experience. As usual, he talks about truth with the terms 'fact' and 'fiction,' and he describes how Wolf provided

No warrant for the fiction I, as fact,
Had treasured in my heart and soul so long –
Ay, mark you! and as fact held still, still hold,
Spite of new knowledge, in my heart of hearts
And soul of souls, fact's essence freed and fixed
From accidental fancy's guardian sheath.   (72–7)

What is 'fact's essence'? Browning provides a clear answer about what it is not, and an ambiguous answer about what it is. It is not moral teaching or precepts, the result of the conative function of literature, so that the young Browning would have learned that

My aim should be to loathe, like Peleus' son,
A lie as Hell's Gate, love my wedded wife,
Like Hector, and so on with all the rest.   (100–2)

Browning might have learned the same lessons from Aristotle's *Nico-*

machean Ethics, all abstract moral teaching with 'no pretty lying' (107), but his assent to such instruction would not match his experience of 'fact's essence.' That essence Browning refers to, enigmatically, as a 'dream,' but the nature of that dream becomes clear when we remember that the boy's first response to the story was 'huge delight,' and that such a response led to a treasuring up of the story in 'my heart and soul so long,' even 'in my heart of hearts / And soul of souls.' Such a response can only be to myth, understood as a story which is important to a nation or race, and myth is 'fact's essence,' 'freed and fixed / From accidental fancy's guardian sheath.' 'Accidental fancy' refers, I think, to the various verbal recensions that preserve the myth, never in the same way twice, and in styles and emplotments as different as the different tellers of the story. One does not get rid of 'accidental fancy' (it is important to note), since no myth is independent of historical times and places, and the naïve empiricist who thinks it possible to apprehend a world of unmediated facts has his or her counterpart in the naïve reader who thinks it possible to possess unhistoricized myth. Moreover, as Browning's 'guardian sheath' metaphor indicates, 'accidental fancy' is armour which protects and preserves the myth. Myth may exist in one's 'heart of hearts / And soul of souls,' but as soon as one recounts it, the telling belongs to a particular time and place. Browning's telling belongs in an age where progress was often a shaping idea and an organizing pattern, and Browning (whose concern in this poem is not the actual retelling of the myth but his changing responses to it) typically thinks of individual experience as progressive. Such growth is indicated by the title of the poem itself and by an allusion to Shakespeare near the end of the poem. (Allusion is another technique of embedding one text in another, and deserves a fuller study than I can give it here.) In line 99 Browning expresses gratitude that his father did not teach him 'by forthrights not meanderings.' The allusion is to *The Tempest,* where Gonzalo complains that the wandering of the court party on the island is 'a maze trod indeed / Through forthrights and meanders' (3.3.2–3). We remember that, in the play, such wandering is a trial and initiation that bring about renewal and make possible the resolution of the comic romance, and by echoing the line Browning draws upon the conventional pattern of comic romance, as he also does in *Balaustion's Adventure,* to strengthen his idea of development.

Balaustion's theory of interpretation – that one sense is essentially related to the others, and so evokes statements that are authoritative, though they are based on imagined rather than actual experience – has its counterpart in the doctrine of the three souls ascribed to John in 'A Death in the Desert.' The idea appears in 'the glossa of Theotypas,' one of the critical commentaries on a text which Browning presents as the product of various witnesses and as the subject of a history, or at least of a provenance, difficult to reconstruct:

> This is the doctrine he was wont to teach,
> How divers persons witness in each man,
> Three souls which make up one soul. (82–4)

The first is our physical being, which receives sensations and acts in accordance with the needs of our earthly existence: it is 'what Does' (86).

> The next soul, which, seated in the brain,
> Useth the first with its collected use,
> And feeleth, thinketh, willeth, – is what Knows. (90–2)

Just as the first two souls differ in their operations but are essentially related, so both are different from but organically linked with the third and last soul. It

> uses both the first,
> Subsisting whether they assist or no,
> And, constituting man's self, is what Is. (95–7)

Theotypas summarizes his commentary in line 103: 'What Does, what Knows, what Is; three souls, one man.' The way in which the three souls work is apparent in John's account of his life.

For the purposes of the poem, Browning accepts as fact the identity of John the author of the fourth gospel, John the letter-writer, and John the recorder of Revelation. He does so because he wants to make a major point about the nature of ongoing interpretation: that when the words of one kind of witness, once adequate in their time, fail, then the words of another kind of witness take over, a refashioning that parallels the casting off of old clothes and the tailoring of new ones in Carlyle's *Sartor Resartus*. In 'A Death in the Desert' the central issue is one of great interest to Victorian thinkers who knew the Higher Criticism: what kind of authority can be claimed by writers who were no longer sensible witnesses to the life of Christ, whose experience of him was not that of eye and ear and hand? The historical moment Browning chooses for the poem dramatizes the issue: John presents himself as the last person in the world to have witnessed the earthly existence of Jesus, and the question he poses is the crucial one:

> 'there is left on earth
> No one alive who knew (consider this!)
> – Saw with his eyes and handled with his hands
> That which was from the first, the Word of Life.
> How will it be when none more saith "I saw"'?   (129–33)

The time Browning chooses is the same (as Elinor Shaffer has pointed out) as that chosen by Coleridge for his planned but never written epic, *The Fall of Jerusalem*: 68–9 AD. 'A history of Jesus written in A.D. 70 was just at the limit of authentic witness, at the point when memories were turning into legend,'[12] historical fact into Christian myth. Like Coleridge, Browning was well aware of the way in which empiricists privileged eyewitness accounts, labelling facts as truth and interpretations not quite as fiction but certainly as opinions created by the mind and therefore less authentic, less reliable, than the original event. Such empiricists would have a very difficult time, then, with Henry Melvill's argument in the 1833 sermon I referred to in chapter 1, 'Truth as it is in Jesus.' 'Those who have not seen,' Melvill says, 'may stand in precisely the same position as those who have; and ... consequently, the absence of what may be called sensible proof, furnishes no ground-work of complaint, that "the former days were better than these."'[13] Melvill is making the same point as Coleridge before him: that we do not see any event in an unmediated way, but always in terms of our expectations, our habits of thought, our concerns, and our judgments. 'Interpretation is embedded in event,' writes Shaffer (46), who quotes Fritz Strich: '"To perceive is to mythologize"' (47). Browning too suggests that the problems of interpretation for those who have not seen are not essentially different from those of eyewitnesses, and he dramatizes that point by having John confess to fleeing from one of the crucial events of the Passion. The reference (in lines 301–11 of the poem) is not to the Crucifixion (as Shaffer, following Renan, says, 193) but rather to Gethsemane, as R.L. Brett pointed out in reviewing Shaffer's book,[14] but nonetheless the flight is a test of the other faculties of one 'who was present from the first!' (301) and saw and heard for himself. Much of John's speech is in fact devoted to witnessing with faculties other than his senses, and, when one becomes inadequate, another takes over in a cooperative and reciprocal relationship. At first John does indeed rely on the evidence of his senses, and that evidence is sufficient to assure believers:

'Since I, whom Christ's mouth taught, was bidden teach,
I went, for many years, about the world,
Saying "It was so; so I heard and saw,"
Speaking as the case asked: and men believed.'   (135–8)

His writing of the Book of Revelation is similarly the result of the evidence of his senses, except that he is not required to judge that evidence or interpret it in any way. He is simply God's passive instrument:

'I was not bidden teach,
But simply listen, take a book and write,
Nor set down other than the given word,
With nothing left to my arbitrament
To choose or change: I wrote, and men believed.'   (140–4)

John's preaching and writing of the Book of Revelation are the result of the activities of his first soul, 'what Does,' and for a time its evidence is sufficient. Then John goes beyond listening and repeating what he has heard in his speech or writing. In the second stage, he reasons from his knowledge (line 147) and writes the letters: '"Friends said I reasoned rightly, and believed"' (151). The third stage gathers up 'what Does' and 'what Knows' in a fuller and more comprehensive interpretation of the life of Christ, the result of which is the fourth gospel:

'Since much that at the first, in deed and word,
Lay simply and sufficiently exposed,
Had grown (or else my soul was grown to match,
Fed through such years, familiar with such light,
Guarded and guided still to see and speak)
Of new significance and fresh result;
What first were guessed as points, I now knew stars,
And named them in the Gospel I have writ.'   (168–75)

The gospel is no more (or less) authentic and authoritative than his first preaching because the doctrine of the three souls (which has parallels in Plato and Neoplatonism)[15] is a trinitarian analogy, as William Whitla (following F.E.L. Priestley) pointed out long ago.[16] The essence of the three souls is the same, whatever the differences in their operation. As with the three senses Balaustion discusses, the stimulation of one leads to the operation of the others because of the interpretive and shaping power they share.

The companion piece to *Balaustion's Adventure* is *Aristophanes' Apology*, and it too is a play within a play within a play, though the second frame of this nesting structure differs from that of the earlier poem. The play at the centre is Euripides' *Herakles*, the 'perfect piece' which Balaustion 'reads' aloud (3534) as part of her debate with Aristophanes – the debate is the second of the plays – and both the Euripidean play and the debate are enclosed within a third play, Balaustion's speech to her husband Euthukles during their voyage home to Rhodes, a speech which she describes as a repetition of the tragedy they have just experienced, the fall of Athens:

> So, Euthukles, permit the tragedy
> To re-enact itself, this voyage through,
> Till sunsets end and sunrise brighten Rhodes!
> Peplosed and kothorned, let Athenai fall
> Once more, nay, oft again till life conclude,
> Lent for the lesson ...   (167–73)

The voice of the poet himself, the containing voice of *Balaustion's Adventure*, is in *Aristophanes' Apology* not explicitly present, but the words are, of course, of his choosing. Because the story here reverses the story of *Balaustion's Adventure*, and because that reversal gives us a sense of things being turned inside out and upside down, the text invites us to begin, not with the innermost of the plays, but with the outermost.

Balaustion's Adventure began, like *The Tempest*, with a tragic action, a ship blown off course and a community threatened with death and destruction. Balaustion's reciting of the *Alkestis* brings about a reversal – 'so turns to comic what was tragic,' says Browning of one of his later stories[17] – and that reversal leads to the kind of ending one would find in comic romance, a successful conclusion of the voyage to Athens, and the marriage of Balaustion and Euthukles. *Aristophanes' Apology* reverses that dénouement as the comedy turns to tragedy: Athens is defeated by Sparta, the defences of the city are pulled down, and Balaustion and her husband are exiled from their cultural and spiritual home. Browning's continuation of the story parallels 'the view of English Comedy of a sagacious essayist' paraphrased but not identified by Meredith in his

1877 lecture on comedy, an essayist 'who said that the end of a Comedy would often be the commencement of a Tragedy, were the curtain to rise again on the performers.'[18] Since *Aristophanes' Apology* is concerned in a central way with the rival claims of tragedy and comedy, and since one of its governing tropes is the turning which translates one genre into another, the plotting of this outermost of the text's plays is a commentary on the debate or contest which makes up the second of the plays, and on Balaustion's way of presenting the *Herakles*, the innermost of these nested plays.

The tragic nature of the outermost play is signalled by a beginning which is the lament of an exile. Though Balaustion and Euthukles are 'homeward-bound' (36), their feelings are not those of anticipation but of overwhelming loss, and a sense of loss coupled with a sense of things breaking up is the conventional mark of tragedy. That sense shapes Balaustion's lament: 'Athenai, live thou hearted in my heart: / Never, while I live, may I see thee more' (4–5). 'The living are the dead now' (104), she says, and they themselves are 'Exiles from dead Athenai' (217). The *ubi sunt* formula is one of the conventional notes of the lament, and Balaustion sounds it when she remembers the companions to whom she told her first adventure: 'Where are the four now'? (190). The natural cycle with which Balaustion associates her present state is the cycle of the day, and the part of that cycle which corresponds to tragedy is the coming of night. The homeward voyage is, in her experience of it, a sunset rather than a sunrise, and she sees it in that way as a result of her night visitor, Aristophanes:

Condense our voyage into one great day
Made up of sunset-closes: eve by eve,
Resume that memorable night-discourse. (223–5)

The voyage, then, is a reenactment of the tragedy (though we note that, just as comedy continued is tragedy, tragedy continued is comedy, a turn Balaustion anticipates when she says that their voyage will last 'Till sunsets end and sunrise brighten Rhodes!' 169).

The tragedy that Balaustion reenacts begins with the death of Euripides, continues through the debate with Aristophanes, and includes her reading aloud of the *Herakles*. That performance is very different from her reciting of the *Alkestis*. Then she had not only repeated the dramatic text but had integrated it with the theatrical production she had witnessed and with her interpretation of both. Now her reading provides nothing beyond the words of Euripides' text: no staging of it in the theatre of her mind, no interpretation of it as she recites it. When Euripides gave her the text, he said (as she reports his speech), '"So, should you croon the ode bewailing Age"' – he is referring to one of the choruses in the play – '"Yourself shall modulate – same notes, same strings – / With the old friend who loved Balaustion once"' (3521–3). The modulation in the voice of Balaustion seems to be not much more than that of Echo's voice, since she is sounding the '"same notes, same strings,"' and since she reads Euripides' text word for word without any additions of her own. All the intelligence, all the interpretive and quickening powers she had brought to the *Alkestis* she here brings not to this text (which in her view is 'perfect' and needs no interpretation) but to her repeating of her debate with Aristophanes. She recounts not only the words of that debate but the looks and gestures, all of which she interprets in terms of motives, feelings, and ideas. Of her reenactment of the debate she says,

> Let us attempt that memorable talk,
> Clothe the adventure's every incident
> With due expression: may not looks be told,
> Gesture made speak, and speech so amplified
> That words find blood-warmth which, cold-writ, they lose?   (233–7)

The *Herakles*, read aloud, remains 'cold-writ'; it is the debate which contains it which she 'amplifies' and in which she finds 'blood-warmth.'

The reenactment of that debate begins with a tragedy, the death of Euripides. Balaustion tells how Euthukles brought her the news of that death, and their memories of the final stages of Euripides' life provide us with the conventional tragic action, the separation of an individual from his society, his exile and finally his death. The news of the death coincides with '"victory / Again awarded Aristophanes"' (346–7), and we remember that Balaustion habitually characterized the *Alkestis* as the 'play that gained no prize' (*Balaustion's Adventure* 2704). Its being passed over is an early indication of its author's gradual exclusion from his society. Euripides' experience of the Athenian theatre was one dominated by criticism and finally the scorn of the audiences, so that he retreated to a 'sea-cave' (284) and then went into exile in Macedonia, where he died. To commemorate their dead hero, Balaustion and Euthukles prepare to read his last gift to them, the *Herakles*, 'writ by his own hand, each line' (522). They do so in the hope of reversing the decline of Euripides' fame and proving the worth of the play. 'What if you and I / Re-sing the song, inaugurate the fame?' (529–30), Balaustion asks. It is at that moment that the mourners are interrupted by revellers, the reading of the tragedy stayed by the appearance of 'the Choros of the Comedy' (574) and then by Aristophanes himself. The juxtaposition of the two groups and their opposing emotions and values lead to the main part of the tragedy, the *agon* or conflict.

Critics have noted how much the main part of *Aristophanes' Apology* depends upon the struggle of opposites. Clyde de L. Ryals, for instance, describes Balaustion as soul, Aristophanes as body; in a later book he expands on a different argument, labelling Aristophanes as being and Balaustion as becoming.[19] Such a struggle not only is a conventional part of the action of tragedy, but also owes something to a poetic genre, the contest or *débat*, where soul is often pitted against body or water against wine. I mention these conventional pairings because both appear in the poem and because they are of some importance in defining the competing claims of the chief antagonists, comedy and tragedy. These claims are bound up with a host of other pairings: drunkenness and sobriety, laughter and tears, virtue and vice, 'low flesh' and 'high soul' (498), earth and heaven, '"ordure-heap"' (479) and '"true lightning overhead"' (481), 'fire and filth' (226), 'deity / And dung' (227–8) – even '"Vowel-buds thorned about with consonants"' (640). Our main concern, however, is with comedy and tragedy and with a pairing which characterizes the language of both: names and nicknames.

The theory of comedy appears in the reported toast of Strattis, who raises his cup

'"To the Comic Muse,
She who evolves superiority,
Triumph and joy from sorrow, unsuccess
And all that's incomplete in human life ..."'   (1353–6)

Joy out of sorrow, triumph out of 'unsuccess,' are phrases that sum up the plot of comedy. Strattis then goes on to draw upon the theory of humours, arguing that comedy takes the unbalanced and the misshapen in human makeup and restores men and women to a harmonious completeness. '"'Fancy's feat,'"' he says, is to

'"right man's wrong, establish true for false,–
Above misshapen body, uncouth soul,

Reach the fine form, the clear intelligence –
Above unseemliness, reach decent law, –
By laughter ...'" (1364–9)

In arguing for the civilizing, harmonizing, and elevating effect of the laughter of comedy, Strattis is anticipating the argument Meredith would advance in his lecture of 1877. Strattis's view, however, is a relatively pure or unmixed one, and he leaves out of his toast other sides of comedy important to Aristophanes, particularly satire and the satyr-play. Balaustion is willing to accept the aim of satire – '"to burn and purify the world, / True aim, fair purpose"' (787–8) – but balks at its unabashed portrayals of the ordinary life of the senses, summed up by Aristophanes thus:

'Grub one's vine,
Romp with one's Thratta, pretty serving-girl,
When wifie's busy bathing! Eat and drink,
And drink and eat, what else is good in life?' (1087–90)

Tragedy elevates, in Balaustion's view, while comedy panders to human sensuality. Friends had accused Balaustion of prudery and ignorance (415–16), and Aristophanes recognizes that she blames '"Both theory and practice – Comedy"' (1764) because it deals with ordinary men and women pursuing ordinary lives.

'I stand up for the common coarse-as-clay
Existence, – stamp and ramp with heel and hoof
On solid vulgar life, you fools disown.' (2683–5)

As Meredith would do, Aristophanes defends comedy as '"Coëval with the birth of freedom"' (1784), and he insists that it is a life-expressing and life-giving genre:

'for I praise the god
Present in person of his minister,
And pay – the wilder my extravagance –
The more appropriate worship to the Power
Adulterous, night-roaming, and the rest:
Otherwise, – that originative force
Of nature, impulse stirring death to life,

Which, underlying law, seems lawlessness,
Yet is the outbreak which, ere order be,
Must thrill creation through, warm stocks and stones,
Phales Iacchos.'   (2357–67)

'"Phallic Bacchus,"' in other words. Hence it is not surprising that Aristophanes attacks tragedy, and specifically Euripides, for his focus on death and a better life rather than on the here and now with its impulses and natural energies:

'I cry "Life!" "Death," he groans, "our better Life!"
Despise what is – the good and graspable,
Prefer the out of sight and in at mind,
To village-joy, the well-side violet-patch,
The jolly club-feast when our field's in soak,
Roast thrushes, hare-soup, pea-soup, deep washed down
With Peparethian [wine] ...'   (1953–9)

In sharp contrast to such earthy views of comedy, Balaustion associates tragedy with the soul, particularly the 'disembodied soul' (43) which is 'Thought-borne' (44) and which, in a spatial metaphor which is typical of her handling of her side of the debate, is 'above / Man's wickedness and folly' (39–40), 'Above all crowding' (45), and 'Above all noise' (46). In an imperative addressed to Perikles, she asks him to build a new Athens, 'some spirit-place no flesh shall find' (108). We begin to realize not only that Balaustion is an apologist for tragedy but also that her way of seeing things at this moment in her life is essentially tragic: in contrast to the comic inclusiveness of Aristophanes, she wants to separate and divide and 'purify'; soul is to be separated from body, virtue from vice, and so on. (To state the contrast as sharply as I have just done does not do justice to Balaustion's intelligence, however, since she listens to Aristophanes with understanding, since their debate is genuine give and take, and since she says such things as 'I thought there might lurk truth in jest's disguise' 1030.) The girlhood episode in which she saw a god rise from the sea defines her view: '"He rose but breast-high. So much god she saw"' (says Balaustion, speaking about herself in the third person) '"So much she sees now, and does reverence!"' (824–5).

It is Aristophanes who, in response to Strattis's toast to comedy, proposes a toast to 'the Tragic Muse':

'"She who instructs her poet, bids man's soul
Play man's part merely nor attempt the gods'
Ill-guessed of! Task humanity to height,
Put passion to prime use, urge will, unshamed
When will's last effort breaks in impotence!
No power forego, elude: no weakness, – plied
Fairly by power and will, – renounce, deny!
Acknowledge, in such miscalled weakness strength
Latent: and substitute thus things for words!'"   (1394–1402)

We note that Aristophanes defines the language of tragedy as equivocal: strength is 'miscalled weakness.' To read a tragedy, then, is to turn to the 'things' – ideas, that is – to which words point in such an ambiguous and riddling way. Aristophanes' understanding of the language of comedy is, as we shall see, the same, and such language, common in nature and function to the two genres, makes possible the turning of one into the other, and ultimately the fusion of the two. Our concern at the moment, however, is with the debate and with the defining of sharply opposed positions, and Aristophanes defines those positions thus: blame comedy, he says,

    'from altitudes the Tragic friend
Rose to, and upraised friends along with him,
No matter how. Once there, all's cold and fine,
Passionless, rational; our world beneath
Shows (should you condescend to grace so much
As glance at poor Athenai) grimly gross –
A population which, mere flesh and blood,
Eats, drinks and kisses, falls to fisticuffs,
Then hugs as hugely ...'   (1764–72)

The world has '"two courses"' (1775): it can '"Unworld itself"' (1776) and pursue philosophy on '"heights serene, fit perch for owls like you"' (1778), Aristophanes says to Balaustion, or it can '"go blackening off / To its crow-kindred"' (1776–7). The debate, in short, is cast in terms of opposites that seem irreconcilable. At the centre of the debate is a characteristic Browning issue: the question of turning something and seeing it from more than one side.

As Aristophanes and Balaustion come more and more to understand their positions, Aristophanes is able to voice a central and damaging charge: that Balaustion and Euripides and the champions of tragedy have a single perspective, while he and the defenders of comedy are capable of multiple ways of viewing. As usual, Browning uses the orb image for the thing which is to be viewed (the image, I suspect, owes something to Quarles and the recurring *pictura* of the world as an orb), but here the viewer is not outside, turning the thing in various ways, but on the inside looking out. Aristophanes contrasts himself and Euripides, both of whom he pictures as suspended inside the orb, so that they become containers within containers in the game of '"kottabos"' (5101), 'a Greek pastime,' in the words of Pettigrew and Collins in the Penguin-Yale edition, 'which involved throwing wine in a carefully prescribed manner from one container to another' (2:1017). The passage is a long one but an important one, and I quote the whole of it:

> 'Take a sphere
> With orifices at due interval,
> Through topmost one of which, a throw adroit
> Sends wine from cup, clean passage, from outside
> To where, in hollow midst, a manikin
> Suspended ever bobs with head erect
> Right underneath whatever hole's a-top
> When you set orb a-rolling: plumb, he gets
> Ever this benediction of the splash.
> An other-fashioned orb presents him fixed:
> Of all the outlets, he fronts only one,
> And only when that one, – and rare the chance, –
> Comes uppermost, does he turn upward too:
> He can't turn all sides with the turning orb.
> Inside this sphere of life, – all objects, sense
> And soul perceive, – Euripides hangs fixed,
> Gets knowledge through the single aperture
> Of High and Right: with visage fronting these
> He waits the wine thence ere he operate,
> Work in the world and write a tragedy.
> When that hole happens to revolve to point,
> In drops the knowledge, waiting meets reward.
> But, duly in rotation, Low and Wrong –
> When these enjoy the moment's altitude,
> His heels are found just where his head should be!
> No knowledge that way! *I* am movable, –

To slightest shift of orb make prompt response,
Face Low and Wrong and Weak and all the rest,
And still drink knowledge, wine-drenched every turn, –
Equally favoured by their opposites.
Little and Bad exist, are natural:
Then let me know them, and be twice as great
As he who only knows one phase of life!'   (5102–34)

Wine, which we must by now recognize as Browning's metaphor for the natural energy which sustains our physical life and creates new life through both the body and the imagination, is common to the writer of tragedy and the writer of comedy, but the former is 'fixed' and 'can't turn all sides with the turning orb' while the latter is 'movable' and sees from multiple perspectives.

At an earlier stage in the debate, Aristophanes linked the multiple perspectives of comedy with equivocation in language. Contrary to the theatre-goers who accuse Balaustion of squeamishness, of not being able to '"bear plain words / Concerning deeds [the world] acts with gust enough"' (407–8) and of not liking a stage '"where truth calls spade a spade!"' (410), Aristophanes argues that the language of comedy, especially when it serves the purposes of satire, is characteristically false. His chief metaphor is a conventional one: the satirist as physician and his satire as physic:

'I dose each culprit just with – Comedy.
Let each be doctored in exact the mode
Himself prescribes: by words, the word-monger –
My words to his words, – my lies, if you like,
To his lies.'   (2490–4)

Hence he uses not names but nicknames: '"Sokrates I nickname thief, / Quack, necromancer"' (2494–5). For the same reason he uses verbal irony, where words mean their opposites:

'Love smiles "rogue" and "wretch"
When "sweet" and "dear" seem vapid: Hate adopts
Love's "sweet" and "dear" when "rogue" and "wretch" fall flat:
Love, Hate – are truths, then, each, in sense not sound.'   (2503–7)

Aristophanes defends such irony as the telling of truth which univocal words would falsify:

'if Love, remaining Love, fell back
On "sweet" and "dear," – if Hate, though Hate the same,
Dropped down to "rogue" and "wretch," – each phrase were
   false.'   (2507–9)

In short, the turning which creates the equivocation also signifies a
fuller truth than the word attached to its conventional idea could ever
do. '"Well, I acknowledge!"' Aristophanes says,

   'Every word [in comedy] is false,
Looked close at; but stand distant and stare through,
All's absolute indubitable truth
Behind lies, truth which only lies declare!
For come, concede me truth's in thing not word,
Meaning not manner!'   (2498–2503)

One should perhaps note that Aristophanes is not expressing the naïve
empiricism of thinkers like those in Swift's Academy of Lagado, where
'things' are material and physical objects. 'Thing' here is closer in meaning to 'idea,' and in particular to idea not as a single abstraction from
sensation but as a many-sided concept, the kind of thing Locke means
by the names of 'mixed modes and relations,' where the mind chooses a
certain number of ideas, connects them into one, and 'ties them together
by a Name' (3.5.4). The name, in Locke's own trope, is a knot, a metaphor Locke uses primarily to indicate the mind's action in fastening
ideas together, but which we can see as signifying a riddle which can be
solved only by following all the twists and turns of the name itself. To
that understanding of words Aristophanes applies two different tropes:
when he must fight his foes, he says, the word becomes his weapon
('"with word, wage war!"' 2515), and when he is dealing with the attitudes of an audience or '"populace,"' the word is yeast that '"leavens
their whole lump / To the right ferment for my purpose"' (2526–7).
Then Aristophanes gives an example of the way in which words work in
comedy. When adversaries differ and people must judge '"which is
right / And which is wrong"' (2532–3), argument is likely to be unintelligible, but nicknames and lies will achieve the writer's purpose without
argument:

'Swear my foe's mother vended herbs she stole,
They [the populace] fall a-laughing! Add, – his household drudge

Of all-work justifies that office well,
Kisses the wife, composing him the play, –
They grin at whom they gaped in wonderment,
And go off – "Was he such a sorry scrub?
This other seems to know! We praised too fast!"
Why then, my lies have done the work of truth,
Since "scrub," improper designation, means
Exactly what the proper argument
– Had such been comprehensible – proposed
To proper audience – were I graced with such –
Would properly result in ...'   (2535–47)

The word 'scrub' means a stunted tree, but figuratively, as the *OED* indicates, refers to 'a mean insignificant fellow, a person of little account or
poor appearance.' Pettigrew and Collins, the editors of the Yale-Penguin
edition of Browning, paraphrase the word as 'drudge,' and that reading
indicates how the foe and the drudge have turned into each other. The
foe is in fact no drudge or 'scrub,' but the word has effected Aristophanes' desired turn in perception. There are moral problems in such
a false use of words, and Balaustion does not let Aristophanes off easily.
When she paraphrases his argument, as she does in lines 3256–70
(where a trireme is named Sokrates), she asks, '"Why must you Comics
one and all take stand / On lower ground than truth from first to last?"'
(3245–6).

Just as words can be turned, so can dramatic genres, the turn resulting
in a fuller, many-sided view of truth which combines both tragedy and
comedy. One might think that the advocate of such turning would naturally be the writer of comedies, since comedy is conventionally the
genre which is characterized by inclusion and reconciliation, but in this
poem such a combination is first suggested by the tragedian Sophokles,
advocated (as we would expect) by Aristophanes, and finally argued for
by Balaustion herself. First, the proposal of Sophokles as reported by
Aristophanes:

'"You know what kind's the nobler, what makes grave
Or what makes grin; there's yet a nobler still,
Possibly, – what makes wise, not grave, – and glad,
Not grinning: whereby laughter joins with tears,
Tragic and Comic Poet prove one power ..."'   (1298–1302)

Then there is Strattis's toast to Comedy, Aristophanes' toast to Tragedy, and the company's applause for the latter: '"He turns the Tragic on its Comic side"' (1433). Aristophanes asks that 'both be praised,' and proposes an ideal combination which he labels 'complex Poetry':

'You who have laughed with Aristophanes,
You who wept rather with the Lord of Tears!
Priest, do thou, president alike o'er each,
Tragic and Comic function of the god,
Help with libation to the blended twain!
Either of which who serving, only serves –
Proclaims himself disqualified to pour
To that Good Genius – complex Poetry,
Uniting each god-grace, including both;
Which, operant for body as for soul,
Masters alike the laughter and the tears,
Supreme in lowliest earth, sublimest sky.'   (1465–77)

Finally, there is Balaustion herself. 'Had you, I dream,' she says to Aristophanes,

                    discarding all the base,
The brutish, spurned alone convention's watch
And ward against invading decency
Disguised as licence, law in lawlessness,
And so, re-ordinating outworn rule,
Made Comedy and Tragedy combine,
Prove some new Both-yet-neither, all one bard,
Euripides with Aristophanes
Coöperant!   (3435–43)

The combination is for Balaustion only a dream, and 'Earth's question' is 'which succeeds, / Which fails of two life-long antagonists?' (3451–2). Aristophanes is more sanguine. When he presents his orb-and-manikin trope, he imagines a third kind of person inside that sphere

'Who, stationed (by mechanics past my guess)
So as to take in every side at once,
And not successively, – may reconcile

The High and Low in tragi-comic verse, –
He shall be hailed superior to us both ...' (5141–5)

The debate we have just been examining frames the innermost of the three plays, the *Herakles* of Euripides, but we note that that text does not stand alone, and that it is answered by the lyric sung by Aristophanes, 'Thamuris marching.' *Herakles*, the 'perfect piece' (3534), is a tragedy which is part of Balaustion's defence of the genre, and 'Thamuris marching' is part of Aristophanes' celebration of his powers as a comic writer. Though both texts can be read independently, Browning clearly places them in a context, so that they must be seen not only as themselves but as part of the containing debate.

Herakles, considered by itself, is a tragedy. Its subject is the last labour of Herakles, the bringing back of Cerberus from Hades. While Herakles is absent, his father, wife, and children are condemned to death by the usurper Lukos. The plot thus establishes itself as that of romantic comedy, with the expectation that Herakles will return, defeat Lukos, save his family, and establish himself in his proper position in Thebes. Heré, however, turns the plot in the opposite direction and afflicts Herakles with madness, so that he slays his wife and children. Released from insanity, Herakles despairs and would kill himself but for the intervention of Theseus, who persuades Herakles to 'bear thy woes' (4947) and to go with him to Athens. The play reverses *Alkestis*. The saviour there becomes the destroyer here; the man who wrestled with death, and won, confronts death here ('my business,' he says, 'is to die defending these' 4170) but becomes the death-dealer himself. 'Reverses are a grave thing' (4923), Herakles says with a grim pun, and he himself sums up 'My life – past, present – as unlivable' (4887). His twelve labours – comic actions all, in the sense of the successful accomplishment of human purposes – have given way to one overwhelming tragedy:

I both went through a myriad other toils
In full drove, as Eurustheus bade, to light
Haides' three-headed dog and doorkeeper.
But then I, – wretch, – dared this last labour – see!
Slew my sons, keystone-coped my house with ills. (4906–11)

Herakles' tragic sense that all his labours have come only to this final turn from good to ill, and his feeling that his life has narrowed to a situation which is 'unlivable,' has its counterpart in Balaustion's aesthetic sense. She introduces the play as 'the perfect piece' (3534), and 'perfect' means primarily 'complete.' It is complete in the Aristotelian sense, in so far as the tragic action has a beginning, a middle, and an end, but it is also complete in another sense that has to do with a reader's response to the text. Balaustion reads the piece and does not add to it in any way, so that for her 'perfect' means that there is nothing more to be said, and tragedy has its ultimate expression in 'the consummate Tragedy' (3526) she presents. It is finished, and it comes to closure. By presenting *Herakles* in this way, Balaustion closes off further possibilities for tragedy, and narrows the genre by suggesting that, with this play, it is fixed for all time. Her reading is followed by a 'long silence' (5085) that seems to confirm her claim.

It is Aristophanes who breaks the silence, who takes something fixed and turns it. His means are equivocal words: '"Our best friend,"' he mutters, '"Lost, our best friend!"' (5085–6). Who is the friend? Is he referring to the last words of the play, where the Chorus laments the loss of 'the greatest of all our friends' (5083), Herakles? Or is he referring to Euripides, now dead? And if he is doing so, whom is he including in 'our'? Does he mean himself and Balaustion? or does he mean his fellow revellers of comedy, and is he therefore suggesting that the tragic playwright is the best friend of comedy, because the end of a tragic action is the beginning of a comic one? Browning's text does not resolve these ambiguities, but it is at this point that Aristophanes goes on with his orb-and-manikin metaphor and its view of comedy as multiple in perspective and open to energies, troped as wine sloshing in from all sides.

In spite of the common context for both *Herakles* and 'Thamuris marching,' and in spite of the fact that both Herakles and Thamuris meet tragic ends by confronting and challenging powers beyond human ones, the texts are very different in their function. Where *Herakles* is 'perfect' or complete, 'Thamuris marching' is a fragment. Aristophanes simply breaks off without any warning: '"Tell the rest / Who may!"' (5265–6), he says to Balaustion. Where *Herakles* ended with weeping and silence, 'Thamuris marching' ends with laughter (5265). Where Balaustion preserves the words of the *Herakles* as a memorial to Euripides and as the way to test 'true godship,' Aristophanes sings a song celebrating not only supernatural powers but a natural energy common to all of creation. It is that same power that Aristophanes had earlier identified with comedy, '"that originative force / Of nature"' (2362–3), the animal and sexual impulse which '"seems lawlessness"' (2364) – the 'seems' is important – and which precedes order. 'Thamuris marching' links that power with language itself.

The lyric begins with the shape of the whole action, for Thamuris journeys from Thrace and successfully accomplishes a number of actions as he moves 'From triumph on to triumph' (5197) until he, like Childe Roland, comes to the spot where he expects to die: he 'came, saw, and knew the spot / Assigned him for his worst of woes, that day' (5198–9). The parenthesis at the beginning of the lyric suggests that the story is to be a cautionary tale, for it is addressed to the 'poet-race,' and its imperative 'Perpend' (weigh or consider) sounds a warning note. The rest of the fragment is exemplary rather than cautionary. Thamuris marches through a landscape where nature has already been given a human shape: the valley is 'some wide / Thick busy human cluster, house and home' (5203–4). More important, the language of the lyric gives the landscape human attributes, for the dominant trope is proso-popoeia: the river, Balura, for instance, 'meets' Thamuris but does not 'menace' him as it 'pursue[s] its lot / Of solacing the valley' (5201–3). When Thamuris actually speaks, he, like the narrator, tropes nature: '"Each flake of foam,"' he says, '"Mocks slower clouds adrift in the blue dome!"' (5206, 5208). His saying this is linked with marching and laughing, the marching indicating a regular beat, the kinesthetic rhythm of his physical being, and the laughter indicating comedy, with its civilizing push towards inclusiveness and integration. The lyric is, in fact, a celebration of the unity of Thamuris and nature, and that unity is figured in a conventional way, as the animating of inanimate things. The 'ravaged tree' laughs, for instance, and in fact everything in nature moves energetically:

Each, with a glory and a rapture twined
About it, joined the rush of air and light
And force: the world was of one joyous mind.   (5221–3)

The antecedent for such oneness is the great Exodus psalm, 114, where 'the mountains skipped like rams, and the little hills like lambs.' The psalm, we remember, is a celebration of liberation, of an epic action which is also a comic action, and that action has a linguistic element as well: the children of Israel are freed 'from a people of strange language' and enter into a landscape animated by 'the presence of the Lord,' 'which turned the rock into a standing water, the flint into a fountain of waters.' To turn is to perform a miracle, but it is also to trope, and so human beings share in the divine power through their language. That same sharing is the theme of 'Thamuris marching.' 'Earth's community of purpose' (5228) is the phrase there, and since all things share that divine but natural energy, it is possible for one thing to become something else:

> Say not the birds flew! they forebore their right –
> Swam, revelling onward in the roll of things.
> Say not the beasts' mirth bounded! that was flight –
>
> How could the creatures leap, no lift of wings?   (5224–7)

The answer to that question is that they share the same energy, so that birds can swim and beasts can fly. That common energy is also the basis of troping. Just as Browning had, in his note in his copy of Donne, suggested that the elements common to all things were the key to metaphysical conceits, so here he suggests that the energy common to all things makes troping possible. The language with which he describes 'earth's fulfilled imaginings' (5229) suggests the metaphor. Twice he uses the word 'transport,' once in line 5231, and again in line 5243, where the carrying across is 'fiery.' The first appearance of the word is in this tercet:

> So did the near and far appear to touch
> I' the moment's transport, – that an interchange
> Of function, far with near, seemed scarce too much.   (5230–2)

The imaginings bring together things widely separated ('near and far') and, through an 'interchange,' attribute the function of one to the other – and all this through 'transport,' the Latin-based synonym of the Greek 'metaphor.' The common energy which makes troping possible is embodied aurally in the *terza rima* which Browning uses as the form of this lyric. Its repeated and interwoven rhymes suggest both something common to all things and something turning into something else.

In the narrative which forms part of the content of this lyric, Thamuris arrives at the site of his crucial struggle: 'he saw, he knew the place' (5253). The moment parallels that moment in '"Childe Roland"' when the questing candidate for knighthood has a sudden flash of recognition: 'This was the place!' (176). And just as Roland issues a challenge by blowing his slug-horn and defining himself by his story ('"Childe

Roland to the dark tower came"'), so Thamuris issues his challenge, singing to the accompaniment of his lyre and confirming his powers of turning. The music, we note, is first without words, and it comes to him on the wind (that conventional metaphor for inspiration) and, more important, as units of equal time: the wind 'arrived with all the rhythms from the plain' (5254). Without words, we cannot say what the meaning of such rhythms are, but through the power of words Thamuris makes explicit the meaning, and 'that grew song which was mere music erst' (5259). The song consists of apostrophes, apostrophe being one of the figures of prosopopoeia, and the verbal action is the turning of one thing into another:

> 'Be my Parnassos, thou Pangaian mount!
> And turn thee, river, nameless hitherto!
> Famed shalt thou vie with famed Pieria's fount!'   (5260–2)

Thamuris is clearly aware of the struggle to come – '"Here I await the end of this ado: / Which wins – Earth's poet or the Heavenly Muse"' (5263–4) – but Aristophanes breaks off here, and the narrative is as open-ended as that of '"Childe Roland."' What are we to make of such a refusal to bring the lyric to closure? Perhaps an affirmation on the part of Aristophanes that there is no such thing as closure. The 'triumph' of Thamuris will give way to defeat, the comedy of his life to its tragedy, but the turning will go on and on and on.

The final part of Balaustion's narrative – after she has finished her account of the debate with Aristophanes – has the shape of tragedy, for she tells of the pulling down of the walls of Athens and her own departure from the city and into exile. The text teaches us, however, that the end of a tragedy is the beginning of a comedy, and that beginning is evident in a number of ways. First of all, Euthukles saves the Akropolis from destruction with a 'choric flower' (5558) from Euripides' *Elektra*. At first it seems that he has saved the whole city, but there is a turn (signalled by 'But next day' in line 5610) when Lusandros and the Spartans change their minds and demolish the 'Long Walls.' They do so, however, to music:

> The very flute-girls blew their laughing best,
> In dance about the conqueror while he bade
> Music and merriment help enginery

Batter down, break to pieces all the trust
Of citizens once, slaves now.   (74–8)

The action is a parody of the building of Troy and Thebes, since the music destroys a city rather than creating one, but Browning would be aware of Carlyle's teaching through his 'organic filaments' metaphor in *Sartor Resartus* that creation and destruction proceed together, and that the new is already forming itself in the ruins of the old. Hence the girls and the dance are associated with comedy, the 'kordax-step' (101) being 'the hearty slapping-dance' (5635) in Old Comedy. Lastly, there is Balaustion's final imperative: 'see if young Philemon ... too have not made a votive verse!' (5692, 5694). She presents Philemon as an admirer of Euripides, and she cannot know, as Browning's readers know, that Philemon, along with Menander, would become one of the chief writers of New Comedy.

It is clear, from these two poems and from the 1877 translation of the *Agamemnon* of Aeschylus, that the nature and purposes of translation occupied Browning's attention through the 1870s. His framing of the translations – the play-within-a-play-within-a-play structure – makes them part of the art of 'complex Poetry' (*Aristophanes' Apology* 1473), and that complexity, the result of the blending of genres and the nesting structure, comes to characterize the language of his translations as well. The preface to his translation of the *Agamemnon* is his chief statement on the art of turning Greek into English. That art, as Yopie Prins has argued in an important article, is in fact a turning or reversal of our usual expectations: where we expect accessible and idiomatic English out of the Greek, we get just the opposite – a defamiliarizing of English, the result of Browning's requirement of the translator 'to be literal at every cost save that of absolute violence to our language,' and his expressed tolerance for 'even a clumsy attempt to furnish me with the very turn of each phrase in as Greek a fashion as English will bear.'[20] 'Browning seems to reverse source language and target language,' Prins writes, and 'the task of the translator, then, is not to make a foreign language one's own but rather to make one's own language foreign.'[21] That act, in Prins's view, depends upon the opposition of spoken and written word, so that the *Agamemnon* 'demonstrates a violent disjunction of text and voice that is present to some degree in all Browning's poetry, but it articulates this juncture to such an extreme that it finally disarticulates itself' (153). Yet the translation is not entirely unsuccessful. George Steiner praises it for sometimes communicating 'an *aural* density vital to Greek drama,' and he characterizes it, interestingly enough, less as a translation than as a transcript: Browning's language is 'a centaur-idiom in which the grammar, the customary cadence, the phrasing, even the word-structure of his own tongue are subjected to the vocabulary, syntax, phonetic patterns of the text which he is translating or, more exactly, seeking to inhabit and only transcribe.'[22]

'Do you say this, or I?': Browning's 'parleyings,' *La Saisiaz, Red Cotton Night-Cap Country,* and *Fifine at the Fair*

The topic of this chapter is one we have already glanced at in *Aristophanes' Apology*, where, we remember, the second of the nested plays was a debate between Balaustion and Aristophanes. The debate is presented entirely through the account of it that Balaustion provides for Euthukles, so that we hear it not in an unmediated way but as represented and interpreted by the voice of one of the participants. Browning often encloses both debate and dialogue in a monologue, and such framing is one of his riddling techniques, since the reader must struggle to keep in mind who says what, or must note whether a passage in quotation marks is actually a quotation or an attributed speech. The mediating voice is shaper and interpreter, like the voice of Balaustion, for instance, or like Browning's own voice in *La Saisiaz* and in the poems of the volume of 1887. As the title of that volume indicates, Browning's own word for poems using this technique is 'parleying.' Browning had used the noun 'confabulations' when describing the volume to Furnivall,[1] and he might, one thinks, have used the word 'dialogue' to indicate the poems' links with the genre he was familiar with in Mandeville and Plato. In them the dialogue is a teaching form, and the instruction is not by direct statement – something Browning too characteristically avoided – but by an argument unfolding through the drama of the give and take of opposing points of view, as in a debate, or through the kind of conversation where one voice – the voice of experience and wisdom – leads another voice – that of the seeker after knowledge – towards illumination. The dialogue may involve the discipline of logic, but it also proceeds under the pressure of actual circumstances, as in *La Saisiaz,* and with regard to the character of the second voice, as in the *Parleyings* of 1887. Perhaps Browning wanted to indicate this combination of logic and drama when he called his various dialogues 'parleyings,' and we can see that such a combination grows out of the 'new logic' of Locke and others that we explored in chapter 1, where reasoning takes into account the limitations of knowledge, human uncertainty about many questions that are of concern to us, and human opinion with all the various forces of actual human experience that go towards its formation. The word 'parleying' is not in Johnson's *Dictionary* (though the *OED* traces its use back to the seventeenth century), but Johnson does include the noun 'parley,' which is 'from the verb' and means 'oral treaty; talk; conference; discussion by word of mouth.' Browning was, as usual, attracted to the use of voices. To present ideas by having actual or fictional voices respond to one another in particular historical circumstances is to conflate debate and conversation – a conflation that characterizes the 'parleying' as Browning develops the genre. What he means by the label may be clearer if we examine two books that explore the dialogue form, one by Mandeville and one by Schleiermacher. Browning owned both.

Mandeville advocates dialogue that is truly debate, genuine give and take which has therefore some dramatic interest, in contrast to dialogue that is only an excuse for the writer to present his or her own views, and where opponents are easily disposed of. His preface to part 2 of *The Fable of the Bees* is his defence of the form, and in Browning's copy, given to him by his father and now in the Beinecke Library at Yale, that preface is marked in pencil in various ways, with underlinings, quotation marks, and lines and other marks in the margins. Two paragraphs in particular are extensively marked, and the number of the page where they appear is one of those listed in pencil on the flyleaf at the back of the volume (such a rudimentary index is a characteristic mark of Browning's having read a book carefully). These are the paragraphs where Mandeville presents the dialogue as a better form than the fable, 'an inconsiderable trifle,' he says;[2] he objects, however, to recent handling of the form: 'It is counted the most unfair manner of writing' because the adversary is 'visibly set up on purpose to be knocked down' (264). Adversaries who are straw men are a major part of the 'ill use' of the form and have brought it 'into disrepute' (264). 'The reason why Plato preferred dialogues to any other manner of writing, he said, was that things thereby might look, as if they were acted, rather than told' (264); this sentence is marked with double quotation marks in the margin, and there are double quotation marks around the conclusion of it: 'the same was afterwards given by Cicero in the same words, rendered into his own language.' Part of the fault, Mandeville argues, lies in the naming of the characters. Names are often 'judicious compounds, taken from the Greek, that serve for short characters of the imaginary persons they are given to, denoting either the party they side with, or what it is they love or hate' (265). Such names indicate 'the event of the battle,' and 'many readers have complained, that they had not sport enough for their money, and that knowing so much before hand, spoiled all their diversion' (265). For his own dialogue, Mandeville chooses characters who are 'real' and 'as faithfully copied from nature as I have been able to take them' (266). He is not averse to making his characters known to his readers ('when I am to converse with people for a considerable time, I desire to be well acquainted with them' 266), but their names do not make them types, and even when he introduces one of them as his defender, he warns the reader, 'when a man professes himself to be an author's friend, and exactly to entertain the same sentiments with another, it must naturally put every reader upon his guard, and render him as suspicious and distrustful of such a man, as he would be of the author himself' (274). Mandeville, then, sees the dialogue in the same way, in one crucial respect, that Wolf sees the Homeric texts: as a coming together of different voices, each one of which must be examined and evaluated and judged. 'Hard battle it is to judge each claim,' says the Chorus of the enmity of Agamemnon and Klutaimnestra in Browning's translation of Aeschylus's play, and the line (1618) could be the motto for every reader confronted with the kind of dialogue Mandeville champions. In such a dialogue, the character type disappears as the basis of our expectations and the guide to our response, and we are left with the speeches themselves, to make sense of and judge as best we may.

Mandeville's reference to Plato reminds us that the model for the dialogue is Plato's use of the form. Among the books in Browning's library was *Schleiermacher's Introductions to the Dialogues of Plato*, where Browning would have found a theory of the dialogue which parallels that of Mandeville, and which is more explicit in defining the form's motives and techniques. Plato, more than other philosophers, creates difficulties for his readers, Schleiermacher says, because he does not use a 'systematic form'[3] for philosophical communication, but chooses instead one which is 'fragmentary' and 'dialogistic' (7). Commenting on the *Phaedrus*, Schleiermacher shows how Plato's use of the form exploits the relation between speech and writing. Oral instruction was Plato's method of teaching, and the dialogues are a 'written imitation' (17) of it, texts requiring of the reader and student a response different from direct spoken reply to one's teacher. Oral instruction is superior because the philosopher can answer, guide, and correct; written instruction, being silent, leaves the student on his or her own, and 'uncertainty' (15) is inescapable. As Schleiermacher writes, 'Plato says, that a sentence orally delivered may always be supported by its Father and receive his protection, and that not only against the objections of one who thinks otherwise, but also against the intellectual stubbornness of one as yet ignorant, while the written sentence has no answer to make to any further inquiries' (15–16). There is yet another element which makes uncertain the teaching in a dialogue: 'that mimic and dramatic quality by means of which persons and circumstances become individualized' (36), a quality which spreads 'beauty and charm' (36) but which increases the difficulties of a student whose object is learning. And then there are the riddling aspects of the dialogue: the indirection, the recommencement of the topic from another point of view, the seemingly capricious and loose progression of the discussion, the mingling of the important and the trifling, the hints and suggestions, 'the dialectic play with ideas' (37). Schleiermacher names three techniques in particular: 'enigma' (17), the veiling of the object of investigation (18), and the sketching of the object 'by a few unconnected strokes' (18). Why create so many difficulties? Why should a philosopher not provide direct instruction? One answer to those questions is that the communication of knowledge is not the philosopher's only end, and learning how to discover knowledge is as important for the student as possessing it. 'To this end, then, it is requisite that the final object of the investigation be not directly enunciated and laid down in words, a process which might very easily serve to entangle many persons who are glad to rest content, provided only they are in possession of the final result, but that the mind be reduced to the necessity of seeking, and put into the way by which it may find it' (17). So the enigma is 'woven out of contradictions, to which the only possible solution is to be found in the thought in view' (18); or 'the real investigation is overdrawn with another, not like a veil, but, as it were, an adhesive skin, which conceals from the inattentive reader, and from him alone, the matter which is to be properly considered or discovered, while it only sharpens and clears the mind of an attentive one to perceive the inward connection' (18); finally, the 'few unconnected strokes' of the sketch require the reader to 'fill up and combine' them, and so arrive at a view of the whole (18). A second answer to the question (why create so many difficulties?) has to do with arousing the reader and giving him or her a motive for discovery. All the techniques of the dialogue are designed to drive the seeker after knowledge to 'an inward and self-originated creation of the thought in view' (17), where the mind is 'brought to so distinct a consciousness of its own state of ignorance, that it is impossible that it should willingly continue therein' (17). Just as the first stage of conversion is a conviction of sin, so the first stage of learning is a conviction of ignorance, and dialogue, like the decalogue, is at this point an adversary and an accuser, challenging, provoking, and prodding to change.

But the written dialogue as adversary is not like the adversary in oral exchange. In the latter, the speaker is an other, separate and distinct from oneself; in the former, opposing positions may both reflect one's own views, which the text prods us to clarify and develop. The written dialogue evokes a more complex response than an opposing voice in an oral debate, and its very existence reminds us that no one apprehends a debate or parleying in an unmediated way. We do not hear an opposing position as it is in itself, but rather as it is in our understanding of it. Hence Browning usually frames a parleying within a single consciousness such as Balaustion's, as we have seen. For all her resistance to Aristophanes' position, she has been thinking along her opponent's lines, and there are points where she might well ask, 'Do you say this, or I?'

That line – the title of this chapter – is from the *Easter-Day* half of *Christmas-Eve and Easter-Day*. It begins with the lines, 'How very hard it is to be / A Christian! Hard for you and me ...' The pronouns establish a dialogue between the narrator and 'a live actual listener' (355), and signposts such as 'you see' and 'I conclude' give the reader the impression of two voices and differing positions. We are not very far into the discussion, however, before the positions blur under the pressure of illation, that aspect of reasoning which is the ordering of 'intermediate *Ideas*,' in Locke's words, 'to discover what connection there is' from one to another (4.17.2). Both speakers are caught up in the chain of ideas – that conventional metaphor for the links the mind makes in moving from one idea to the next – and the inferences of one speaker may just as well be those of the other, thanks to that common human faculty that Locke called reason, that process 'whereby the Mind comes to see, either the certain Agreement or Disagreement of any two *Ideas*, as in Demonstration, in which it arrives at Knowledge; or their probable connexion, on which it gives or with-holds its Assent, as in Opinion' (4.17.2). So the debate and the two voices begin to sound like a complex argument comprehended by a single consciousness and advanced by a single voice, especially when one speaker proposes or conjectures positions for the other. Most of the narrator's verbs in *Easter-Day* are in the declarative mood and present tense ('you say'), but there is the future as well ('you will say' 13, or 'you'll find sufficient' 195), and that future shades into wishing or speculating that requires the subjunctive mood. Browning in fact does not use that mood to introduce the speeches of the other voice in this particular dialogue ('you would say' and 'you might say' do not appear), but it is characteristic of him to blur opposing positions or to make it difficult for his readers to distinguish between or among the various voices in his poems, so that one has a good deal of sympathy with Alfred Domett's puzzled 'Who says this?' when he is trying to make sense of *Sordello* and, as he records in his diary, 'scribbled in pencil' on his presentation copy from Browning 'two or three impatient remarks.'[4]

In Browning's hands, then, a 'parleying' is a combination of debate and conversation mediated by a single consciousness. The *OED* labels the word a 'verbal substantive' (one of the dictionary's three examples is the title of Browning's 1887 volume), and the label indicates that 'parleying' is a gerund, uniting subject and action, content and performance. At the centre of a 'parleying' is a debate which Browning imitates in his poetic text. That text, like his dramatic texts in relation to a theatrical performance, is designed to be read silently, the argument playing itself out in the hall or legislature of the reader's own mind. Browning places the debate itself at two removes from the reader of his poetic text, a technique which Schleiermacher might call 'veiling' or 'indirection,' since the reader faces the problem of interpreting and judging not only the opposing positions, but the understanding of them by the character who recounts the argument. Such a technique also indicates why 'parleying' is a gerund. The reader of Browning's text must not only comprehend the subject and the opposing positions taken – the content of a 'parleying' – but also evaluate the acts of argument and interpretation of the participants and of the framing voice.

The form as Browning actually uses it encompasses a range of ways of presenting the voices in dialogue. Sometimes (but not very often), Browning specifically labels the speeches with the names of the speakers, as he does in the Epilogue to *Dramatis Personae* or in 'Apollo and the Fates' and 'Fust and His Friends,' the prologue and epilogue to the *Parleyings with Certain People of Importance in Their Day.* At the other extreme, Browning conceals the form, and one favourite technique is to give one side of the dialogue only, so that the reader must infer the words and perspective of the opponent. Such a technique is characteristic of the dramatic monologues, and we begin to realize that the monologue, considered as a subgenre of the parleying in Browning's hands, depends for its stimulating of the reader's mind on the fragmentary and the elliptical: the leaving out of one voice. One could point to 'Fra Lippo Lippi' or 'Bishop Blougram's Apology' or 'Mr. Sludge, "The Medium,"' but those texts are relatively easy puzzles since they provide us with a number of clues about the night watchman or Gigadibs or the angry 'sir' whom Horsefall addresses. More enigmatic are those texts, like *Prince Hohenstiel-Schwangau*, where the listener is not an opponent at all (she turns out to be imaginary too), and where the debate is internalized. There the character of the speaker is (to use Schleiermacher's term) an 'adhesive skin' over the matter and purpose of the debate, and the attentive reader will be aware of the extent to which the Prince condemns himself when he says, 'Give me the inner chamber of the soul / For obvious easy argument' (2126–7). More usually, the internalized dialogue is a genuine debate, an incident in the development of the soul, in Browning's understanding of it, because the outcome is of some importance in both one's earthly life and ultimate destiny. I want to examine in some detail three different 'parleyings,' and explore the range and varying dynamics of the form. One such 'parleying' – *La Saisiaz* – is an inner debate, and the most personal of Browning's late poems; one – *Red Cotton Night-Cap Country* – is Browning's imitation of an oral debate with a friend, Annie Thackeray; and one – *Fifine at the Fair* – is a debate where the central character may or may not supply the voices of the others. Moreover, all three of these 'parleyings' turn, to a greater or lesser extent, on a central issue in language theory: the nature of naming, and the relation between a name and the idea it signifies.

We begin with *La Saisiaz*. The subject of the dialogue is faith and its goal is assent, but Browning, like Schleiermacher, knows the value of 'not directly enunciating and laying down in words' the 'final object of the investigation,' and has only contempt for the reader who would have faith because 'the famous bard believed!' (572): '"Well? Why, he at least believed in Soul, was very sure of God"' (604). Browning knows that faith is not something one has, but something one is always struggling to affirm, and his problem is like that of Lazarus in 'An Epistle': 'How can he give his neighbour the real ground, / His own conviction?' (216–17). He can't, but through a 'parleying' he can prod the reader to work out his or her own faith. So the poet's debate with himself becomes a debate with the reader, a challenge to every person who faces the situation the poet faces: the sudden and unexpected death of a close friend.

The occasion of the poem is well known, and Browning describes it in the opening sections: he had planned to climb a mountain with Anne Egerton Smith, the 'tall white figure' of the narrative, only to discover that, on the very morning of their proposed excursion, she had died. 'No premonitory touch,' Browning writes, 'As you talked and laughed ('tis told me) scarce a minute ere the clutch / Captured you in cold forever' (109–11). Her death, sudden and unexpected, raises crucial questions for Browning, and he asks them when he, alone, climbs La Salève: 'here I stand: but you – where?' (139). That question leads to others: '"Does the soul survive the body? Is there God's self, no or yes?"' (144); '"Was ending ending once and always, when you died?"' (172). He and Smith had debated such questions as a result of having read Frederic Harrison's essay 'The Soul and Future Life,' but they had done so by 'passing lightly in review / What seemed hits and what seemed misses' (162–3). Now the questions cannot be considered playfully, and he has no 'heart to palter' (171), to play fast and loose with the issues, to equivocate. The questions are urgent and crucial:

> I will ask and have an answer, – with no favour, with no fear, –
> From myself. How much, how little, do I inwardly believe
> True that controverted doctrine? Is it fact to which I cleave,
> Is it fancy I but cherish ... [?]   (208–11)

F.E.L. Priestley's analysis, published in 1955, is still the best guide to the way the argument proceeds.[5] To that analysis we need to add an awareness of how Lockeian the argument is. The parleying is an internal debate between Fancy and Reason, and that 'Amicable war' (403) is the final stage of a process of thinking which Locke would call illation. The language is explicitly one without any claims to revelation or divine authority, and is only the arbitrary attaching of verbal sign to the meaning signified. The poem explores the nature and possibilities of such a view of language, chosen because it is (in a society dominated by empiricism) the least subject to question or doubt, and because it is (for a man coping with the grief of a sudden death and determined to face the truth of things without clinging to illusion or resorting to fiction) the least likely to offer easy answers or to base itself on shaky assumptions about divine origins and authority.

Locke, as we have already noted, is always reminding his readers of the limitations of knowledge, and always pointing out that those things of which we can be certain are not a sufficient guide for conduct, so that we must govern our actions as much by our judgment of probability as by the knowledge derived from sensory experience. Where knowledge is scanty or lacking, we must resort to inference. Inference is the chief act of reason, and it produces a sequence of ideas which Locke tropes as a chain, 'each intermediate *Idea* agreeing on each side with those two it is immediately placed between' (*Essay* 4.17.4). Reason is one of Browning's voices in this internal debate, and its dialogue with Fancy, 'from fact educing fit surmise' (522), produces a sequence of thoughts for which Browning uses the same chain metaphor. His starting point – two points, actually – is the same as that in Locke's reasoning for the existence of God. Here is how Browning establishes his argument:

> I have questioned and am answered. Question, answer, presuppose
> Two points: that the thing itself which questions, answers, – *is*, it knows;
> As it also knows the thing perceived outside itself, – a force
> Actual ere its own beginning, operative through its course,
> Unaffected by its end, – that this thing likewise needs must be;
> Call this – God, then, call that – soul, and both – the only facts for me.
>
> (217–22)

Locke uses those same two facts for his chapter 'Of our Knowledge of the Existence of a GOD,' chapter 10 of the fourth and climactic book of *An Essay Concerning Human Understanding*. He insists that our knowledge of our own existence is sure and certain: 'In every Act of Sensation, Reasoning, or Thinking, we are conscious to our selves of our own Being; and, in this Matter, come not short of the highest degree of *Certainty*' (4.9.3). Our knowledge of the existence of God is a matter of reasoning: 'we know there is some real Being, and that Non-entity cannot produce any real Being,' and such reasoning is demonstration that 'from Eternity there has been something' (4.10.3). That something is demonstrably powerful, and also (since human beings have perception and knowledge) 'some knowing intelligent Being' (4.10.5). 'Thus from the Consideration of our selves, and what we infallibly find in our own Constitutions, our Reason leads us to the Knowledge of this certain and evident Truth, That *there is an eternal, most powerful, and most knowing Being*' (4.10.6). Browning considers the same demonstration and, like Locke, considers its limitations, when we would like 'all-potent' and 'all-wise' to be 'all-good' also (336). He is even more at a loss when he asks the question about immortality – 'Can it be, and must, and will it?' (390) – and receives only silence for an answer. He is left with 'surmise,' and fact would 'stop the mouth' of surmise, except that fact (as Locke constantly insists) does not meet all human needs and aspirations. So knowledge, in Locke's terms, shades into opinion and belief, and reason, guided by human needs and concerns, supplies probabilities where sure and certain knowledge is lacking. Hence Browning stages a debate between Reason and Fancy, the umpire being the soul. Fancy grants the assumptions which cannot be proved, and Reason integrates those assumptions into a sequence of thoughts which do in fact provide a sufficient basis for conduct and which compensate for the limitations of our knowledge. Immortality may not be a fact, but Fancy immediately 'concede[s] the thing refused' (405) and makes 'this mere surmise that after body dies soul lives again' (406) the third fact, not to be proved, but to be 'put ... to use in life.' Reason immediately picks up on that point, finding that the third 'fact' 'promises advantage, coupled with the other two' (410). So the debate proceeds, through two more 'facts' – heaven and hell – to a sixth, reward and punishment for good or evil done on earth. Not one of these 'facts,' we note, is a matter of revelation. Browning arrives at them on the basis of his own actual experience, resolutely faced and accepted without shirking or self-deception.

The kind of language which goes along with such illation is also Lockeian in its orientation. When Browning insists on facing truths, however painful, he also insists that his speech can claim to be no more than '"man's truest answer,"' not God's response. God may be all-seeing and all-hearing, but the poet is not:

> Can I make my eye an eagle's, sharpen ear to recognize
> Sound o'er league and league of silence? Can I know, who but surmise?
>
> (159–60)

The answer to those questions can only be no. Hence, by analogy, Browning insists that his language is only human, and not divine or revelatory: how can it be an imitation of a speech which is unknowable?

> 'I shall no more dare to mimic [God's] response in futile speech,
> Pass off human lisp as echo of the sphere-song out of reach ...'   (153–4)

Words are human inventions, then, and they are articulate sounds attached, arbitrarily, to ideas. There is no necessary or inevitable connection between word and idea, nor is the word commensurate with the idea. Moreover, a word gives only the nominal essence of something, not its real mode of existence. So, when Browning arrives at the first two facts, 'the thing itself which questions' (218) and 'the thing perceived outside itself' (219), he names them by attaching a single articulate sound to each: 'Call this – God, then, call that – soul' (222). The names, we note, are (as in Tooke) abbreviations for a number of words (here a noun with a restrictive clause), and they are tools to argue with, not a means to enter into a world beyond our senses. Locke, interestingly enough, goes about naming in exactly the same way in his chapter on the existence of God. When he has demonstrated the existence of *an eternal, most powerful, and most knowing Being,*' he adds, 'which whether any one will please to call *God,* it matters not' (4.10.6). The name is only a convenience, and even the idea of which it is the label is no proof that God is: '*How far the* Idea *of a most perfect Being,* which a Man may frame in his Mind, does, or does not prove the *Existence of a* GOD, I will not here examine' (4.10.7).

While an idea is at one remove from the thing or things which give rise to it, the name of an idea is at two removes – the 'mark' or 'sign' of an idea, in Locke's terms, 'thought's echo' (195) in Browning's wording in this poem. Whenever he refers to naming in *La Saisiaz* – and he does so when he uses the verbs 'style' or 'call' or 'say' – the name is at best convenient but more usually limited or relative. 'Much conjecture styled belief' (233), he says in the context of his rush-in-the-stream analogy, where the rush cannot know either the source or the end of the stream but nonetheless 'conceives [what] the stream means' (234). Or the speaker for whom grass is green, and his colour-blind neighbour, for whom it is red: 'which employs the proper term?' (276). Or Fancy seeking quick and convenient labels for the 'next life' that human beings 'darkling' descry: 'call it, heaven' (462) and 'say, hell' (463). Reason assures Fancy that 'next life will give the power of speech' (470), but that assurance is hardly a help for the actual living of one's life now. So we must name as best we can, though the articulate sounds we choose as signs have no knowable connection with the reality of things. They do, however, have a connection with our ideas of the reality of things, and the poem suggests, in ways that we must now explore, that naming is not quite so limited as it at first seems.

Naming, as Browning treats that act in the poem, is a heuristic, and it serves to find out a pattern of relations which appears in the poem as pairings. Sometimes Browning sets words side by side and uses sounds to hold them together, as with fact and fancy, which are tied by both alliteration and assonance though opposite in meaning; sometimes he pairs the names of two images; and sometimes he doubles verbs or adverbs or adjectives. In all of these pairings, he is exploring the way in which things are held together, usually as opposites, but also in sequence (intention and deed, for instance), and occasionally as repetition. The pairings, which are so pervasive in the poem, indicate that nothing we experience is ever experienced in isolation, and the context or relation is that which gives meaning to the name we attach to the experience. When the relation is one of opposites, one of the pair often names something known by experience and the other something inferred, so that the relation parallels that between verbal sign and idea signified in Locke's language theory: it is a relation which is arbitrary because it depends upon human judgment, and because the name is no indication of the real essence of the thing named. Still that relation is not without its foundation and authority. Its foundation is human needs and concerns, and its authority rests upon the extent to which it enables us, in Locke's words, 'to spend the days of this our Pilgrimage with Industry and Care, in the search, and following of that way, which might lead us to a State of greater Perfection' (4.14.2).

The poem begins with a pair of verbs, 'Dared and done,' a phrase borrowed from the last line of Smart's *Song to David* and held together by alliteration. The words refer to the verbal arrangements between Browning and Smith about 'the climbing both of us were bound to do' (2). The daring – '"Why not try for once the mountain [?]"' (29) – leads to the done – 'at last I stand upon the summit' (1) – and so the pairing involves keeping one's word: constructing an action in one's mind and matching it to its physical enactment, so that intention and deed become one. In a juxtaposition which is crucial to the poem as a whole, Browning contrasts 'Dared and done' with another pair, 'here' and 'there.' Physically, 'here' is the summit of La Salève, 'there' is Collonge, but Collonge is Smith's burial place, and so 'here' is in fact life and 'there' death. Between the two in this pair there is a gap, and the adverbs pull so far apart from each other that Browning tropes the gap as a barrier, deeper than the mountain valley he calls 'Yon Profound' (19) and absolutely impassable: 'barrier this, without a bound!' (20). The alliteration holds together 'barrier' and 'bound,' and the words are synonyms, but the paradox indicates opposites juxtaposed without any possibility of resolution. 'Disjoints' (24) is Browning's verb when he mentions a related pair, past and present (25), and the word which establishes the nominal relation between them is not 'and' but 'from.' The severing of a pair has its emblematic image in Browning's lonely climb – he twice uses the adverb 'singly' (2, 12) – in contrast to the planning of the excursion, done 'arm in arm' (27, 134), and in contrast to their walking and talking when they had discussed Harrison's essay, their conversation indicating mutual respect, responsibility, and love. The central part of the poem, the parleying with the self, turns upon more pairings: body and soul, knowing and surmising, fact and fancy, fancy and reason – as well as the pairing which is the verbal form of this internal debate, question and answer: 'I have questioned and am answered' (217). In all of these relationships, the barrier between the two, as Browning explores it, is not absolute.

One pair, question and answer, 'presuppose' (217) another pair, me and not-me, the first two 'facts' of this internal debate. 'Fact' is a noun Browning has already paired with 'fancy,' and his understanding of the two is Lockeian: 'fact' is a generalization from sensory experience, while 'fancy' is something made up by the mind, something which does not correspond to the relations we actually observe outside us. To 'prove' a fact is to point to those actual relations, but Browning (unexpectedly) does not treat his first two 'facts' in that way:

> Prove them facts? that they o'erpass my power of proving, proves them such:
> Fact is it I know I know not something which is fact as much.   (223–4)

Line 224 is Browning's version of Meno's paradox in Plato's dialogue of that name. 'How will you investigate,' Meno asks Socrates in Jowett's translation, 'that of which you know nothing at all? Where can you find a starting-point in the region of the unknown? And even if you happen to come full upon what you want, how will you ever know that this is the thing which you did not know?' (*Meno* 80d).[6] Browning's solution to that paradox involves the pairing of opposites we have been exploring. We think in terms of opposites, and language makes possible the opposite of everything, so that we infer the negative of every affirmation, and need only insert a 'not' in every proposition to explore another possible truth. So the gap between knowing and not knowing seems a little less obvious. It is true, as Browning goes on to argue, that we truly cannot know either the causes or effects of many things, just as the rush cannot know the source or end of the stream which moves it, but we can experience a relationship of opposites at (what Browning calls) 'the midway point' (255) between cause and effect, and 'in that narrow space [we] must cram / All experience' (256–7). Hence Browning says of body and soul, the culminating pair of a series of opposites that begins with right and wrong and moves through hope and fear, 'Truce to such old sad contention' (249). The truce comes about through a musical metaphor:

'But the soul is not the body': and the breath is not the flute;
Both together make the music: either marred and all is mute.   (247–8)

Life is possible, in other words, in the 'truce' of opposites, not in the defeat of one or the other, but in the struggle between them. The 'Amicable war' of Fancy and Reason is thus paradigmatic.

The debate in the poem is open-ended and unresolved. The refusal to come to closure is the result of Browning's honesty in examining his own ideas and beliefs, and he presents that refusal in a final pair of opposites, the circle and the straight line or chain. Illation leads him in both ways. The circle image is the first to appear, and it does so when Reason returns to the first two 'facts' (the soul and God), and to earth, the theatre in which the soul and God act out their relationship:

wherein, by hypothesis,
Soul is bound to pass probation, prove its powers, and exercise
Sense and thought on fact, and then, from fact educing fit surmise,
Ask itself, and of itself have solely answer, 'Does the scope
Earth affords of fact to judge by warrant future fear or hope?'   (520–4)

We note that the phrase 'from fact educing fit surmise,' which I have already quoted, is an apt summary of illation, and that the sequence of inferences and judgments, as Browning presents it here, brings him back to the question with which he started. 'Thus,' he says,

have we come back full circle: fancy's footsteps one by one
Go their round conducting reason to the point where they begun.   (525–6)

The circling round might elsewhere suggest frustration, but Browning here links it with hope and with resignation to life as it is. 'Hope the arrowy' (543), he says, troping the abstraction in a way that suggests skill in making and judging. In these same lines he uses the plumb-line image:

I can fathom, by no plumb-line sunk in life's apparent laws,
How I may in any instance fix where change should meetly fall
Nor involve, by one revisal, abrogation of them all.   (536–8)

Locke, too had used the plumb-line image to indicate both the limitations and the adequacy of human knowledge: "'Tis of great use to the
Sailor to know the length of his Line, though he cannot with it fathom
all the depths of the Ocean. 'Tis well he knows, that it is long enough to
reach the bottom, at such Places, as are necessary to direct his Voyage,
and caution him against running upon Shoals, that may ruin him. Our
Business here is not to know all things, but those which concern our
Conduct' (1.1.6). So the illation ends with an imperative – 'hope!' (545) –
which is not the end of the poem. The circle becomes a line, and it does
so when Browning inserts the passage on fame, the passage in which he
warns his readers that every human being must work out his or her own
beliefs and not make affirmations because 'the famous bard believed!'
(572). The last fourteen lines of the poem indicate that faith is no such
easy matter:

> Not so loosely thoughts were linked,
> Six weeks since as I, descending in the sunset from Salève,
> Found the chain, I seemed to forge there, flawless till it reached your grave.
>   (606–8)

The lines are ambiguous and troubling. We note, to begin with, that
the context suggests that the writing of the poem 'Here in London's
mid-November' (606) forges a chain different from the one he made
the day he climbed La Salève. The latter chain is straight and without
tangles:

> And since I found a something in me would not rest
> Till I, link by link, unravelled any tangle of the chain,
> – Here it lies, for much or little!   (610–12)

The former chain was even better – it was 'flawless' – 'till it reached
your grave'; and then we note that Browning says, of the making of that
former chain, that he 'seemed to forge' it. Did he make only an appearance of a chain, and then make an actual one now, six weeks later? And
if he did make one then, why were the thoughts 'Not so loosely ...
linked' but rather more tightly than they are now? Finally, what are we
to make of that crucial clause, 'till it reached your grave'? Priestley asks
the right questions: 'When he says that then he found the chain flawless
till it reached Miss Smith's grave, does he mean that it was flawless to
that point but not beyond? that the chain broke at the grave? or that the
chain firmly joined himself and the grave?' (58). There is no answering

any of these questions with assurance, and the clause is an enigma in Schleiermacher's sense: the 'till' makes the clause 'woven out of contradictions, to which the only possible solution is to be found in the thought in view.' The 'thought in view' is not that faith prevails to Miss Smith's grave and beyond, or that faith fails at Miss Smith's grave. Rather, 'till' holds together both meanings, and indeed the meaning could not be the meaning without our awareness of its opposite. There can be no fact without fancy, no fancy without reason, no body without soul, in the linguistic system by which we make sense of our experience. So there can be no life without death, no mortality without immortality. In every instance, the idea signified by the word would be unintelligible without its opposite. Naming opposites is no guarantee that such things exist, and to name the soul and immortality is not evidence of the actual existence of such things. But then, our names for the things we observe are only names too, and no evidence of their real mode of existence. We assume, as Locke points out – and the assumption is a matter of faith – 'that our Faculties act and inform us right' and 'do not herein deceive us' (4.11.3), and Browning too affirms that 'things there are' (259), but he is as sceptical as Locke is about knowledge: 'things may be as I behold,' Browning says, 'Or may not be' (258–9). Browning suggests, however, that the dialectical play of ideas is not without purpose, for he ends the poem with a crucial pairing: 'Least part this: then what the whole?' (618).

Browning supplied Mrs Orr with a prose statement of the argument of *La Saisiaz* for her *Handbook*,[7] and the statement confirms the need for fancy to complete fact. 'Everything,' Browning begins, 'in my experience – and I speak only of my own – testifies to the incompleteness of life, nay, even to its preponderating unhappiness. The strong body is found allied to a stunted soul. The soaring soul is chained by a bodily weakness to the ground.'[8] After more examples, Browning proceeds with syntax which parallels the illation in the poem, from conditional clause ('If we regard') to consequence ('we must relinquish'), from speculation ('But let us once assume') to confident statement ('every difficulty is solved'), and finally to a conclusion which involves the reader in the affirmation the poet himself makes ('May I then accept the conclusion ...?'). Mrs Orr misses the conditional, so that her comment is misleading: 'Mr. Browning initiates his final inquiry by declaring that he will accept only the testimony of fact. He rejects surmise' (191). She is paraphrasing the lines that introduce the debate between Fancy and Reason, where surmise is prepared to 'dispute / Fact's inexorable ruling, "Outside fact, surmise be mute!"' (391–2), and where the poet himself says, "'T is surmise I stop the mouth of' (394) – but only with a crucial condition: 'if fact's self I may force the answer from!' (393). How may he 'force the answer'? By Fancy.

The parleying of *Red Cotton Night-Cap Country* serves as a frame for the narrative and provides the motive for Browning's interpretation of the life and death of Léonce Miranda. The poem is thus made up of two texts: the dialogue with Annie Thackeray (the 'fair friend' to whom the poem is addressed and dedicated), and the story of the Miranda family, a story Browning first heard from Milsand (mentioned at line 2945 of the poem). He claims (in an 1889 letter to Nettleship) historical truth for his narrative ('Indeed the facts are so exactly put down, that, in order to avoid the possibility of prosecution for Libel – that is, telling the exact truth – I changed all the names of persons and places') and he claims truth for his understanding of the motives of Miranda's death ('occasioned,' he writes to Nettleship, 'by religious considerations as well as passionate woman-love, – and I concluded that there was no intention of committing suicide').[9] The poet procured the legal documents (as he had for *The Ring and the Book*)[10] and collected newspaper stories and the oral accounts of people in the neighbourhood, visited house and grounds, and even (as he records in the poem) saw the heroine of the story ('Do you know / I saw her yesterday – set eyes upon / The veritable personage, no dream?' 821–3). Moreover, the framing parleying is firmly based on the poet's own experience: Browning speaks in his own voice, to an actual friend, and makes full use of his personal knowledge of the Normandy countryside around Saint Aubin, where he vacationed in 1870 and 1872. A critical reader of the poem may well ask what authority Browning can claim for his shaping and interpreting of the historical materials. The answer to that question lies in the issue common to both texts: the nature of naming or (to use the noun Browning uses in the poem) 'nomenclature.' The theory of naming in the parleying is empiricist, while that in the framed story is idealist. In this poem, in contrast to *La Saisiaz*, Browning criticizes the former to claim truth for the latter.

The parleying begins in the manner of an emblem, with a visual image – the Normandy countryside – and the question of its meaning. Even at this early stage, Browning (whose role in the debate will be to attack the limitations of the empiricist theory of naming) suggests that the relation of sign and signified goes beyond the arbitrary and conventional relationship which is the essence of Locke's language theory. Each place on earth, Browning argues, has its 'proper service,' which is 'To give [man] note that, through the place he sees, / A place is signified he never saw, / But, if he lack not soul, may learn to know' (60–3). Locke, we ought to remind ourselves, bases his theory of naming on the actions of abstracting and generalizing from sensory experience, and would label as fiction the idea that a name may signify something not seen. Thackeray's understanding of naming, an understanding which defines her role in the debate, is both Lockeian and Tookeian. She names the country '"White Cotton Night-cap Country"' (146) and she defends the name in a long speech (195–243) where she argues that 'Night-cap' is (as in Locke) an abstraction from all individual experiences of that article of clothing, and (as in Tooke) an abbreviation for all particular night-caps, an abbreviation that makes verbal communication swift and economical. Names 'comprehend several particular Things,' says Locke, 'For the multiplication of Words would have perplexed their Use, had every particular thing need of a distinct name to be signified by' (3.1.3); hence we make an idea general by abstracting or separating it from 'the circumstances of Time, and Place, and any other Ideas' (3.3.6). In the first chapter of The Diversions of Purley, Tooke praises 'Mr. Locke's Essay' as our 'best guide' to abbreviations in 'terms,'[11] and he is referring to abstraction. So Thackeray answers Browning's question, '"Which sort of Night-cap have you glorified?"' (193), with '"What other Night-cap than the normal one?"' (195). By 'normal' she seems to mean the kind which is, in ordinary experience, the most numerous, though 'form and fashion vary, suiting so / Each seasonable want of youth and age' (200–1). At the end of her defence of naming, she returns to the generalization, calling it 'Night-cap pure and simple':

> 'What should Night-cap be
> Save Night-cap pure and simple? Sorts of such?
> Take cotton for the medium, cast an eye
> This side to comfort, lambswool or the like,
> That side to frilly cambric costliness,
> And all between proves Night-cap proper.'   (239–43)

Browning himself alludes to Tooke when he asks about Thackeray's intention:

> You mean to catch and cage the wingèd word,

And make it breed and multiply at home
Till Norman idlesse stock our England too?   (158–60)

'Wingèd words' is the translation of the Greek title of *The Diversions of Purley* (a copy of which was, as we have already noted, in Browning's father's library), and the metaphor is, as Thackeray would hear it, neither revelatory nor apocalyptic but descriptive: '*Abbreviations* are the *wheels* of language, the *wings* of Mercury,' Tooke says (13); 'Words have been called *winged*; and they well deserve that name, when their abbreviations are compared with the progress which speech could make without these inventions' (14–15).

'Happy nomenclature' (155), Browning calls Thackeray's 'wingèd word,' and it is 'happy' because Browning knows (as does Thackeray, finally) that the name is not 'pure and simple,' a sound arbitrarily attached to an idea, but a sign which is attached to unnamed feelings, associations, and ideas beyond that one idea which is explicitly named. The feelings attached to the word are suggested when Browning praises Thackeray's eye as more than a receiver of physical sensation: 'The learned eye is still the loving one!' (109). The associations and ideas appear when Browning treats the name as an image in an emblem, and gives its meaning by troping it: the white cotton night-cap is 'This badge of soul and body in repose' (149). The poet not only carries the night-cap across to another image ('This badge') but to an idea: it is the emblem of rural contentment, of the pastoral ideal. Then he carries the night-cap across to still another image – it is the 'crown' (141) of the country, 'the Cap / That crowns the country!' (170–1) – and the 'happy nomenclature' begins to seem problematic. 'Crown,' the conventional emblem of the court, and 'cap,' here the emblem of the country, are usually juxtaposed, and each has its conventional character and values: action as opposed to contemplation, the aspiring mind rather than the contented mind, duplicity as opposed to simplicity, and so on. The point is that the noun 'night-cap,' initially so 'proper,' 'pure and simple,' seems to be turning into its opposite, and that impression is strengthened by the later appearance of the historical crowns Miranda orders made for the Madonna and child, where the crowns, designed to honour one thing, seem to mark an obsession with its opposite. The jeweller may be a 'country-gentleman, / And most undoubted devotee [of the Virgin] beside!' (523–4), but when one considers the names for the Virgin, that devotion seems as much erotic as it is religious. The 'Belovèd of his soul, La Ravissante' (752) – a name which, in his view, 'fell fit / From the Delivering Virgin, niched and known' (1184–5) – is, Browning tells Thackeray, a corruption of 'The proper name which erst our province bore' (1189), 'a pleasantry, / A pious rendering of Rare Vissante' (1188–9). So the name of the country becomes the name of the Virgin and her church, but it is hardly a 'pious rendering,' for 'La Ravissante' suggests the allures and enticements of a siren rather than the Virgin, and a love which is a seizing and a carrying off by force rather than the quiet and freely chosen relation of the pastoral ideal. As Browning treats the 'happy nomenclature,' then, 'night-cap' becomes part of a configuration of images and ideas where one thing not only turns into something else but becomes its opposite. As Browning was to say in 1882 about another quiet corner of France, 'By a law of the association of ideas – *contraries* come into the mind as often as *similarities* – and the peace and solitude readily called up the notion of what would most jar with them.'[12] Hartley may provide the psychology for such turnings, but in *Red Cotton Night-Cap Country* Browning argues that the pursuit of meaning itself, the tracing of words through their shifts and transformations, will yield 'contraries' as frequently as 'similarities.'

Browning's function in this parleying is to turn or reverse Thackeray's argument, the verbal signs being a conjunction like 'Yet' (180) or an adverb like 'only' (245):

Only, your ignoramus here again
Proceeds as tardily to recognize
Distinctions: ask him what a fiddle means.   (245–7)

The chief reversal in fact turns on the word 'fiddle,' for Browning says, after presenting Thackeray's argument for naming the 'Night-cap pure and simple,' 'Add / "Fiddle!" and I confess the argument' (243–4). The exclamation would dismiss the argument as trifling, frivolous, and absurd, but the poet, in yet another turn, would admit the validity of the argument, and would do so, paradoxically, only when his opponent would admit its invalidity. No wonder, then, the poet says to Thackeray, 'Ask him what a fiddle means' (247), for the word is obviously more than a label for a class of musical instruments. '"Just a fiddle" seems the apt reply' (248), but it is 'apt' only in an ironic sense: 'just a fiddle' is the response of the impatient empiricist who insists that words mean what they say, that they are limited to naming things. Browning knows perfectly well that words mean more than they say, and that pursuing meaning is not a reductive but rather an increasingly inclusive activity, of which the main parts are interpretation, reversal, and ultimately discovery.

Browning's first step in saying 'what a fiddle means' is to reverse the Lockeian process of abstraction and return to the concrete and particular. He describes in detail 'A special Fiddle-Show' (251), an actual exhibition mounted in South Kensington, with fiddles of all makes, materials, and designs: 'Three hundred violin-varieties / Exposed to public view!' (274–5). The point he is making is that the word 'fiddle' can have no meaning as an abstraction without our experience of many particular instruments from which our minds create the generalization or idea that we name 'fiddle.' 'So we profit by the catalogue' (292), Browning says, as he envisages 'Quite as remarkable a Night-cap-show' (277), with the caps of Pope and Voltaire, Hogarth and Cowper – and the hangman. Each cap, from Pope's 'sickly head-sustainment' (282) to Voltaire's 'imperial velvet' (287), is the outward and visible sign – the clothing –of the inward and spiritual self, the sign of his character and social function. So Browning pushes the word 'night-cap' from an abstraction or abbreviation in the Lockeian and Tookeian senses to a metaphor in the Carlylean sense. Indeed (as critics have long recognized) he borrows heavily from Carlyle's *The French Revolution* for his central metaphor, the red cotton night-cap. It is, as in Carlyle, 'The Phrygian symbol, the new crown of thorns, / The Cap of Freedom' (313–14). Hence, says Browning to his 'fair friend,' 'Why not Red Cotton Night-cap Country too?' (332). Thackeray replies by arguing for a name which is a sign of the typical, the normal, and the numerical majority:

> 'Why not say swans are black and blackbirds white,
> Because the instances exist? ...
> Enough that white, not red, predominates,
> Is normal, typical, in cleric phrase
> *Quod semel, semper, et ubique.'*   (333–7)

She imagines a show of night-caps with the red-cap shelf a 'vacancy' (372) while 'Whites heap your row of pegs' (374).

So the issue is defined and the sides established. The poet images the parleying as a battle:

> You put me on my mettle. British maid

> And British man, suppose we have it out
> Here in the fields, decide the question so?   (381–3)

The battle, as in Carlyle's history, will be a verbal one, and the passage in *The French Revolution* where Carlyle contrasts two kinds of warfare, 'the modern *lingual* or Parliamentary-logical kind, and the ancient or *manual* kind in the steel battlefield,' can be read as a comment not only on the dialogue form but on the theory of naming Browning is exploring. In manual fighting, the foe 'does honestly die, and trouble you no more.' In verbal battles, however, 'no victory yet definable can be considered as final.'[13] Arguments defeated today will appear again tomorrow, like fashions in music and partial truths, as Browning will later say in the 'Parleying with Charles Avison': 'Never dream / That what once lived shall ever die!' (328–9). So revivals and reversals characterize a parleying – and a blessing it is that they do, for Browning associates them with the chief religious experience of his independent tradition, conversion or re-creation. The 'march-tune' (401) for their verbal battle is a verse from Isaiah 1:18: 'though your sins be as scarlet, they shall be as white as snow; though they be red like crimson, they shall be as wool.' The battle is thus a saving one, and salvation could not be its end without the reversals language makes possible.

While the empiricist theory of naming is the subject of the parleying, the idealist understanding of names is the governing idea in the narrative itself. From one idealist perspective – it is not the one Browning defends in this parleying – the verbal sign and the thing signified are not related in a conventional and arbitrary way; rather, the name participates in the essential character of the thing signified, as it does in the argument advanced by Cratylus in Plato's dialogue of that name and as is suggested by Adam's naming of the beasts. Browning glances at such a theory in a taunting way when he says in a parenthesis after he has introduced Clara de Millefleurs, 'note the happy name' (1513). From another idealist perspective, the name is a living power which begins as the label of a sensible object and expands to shape everything around it into an all-embracing configuration. Such an understanding of naming is an elaboration of Carlyle's theory of symbols, where the sensible object, viewed with the 'philosophic eye,' is the manifestation of spirit, the window, in Teufelsdröckh's metaphor, through which we look '"into Infinitude itself."'[14] Carlyle's usual metaphor for spirit is light, which appears most memorably as the 'stream of fire' in Teufelsdröckh's 'Baphometic Fire-baptism,' and Browning uses parallel metaphors in the words 'gleams' and 'flash.' Both are associated with the 'visionary,' a word which points to sight beyond that of the physical eye, but Browning, like Carlyle, never dispenses with the physical, and in fact can be seen as exploiting the idealist implications of the empiricist theory of naming.

So Browning, beginning like Locke with the data of sensations, bids his 'fair friend' to see: 'Look, lady!' (548), he says, at the 'park and domicile,' the 'country-seat / Of this same good Miranda!' (551–2). Then he defines the goal of the quest and his purpose in parleying. The goal, as in '"Childe Roland,"' is a tower, this time a house with 'the tower a-top' (677), the 'Pillared and temple-treated Belvedere' (679), and the word 'belvedere,' which means 'fair seeing' or 'beautiful sight,' hints at the expanded perspective and understanding which are the end of the quest. The purpose of the parleying he defines thus:

> Or there, or nowhere else,
> Will I establish that a Night-cap gleams
> Of visionary Red, not White for once!   (553–5)

The red night-cap is one particular article of clothing, the one the gardener names as he raises the head of the dead Miranda and tropes the cracked and bloodied skull (3600). The emblem of a bloody revolution thus becomes the emblem of an individual's violent death, but Browning maintains the link with revolution by insisting on a turn in Thackeray's understanding of the word 'Night-cap' and in her understanding of that death itself. The red is not only a contrast to the white Thackeray says is 'normal' and 'typical,' but a 'visionary' colour which 'gleams' (554–5). That verb and that adjective suggest that we are to see the cap in a Carlylean way, and in fact Browning quotes a sage who is apparently his old friend:

> 'Heaven' saith the sage 'is with us, here inside
> Each man:' 'Hell also,' simpleness subjoins,
> By White and Red describing human flesh.   (556–8)

Everything depends, then, on the activity of the seeing eye, and Browning brings all his insight to the name of his central figure. That name is his authority for his shaping of the story.

Browning introduces the authority of the name in association with a recurring image in the poem, the 'shaft' or 'arrow-flash' of light:

I – sceptical in every inch of me –
Did I deserve that, from the liquid name
'Miranda,' – faceted as lovelily
As his own gift, the gem, – a shaft should shine,
Bear me along, another Abaris,
Nor let me light till, lo, the Red is reached,
And yonder lies in luminosity!   (541–7)

In analysing these lines, we should first clear out of the way a difficulty posed by the history of the text. As Browning told Nettleship, he intended to use the actual historical names, but on legal advice and out of fear of libel changed them when the poem was in proof. The legal difficulty, however, served Browning's artistic purposes in a sly and unexpected way. He refers Nettleship to the list of changes as given in Mrs Orr's *Handbook*, and that list invites us to read Browning's names as fiction and the historical names as truth. Miranda 'is really' Mellerio, and so on. Mrs Orr's own phrasing invites such a reading: 'Mr. Browning allows me to give the true names of the persons and places concerned in the story' (*Handbook* 261). The poet himself uses the same words when he promises to send to Furnivall 'a list of the true names of men, things, and places in "Red Cotton Night-Cap Country"' (*Browning's Trumpeter* 25). Browning's argument in the poem, however, reverses our understanding of that truth: Mellerio's name 'is really' Miranda, and it is (as Browning's happy choice of a fictitious name reveals) a wonder. (So Ferdinand calls the heroine of *The Tempest* a 'wonder' (1.2.427) before he learns her 'real' name and puns on its etymology with 'Admired Miranda!' (3.1.37)). The name reveals the essence of the person (that essence being revealed, as always in Browning, in the choices and actions that make up an individual's life). In Browning's troping of the name, it is a gem from which a shaft of light shines, light being a conventional metaphor for the spirit or essence within. It is the allusion to Abaris, however, which confirms this understanding of naming as idealist. Abaris was the priest of Apollo, and he carried about with him an arrow, the symbol of the god he served, and on which he rode through the air. The arrows of Apollo figure his rays and also his words; an arrow aimed at and hitting a target is a conventional image for correct judgment (when Browning charges Thackeray with wrong judgment, he says she is 'Farther than ever from the mark' 791); finally, the priest who is held up by the arrow is a figure for the understanding; that is, the arrow or name which the priest aims stands under the appearance of the thing named and holds it up, because the name is a power or form in the mind which is prior to sensory experience, and without which sensory experience would be unintelligible. 'Shaft,' 'arrow,' and 'flash' are a cluster of images that Browning returns to in the poem, and all are linked with the idealist view of naming. Browning pictures himself as Abaris when he says that 'the Stone' (the gem in the Virgin's crown) 'Gratefully bore me as on arrow-flash / To Clairvaux, as I told you' (753–5). 'Flash,' 'flashing,' and 'flashed' all appear in the last few lines of the poem, when Browning asks his companion to judge his argument ('How say you, friend? / Have I redeemed my promise?' 4229–30). 'Flash,' as Browning uses that word in the last lines, is a sudden illumination ('that moment's flashing' 4236) conveyed through a particular setting ('what Saint-Rambert flashed me in a thought' 4239) and containing the whole story and its shape and meaning ('All this poor story – truth and nothing else' 4235). The 'flash' is the plot, the shape provided by the mind (as in the idealist theory of naming) which makes sense of facts that would otherwise be only a miscellany. The emblem of that shape is the red cotton night-cap itself.

Our sense of a perceiving and shaping mind which holds up the story and makes it intelligible is strengthened when we consider the relation of the two texts of the poem, the parleying and the narrative. The narrative is a story about that familiar Victorian type, the individual with the divided mind, torn between opposites that he or she cannot reconcile. The parleying, also a battle of opposing positions, has as its central figure a man who urges opposites upon his companion, but he, unlike Miranda, is capable of holding opposites together without being destroyed by them and without diminishing their character or significance. Miranda, the artificer and goldsmith, fails, at crucial moments, both to name and to pursue competently the meaning of the names for complex ideas; Browning, also the artificer, proves himself the master of names and the master manipulator of complex ideas.

Miranda is a man at war with himself. From his father he has 'Castilian passionate blind blood,' from his mother a gift 'Of spirit, French and critical and cold': 'Such mixture makes a battle in the brain' (1152–5) and his life is a sad story of 'inward strife' (3167). He is brought up 'dutiful / To altar and to hearth' (1332–3):

Father and mother hailed their best of sons,
Type of obedience, domesticity,
Never such an example inside doors! (1341–3)

Then he 'changed mask, / And made re-entry as a gentleman / Born of the Boulevard' (1328–30). Towers give way to turf, soul to body, the Virgin to the enchantress in the person of Clara. Thereafter Miranda is torn between Paris and Normandy, his mother and Clara, sacred and profane love, the spirit and the flesh. The long speech – actually unspoken thought – that Browning provides for Miranda just before he leaps from the tower focuses on these contraries that Miranda cannot reconcile. His failure is, as it is presented in that passage, a failure to name. Miranda begins by naming and addressing the Virgin – '"Behold me, Lady called The Ravissante!"' (3297) – and he poses a problem: 'how shall I denominate / The unrobed One?' (3311–12):

> Robed you go and crowned as well,
> Named by the nations: she is hard to name,
> Though you have spelt out certain characters
> Obscure upon what fillet binds her brow,
> *Lust of the flesh, lust of the eye, life's pride.*
> 'So call her, and contemn the enchantress!' – 'Crush
> The despot, and recover liberty!' –
> Cried despot and enchantress at each ear.   (3312–19)

The names Miranda comes up with –'lust,' 'pride' – are not only abstractions (presented like the motto in an emblem, in a band around the *pictura*) but also (in Locke's terminology) 'complex ideas,' collections of simple ideas 'put together in the Mind, independent from any original Patterns in Nature,' and tied together by a name (3.5.5, 4). Such names are 'the free choice of the Mind, pursuing its own ends' (3.5.6), but Locke thinks of them as an imperfection of language unless we are able to distinguish clearly the particular ideas thus tied together. Browning criticizes Miranda for failing to understand properly the name of a complex idea like love, and for failing to infer from it a course of action which is not self-destructive:

> Miranda hardly did his best with life:
> He might have opened eye, exerted brain,
> Attained conception as to right and law
> In certain points respecting intercourse
> Of man with woman – love, one likes to say.   (3997–4001)

Browning, however, also criticizes the kind of analysis of the name of a complex idea suggested by Locke, where the name is divided into its constituent parts or ideas, and those ideas are traced back to their 'originals,' the data provided by our five senses. I quote again the passage from book 3 of Locke's *Essay*, because I want to focus on the word 'original' and Browning's use of it. 'It may also lead us a little towards the Original of all our Notions and Knowledge,' Locke writes, 'if we remark, how great a dependance our *Words* have on common sensible *Ideas*; and how those, which are made use of to stand for Actions and Notions quite removed from sense, *have their rise from thence, and from obvious sensible* Ideas *are transferred to more abstruse significations*, and made to stand for *Ideas* that come not under the cognizance of our senses' (3.1.5). The notion 'quite removed from sense' with which both Browning and Miranda are concerned is 'faith,' and Browning firmly rejects a Lockeian analysis of it: 'Now, into the originals of faith, / Yours, mine, Miranda's, no inquiry here!' (2950–1). Then Browning goes on to explain at length the difficulties, and finally the inefficacy, of such an analysis. His criticism turns on a question of naming: 'How substitute thing meant for thing expressed?' (2959). Here is the whole passage:

Of faith, as apprehended by mankind,
The causes, were they caught and catalogued,
Would too distract, too desperately foil
Inquirer. How may analyst reduce
Quantities to exact their opposites,
Value to zero, then bring zero back
To value of supreme preponderance
How substitute thing meant for thing expressed?
Detect the wire-thread through that fluffy silk
Men call their rope, their real compulsive power?
Suppose effected such anatomy,
And demonstration made of what belief
Has moved believer – were the consequence
Reward at all? would each man straight deduce,
From proved reality of cause, effect
Conformable – believe and unbelieve
According to your True thus disengaged
From all his heap of False called reason first?   (2952–69)

The passage suggests a disjunction between words, which can be traced back to their 'originals' in sensory experience, and meaning, the shapes or forms in the mind which must nonetheless make use of materials derived from sense. To catch and catalogue each idea which makes up faith, and to trace each of those ideas back to its 'original' in a sense datum, is, as Browning criticizes that procedure here, to reduce and negate: it reduces spirit to sense, idea to matter, an organic configuration to nothing more than the sum of its parts. So quantities are reduced 'to exact their opposites, / Value to zero.' Anyway, Browning goes on to ask, would such an analysis lead human beings to 'believe and unbelieve'? In asking this question, he uses the words 'True' and 'False,' and he seems to be using them in his usual ironic way, the 'True' being that which can be confirmed by sensory experience and the 'False' that which the mind makes up. What the mind makes up is usually attributed to the imagination, but Browning here attributes it to reason, Locke's term for the chain of 'Inferences in Words' (4.17.18) or 'Illation,' that ordering of 'the intermediate Ideas, as to discover what connection there is in each link of the Chain, whereby the Extremes [the beginning and end of the chain of ideas] are held together' (4.17.2). Inference, 'the great Act of the Rational Faculty' (4.17.4), and illation are activities of the mind which compensate for our lack of sure and certain knowledge. Yet so powerful is our assumption that only those propositions are true which correspond with the observed relations of things, that we label as false any relations which the mind establishes without complete proof or demonstration. Browning suggests in this passage that the 'False called reason' is just as essential to faith as the 'True' which is demonstrable, and he uses an image parallel to Locke's chain – 'the wire-thread through that fluffy silk / Men call their rope' – to suggest that the 'True' could not be held together at all without the strong central 'wire-thread,' the ability of the mind to order ideas and reach conclusions where full and complete knowledge is lacking.

Thus Browning discourages the kind of analysis which attempts to return to 'originals,' the sensory data which are the basis of our generalizations and hence of our names for things, but he does encourage another kind of analysis, the identification and assessment of each step in illation. Indeed, in a passage which sounds like a summary of Locke on reason, he advises Thackeray to accept the conditions under which each one of us lives his or her life – 'Little you change there!' (3010) – and to assess instead that which each one of us does with those conditions. Leave the first stage, Browning says, the stage of 'apprehension' (3007):

                    What comes afterward –
From apprehended thing, each inference
With practicality concerning life,
This you may test and try, confirm the right
Or contravene the wrong which reasons there.   (3010–14)

Browning is here defining his own treatment of Miranda's actions. The process involves the apprehending of those actions – Miranda's thrusting of his hands into the fire, his leap from the belvedere – and then the reasoning about them so as to arrive at conclusions about the nature of the acts themselves, and about Miranda's character. In Lockeian terms, Browning is taking knowledge – the eyewitness accounts of those physical acts – and making inferences which will enable him to judge them and so arrive at their significance. For example, in Browning's account of Miranda's burning of his hands and subsequently painting with his mouth and playing the piano with his feet, Browning says, 'I infer / He was not ignorant what hands are worth, / When he resolved on ruining his own' (3215–17). So too with Miranda's leap from the belvedere:

                    I see no slightest sign
Of folly (let me tell you in advance)
Nothing but wisdom meets me manifest
In the procedure of the Twentieth Day
Of April, 'Seventy ...   (3229–33)

Hence Browning's conclusion about the leap. He quotes the gardener who witnesses it and who arrives at his own conclusion when he (like the poet) puts together a statement of Miranda and the act itself:

'This must be what he meant by those strange words
While I was weeding larkspurs yesterday,
"Angels would take him!" Mad!'   (3601–3)

The poet arrives at the opposite conclusion from the same evidence:

                    No! sane, I say,
Such being the conditions of his life,
Such end of life was not irrational.   (3603–5)

'Not irrational': the adjective is Lockeian in its implications, but the context in which Browning places it suggests the idealism of the Germano-Coleridgian tradition.

That context is the metaphor 'flash,' and it means, as we have already seen, a sudden illumination which provides a configuration or shape or context for a single act, like the leap from the belvedere, or a single name, like Miranda itself. Browning is making the same point that Coleridge had made long before in an 1801 letter to Josiah Wedgwood, that no one name or sensory experience has any significance outside the system of relations which make up a language, or outside the connections with other sensory experiences. ('Both Words & Ideas derive their whole significancy from their coherence,' Coleridge tells Wedgwood; 'The simple *Idea* Red disserved from all, with which it had ever been conjoined would be as unintelligible as the word *Red*; the one would be a *sight*, the other a Sound, meaning only themselves, that is in common language, meaning nothing.')[15] Browning's metaphor for the leap from the belvedere is 'A flash in middle air' (3593), and Miranda's thought which precedes it is a flash too. Browning does not actually use that word for the thought, but he does say that the three hundred lines occur 'in a minute's space' (3286), and he does indicate that he is providing 'The thoughts which give the act significance' (3280). The etymology of the word 'significance' is helpful for our understanding of Browning's use of it here. A combination of *signum*, 'sign,' and *facio*, 'to make,' the word suggests something other than the Lockeian understanding of 'sign,' where a name has a one-to-one relation with an idea. To identify the idea, however, is not to account for the meaning of the name, which lies in a system of relationships with all other names, nor to give its significance, which depends upon the ability of the mind to infer those relationships from the data which make up our knowledge, and to arrange names in ways which meet human needs and concerns. So Browning distinguishes between act and thought, a datum (apprehended by our senses) and the inferences which make that datum significant. Here is how he introduces the three hundred lines that reveal the meaning of Miranda's act:

He thought ...
          (Suppose I should prefer 'He said'?
Along with every act – and speech is act –
There go, a multitude impalpable
To ordinary human faculty,

The thoughts which give the act significance.
Who is a poet needs must apprehend
Alike both speech and thoughts which prompt to speak.
Part these, and thought withdraws to poetry:
Speech is reported in the newspaper.)

He said, then, probably no word at all,
But thought as follows – in a minute's space. (3276–86)

Act is 'palpable' – observed by the senses, that is, and so, in Locke's terms, a matter of knowledge – but 'significance' can only be determined by illation, that activity of the reason which infers and judges (and which is in turn to be judged by every other reasoning human creature). So Browning, using his own powers of inference, provides the 'thought' of Miranda and claims truth for his attributions, though he certainly does not preclude the judgment of others, and in fact is always inviting it. Nor does he draw much attention to the source and authority of his powers of inference, though the source is the shapes within the mind that make naming possible and their authority the quickening God-given spirit within each human being.

Fifine at the Fair is a parleying which is contained within the understanding of the central male figure, whose situation can best be pictured in an emblematic way: he is flanked by two female figures, who contrast with each other and who are not only characters in their own right but projections of conflicting values and desires of the hero. One thinks of Scott's Waverley moving between Flora MacIvor and Rose Bradwardine, Ivanhoe's involvement with Rebecca and Rowena, Thackeray's Pendennis torn between Laura and Blanche – even (in Juliet McMaster's view) the reader of *Vanity Fair* drawn to both Becky and Amelia.[16] In Browning's poem, Don Juan has Elvire on his arm and Fifine in his sight, and his speech, ostensibly voiced to them both, is in fact an internal dialogue in which he assigns to the women opposing characteristics, frequently through attributed or imaginary speeches. The starting point of the dialogue is a visual image, and the naming and interpreting of it introduce the linguistic issues in the poem. Those issues all involve separation: of *pictura* and *explicatio*, of sign and idea, of image and interpretation, of order and lawlessness, of impulse and control – and of Elvire and Fifine. Language inevitably reflects such separation, and so is a maze of opposites. Juan revels in the chaotic energy of our ordinary experience and of the language which represents it, but he also dreams of another world where language disappears, and he affirms that God is the ultimate Word that makes sense of all the limitations and paradoxes of human language.

The image with which Juan begins is the fair itself, and he responds primarily to its vitality: its sudden appearance overnight, its miscellany of sights, its confused and confusing vigour and power. The 'pennon' focuses that energy for him – it is 'Frenetic to be free' (38) – and he associates it with passion, 'fever,' and 'lawlessness,' with that same natural energy Aristophanes celebrates in *Aristophanes' Apology*, that 'originative force / Of nature,' that 'impulse' which, 'underlying law, seems lawlessness' (2362–4). That energy is Don Juan's inspiration, and he describes his response to it as an internalizing of it, his metaphor being not a correspondent breeze but a correspondent fever:

> Frenetic to be free! And, do you know, there beats
> Something within my breast, as sensitive? – repeats
> The fever of the flag? My heart makes just the same
> Passionate stretch, fires up for lawlessness, lays claim
> To share the life they lead; losels, who have and use
> The hour what way they will ...   (43–8)

'Losels,' we remember, are good-for-nothings, scoundrels, so that the energy associated with them is a threat to society and to social order. They are 'without the pale' (100) and 'sell what we most pique us that we keep!' (102) – we being 'God-fearing householder[s]' (134). Don Juan's subject is not so much the question of choosing between one and the other, but rather how one turns into the other. Section 13 establishes this issue, and the crucial verbs are 'returns' and 'turns':

> Now, what is it? – returns
> The question – heartens so this losel that he spurns
> All we so prize? I want, put down in black and white,
> What compensating joy, unknown and infinite,
> Turns lawlessness to law, makes destitution – wealth,
> Vice – virtue, and disease of soul and body – health?   (138–43)

The answer to these questions lies in a characteristic Browning activity: the reading and interpreting of visual images. He cannot read 'the slow shake of head, the melancholy smile' (144) of Elvire, and so he turns to Fifine: 'Here's she, shall make my thoughts be surer what they mean! / First let me read the signs' (149–50). The signs are the features of Fifine's physical appearance, catalogued in a way that suggests the blazon of Renaissance love poetry, and contrasting with the 'Sexless and bloodless sprite' (173) who is Elvire. Fifine, the gypsy (151), is all erotic energy and lawlessness, Elvire, the wife, 'loveliness for law / And self-sustainment made morality' (175). Juan sets the figures in motion in a 'pageant' (201) which turns out to be a masque (251), with the conventional action of the genre – a procession – and the conventional approach of the various figures to the couple who are to be honoured – in this instance, the couple who are to be enlightened, Juan and Elvire. The sequence of figures has a moral order, proceeding as it does from siren to saint – 'See, Helen!' (210), 'See, Cleopatra!' (218), 'What say you to Saint ...' (228) – but the sense of steady upward progress is upset when the procession concludes with another siren: 'who concludes the masque with curtsey, smile and pout, / Submissive-mutinous? No other than Fifine' (251–2). In terms of morality, then, the procession circles round to its beginning. Again there is a push for meaning, this time on the part of Elvire, or at least in words that Don Juan attributes to Elvire: '"Well, what's the meaning here, what does the masque intend ...?"' (254).

In spite of the apparent dialogue, Browning blurs the distinction between his speakers. We can never be sure that Elvire is actually speaking, and all too often we suspect that her words, like the masque Juan conjures up, are attributed to her rather than actually spoken by her. That blurring of speakers is partly a result of verbal echoes, where Juan quotes from Elvire words that he also uses himself. We have already heard one question of Juan's echoed by Elvire (149, 199), and a second question, arising out of Juan's imperative, 'Judge and be just!' (200), is also repeated: '"What puts it in my head to make yourself judge you?"' (303). The line is in quotation marks. Is Juan echoing a question of Elvire's? Or is he quoting himself? And to whom do the pronouns refer? We note that the expected 'I judge you' is replaced by 'yourself' judging 'you,' so that the act is an internal one, and what comes from without is not the content of the judgment but the stimulus to make it. The stimulus is a divided self, presented by Juan in the myth of the phantom Helen and the 'true Helen' (318) and repeated in 'the phantom-wife' and 'the tearful true Elvire' (325–6). That division, Juan says (echoing line 303), 'put it in my head, / To make yourself judge you' (324–5). Here 'you' clearly refers to Elvire, but the act of making or compelling turns back upon the agent, since Juan is himself divided, and the judgment Elvire is to make is a judgment Juan will make of the Elvire within him.

The riddle – who is speaking? – becomes more convoluted when Juan attributes speech to Fifine, who in turn attributes speech to others, this time the figures in Juan's life and masque. The sequence (section 32) begins in the manner of the emblem, with Juan taking the picture he sees and making it speak: 'To me,' he says, 'that silent pose and prayer proclaimed aloud' the words which follow in quotation marks. The affirmation Juan attributes to Fifine is simple enough – '"all I plead is 'Pay for just the sight you see"'' (410) – but it is followed by a series of possible speeches by Fifine, all introduced in the same way: '"Do I say, like your Love?"' (412); '"Do I say, like your Wife?"' (414); '"Do I say, like your Helen?"' (416) – and '"like your Queen of Egypt"' (436) and '"like your Saint"' (448) and, finally, '"like Elvire"' (462). The repeated question '"Do I say?"' makes the fictional speeches conditional, but then, in a parenthesis not included within the quotation marks of the attributed speech, Juan makes the fiction truth and the conditional declarative. To Elvire he says directly, '(Your husband holds you fast / Will have you listen, learn your character at last!)' 462–3. The attributions turn out to be the means of speaking to Elvire, and indirection turns out to be direction. There is the same mingling of attribution and indirection in the next section. Most of section 33 is a speech Juan attributes to Fifine – it makes up lines 462 to 507 – who in turn attributes a speech to Elvire, who, in that conditional and fictional speech, pleads for Juan's love and judges Fifine as a '""fizgig"''' (507). The only way in which the reader of Browning's text can find directions through this maze is to look for the quotation marks, but when he or she finds quotation within quotation within quotation, and attributed speech within attributed speech within attributed speech, even the quotation marks are not enough. A poet who once championed the silent reading of a dramatic text as the way to enter into possession of the inner workings of a character's mind is here developing that method of presentation into a visual and semantic puzzle: who says what? who might say what? and how are we to judge the truth of a speech within a speech within a speech? The search for meaning is the continuous frustration of meaning, and the only way out of the maze of words, at least in this text, seems to be an exploration of the nature of naming itself. Juan deals with that issue by exploring the relation of body and soul.

'The mask / Of flesh,' Juan says, is 'meant to yield ... precise the features of the soul' (649–51) and 'show on the outside correspond / With inward substance' (659–60). So names ought to give essences, but they don't, any more than the faces Juan draws in the sand. Faces ought to yield 'a type' (653) but in fact are a 'mystery' (663), 'a plaguy puzzle' (664), because they are so obviously different and so often 'Retire from beauty, make approach to ugliness' (670). The faces he draws are caricatures, and his question about them is one that all users of names must ask when confronted with individual instances: 'what may that face mean, no matter for its nose, / A yard long, or its chin, a foot short?' (702–3). The answer is a variation on a favourite Browning idea, that imperfection means perfection hid, and so the exaggerations and deficiencies all turn out to be stimuli that lead the gazer to see the type or pattern. The perceiving agent who is stimulated by these hints and imperfections is the soul itself, understood as the interpretive power within us, and without which the material world would be a dead thing instead of a living sign. In vain would we 'attempt to make account / Of what the sense, without soul's help, perceives' (793–4). Juan's account of the soul's acts yields an idealist theory of naming:

> Since, in the seeing soul, all worth lies, I assert, –
> And naught i' the world, which, save for soul that sees, inert
> Was, is, and would be ever, – stuff for transmuting, – null
> And void until man's breath evoke the beautiful –
> But, touched aright, prompt yields each particle its tongue
> Of elemental flame ...   (824–9)

The words 'man's breath' suggest that each human being repeats the divine act of inspiration, and the result is 'transmuting,' the changing or turning of the 'stuff' or matter of this world. The imagery in the passage is pentecostal, and the 'tongue / Of elemental flame' that each 'particle' (a materialist word) yields is not only the divine spirit dwelling in each thing but a 'tongue,' the conventional synecdoche for the language by which each thing speaks, 'Fling[s] out broad its name' (in the words of Hopkins's 'As kingfishers catch fire') and declares its meaning. That meaning is an indwelling quality in each thing, and is to be discovered rather than invented. Discovery, however, is no easy matter, since so many things in our experience seem to be in conflict with each other: body and soul, truth and falsehood, articulate sounds themselves and the ideas of which they are the signs.

Juan's central metaphor for such opposites is the conflict between water and air experienced by the swimmer, a conflict from which the soul benefits, particularly in its use of language. The water is the false, the air the true, but one cannot 'Be in the air and leave the water altogether' (1030), and so 'the adept swims, this accorded, that denied; / Can always breathe, sometimes see and be satisfied!' (1037–8):

> I liken to this play o' the body, – fruitless strife
> To slip the sea and hold the heaven, – my spirit's life
> 'Twixt false, whence it would break, and true, where it would bide.
> I move in, yet resist, am upborne every side
> By what I beat against, an element too gross
> To live in, did not soul duly obtain her dose
> Of life-breath, and inhale from truth's pure plenitude
> Above her, snatch and gain enough to just illude
> With hope that some brave bound may baffle evermore
> The obstructing medium, make who swam henceforward soar.   (1039–48)

The false turns out to have its use and purpose:

> We must endure the false, no particle of which
> Do we acquaint us with, but up we mount a pitch
> Above it, find our head reach truth, while hands explore
> The false below: so much while here we bathe, – no more!   (1059–62)

The lesson: 'By practice with the false, I reach the true' (1069). That argument may seem self-serving when, at the end of the poem, Juan apparently opts for an assignation with Fifine, but that same statement is a general truth which characterizes the human use of language.

In a life where our ordinary experience is characterized by opposites, words too are inevitably double, naming physical things but produced by a soul which is immaterial and immortal. The soul may intuit 'Truth' (945) directly, and words might be the signs of such intuitions ('Truth,' Juan says, might be 'reached ... easily by thought / Reducible to word' 946–7), but words can only struggle towards Truth, weighed down as they are by their ties to the physical world. Music, Juan says (in a way which reflects his creator) may

> tricksily elude what words attempt
> To heave away, i' the mass, and let the soul, exempt
> From all that vapoury obstruction, view, instead
> Of glimmer underneath, a glory overhead.   (952–5)

Words, however, are 'weary' (961). Juan tropes them as carrying a 'burthen' (962), the appearances or 'shows of things,' weighty and material. So, Juan says,

> Words struggle with the weight
> So feebly of the False, thick element between
> Our soul, the True, and Truth!   (943–5)

Not so thick, however, as to be wholly opaque. 'At least permit they rest their burthen here and there, / Music-like: cover space!' (962–3). The simile is crucial. The space to be covered is the blank page of a printed book, where the inked words, like the notes in a musical score, rest themselves 'here and there.' The words, like a musical score, have the potential to be brought to life and to make the space in which we exist intelligible. So, Juan says when he and Elvire are about to descend to the beach, the moment is 'just the time, / The place, the mood in you and me, when all things chime' (966–7), when there is the possibility of hearing 'Reverberated notes whence we construct the scale / Embracing what we know and feel and are!' (970–1). Hence he comes to the possibility of closing the gap between sign and signified.

The separation of sign and signified is a mark of our fallen state (Boehme, we recall, describes the fall in just that way in his *Mysterium Magnum*), and the limited reason of fallen human beings makes every interpretation tentative and suspect. Juan dreams, however, of another and higher order of being, a restoration where images and meaning are one, instantly grasped by both eye and mind. In this order of being, words are no longer necessary. That possibility occurs to Juan in a dream-vision inspired, significantly, by music. The music is 'Schumann's "Carnival"' (1588), a piece which, as Juan treats it, unites the lawless energy of the fair with the insights and feelings only music can manage. (And so music 'puts poetry to shame' 1572). The fair or carnival expands into the whole of the created world, the expansion imaged as a circling:

> Lo, link by link, expands
> The circle, lengthens out the chain, till one embrace
> Of high with low is found uniting the whole race,
> Not simply you and me and our Fifine, but all
> The world: the Fair expands into the Carnival,
> And Carnival again to ... ah, but that's my dream!   (1606–11)

The dream is a dream of Venice as 'a prodigious Fair' (1690), with a

'Concourse immense of men and women' (1691), all masked. The sight is a riddle (Juan explicitly labels it as such), and the puzzle is that 'from all these sights beneath / There rose not any sound: a crowd, yet dumb as death!' (1723–4). 'Propose a riddle, and 'tis solved / Forthwith – in dream!' (1725–6), Juan says. The solution is not (as we might expect) the identity of word and meaning, of sign and signified, but the dispensing with words entirely, so that image and meaning are one, and the eye is sufficient where the tongue would be deficient. It 'devolved [on me] / To see, and understand by sight' (1726–7), Juan says. The crowd in fact speaks (1726), but Juan in his dream has no need of their words:

> 'myself it is that, seeing, know,
> And, knowing, can dispense with voice and vanity
> Of speech.'　(1732–4)

That last phrase, '"vanity / Of speech,"' is consistent with Browning's views elsewhere: that words, tied as they are to the 'false shows of things,' are empty. Since most human beings cannot claim the kind of perception Juan claims in his dream, they must rely on words, which are not so hollow that they do not point towards truth. So, in the words Juan attributes to his 'thought' in the dream,

> 'He who cannot see, must reach
> As best he may the truth of men by help of words
> They please to speak, must fare at will of who affords
> The banquet ...'　(1728–31)

Human words belong to a fallen world, and are evidence of the division between that world and our understanding of it. Hence, when Juan observes the men and women of the 'prodigious Fair' talking to each other, he says that

> all seemed out of joint
> I' the vocal medium, 'twixt the world and me. I gained
> Knowledge by notice, not by giving ear, – attained
> To truth by what men seemed, not said: to me one glance
> Was worth whole histories of noisy utterance,
> – At least, to me in dream.　(1760–5)

In the waking world, however, sight alone is not sufficient, and we cannot dispense with words. The world as we know it is invariably double, and the linguistic form of that doubleness is the oxymoron or the paradox.

Juan's oxymoron – 'honest cheating' (1517) – is his reason for prizing 'stage-play.' The 'inmost charm of this Fifine and all her tribe' (1474), he says, lies in the fact that they are actors:

> We also act, but only they inscribe
> Their style and title so, and preface, only they,
> Performance with 'A lie is all we do or say.' (1475–7)

That inscription is like a motto in an emblem, and it is a paradoxical one. If all that they say is a lie, then the motto is itself a lie, and they are speaking the truth. There is no way out of the logical maze which a statement of this sort creates, but Juan does argue that a frank and open embracing of falsehood is, paradoxically, a means of grace. The argument appears in the lines where Juan is interpreting, the sign of his interpreting being the verb 'means': 'To feign, means – to have grace / And so get gratitude!' (1482–3). That paradox becomes intelligible when we read the entry for 'feign' in Johnson's *Dictionary*. The meaning which seems to us most familiar – 'to dissemble; to conceal' – Johnson labels as 'obsolete,' and the first meaning he gives is 'to invent.' Even when the meaning is 'to relate falsely,' Johnson links that sense with 'to image from the invention,' and his example is a quotation from Shakespeare about the poet's feigning. Johnson's primary sense is thus close to the Latin root of the word, the verb *fingere*, 'to fashion, form, mould,' and such invention is possible because of the living spirit within us, 'grace' being, in Johnson's words, the 'favourable influence of God on the human mind.' 'To have grace / And so get gratitude' can be read in two contexts. One is that of the theatre or fair, where the actor and the character played are, we know, clearly separate ('the man who wept the tears was, all the time, / Happy enough' 1493–4), and where the 'grace' or skill of the man makes the character come alive ('The histrionic truth is in the natural lie' 1492). The other is that of the fallen world, where we all can form or shape things because of the divine influence. Shaping and moulding are the essential human activities, initiated and sustained by the Holy Spirit, so that making things up turns out to be the way upwards to truth. That idea brings us back to Juan's swimming metaphor. He had, in pursuing that metaphor, affirmed 'One truth more true for me than any truth beside – / To-wit, that I am I, who have the power to swim, / The skill to understand' (1064–5). That power and skill are the indwelling grace in him, which enables him to master the water, so that 'By practice with the false, I reach the true' (1069). The antithesis of that line is yet another version of the verbal contradictions inevitable in human speech.

I use the word 'version' deliberately, because the contradictions are not static or arranged, like poles, at the extreme ends of a straight line. Instead, they are parts of constant change which falls into a circular and ultimately a spiral pattern. Juan suggests that pattern first when he describes 'man' as 'one stuff miscalled by different names' (1875). At first glance, such naming seems entirely false, and that impression is strengthened by the participle 'miscalled,' but the names turn out to be true to levels of development, for they are 'According to what stage i' the process turned [man's] rough ... to smooth' (1876–7). The names are in fact the instruments of that turning, and have a place in cycles of change that Juan goes on to describe at length. Those cycles proceed from creation through destruction to recreation; temples and academies 'subdivide, collapse, / And tower again, transformed' (1913–14); churches and colleges 'grow nothing, soon to reappear no less / As something, – shape reshaped, till out of shapelessness / Come shape again as sure!' (1961–3). Truth itself '"builds upon the sands, / Though stationed on a rock: and so her work decays, / And so she builds afresh, with like result"' (1944–6). '"All is change"' and '"All is permanence"' (2009, 2010) – those two 'preachments,' like the sand and the rock, are opposites not to be reconciled, but both must be held together, and both are truths.

Both are truths because both are 'variants' of the Word itself, defined by Juan as 'the Protoplast,' the first fashioner or creator ('God said, Let there be light: and there was light'), and the name of God, the tetragrammaton revealed to Moses out of the burning bush. The King James translation of that name, 'I am that I am,' suggests a changeless and eternal being, but the Hebrew verb, as Bernhard Anderson points out in *Understanding the Old Testament*, differs from the English 'to be' in suggesting ongoing activity, creativity, the divine guidance of earthly events, and the future accomplishment of divine purpose.[17] The Word is both permanence and change. When Juan is describing the pulling down and building up of temple stones, he hears 'at the core, / One and no other word' (2171–2):

> For as some imperial chord subsists,
> Steadily underlies the accidental mists

Of music springing thence, that run their mazy race
Around, and sink, absorbed, back to the triad base, –
So, out of that one word, each variant rose and fell
And left the same 'All's change, but permanence as well.' (2175–80)

Because all words are emanations of the Word, God is in falsehood as much as he is in truth, and partial or contingent truths are the means of rising into fuller truth. '"Truth successively takes shape, one grade above / Its last presentment"' (2192–3), and from the next level up those previous truths reveal themselves as lies. But '"Then do we understand the value of a lie"' (2200), says Juan: '"Each lie, superfluous now, leaves, in the singer's stead, / The indubitable song"' (2202–3).

All this teaching about the nature and function of language is a commentary on the narrative of the poem. The story is circular. At the beginning of the poem, Juan draws attention to the cycles of the day and the year (the time is afternoon, the season autumn), to the appearance of the fair in the morning. The time proceeds from daylight and waking life to darkness and dreaming ('How quickly night comes!' 1462) and then to waking again (2238). The physical movement of Juan and Elvire is also a circle. They attend the fair, descend to the beach, confront the Druid monument, and return to 'villa-door' (2305). Juan makes the circular pattern even more explicit with an allusion to Donne's 'A Valediction: Forbidding Mourning':

Awaking so,
What if we, homeward-bound, all peace and some fatigue,
Trudge, soberly complete our tramp of near a league,
Last little mile which makes the circuit just, Elvire?
We end where we began ... (2238–42)

The journey, in short, is the visible embodiment of the circling round of language, and that circling has its climactic moment in the confrontation with a ruined tower, as in '"Childe Roland."'

The tower is the Druid monument. It is a 'construction gaunt and grey' (2048), and it appears 'I' the solitary waste we grope through' (2051). The diction suggests the romance quest, and its climactic moment conventionally is a confrontation with the self, as the dark tower certainly is for Roland. The monument here is not so obviously Juan's self. It has two parts: there is the 'caverned passage' with its 'monstrous door / Of granite' and a 'cold dread shape' at the end (2053–

7) – a cross – and there is the 'huge stone pillar, once upright, / Now laid at length, half-lost' (2104–5). The text itself indicates that the pillar is a phallic symbol – 'go and ask our grandames how they used / To dance around it' (2146–7) – while the 'caverned passage' is a vaginal one. There is a problem with interpreting the 'huge stone pillar.' The Curé insists that it is a ladder like Jacob's ladder, 'A staircase, earth to heaven' (2115), but to trope it thus is, in Juan's view, to 'refine / To inspidity' (2143–4). The people think that 'what once a thing / Meant and had right to mean, it still must mean' (2126–7). Juan combines both meanings when he affirms that one approaches God – the 'arch-word' (2130) – better through crude energy than through elegant order.

> So cling
> Folk somehow to the prime authoritative speech,
> And so distrust report, it seems as they could reach
> Far better the arch-word, whereon their fate depends,
> Through rude charactery, than all the grace it lends,
> That lettering of your scribes!   (2127–32)

The parleying, in Browning's hands, is a genuine clash of opposites, and, as in Carlyle's warfare of 'the modern *lingual* or Parliamentary-logical kind,' 'no victory yet definable can be considered as final,' either within the poetic text itself, or in the parleying of the text with its reader. In such a debate or argument, language is both the record of human knowledge and the expression of human judgment; hence it involves both the naming of things and ideas, and the turning, troping, or interpreting of the name, those actions by which we assert its meaning. The speakers in a parleying often consider the nature of language itself, and they do so for the same reason that Locke includes book 3 in his *Essay*. 'It is impossible,' Locke says at the end of book 2, 'to speak clearly and distinctly of our Knowledge, which all consists in Propositions, without considering, first, the Nature, Use, and Signification of Language' (2.33.19). Words are both instrumental (as the means of communication) and arguable (as the expression of human judgment), and so a 'parleying,' in Browning's sense of the word, is natural to language itself.

Overview and Conclusion

The reader may find useful an attempt to summarize Browning's understanding of the nature and use of language. In his view, language is the chief means of our moral and spiritual progress, the conditions of which determine the nature of words and syntax. That progress Browning refers to in the 1863 dedication to *Sordello* as 'incidents in the development of a soul,' and he tells Milsand, to whom the dedication is addressed, 'little else is worth study.' Two major functions of language are indicated by this statement. First of all, the incidents which are crucial for an individual are judgments made by the mind, realized in conduct, and expressed in language, the mind being, in Browning's view, the 'servant' of the soul (that 'the soul is above and *behind* the intellect' was a 'momentous' doctrine for him, Browning told Mrs FitzGerald). Secondly, every 'incident' which is important for one person is 'worth study' by another, and since the soul can be known only through the mind, and the mind in turn only through the language by which it expresses and communicates its decisions, language is, for every student of it, both heuristic and conative. As the instrument of the mind, it serves to find out, obliquely, the soul itself; and as the basis of conduct, it presents shapings and interpretations that are both exemplary and cautionary. Hence language offers itself to the reader for both discovery and judgment, and so it is like a riddle, the solution to which is an incident in the development of the reader's own soul.

The conditions under which such development takes place determine the nature of language. Browning was brought up in the Congregational church and in the Puritan tradition, and in the statement of faith adopted by the York Street Chapel (the Westminster Confession of 1646–8), human beings live in a fallen world; they are 'dead in sin, and wholly defiled in all the faculties and parts of soul and body.' In such a desperate state, however, they have the hope and comfort of the 'Covenant of Grace,' God's freely offered gift of 'salvation by Jesus Christ' and of the Holy Spirit, who makes human beings 'willing and able to believe.' 'Able' is a crucial word, for the Holy Spirit is that power which gives us the ability to understand and interpret – crucial actions in a fallen world where sign and signified are no longer one. In an unfallen world, a word is synecdochic, the articulate sound participating in the essential being of that of which it is the sign. Browning thinks of such primal unity in language as a goal, and explores it in his reading and use of Boehme and perhaps of Swedenborg, but he knows that the actual relation of sign and signified, in our ordinary experience, is just the opposite: there is no necessary connection between the two, and the articulate sound which is the name of an idea is conventional and arbitrary, not natural and inevitable. The language theory with which Browning's has most in common is Locke's. Browning seems to have had little interest in the new philology of his day, the historical and comparative studies of languages as defined by the work of Sir William Jones, continued in Germany by the brothers Grimm and others, and later championed in England by scholars like Trench and Kemble, who were Coleridgians. Browning, however, told Mrs Orr 'that he knew neither the German philosophers nor their reflection in Coleridge.' The philosophy he did know was British empiricism.

There is plenty of evidence for Browning's knowledge of language as it is understood by the empiricists, though the theory probably came to the poet not primarily from *An Essay Concerning Human Understanding* (in spite of the copy in Browning's library) but through Johnson's *Dictionary*, which the poet read carefully, and through his father's eccentric and certainly eclectic reading, especially in the so-called 'new logic' which was a development both of the *Essay* and of Locke's *Conduct of the Understanding*. The important parts of that tradition for Browning are the acts of naming and interpreting. Names, Locke had taught, are conventional, the act of naming being 'voluntary' or willed, and the relation between sound and idea being 'arbitrary.' Naming is thus an act by which the mind makes known its own concerns and pursues its own ends, and names themselves, far from being merely fanciful or whimsical, are the result of judgment, as the etymology of 'arbitrary' indicates. Words and all their relating and sorting out of ideas are (to use Locke's phrase) 'the Workmanship of the Understanding,' and the entries in

Johnson's *Dictionary* – the one Browning claimed to have read in its entirety, and digested, in preparation for his being a poet – are all manifestations of the soul, for which the understanding is an agent. Every act of naming is an act of interpretation and judgment, which in turn must be interpreted and judged by every reader. The entries in the *Dictionary* are a record of such acts, but Browning as poet is especially interested in interpretation involving an act Locke distrusted: the turning or troping of a word. For Locke, the figures of rhetoric – metaphor, simile, and so on – are a 'perfect cheat' because propositions using them ('this is that,' for instance) assert relations other than those we actually observe in the world around us, where 'this' clearly is not 'that.' For Browning, however, such turning, especially when it involves a reversal ('this' becomes its opposite, 'that'), holds out the promise of repairing the breakup of all things at the fall. Such a faith in troping, I argue, comes from the experience at the centre of the dissenting religious tradition in which Browning was raised: conversion. It too (if we look at 'conversion' etymologically) is a turn, from being 'dead in sin' to being alive in grace, and such a reversal, such a radical shift from one state to its opposite, is a circling round that becomes, in Browning's view, a spiralling upwards. Browning does not hesitate to suggest that wrestling with the meaning of words, interpreting them and turning them, are activities which will save the soul (as he affirms at the end of *The Ring and the Book*), and he often suggests, too, that interpretation is possible because of a spirit which animates the understanding, though it does not limit the mind's freedom of choice (the doctrine of Christian liberty being as important for Browning as it is for Milton).

Browning typically deals with poetry in relation to two other arts in which he had a lifelong interest, painting and music. Poetry is conventionally linked with the appeal to the sense of sight through the Horatian tag *ut pictura poesis*, and when one considers prosody and its appeal to the ear, one thinks that Horace ought also to have said *ut musica poesis*. The analogies fill out our understanding of the language of poetry as Browning treats it. Visual images are, without words, puzzles for the mind, and need the agency of language so that the viewer can say, 'this means that.' Browning's model for such an act of interpretation is the emblem, which he knew primarily through the work of Quarles. In that genre, *pictura*, motto, and *explicatio* carry the image across both to other images and to ideas, a sequence which occurs frequently in Browning's poetry. 'Do you see?' he asks in the first line of *The Ring and the Book*, and the initial appeal to the physical eye develops into a challenge to the eye of the understanding. Musical sounds, in contrast to visual images, are not so easily carried across to ideas, but when Browning does treat music as a theme, he thinks of its sounds as things which are themselves, 'whole' and 'sole,' and not the signs of ideas. Hence music suggests that ideal language where sign and signified are one, a state Browning associates with play. The actual music of Browning's poetry is an approach to such an ideal state. The music of his poetry lies, not in pleasing or smooth sounds, or in lengthened vowel sounds (as in Tennyson), but rather in keeping time, in organizing varying numbers of syllables into isochronous units. Rhyme (Browning prided himself on being a virtuoso rhymester) is a 'time-beater' (in Coventry Patmore's terminology), and 'beat' is neatly double: it is both the ictus or strong accent that marks the beginning of each unit or bar, and the overcoming or transcending of time by the skilful use of it. Browning has only contempt for thumpingly obvious rhythms, and his 'thought-tormented music' (to use Gabriel Conroy's words from Joyce's 'The Dead') or 'monstrous music' (to use Gilbert's phrase from Wilde's 'The Critic as Artist') is part of the art of 'complex Poetry.'

The complexity arises out of Browning's characteristic desire to be inclusive and encyclopedic, and to go, like his David, 'the whole round of creation.' It also arises out of his characteristic purpose: to teach his readers and 'make' them 'see.' Locke and those who followed him in developing the 'new logic' distinguished between the discovery of knowledge and the communication of it, and Browning, like his Paracelsus, knows that 'to possess [is] one thing – to display / Another.' He knew that his readers often wanted ends or conclusions presented in plain language and in the poet's own voice, and didn't like going to the trouble of working out the meaning for themselves. Only in one's striving for meaning, however, could truths come alive, not just in the mind but in the heart; only in struggle could one's soul wake and grow. Hence Browning creates texts designed to be the site of the growth of the reader's soul, and he teaches not just truths but also methods of approaching truth. He sometimes fragments or defamiliarizes language (he breaks up syntax in *Sordello*, for instance), but more characteristically he uses techniques of indirection: he multiplies his own voice in the voices of all the characters he creates, and forces the reader to assess the mind which mediates the subject. He blurs the distinctions between speakers in a parleying, or he constructs a verbal maze when he creates a character who in turn attributes speeches to others. He encloses a text or story within a parleying within yet another parleying, and this 'art of narrative strip-tease' (I am borrowing David Shaw's words)[1] forces the reader into multiple perspectives. Language is the sole medium of all these textual puzzles, and (largely as a result of his experience as a playwright) Browning insists upon the reader's silent confrontation with the words of his texts. Nothing must come between reader and word – not the sights and sounds of a theatrical performance, not even his own reading aloud of his poems. Actual sights and voices provide only one interpretation of a text; language alone, absorbed silently and privately, makes possible varying or even contradictory interpretations, to be played out in the theatre or lecture room or debating hall of the reader's own mind. Browning's language is that of the 'Maker-see,' and it makes us see by jarring us out of a single perspective into a struggle of contradictions which (Browning hopes for both himself and us) will eventually round to a whole.

With such a strong sense of development as the governing pattern of the individual human life, Browning might reasonably be expected to have changed his views of language over time. The writing of this book has led me to the conclusion, however, that Browning's views did not change in any fundamental way in the course of a long career. Language is for him a given, and Browning's use of it is not a matter of invention but of discovery. The given was specifically Johnson's *Dictionary*, and in it Browning explored the nature of words and discovered the acts of the mind lying behind every name and every proposition. Browning is typically ironic and circumspect about the truth of such acts, labelling them (in *The Ring and the Book* 1. 859) 'swerving,' as if truth were a straight line and the mind's apprehension of it a deviation. Browning knows, however, that no truth is ever apprehended in an unmediated way, and hence truth is to be found, paradoxically, in 'swerving.' That paradox can be seen as a revolution in our understanding of the word 'arbitrary.' The adjective is the one Locke uses for the relation between sign and idea, and we ordinarily understand it as the expression of 'mere opinion,' in the words of the *OED*, as something 'capricious.' Opinion, in Browning's view, is never 'mere,' and his poetry leads us back through the etymology of 'arbitrary,' to the judgment made by the mind and to the revelation of human concerns in every linguistic act. Truth for Browning lies in the 'arbitrary.' It cannot be discovered in any other way, and so one must pick through the 'filthy rags of speech' (*The Ring and the Book* 10.372), turning out every seam and thread to examine the connections and patterns which are the evidence, however adequate, of truth. This statement leads to a yet further conclusion: that words have a worth which, I hope, will be more fully realized in Browning criticism.

No critic works in isolation, and the argument I have been pursuing is my addition to work which has been under way for a decade or so. To be a critic is 'to enter into a body of thought' (to use Northrop Frye's comment on thinking as a discipline) 'and to try to add your own thinking to it.'[2] Nearly everyone who has written about Browning has had something to say about his language, and two recent books are immensely useful surveys of that large body of work: Patricia O'Neill's *Robert Browning and Twentieth-Century Criticism* (1995) and John Maynard's *Browning Re-viewed: Review Essays, 1980–1995* (1998).[3] Among all the books and articles and editions which they describe and evaluate, I am particularly conscious of adding to the work of three critics for whom Browning's language is a central concern: David Shaw, Hillis Miller, and Isobel Armstrong.[4]

It is David Shaw who has provided critics with the best guide to 'philosophy among the poets.' That phrase is one of Shaw's headings in *The Lucid Veil* (1987), and in both that book and *Victorians and Mystery: Crises of Representation* (1990), Shaw explores the multiple links between philosophy and poetic language. Shaw's model is Abrams's *The Mirror and the Lamp*, but *The Lucid Veil* is (to use Coleridge's distinction) an imitation and not a copy. Like Abrams, Shaw has his organizing metaphors, and the shift from Abrams's antithesis to Shaw's oxymoron (borrowed from Tennyson) is an indication of the Victorian attempt to mediate between the two philosophical traditions (usefully summed up in Mill's essays on Bentham and Coleridge) which the age inherited. The empiricists provide us with the metaphor of the mind as the mirror of nature, a metaphor which is modified by the idealists, for whom the world is framed by a self-conscious subject, so that the mind becomes a window on nature, a glass through which we see, usually 'darkly.' Browning, as I have tried to show, is not much interested in nature or in the echo which is the aural equivalent of the mirror, but he is excited by frames and glasses, the metaphors for the linguistic acts by which we make sense of the world and our experience of it. Hence I have tried to add to Shaw's criticism a fuller understanding of Locke, for whom a word is not the sign of a thing but of an idea. Locke had found an examination of language necessary in his drive towards establishing a reasonable basis for conduct, and Browning too, aware of the fact that readers usually look through language at something else, wants us to look *at* language in (what Hillis Miller calls) 'the linguistic moment.'

The phrase is the title of Miller's 1985 book (*The Linguistic Moment: From Wordsworth to Stevens*), and it points to 'moments of suspension within the texts of the poems, not usually at their beginnings or ends, moments when they reflect or comment on their own medium.' These moments are not just casual or incidental, but tend 'to spread out and dominate the functioning of the whole poem.' Such moments are 'a breaking of the illusion that language is a transparent medium of meaning' (xiv). In his Browning chapter, which is a superb analysis of 'The Englishman in Italy,' Miller deals with topics which are also concerns of this book: the encyclopedic thrust of the speaker's interests, his desire to possess his world through language, his attempt to conquer time, his longing for symbols when words are only signs, and his 'ascending spiral' (192) towards totality (a movement which is inevitably frustrated). The same themes and patterns emerge from the texts of Browning's whole career, as I have tried to show, and I have attempted to work out more fully the implications of such designs and ideas. Miller begins his book with one idea which is crucial for Browning: that every text is an interpretation of other texts, and that, as Miller (quoting Foucault) points out, one can never go so far back as to discover something that is not already an interpretation (3). Such an 'abyss of interpretation' (3) is an idea Browning applies to language as well. Browning, as I have said, was not much interested in the origin of language, though the question had been central to scholarly debate (the assumption being that origins define the nature of one's subject); Browning saw no need to go to origins, since every utterance, past or present, reveals that words are interpretation.

Isobel Armstrong's treatment of Browning's language in *Victorian Poetry: Poetry, Poetics and Politics* (1993) anticipates the argument I have been making about the 'arbitrary.' Like me, Armstrong places Browning in the empiricist tradition, and focuses in particular on Bentham's theory of fictions as a guide to understanding Browning's poetic language. The theory

> neither consolidates pure representation nor identifies the sign and the thing signified. Curiously, its advantage to an artist is that it confirms the necessity of fictions and places them as central to the process of thinking, in spite of the discreditable purposes to which they may be put. Moreover, it asserts that fictional constructs intervene substantively in the world and affect choices and actions however fictional they may be. They are as enabling as they are disreputable.   (150)

'Bentham's willingness to speak of a fiction "as if it were real"' is, Armstrong remarks, 'a flagrantly, almost perversely, paradoxical theory' (150), but it is a paradox which illuminates the nature of Browning's poetic enterprise, an enterprise in which, Armstrong remarks, language is central (299). Like me, Armstrong wants readers to see the worth of the 'arbitrary,' which for her is largely performative: 'the connection between a word and its import is "altogether arbitrary" but coercive' (151). Hence Armstrong uses the Benthamite theory of fictions to explore the dramatic monologue and the link of poetry and politics, and I have tried to add an exploration of the link between the arbitrary and the 'development of the soul.'

'Here were an end, had anything an end' (to borrow Browning's words from the last book of *The Ring and the Book*), and my end (to play upon the word) has been not only to see Browning plain (like the man in 'Memorabilia' who saw Shelley) but to see him whole, and to do so through that which was of most concern to him, the medium of his art. What kind of artist do we see? The creator of complex dramatic texts, the master rhymester – and the 'philosophical and religious teacher' (to borrow from the title of Henry Jones's 1891 book), the Protestant and the dissenter too, though an understanding of the poet's language gives us a new take on those old aims and positions. That list of nouns brings us to an end, but Browning's Pope (quoting the preacher in Ecclesiastes) reminds us that 'of the making books there is no end.' My conclusions are only interpretations, ready to be interpreted in turn, and judged.

Notes

Introduction

1 *Letters of Robert Browning Collected by Thomas J. Wise*, ed. Thurman L. Hood (London: Murray, 1933) 165.
2 Hallam Tennyson, *Alfred Lord Tennyson: A Memoir by His Son* (London: Macmillan, 1899) 524.
3 *Dearest Isa: Robert Browning's Letters to Isabella Blagden*, ed. Edward C. McAleer (Austin: U of Texas P, 1951) 180–1.

Chapter One: 'The world of words'

1 K.M. Elisabeth Murray, *Caught in the Web of Words: James A.H. Murray and the 'Oxford English Dictionary'* (New Haven: Yale UP, 1977) 235.
2 Mrs Sutherland Orr, *Life and Letters of Robert Browning*, 2nd ed. (London: Smith, Elder, 1891) 53.
3 John Maynard, *Browning's Youth* (Cambridge, Mass.: Harvard UP, 1977) 297.
4 *Dearest Isa: Robert Browning's Letters to Isabella Blagden*, ed. Edward C. McAleer (Austin: U of Texas P, 1951) 353.
5 John Woolford, intro. *Sale Catalogues of Libraries of Eminent Persons*, vol. 6, Poets and Men of Letters (London: Mansell, 1972) 3; Maynard, 86.
6 William Irvine and Park Honan, *The Book, The Ring, and The Poet: A Biography of Robert Browning* (New York: McGraw, 1974) 6–7.
7 *Learned Lady: Letters from Robert Browning to Mrs. Thomas FitzGerald 1876–1889*, ed. Edward C. McAleer (Cambridge, Mass.: Harvard UP, 1966) 193.
8 George Bornstein, 'Pound's Parleyings with Browning,' *Poetic Remaking: The*

Art of Browning, Yeats, and Pound (University Park: Pennsylvania State UP, 1988) 124.

9 All quotations from Johnson's Preface are from *A Dictionary of the English Language*, 2 vols. (1755; New York: AMS, 1967). The pages are unnumbered.

10 Qtd. in Robert DeMaria, Jr, *Johnson's 'Dictionary' and the Language of Learning* (Chapel Hill: U of North Carolina P, 1986) ix.

11 The statistics given by Elizabeth Hedrick qualify this statement. She points out that 'nearly 67% of the entries in the *Dictionary* – to the extent that Johnson's treatment of words beginning with the letter F is representative of his work throughout – are given only one meaning ... All the same, Johnson is decidedly more interested in multiple meanings than any of his lexicographic predecessors.' 'Locke's Theory of Language and Johnson's *Dictionary*,' *Eighteenth-Century Studies* 20 (1987) 433.

12 N. Dralloc [John Collard], *An Epitome of Logic, in four Parts* (London: Printed for the Author, 1795) 35n.

13 All quotations from *An Essay Concerning Human Understanding* are from the edition of Peter H. Nidditch (Oxford: Clarendon, 1975). Quotations are identified by book, chapter, and paragraph numbers. This particular quotation is from book 3, chapter 10, paragraph 5.

14 Thomas Carlyle, *On Heroes, Hero-Worship, and the Heroic in History*, ed. Archibald MacMechan (Boston: Ginn, 1901) 210; Frederick Denison Maurice, *The Friendship of Books and Other Lectures*, ed. Thomas Hughes, 2nd ed. (London: Macmillan, 1874) 44.

15 Nor was Browning much interested in the origin of language, a question that had been central to debates about language in the seventeenth and eighteenth centuries. Ripert-Monclar had given him, in 1834, a copy of a book by his uncle, the Marquis de Fortia d'Urban, *Essai sur l'Origine de l'Ecriture*, which deals with the origin of language as well as writing, but though one or two passages are marked in pencil, the question of origins seems not to have engaged Browning's interest.

16 Qtd. in Murray 235.

17 Hans Aarsleff, *The Study of Language in England 1780–1860* (Princeton: Princeton UP, 1967) 31.

18 *The [Westminster] Confession of Faith; The Larger and Shorter Catechisms* (Edinburgh: Johnstone, 1868) 32.

19 The quotation is from 'A succinct Account of the origin and progress of the Church of Christ assembling at Lock's Fields Meeting House Walworth in the Parish of Newington Butts in the County of Surrey,' a handwritten account of the York Street Chapel, 'of the rise and progress of the Church and of the principles on which it was formed,' by John Flint and Richard Smales.

I am indebted to the Reverend Clive R. Dunnico for supplying me with photocopies of this document, one from 'The Church Book' and the other from the 'Register of Church Members.'

20 Williston Walker, *The Creeds and Platforms of Congregationalism* (1893; Philadelphia: Pilgrim, 1960) 374.

21 *The Letters of Robert Browning and Elizabeth Barrett Barrett 1845–1846*, ed. Elvan Kintner (Cambridge, Mass.: Belknap, 1969) 919. Hereafter referred to as Kintner.

22 This statement needs qualification. There are 25 entries for 'puff' and its variants in *A Concordance to the Poems and Plays of Robert Browning*, compiled by Richard J. Shroyer and Thomas J. Collins, 7 vols. (New York: AMS, 1996). By way of contrast, there are 671 entries for 'true' and 856 for 'truth.'

23 Quotations from *Aurora Leigh* are from the text edited by Margaret Reynolds, Norton Critical Edition (New York: Norton, 1996).

24 Again, I am quoting from the handwritten 'succinct Account' signed by Clayton.

25 George Clayton, *A Course of Sermons on Faith and Practice*, delivered by the Rev. George Clayton, at York Street Chapel, Walworth, 1838–39 (London: Ward, 1839) 3.

26 *The [Westminster] Confession of Faith; the Larger and Shorter Catechisms* (Edinburgh: Johnstone, 1868) 196–7.

27 Maynard, 315, 134. Much later in his life, Browning responded to William Hale White ('Mark Rutherford'), who had written to the poet after reading his 1879 'Ned Bratts,' and focused on their common interest: 'a lover of Bunyan too, the object of my utmost admiration and reverence.' *New Letters of Robert Browning*, ed. William Clyde DeVane and Kenneth Leslie Knickerbocker (London: Murray, 1951) 251. 'Ned Bratts,' from the 1879 *Dramatic Idyls: First Series*, is the poem in which Browning makes the fullest and most explicit use of Bunyan.

28 All quotations from *The Pilgrim's Progress* are from the text edited by James Blanton Wharey and Roger Sharrock, 2nd ed. (Oxford: Clarendon, 1960). This quotation is on page 8.

29 See especially Eleanor Cook's chapter, 'Mage and Prophet,' in her *Browning's Lyrics: An Exploration* (Toronto: U of Toronto P, 1974) 229–38; and George P. Landow, 'Moses Striking the Rock: Typological Symbolism in Victorian Poetry,' in *Literary Uses of Typology from the Late Middle Ages to the Present*, ed. Earl Miner (Princeton: Princeton UP, 1977) 315–44; and 'The Smitten Rock' in *Victorian Types Victorian Shadows: Biblical Typology in Victorian Literature, Art, and Thought* (London: Routledge, 1980) 65–94.

30 George Clayton, *Christian Unity. The Principle of Union, among the disciples of Christ, explained and enforced: A Sermon, delivered at York Street*

Chapel, Walworth, on Sunday, February 21, 1836 (London: Hatchard;
Westley and Davies; Hailes, 1836) 13, 9.
31 Richard J. Helmstadter, 'The Nonconformist Conscience,' in *The Conscience of
the Victorian State*, ed. Peter Marsh (Syracuse, NY: Syracuse UP, 1979) 141.
32 David Bebbington, *Victorian Nonconformity*, Headstart History Papers
(Bangor, Wales: Headstart History, 1992) 64–6.
33 'Congregationalists felt that they had a special claim on the Brownings,'
writes R. Tudur Jones in his *Congregationalism in England 1662–1962* (London:
Independent Press, 1962) 295. 'Elizabeth Barrett had been baptized at
Paddington Chapel and Robert Browning at York Street, Walworth' (295).
Elizabeth had in fact been baptized at Kelloe Church in the County of
Durham (*Correspondence* 1: xlv).
34 Hans Aarsleff, *From Locke to Saussure: Essays on the Study of Language and Intellectual History* (Minneapolis: U of Minnesota P, 1982) 120–45.
35 John Stuart Mill, 'Coleridge,' in *Essays on Ethics, Religion and Society*, ed. J.M.
Robson, vol. 10 of *Collected Works of John Stuart Mill* (Toronto: U of Toronto P,
1969) 125.
36 Qtd. in Kelley and Coley, item A680.
37 For an account of the systematic way in which Browning's father read a
book, see Albert Foster Butler, *Robert Browning's Father: His Way with a
Book* (Ann Arbor: privately printed, 1969). Butler deals with one book only,
the father's copy of John Landseer's *Lectures on the Art of Engraving
Delivered at the Royal Institution of Great Britain* (item A1417 in Kelley and
Coley).
38 Wilbur Samuel Howell, *Eighteenth-Century British Logic and Rhetoric* (Princeton: Princeton UP, 1971) 695.
39 Qtd. in W.G. Collingwood, *The Life and Work of John Ruskin*, 2nd ed. (London:
Methuen, 1893) 1: 200–1. All subsequent quotations from this letter are from
these same two pages.
40 Eleanor Cook, 'The Function of Riddles at the Present Time,' in *The Legacy of
Northrop Frye*, ed. Alvin A. Lee and Robert D. Denham (Toronto: U of Toronto
P, 1994) 327–8.
41 Karl Josef Höltgen, *Aspects of the Emblem: Studies in the English Emblem Tradition and the European Context* (Kassel: Reichenberger, 1986) 31.
42 Gerard de Lairesse, *The Art of Painting*, trans. John Frederick Fritsch (London:
Vandenburgh, 1778) 54.
43 Peter M. Daly, 'The Cultural Context of English Emblem Books,' in *The
English Emblem and the Continental Tradition*, ed. Peter M. Daly (New York:
AMS, 1988) 2.
44 Rosemary Freeman, *English Emblem Books* (London: Chatto, 1948) 238–9.

45 Sally N. Lawall, 'Ut Pictura Poesis,' in *Princeton Encyclopedia of Poetry and Poetics*, ed. Alex Preminger (Princeton: Princeton UP, 1974) 881–2.

46 Barbara Kiefer Lewalski, *Protestant Poetics and the Seventeenth-Century Religious Lyric* (Princeton: Princeton UP, 1979) 180.

47 Francis Quarles, *Emblems Divine and Moral: Together with Hieroglyphics of the Life of Man* (London: Trapp, 1777), no pagination.

48 Qtd. in U. Milo Kaufmann, *'The Pilgrim's Progress' and Traditions in Puritan Meditation*, Yale Studies in English 163 (New Haven: Yale UP, 1966) 20.

49 Peter M. Daly, *Literature in the Light of the Emblem: Structural Parallels between the Emblem and Literature in the Sixteenth and Seventeenth Centuries* (Toronto: U of Toronto P, 1979) 173.

50 Fannie Barrett Browning, *Some Memories of Robert Browning* (Boston: Jones, 1928) 22.

51 Henry Melvill, *Sermons*, 2 vols., ed. C.P. M'Illvaine (New York: Miller, 1870) 1:7.

52 Herbert L. Sussman, *Fact into Figure: Typology in Carlyle, Ruskin, and the Pre-Raphaelite Brotherhood* (Columbus: Ohio State UP, 1979) 3.

53 George P. Landow, *Victorian Types Victorian Shadows: Biblical Typology in Victorian Literature, Art, and Thought* (Boston: Routledge, 1980) 5.

54 John Donne, *The Poetical Works of Dr. John Donne, Dean of St. Paul's, London*, Bell's Edition, 3 vols. (Edinburgh: Martins, 1779). The note appears at the bottom of page 128 in volume 1, and I quote it here with the kind permission of Mr Michael Meredith, Librarian, Eton College.

55 Jolande Jacobi, glossary in *Paracelsus: Selected Writings*, ed. Jolande Jacobi, Bollingen Series 28 (Princeton: Princeton UP, 1951) 252.

56 Louis L. Martz, *The Poetry of Meditation: A Study in English Religious Literature of the Seventeenth Century* (New Haven: Yale UP, 1954) 25–39; Kaufmann, 118–50.

57 George Clayton, *The Frailty of Human Life illustrated; and the Providential Agency of God improved*: in two sermons occasioned by the lamented death of Her Royal Highness the Princess Charlotte of Wales, delivered at Walworth, on Sunday the 16th and Wednesday the 19th of November (London: Black, Kingsbury, Parbury, and Allen, 1817) 5; and *The Triumph of Faith, in the Prospect and Crisis of Death. A Funeral Sermon occasioned by the decease of the Rev. Robt. Simpson, D.D.*, late theological tutor of the Hoxton Academy (London: Black, Kingsbury, Parbury, and Allen, 1818) 5.

58 *Learned Lady: Letters from Robert Browning to Mrs. Thomas FitzGerald 1876–1889*, ed. Edward C. McAleer (Cambridge, Mass.: Harvard UP, 1966) 34–5. Browning's references are puzzling. If one turns to the three-volume *Works of the Rev. Robert Hall*, ed. Olinthus Gregory (New York: Harper, 1833), one

finds, at the beginning of volume 3, a 'brief memoir' of Hall by Gregory, in which Gregory describes Hall's mental breakdown and prints the letter Hall received from Sir James Mackintosh during that time. Though one can read some of the passages in the light of the epistemology I am exploring, there is nothing explicit about the relations of mind and soul.

59 John Horne Tooke, ΕΠΕΑ ΠΤΕΡΟΕΝΤΑ, *or The Diversions of Purley*, ed. Richard Taylor (London: Tegg, 1840) 14.

60 *New Letters of Robert Browning*, ed. DeVane and Knickerbocker 272.

61 Thomas Dale, *An Introductory Lecture delivered in the University of London, on Friday, October 24, 1828* (London: Taylor, 1828) 24.

62 Charles Richard Sanders, *The Carlyle-Browning Correspondence and Relationship* (Manchester: John Rylands University Library, 1975).

63 *'Sartor' Called 'Resartus': The Genesis, Structure, and Style of Thomas Carlyle's First Major Work* (Princeton: Princeton UP, 1965) 265.

64 Thomas Carlyle, *Sartor Resartus*, ed. Charles Frederick Harrold (New York: Odyssey, 1937) 72.

65 'The Plan of a Dictionary of the English Language,' in *Johnson: Prose and Poetry*, ed. Mona Wilson (Reynard Library. Cambridge, Mass.: Harvard UP, 1967) 132.

66 Francis Quarles, *Emblemes* (London: Freeman, [1710?]) 287. This is the copy of Quarles given to Browning by his mother (as he notes on the flyleaf) and now in the Balliol College Library. It is item A1912 in *The Browning Collections*.

Chapter Two: Parleying, Troping, and Fragmenting

1 William S. Peterson and Fred L. Standley, 'The J.S. Mill Marginalia in Robert Browning's *Pauline*: A History and Transcription,' *Papers of the Bibliographical Society of America* 66 (1972) 168.

2 Qtd. in W.G. Collingwood, *The Life and Work of John Ruskin*, 2 vols., 2nd ed. (London: Methuen, 1893) 1: 201.

3 Oscar Wilde, *Intentions* (London: Methuen, 1891) 139, 146, 150, 140.

4 F.R.G. Duckworth, *Browning: Background and Conflict* (London: Benn, 1931). For a recent assessment of Duckworth's importance as a critic, see Patricia O'Neill, *Robert Browning and Twentieth-Century Criticism* (Columbia, SC: Camden House, 1995) 57–65.

5 All quotations from *Pauline* are from the texts edited by Ian Jack and Margaret Smith in *The Poetical Works of Robert Browning*, vol. 1 (Oxford: Clarendon, 1983). Jack and Smith print the texts of 1833 and 1888 side by side. The quotations, unless otherwise indicated, are from the 1833 text.

6 Herbert F. Tucker Jr's thesis that 'Browning's moral doctrine of incompleteness finds a clear aesthetic analogue in his poetics,' in *Browning's Beginnings: The Art of Disclosure* (Minneapolis: U of Minnesota P, 1980) 5, is a useful parallel to this argument.

7 Carol Christ, in her *Victorian and Modern Poetics* (Chicago: U of Chicago P, 1984), argues that 'Browning's dramatic monologues characteristically concern the prison of self which the speaker constructs in attempting to encompass and control his world' (19). For another view of the limitations of approximating the totality of things, see the chapter on Browning in J. Hillis Miller's *The Linguistic Moment: From Wordsworth to Stevens* (Princeton: Princeton UP, 1985). Miller, whose text is 'The Englishman in Italy,' argues that such an attempt at totality can never be complete, and the effort itself remains 'paratactic, one item after another' (218). 'There is no possibility of an exhaustive inventory, accounting, or telling over. There is no possibility that the part or a finite collection of parts should adequately stand for the whole' (225). At the same time, however, '"The Englishman in Italy" is a magnificently positive poem dramatizing a taking-possession of a real place through words, and through that act appropriating another person, all time and space, the infinite moment beyond time and space' (220). The poem itself is not a failure, but 'a magnificent verbal notation of failure' (228).

8 Eleanor Cook, *Browning's Lyrics: An Exploration* (Toronto: U of Toronto P, 1974) 107–10.

9 John Maynard is enlightening on this topic. See his *Browning's Youth* (Cambridge, Mass.: Harvard UP, 1977) 135–6, 140–3, and 151–3.

10 Clyde de L. Ryals, 'Browning's *Pauline*: The Question of Genre,' *Genre* 9 (1976) 231–45, and *Becoming Browning: The Poems and Plays of Robert Browning, 1833–1846* (Columbus: Ohio State UP, 1983) 26.

11 Henry Kozicki, 'Browning, *Pauline*, and Cornelius Agrippa: The Protagonist as Magus,' *Victorian Poetry* 28 (1990): 17–38. The quotations in the sentence which follows are all from pages 17 and 18 of this article.

12 Henry Cornelius Agrippa, *Of the Vanitie and Uncertaintie of Arts and Sciences* [trans. James Sanford 1569], ed. Catherine M. Dunn (Northridge: California State University, 1974) 11.

13 John Maynard, 'Speaker, Listener, and Overhearer: The Reader in the Dramatic Poem,' *Browning Institute Studies* 15 (1987) 107. See also Maynard's 'Reading the Reader in Robert Browning's Dramatic Monologues,' in *Browning e Venezia*, ed. Sergio Perosa (Firenze: Olschki, 1991) 165–77. A. Dwight Culler anticipates my argument in 'Monodrama and the Dramatic Monologue,' *Publications of the Modern Language Association* 90 (1975) 368.

14 *Browning's Trumpeter: The Correspondence of Robert Browning and Frederick J. Furnivall 1872–1889*, ed. William S. Peterson (Washington: Decatur House, 1979) 34.

15 J. Hillis Miller, *Fiction and Repetition: Seven English Novels* (Cambridge, Mass.: Harvard UP, 1982) 20.

16 J. Hillis Miller, 'Catachresis, Prosopopoeia, and the Pathetic Fallacy: The Rhetoric of Ruskin,' in *Poetry and Epistemology*, ed. Roland Hagenbüchle and Laura Skandera (Regensburg: Pustet, 1986) 398–407; and 'Prosopopoeia and *Praeterita*,' in *Nineteenth-Century Lives: Essays Presented to Jerome Hamilton Buckley*, ed. Laurence S. Lockridge, John Maynard, and Donald D. Stone (Cambridge: Cambridge UP, 1989) 125–39. The quotation is on page 127 of the second essay.

17 On the various meanings of *symbolon*, see Marc Shell, *The Economy of Literature* (Baltimore: Johns Hopkins UP, 1978) 32–6.

18 George P. Landow, *Victorian Types Victorian Shadows: Biblical Typology in Victorian Literature, Art, and Thought* (Boston: Routledge, 1980) 11.

19 John Hollander, *The Figure of Echo: A Mode of Allusion in Milton and After* (Berkeley: U of California P, 1981) 8.

20 *Letters of Robert Browning Collected by Thomas J. Wise*, ed. Thurman L. Hood (London: Murray, 1933) 92.

21 F.E.L. Priestley, 'The Ironic Pattern of Browning's *Paracelsus*,' *University of Toronto Quarterly* 34 (1964) 68.

22 Qtd. in Ian Jack and Margaret Smith's edition of *The Poetical Works of Robert Browning* (Oxford: Clarendon, 1983) 2:189.

23 David E. Latané, Jr, *Browning's 'Sordello' and the Aesthetics of Difficulty* (Victoria, BC: English Literary Studies, U of Victoria, 1987) 44.

24 Isobel Armstrong, *Language as Living Form in Nineteenth-Century Poetry* (Brighton: Harvester, 1982) 141.

25 Eleanor Cook, 'The Function of Riddles at the Present Time,' in *The Legacy of Northrop Frye*, ed. Alvin A. Lee and Robert D. Denham (Toronto: U of Toronto P, 1994) 327.

26 *Browning's Essay on Chatterton*, ed. Donald Smalley (Cambridge, Mass.: Harvard UP, 1948) 111.

27 See, for instance, Thomas J. Collins, *Robert Browning's Moral-Aesthetic Theory 1833–1855* (Lincoln: U of Nebraska P, 1967) 69.

28 I am here borrowing from the last part of Peter Allan Dale's argument in '*Paracelsus* and *Sordello*: Trying the Stuff of Language,' *Victorian Poetry* 18 (1980) 359–69. The relevant paragraph is on page 369.

29 Barbara Herrnstein Smith, *Poetic Closure: A Study of How Poems End* (Chicago: U of Chicago P, 1968) 71.

Chapter Three: 'Why need I speak, if you can read my thought?'

1 Hallam Tennyson, *Alfred Lord Tennyson: A Memoir by his Son* (London: Macmillan, 1899) 563–4.
2 *The Brownings to the Tennysons: Letters from Robert Browning and Elizabeth Barrett Browning to Alfred, Emily, and Hallam Tennyson*, ed. Thomas J. Collins (Waco, Tex.: Armstrong Browning Library, 1971) 36.
3 'Gentlemen,' Browning said, according to the printed 'Report of the Anniversary of 1846,' 'I feel so deeply impressed with your kindness, that I am really quite unable to do more than thank the learned Serjeant for the eloquent and indulgent manner in which he has proposed this toast, and to thank you for the warmth and cordiality with which you have responded to it (cheers). I assure you I feel it a privilege to have attended this anniversary, and I beg most cordially to express my warm interest in the prosperity of the Institution.' *Royal Corporation of the Literary Fund: List of Members, etc.* (London, 1846) 33.
4 *Royal Corporation of the Literary Fund*, 'Report of the Anniversary of 1846,' 33.
5 Shou-ren Wang has also used the image in the title of his *The Theatre of the Mind: A Study of Unacted Drama in Nineteenth-Century England* (Basingstoke: Macmillan, 1990).
6 The essay by Michael Mason is 'Browning and the Dramatic Monologue,' in *Robert Browning*, ed. Isobel Armstrong (London: Bell, 1974) 231–66. The 'deep roots' metaphor appears on page 232. Shou-ren Wang has more recently provided a more comprehensive account of the historical context in the introduction to his *The Theatre of the Mind*.
7 F.E.L. Priestley, 'Drama and the Social Historian,' *Transactions of the Royal Society of Canada*, 3rd ser. 51 (1957) 27.
8 F.G. Tomlins, *A Brief View of The English Drama, from the Earliest Period to the Present Time: with suggestions for elevating the present condition of the art, and of its professors* (London: Mitchell, 1840) 73, 76.
9 The pamphlet is item A2332 in *The Browning Collections*.
10 F.G. Tomlins, *The Past and Present State of Dramatic Art and Literature; addressed to Authors, Actors, Managers, and the Admirers of the Old English Drama*, 2nd ed. (London: Mitchell, 1839) 6.
11 Edward Mayhew, *Stage Effect: or, the principles which command Dramatic Success in the Theatre* (London: Mitchell, 1840) 31.
12 Sir Walter Scott, 'The Drama,' in *Essays* (Paris: Galignani, 1828) 2:105.
13 F.G. Tomlins, 'The Relative Value of the Acted and the Unacted Drama,' *Monthly Magazine* 3rd ser. 5 (1841) 329.
14 R.H. Horne, ed., *A New Spirit of the Age* (New York: Garland, 1986) 2:85, 99.

15 Charles Lamb, 'On the Tragedies of Shakspeare, Considered with Reference to their Fitness for Stage Representation,' *The Works of Charles and Mary Lamb*, ed. E.V. Lucas (London: Methuen, 1903) 1:99.

16 Charles Dickens, *Little Dorrit*, ed. Harvey Peter Sucksmith, World's Classics (Oxford: Oxford UP, 1982) 255.

17 Stephen K. Land, *The Philosophy of Language in Britain: Major Theories from Hobbes to Thomas Reid* (New York: AMS, 1986) 35.

18 James Engell, *The Creative Imagination: Enlightenment to Romanticism* (Cambridge, Mass.: Harvard UP, 1981) 17–21.

19 Edmund Burke, *A Philosophical Enquiry into the Origin of our Ideas of the Sublime and Beautiful*, ed. James T. Boulton (1757; Notre Dame: U of Notre Dame P, 1968) 170.

20 A. Dwight Culler, 'Monodrama and the Dramatic Monologue,' *Publications of the Modern Language Association of America* 90 (1975) 382.

21 John Maynard, *Browning's Youth* (Cambridge, Mass.: Harvard UP, 1977) 79.

22 *The Characters of Theophrastus*, trans. and ed. by Francis Howell (London: Taylor, 1824) 165.

23 William Allingham, *A Diary*, ed. H. Allingham and D. Radford (1907; Harmondsworth: Penguin, 1985) 249.

24 *More Than Friend: The Letters of Robert Browning to Katharine de Kay Bronson*, ed. Michael Meredith (Waco, Tex.: Armstrong Browning Library, 1985) 52.

25 The words are on page 4 of Browning's childhood copy of Quarles's *Emblemes*, now in the Balliol College Library, and are quoted here with the kind permission of The Master and Fellows of Balliol College, Oxford.

26 R.J. Berman, *Browning's Duke* (New York: Richards Rosen, 1972) 103–8.

27 Harold Bloom, 'Browning: Good Moments and Ruined Quests,' in *Robert Browning: A Collection of Critical Essays*, ed. Harold Bloom and Adrienne Munich (Englewood Cliffs, NJ: Prentice, 1979) 142.

28 Harold Bloom, *A Map of Misreading* (New York: Oxford UP, 1975) 93, 106.

29 Roland may consciously be questing for some other (unspecified) goal, and may have been trained to avoid the tower which is associated with the failure of his predecessors and linked by himself with the experience of being trapped. At the same time, he does seem to know that he must confront the tower, yet its unknown terrors are such that he would not deliberately choose to confront them, and would do so only when the confrontation is inevitable. Hence his attitude to the cripple may be not so much distrust as it is fear that the cripple may be the agent of necessity, pushing him towards dangers for body and soul. For this line of argument, I am indebted to one of the anonymous readers for University of Toronto Press.

30 *The [Westminster] Confession of Faith; The Larger and Shorter Catechisms* (Edinburgh: Johnstone, 1868) 32.

31 Williston Walker, *The Creeds and Platforms of Congregationalism* (1893; Philadelphia: Pilgrim, 1960) 374; the words 'and power of acting upon choice' are the Congregationalists' addition to the Westminster Confession.

32 Thomas Carlyle, *Sartor Resartus*, ed. Charles Frederick Harrold (New York: Odyssey, 1937) 67.

33 Susan Hardy Aiken, 'Structural Imagery in "Childe Roland to the Dark Tower Came,"' *Browning Institute Studies* 5 (1977) 33–4.

34 Clyde de L. Ryals, *The Life of Robert Browning: A Critical Biography* (Oxford: Blackwell, 1993) 225.

35 Thomas Carlyle, *The French Revolution*, ed. K.J. Fielding and David Sorensen, World's Classics (Oxford: Oxford UP, 1989) 1: 317. In Carlyle's division, the passage appears in part 2, book 1, chapter 2.

36 W. David Shaw, *The Lucid Veil: Poetic Truth in the Victorian Age* (London: Athlone, 1987) 86.

37 Richard Chenevix Trench, *On the Study of Words*, 18th ed. (London: Macmillan, 1882) 5–6.

Chapter Four: 'I kept time to the wondrous chime'

1 *Browning's Trumpeter: The Correspondence of Robert Browning and Frederick J. Furnivall 1872–1889*, ed. William S. Peterson (Washington, DC: Decatur House, 1979) 143.

2 *Letters of Robert Browning Collected by Thomas J. Wise*, ed. Thurman L. Hood (London: Murray, 1933) 130–1.

3 *Learned Lady: Letters from Robert Browning to Mrs. Thomas FitzGerald 1876–1889*, ed. Edward C. McAleer (Cambridge, Mass.: Harvard UP, 1966) 180.

4 Ian A. Gordon, *The Movement of English Prose* (London: Longman, 1966) 16, 19–20.

5 The most recent study of Browning and music is Nachum Schoffman's *There Is No Truer Truth: The Musical Aspect of Browning's Poetry* (New York: Greenwood, 1991).

6 E.A.W. StGeorge, *Browning and Conversation* (Basingstoke: Macmillan, 1993).

7 Sidney Colvin, *Memories and Notes of Persons and Places 1852–1912* (London: Arnold, 1921) 81.

8 Fannie Barrett Browning, *Some Memories of Robert Browning* (Boston: Jones, 1928) 16.

9 Anne Ritchie, *Records of Tennyson, Ruskin, Browning* (New York: Harper, 1893) 168–9.

10 Qtd. in Clyde de L. Ryals, *The Life of Robert Browning: A Critical Biography* (Oxford: Blackwell, 1993) 111.

11 F. Max Müller, 'Literary Reminiscences – III,' *Cosmopolis* 5 (1897) 666.

12 William Irvine and Park Honan, *The Book, the Ring, and the Poet: A Biography of Robert Browning* (New York: McGraw, 1974) 331. In his *Retrospects* (London: Smith, Elder, 1904), William Angus Knight had also reported that Browning's 'reading was not so musical as Tennyson's, but it was clearer and crisper, and had occasionally a torrent rush' (99).

13 Northrop Frye, *Anatomy of Criticism: Four Essays* (Princeton: Princeton UP, 1957) 255.

14 Harlan Henthorne Hatcher, *The Versification of Robert Browning* (Columbus: Ohio State UP, 1928) 4–5.

15 John Neubauer, *The Emancipation of Music from Language: Departure from Mimesis in Eighteenth-Century Aesthetics* (New Haven: Yale UP, 1986) 2.

16 Charles Avison, *An Essay on Musical Expression* (1753; facsimile ed. New York: Broude, 1967); no pagination for this passage in the Advertisement.

17 Dennis Taylor, *Hardy's Metres and Victorian Prosody* (Oxford: Clarendon, 1988) 4, 49.

18 Coventry Patmore, 'English Metrical Critics,' *North British Review* 27 (1857) 128.

19 Loy D. Martin, in scanning the lines as I do, remarks that 'the most prominent stress pattern is one of four heavy beats per line, and this pattern is far more regular than that measured by the iambic metre.' *Browning's Dramatic Monologues and the Post-Romantic Subject* (Baltimore: Johns Hopkins UP, 1985) 116.

20 Stephen H. Ford gives a detailed account of the form of the poem as a musical analogy: 'the double octave in which there are fifteen steps.' See 'The Musical Form of Robert Browning's "A Toccata of Galuppi's,"' *Studies in Browning and His Circle* 14 (1986) 22–4.

21 Paul Fussell, *Poetic Meter and Poetic Form*, rev. ed. (New York: Random, 1979) 91.

22 For a different way of reading the lines, see Russell Astley, 'Browning's Logaoedic Measures,' *Victorian Poetry* 16 (1978) 366–7. Astley argues that we hear two metres in each long line: one is five trochaic feet and one monosyllabic foot, the other two third paeonics and an anapest. The latter is a rising rhythm, the former a falling rhythm, and 'the resultant music strikes my ear as delicate and unique' (367). Perhaps because he does not tie the metre to the content and point of view, Astley has 'no feeling of a struggle between two antagonistic metres' (367).

23 Robert J. Getty, 'Anacrusis,' in *Princeton Encyclopedia of Poetry and Poetics*, ed. Alex Preminger (Princeton: Princeton UP, 1974) 33.

24 Qtd. in W.G. Collingwood, *The Life and Work of John Ruskin*, 2 vols. (London: Methuen, 1893) 1: 201.
25 I am indebted to Eleanor Cook's analysis of this lyric in *Browning's Lyrics: An Exploration* (Toronto: U of Toronto P, 1974) 163–73.
26 Thomas Carlyle, *Sartor Resartus*, ed. Charles Frederick Harrold (New York: Odyssey, 1937) 262, 260.
27 *New Letters of Robert Browning*, ed. William Clyde DeVane and Kenneth Leslie Knickerbocker (London: Murray, 1951) 263.
28 I am indebted to Arden Reed's analysis of *The Rime of the Ancient Mariner*, and particularly his comments on the stanza I have just quoted. See 'The Mariner Rimed,' in *Romanticism and Language*, ed. Arden Reed (Ithaca: Cornell UP, 1984) 168–201.
29 The quotations are from Pater's 'The School of Giorgione,' first published in the *Fortnightly Review* in 1877. The page references in William E. Buckler's edition, *Walter Pater: The Major Texts ('The Renaissance,' 'Appreciations,' and 'Imaginary Portraits')* (New York: New York UP, 1986) are 156 and 158.
30 Kevin Barry, *Language, Music and the Sign: A Study in Aesthetics, Poetics and Poetic Practice from Collins to Coleridge* (Cambridge: Cambridge UP, 1987) 33.
31 James Beattie, *Essays* (1776; New York: Garland, 1971) 465.
32 Gerald F. Else, *Aristotle's Poetics: The Argument* (Cambridge, Mass.: Harvard UP, 1967) 63.
33 Qtd. in John Pettigrew and Thomas J. Collins, *Robert Browning, The Poems* (Harmondsworth: Penguin, 1981) 2: 1030.
34 'Prose is where all the lines but the last go on to the margin – poetry is where some of them fall short of it.' Qtd. in Stephen J. Adams, *Poetic Designs: an Introduction to Meters, Verse Forms, and Figures of Speech* (Peterborough: Broadview, 1997) 152 n.
35 Alfred Austin, 'The Poetry of the Period,' in *Browning: The Critical Heritage*, ed. Boyd Litzinger and Donald Smalley (London: Routledge, 1970) 346–7.
36 *Letters of Robert Browning Collected by Thomas J. Wise*, ed. Thurman L. Hood (London: Murray, 1933) 130.
37 *Dearest Isa: Robert Browning's Letters to Isabella Blagden*, ed. Edward C. McAleer (Austin: U of Texas P, 1951) 196. The reference is to a review by William Stigand in the *Edinburgh Review* 120 (October 1864) 537–65.
38 Mrs Sutherland Orr, *A Handbook to the Works of Robert Browning*, 6th ed. (London: Bell, 1913) 342.

Chapter Five: 'Adjust Real vision to right language'

1 *Browning's Trumpeter: The Correspondence of Robert Browning and Frederick J.*

Furnivall 1872–1889, ed. William S. Peterson (Washington, DC: Decatur House, 1979) 145.

2 This paragraph and the next three are taken (in a partly revised form) from my 'Browning's Palace of Art,' *University of Toronto Quarterly* 48 (1978–9) 116–18, and are used here with the kind permission of the Journals Division at University of Toronto Press.

3 Frances Yates, *Theatre of the World* (Chicago: U of Chicago P, 1969).

4 Thomas Carlyle, *Sartor Resartus*, ed. Charles Frederick Harrold (New York: Odyssey, 1937) 263.

5 Samuel Taylor Coleridge, *Aids to Reflection*, ed. John Beer, *The Collected Works of Samuel Taylor Coleridge* 9 (London: Routledge, 1993) 181. Coleridge's translation of the tetragrammaton is quoted by James C. McKusick, *Coleridge's Philosophy of Language* (New Haven: Yale UP, 1986) 137.

6 I borrow this sentence and some earlier clauses from my *Tennyson's Language* (Toronto: U of Toronto P, 1991) 80.

7 Jean-Jacques Rousseau, 'Essay on the Origin of Languages,' in *The First and Second Discourses ... and Essay on the Origin of Languages*, ed. and trans. Victor Gourevitch (New York: Harper, 1986) 286.

8 Jean-Jacques Rousseau, *Dictionnaire de Musique* (1768; Hildesheim: Olms, 1969) 15–16.

9 Nachum Schoffman, *There Is No Truer Truth: The Musical Aspect of Browning's Poetry* (New York: Greenwood, 1991) 75.

10 Suzanne Edwards, 'Robert Browning's "Saul": Pre-Raphaelite Painting in Verse,' *Journal of Pre-Raphaelite Studies* 6. 2 (1986) 53–9.

11 Patrick Fairbairn, 'the great Victorian student of typology,' defines these words and gives their history in *The Typology of Scripture* (1845–7), 'probably the finest work written on the subject.' See George P. Landow, *Victorian Types Victorian Shadows: Biblical Typology in Victorian Literature, Art, and Thought* (Boston: Routledge, 1980) 34, 40. My quotations of Fairbairn are from a modern reprinting (Grand Rapids: Kregel, 1989) of the New York edition of 1900, 1. 11.

12 Glenn Everett, 'Typological Structures in Browning's "Saul,"' *Victorian Poetry* 23 (1985) 271.

13 Samuel Taylor Coleridge, *Aids to Reflection*, ed. John Beer (London: Routledge, 1993) 205.

14 Henry Melvill, *Sermons*, ed. C.P. M'Illvaine (New York: James Miller, 1870) 1:117.

15 Eleanor Cook, *Browning's Lyrics: An Exploration* (Toronto: U of Toronto P, 1974) 4.

16 *Letters of Robert Browning Collected by Thomas J. Wise*, ed. Thurman L. Hood (London: Murray, 1933) 104.

17 William Law, 'The Life of Jacob Behmen, the Teutonic Theosopher,' *The Works of Jacob Behmen*, vol. 1 (London: Richardson, 1764) xiii.

18 Jacob Boehme, *The Signature of All Things and Other Writings* (Cambridge: Clarke, 1969) 9–10.

19 [Jacob Boehme] *Mysterium Magnum* 1.19.22, in *The Works of Jacob Behmen, The Teutonic Theosopher* (London: Richardson, Robertson, 1764–81) 3. 80.

20 Richard Lines, lecture, 'Swedenborg and the Brownings,' The Browning Society, London, 16 March 1996.

21 Emmanuel Swedenborg, *A Treatise concerning Heaven and Hell, and of the Wonderful Things therein*, 2nd ed. (London: Hindmarsh, 1784).

Chapter Six: 'For how else know we save by worth of word?'

1 Oscar Wilde, *Intentions* (London: Methuen, 1947) 121, 143.

2 A.N. Kincaid, 'The Ring and the Scholars,' *Browning Institute Studies* 8 (1980) 151–9.

3 Marc Shell, *The Economy of Literature* (Baltimore: Johns Hopkins UP, 1978) 32–3.

4 Richard Chenevix Trench, *On Some Deficiencies in Our English Dictionaries* (London: Parker, 1857) 35.

5 William E. Baker, *Syntax in English Poetry 1870–1930* (Berkeley: U of California P, 1967) 99.

6 *The Letters of Robert Browning and Elizabeth Barrett Barrett 1845–1846*, ed. Elvan Kintner (Cambridge, Mass.: Belknap, 1969) 1069.

7 Qtd. in W.G. Collingwood, *The Life and Work of John Ruskin* (London: Methuen, 1893) 1. 200.

8 Richard Altick's note to 1. 155, on page 638 of his edition of *The Ring and the Book* (Harmondsworth: Penguin, 1971).

9 Eric Griffiths, *The Printed Voice of Victorian Poetry* (Oxford: Clarendon, 1989).

10 Boyd Litzinger, 'The Structural Logic of *The Ring and the Book*, ' *Nineteenth-Century Literary Perspectives: Essays in Honor of Lionel Stevenson*, ed. Clyde de L. Ryals (Durham: Duke UP, 1974) 105–14.

11 Daniel Karlin, *Browning's Hatreds* (Oxford: Clarendon, 1993) 227.

12 Thomas Carlyle, *Sartor Resartus*, ed. Charles Frederick Harrold (New York: Odyssey, 1937) 218–19.

13 Sir Walter Scott, 'Essay on Romance,' *Essays on Chivalry, Romance, and the Drama* (1818; London: Murray, 1870) 231.

14 E.P. Thompson, *Witness against the Beast: William Blake and the Moral Law* (Cambridge: Cambridge UP, 1993) 176–7.

15 *Robert Browning and Julia Wedgwood: A Broken Friendship as revealed in their Letters*, ed. Richard Curle (London: Murray, 1937) 177.

16 Richard D. Altick and James F. Loucks, II, *Browning's Roman Murder Story: A Reading of 'The Ring and the Book'* (Chicago: U of Chicago P, 1968) 123.

Chapter Seven: 'One thing has many sides'

1 *New Letters of Robert Browning*, ed. William Clyde DeVane and Kenneth Leslie Knickerbocker (London: Murray, 1951) 292.
2 Oscar Wilde, *Intentions* (London: Methuen, 1947) 139, 140.
3 W. David Shaw, *The Lucid Veil: Poetic Truth in the Victorian Age* (London: Athlone, 1987) 49.
4 Qtd. in K.M. Elisabeth Murray, *Caught in the Web of Words: James A.H. Murray and the 'Oxford English Dictionary'* (New Haven: Yale UP, 1977) 235.
5 William Clyde DeVane, *A Browning Handbook*, 2nd ed. (New York: Appleton, 1955) 354.
6 Nathan A. Greenberg, 'Browning and *Alcestis*,' *Classical and Modern Literature* 9 (1989) 131.
7 J. Hillis Miller, *Fiction and Repetition: Seven English Novels* (Cambridge, Mass.: Harvard UP, 1982) 1–21.
8 J. Hillis Miller, 'The Critic as Host,' *Critical Theory since 1965*, ed. Hazard Adams and Leroy Searle (Tallahassee: Florida State UP, 1986) 452–68.
9 Shaw, 198–202. The quotation appears on page 198.
10 Joseph H. Friend, 'Euripides Browningized: The Meaning of *Balaustion's Adventure*,' *Victorian Poetry* 2 (1964) 179.
11 Friedrich August Wolf, *Prolegomena to Homer* (1795), trans. with intro. and notes by Anthony Grafton, Glenn W. Most, and James E.G. Zetzel (Princeton: Princeton UP, 1985) 44.
12 E.S. Shaffer, *'Kubla Khan' and 'The Fall of Jerusalem': The Mythological School in Biblical Criticism and Secular Literature 1770–1880* (Cambridge: Cambridge UP, 1975) 55.
13 Henry Melvill, *Sermons* (New York: Miller, 1870) 1: 116.
14 R.L. Brett, rev. of *'Kubla Khan' and 'The Fall of Jerusalem'* by E.S. Shaffer, *Victorian Studies* 20 (1977) 223–5.
15 See Elizabeth Bieman, 'Triads and Trinity in the Poetry of Robert Browning,' *Cithara* 19. 2 (1980) 31–2.
16 William Whitla, *The Central Truth: The Incarnation in Browning's Poetry* (Toronto: U of Toronto P, 1963) 32–4.
17 The quotation is line 62 in 'Pietro of Abano,' from the 1880 *Dramatic Idylls: Second Series*.
18 George Meredith, 'Essay: On the Idea of Comedy and of the Uses of the Comic Spirit' (1877), *Miscellaneous Prose*, vol. 23 of *The Works of George Meredith*, Memorial Edition (1909–12; New York: Russell, 1968) 8.

19 Clyde de L. Ryals, *Browning's Later Poetry 1871–1889* (Ithaca: Cornell UP, 1975) 108; *The Life of Robert Browning: A Critical Biography* (Oxford: Blackwell, 1993) 197.

20 *The Agamemnon of Aeschylus*, in *The Works of Robert Browning*, Centenary Edition, vol. 8 (New York: AMS, 1966) 293.

21 Yopie Prins, '"Violence bridling speech": Browning's Translation of Aeschylus' *Agamemnon*,' *Victorian Poetry* 27 (1989) 151–2.

22 George Steiner, *After Babel: Aspects of Language and Translation* (London: Oxford UP, 1975) 314–15.

Chapter Eight: 'Do you say this, or I?'

1 *Browning's Trumpeter: The Correspondence of Robert Browning and Frederick J. Furnivall 1872–1889*, ed. William S. Peterson (Washington, DC: Decatur House, 1979) 143.

2 Bernard de Mandeville, *The Fable of the Bees; or, Private Vices, Public Benefits. With ... A Vindication of the Book ...* (London: Bathurst et al., 1795) 262.

3 Friedrich Daniel Ernst Schleiermacher, *Schleiermacher's Introductions to the Dialogues of Plato*, trans. William Dobson (Cambridge: Deighton, 1836) 5.

4 *The Diary of Alfred Domett 1872–1885*, ed. E.A. Horsman (London: Oxford UP, 1953) 49.

5 F.E.L. Priestley, 'A Reading of *La Saisiaz*,' *University of Toronto Quarterly* 25 (1955) 47–59.

6 *The Dialogues of Plato*, trans. B. Jowett, 5 vols., 2nd ed. (Oxford: Clarendon, 1875) 1:281.

7 Peterson supplies the evidence for Browning's part in the section on *La Saisiaz* in *Browning's Trumpeter* 124, note 5.

8 Mrs Sutherland Orr, *A Handbook to the Works of Robert Browning*, 6th ed. (1892; London: Bell, 1913) 190.

9 *Letters of Robert Browning Collected by Thomas J. Wise*, ed. Thurman L. Hood (London: Murray, 1933) 309.

10 Mark Siegchrist provides these documents and more in his *Rough in Brutal Print: The Legal Sources of Browning's 'Red Cotton Night-Cap Country'* (Columbus: Ohio State UP, 1981).

11 John Horne Tooke, *The Diversions of Purley*, ed. Richard Taylor (London: Tegg, 1840) 15.

12 *Learned Lady: Letters from Robert Browning to Mrs. Thomas FitzGerald, 1876–1889* (Cambridge, Mass.: Harvard UP, 1966) 152. Park Honan has remarked that Browning 'had never acknowledged an indebtedness to a law of Wordsworth's and Hartley's more explicitly – or succinctly.' William

Irvine and Park Honan, *The Book, the Ring, and the Poet: A Biography of Robert Browning* (New York: McGraw, 1974) 505.
13 The Carlyle passage is in volume 1, part 2, book 1, chapter 2 ('In the Salle de Manège'). Thomas Carlyle, *The French Revolution: A History*, ed. K.J. Fielding and David Sorensen, World's Classics (Oxford: Oxford UP, 1989) 1: 317.
14 Thomas Carlyle, *Sartor Resartus*, ed. Charles Frederick Harrold (New York: Odyssey, 1937) 72.
15 *Collected Letters of Samuel Taylor Coleridge*, ed. Earl Leslie Griggs (Oxford: Clarendon, 1956) 2: 698.
16 Juliet McMaster, *Thackeray: The Major Novels* (Toronto: U of Toronto P, 1971) 63.
17 Bernhard W. Anderson, *Understanding the Old Testament*, 3rd ed. (Englewood Cliffs: Prentice, 1975) 54–6.

Overview and Conclusion

1 W. David Shaw, *The Lucid Veil: Poetic Truth in the Victorian Age* (London: Athlone, 1987) 64.
2 Frye makes the comment in a 1969 interview with Eli Mandel, 'The Limits of Dialogue,' in *A World in a Grain of Sand: Twenty-Two Interviews with Northrop Frye*, ed. Robert D. Denham (New York: Lang, 1991) 11.
3 Patricia O'Neill, *Robert Browning and Twentieth-Century Criticism* (Columbia, SC: Camden House, 1995); John Maynard, *Browning Re-viewed: Review Essays, 1980–1995* (New York: Lang, 1998).
4 The books which are the subjects of the next three paragraphs are as follows: W. David Shaw, *The Lucid Veil: Poetic Truth in the Victorian Age* (London: Athlone, 1987) and *Victorians and Mystery: Crises of Representation* (Ithaca, NY: Cornell UP, 1990); J. Hillis Miller, *The Linguistic Moment: From Wordsworth to Stevens* (Princeton: Princeton UP, 1985); Isobel Armstrong, *Victorian Poetry: Poetry, poetics and politics* (London: Routledge, 1993).

Index